Daughters of Infamy

The Stories of the Ships That Survived Pearl Harbor

by

David Kilmer

iUniverse, Inc.
Bloomington

Daughters of Infamy
The Stories of the Ships That Survived Pearl Harbor

iUniverse books may be ordered through booksellers or by contacting:

iUniverse
1663 Liberty Drive
Bloomington, IN 47403
www.iuniverse.com
1-800-Authors (1-800-288-4677)

Because of the dynamic nature of the Internet, any web addresses or links contained in this book may have changed since publication and may no longer be valid. The views expressed in this work are solely those of the author and do not necessarily reflect the views of the publisher, and the publisher hereby disclaims any responsibility for them.

Any people depicted in stock imagery provided by Thinkstock are models, and such images are being used for illustrative purposes only.

Certain stock imagery © Thinkstock.

ISBN: 978-1-4620-6252-2 (sc)
ISBN: 978-1-4620-6251-5 (hc)
ISBN: 978-1-4620-6250-8 (e)

Library of Congress Control Number: 2011919357

Printed in the United States of America

iUniverse rev. date: 11/10/2011

CONTENTS

PART I: ONE HUNDRED ELEVEN SURVIVORS

PART II: THREE GRAVES

PART III: THE JAPANESE

APPENDIX

<u>*Dedication*</u>

This book is gratefully and lovingly dedicated to

my parents, Robert and Marion Kilmer

who instilled in me the

joy and satisfaction of learning,

and to

the personnel of the United States Navy

who fought and won the war on the sea

during World War II,

to whom the people of the world owe so much.

Acknowledgements

So much of writing a book is a solitary process. Before you set down even one word it is a never-ending journey of research that seems like it could go on forever. Then you realize it indeed could go on forever. At some point the research has to stop and you have to start writing. Only when you set out on a project like this does the enormity of what you have started begin to sink in. For unending hours it is just you and the computer and piles of research and resource material. It is thinking of what to say and how to say it. It is a nightmare and a wonderful dream dancing together. Many times you wonder why you even started this.

When I first thought of writing this book I wrote down several sample ships' profiles just to get a feel for the writing and the format that I had chosen. The next step was the most difficult. That was to reveal these samples to people and ask for their opinions. That is such a risky thing to do. To write is to reveal yourself on so many different levels. To share your writing with somebody for the first time is a scary experience.

One of the first people I showed the samples to was Mirjana Urosev. She is Professor of Literature at a private university in California. I had the temerity to ask her to look at my writing on the first day I met her. She graciously said she would look at it. It was her positive reaction and evaluation that convinced me to write this book. For that encouragement, for her continued guidance, and for her superb tutelage I will be forever thankful.

Allyson West read every word of this book before anyone else. She is one of the smartest people I know when it comes to spelling, grammar, and the written word. She abhors the misplaced apostrophe, the incorrect comma, and very understandably, any sentence that ends in a preposition. She was also a superb guide in my quest to make this story accessible to people who know little or nothing of war, ships, and the Navy. She continually kept me on a path that would make it reader-friendly in order to appeal to an audience larger than the military or World War II aficionado. She was also my number one cheerleader and continues to be so. Words are totally inadequate to thank her. She is very much a part of this book.

Coming to this project about halfway through was my oldest brother Lieutenant Colonel Robert Kilmer, Jr., U.S. Army (Ret.). His last assignment in the Army was as an instructor at the United States Army Command and General Staff College at Fort Leavenworth, Kansas. His experience and knowledge in writing and military history was more than invaluable. He sent me back to my research and sources on innumerable occasions when he challenged me as to accuracy and clarity on all military matters. He made me demand more of myself and the book is better for that.

I would like to thank Rear Admiral Dixon R. Smith, commanding officer of Navy Region Hawai'i and commander, Naval Surface Group Middle Pacific, for his help and that of those under his command. Master Chief Petty Officer Bart Bauer and the staff of the Pearl Harbor Public Affairs Office were extremely kind to a first time author. Jim Neumann is the Pearl Harbor base historian, which has got to be one of the best jobs in the world. Jim did a splendid job for me. He not only arranged for a boat tour of the entire harbor, but he personally took me on a tour of the base, taking me anywhere I wanted to go.

The experience of these two tours was priceless. Because of these tours I have been to every location at Pearl Harbor that I write of in the book. From the coaling docks, to Hospital Point, the submarine base, Ford Island, and Merry Point landing. I have stood on the shore of the main channel and seen how extraordinarily narrow it is. I have knelt down on the old seaplane ramp on Ford Island and put my fingers in bullet holes in the concrete left by strafing Japanese planes. Because of these experiences I have a better understanding of what the sailors and Marines saw and felt on December 7, 1941.

I would like to thank Mr. David Hoffert and his history class at Northfield Junior and Senior High School in Wabash, Indiana. Several years ago as a class project they began contacting Pearl Harbor veterans asking them to relate their stories of the attack and their war experiences. The result is a vast wealth of hitherto unheard stories and perhaps more importantly a permanent connection and relationship between the veterans and the students. Mr. Hoffert has created a home for this treasure of personal history on the Internet. I used it extensively for this book and am grateful to him, his students, and of course the veterans who shared their always honest, sometimes funny, and sometimes very painful stories.

Lastly I would like to thank the four Pearl Harbor survivors that I personally interviewed: Elbert Lee Brown of the coastal minesweeper USS COCKATOO, AMc-8; Ernest Wilkins of the coastal minesweeper USS CROSSBILL, AMc-9; Pat Douhan of the destroyer USS HULL, DD-350; and Arthur Herriford of the light cruiser USS DETROIT, CL-8, who at the time of our interview was president of the Pearl Harbor Survivors Association. I would like to thank them not only for showing kindness to a fledgling author who asked very personal questions but also thank them and their comrades for their service to our country and to the world.

FOREWORD

Almost seventy years have passed since that fateful Sunday in December 1941, when the Japanese attack on Pearl Harbor catapulted America into World War II. Many books have been written about that day and the events leading up to it, and it remains a subject of enduring fascination and speculation.

Dave Kilmer has now added a new and unique perspective to the Pearl Harbor saga, the stories of the United States Navy ships caught in the harbor that morning and of their subsequent careers throughout the next three and a half years of war. These ships belonged to a unique sorority that shared a defining moment in American and world history. There was much fighting ahead and most of the veterans of that first day of war were in the thick of it. The battleship *Nevada* was raised from the mud to pound German positions behind Utah beach, helping pave the way for the Normandy landings. Another battleship, *Pennsylvania*, Pacific Fleet flagship on December 7, 1941, was one of the first ships damaged in the war. And one of the last, struck by a torpedo in Buckner Bay, Okinawa, while the fleet, and the nation, waited for word of the Japanese surrender. The destroyers *Monaghan* and *Hull* survived the attack together only to die together in a typhoon three years later. Yet others served quietly, like the little harbor ferry *Nihoa*, destined to spend the war where she began it, plying the waters of Pearl Harbor. Dave does not ignore the human side either. There is the gunner's mate aboard the destroyer *Phelps* at anchor in San Francisco Bay, marveling at the bright lights of Oakland and San Francisco sparkling across the water, the first lights he had seen at night since the war began.

The book also tells the ultimate fate of each of those special ships, whether a war casualty like the tanker *Neosho*, service in another navy like the cruiser *St. Louis*, or as was the fate for most, the scrapper's torch. All however were linked by a common thread, for the ships belonged to a special sisterhood as a participant in the attack that galvanized and united a nation. They were indeed the Daughters of Infamy, and Dave Kilmer ably tells their stories.

Daniel Madsen

Dan Madsen is the author of *Forgotten Fleet: The Mothball Navy* and *Resurrection: Salvaging the Battle Fleet at Pearl Harbor*.

PREFACE

Back in 1994 I made my first trip to Pearl Harbor. While I never considered myself an expert on the events of December 7, 1941, I always felt that I was more than just a little knowledgeable about it. At that time I purchased a map at the visitors center. The map titled "Air Raid, Pearl Harbor. This is Not Drill", (the name is taken from the text of the message transmitted to all U.S. Navy vessels announcing the Japanese attack), published by O.S.B. Mapmania Publishing, contains a thumbnail historical account of the raid and all kinds of ancillary information. It does indeed include a map of Pearl Harbor, and more importantly a list and the location of every ship in the harbor on December 7, 1941.

I had kept it neatly tucked away on my bookshelf between Gordon Prange's, "At Dawn We Slept" and one of my most cherished possessions, my father's 1944 edition of the Bluejackets' Manual that he received when he went through boot camp in World War II. Occasionally, as I read something about Pearl Harbor or just wanted to relive my visit there, I would pull it out and look at it. One day while perusing it the idea of a project came to mind. When I retired from work I would need a grand retirement venture to work on. The map gave me an idea. Why not make a model, a diorama, of Pearl Harbor at the instant the war broke out, with little Japanese planes flying overhead and the first torpedoes in the water. Perhaps I could make a 3D representation of one of the famous photos taken by the Japanese pilots. I liked the idea. So I began researching the project.

I discovered that the damaged incurred by some ships was of such a minor nature that they were battle ready within months or weeks if not days. I also discovered, much to my surprise that most of the ships at Pearl Harbor suffered no damage at all! I discovered that with the exception of three ships, ARIZONA, OKLAHOMA and UTAH, all the ships that were sunk that day were refloated, repaired, refurbished and ultimately entered the war to avenge themselves against the Imperial Japanese Navy. Finally I ran across the ultimate fact. Two ships at Pearl Harbor on December 7, 1941, one of which was sunk, were also present at the Japanese surrender in Tokyo Bay on September 2, 1945. This intrigued me and of course prompted the next question; If these two ships survived the attack on Pearl Harbor, survived the war and made it all the way to the surrender, what happened to the other ships of Pearl Harbor? When I attempted to find the book that would answer that question I discovered a new fact. There wasn't one. So the reason this book exists is that I wanted to read it and no one had yet written it.

This book is not intended to be a complete in depth history of every ship that survived Pearl Harbor. That could never be done in a single volume. Nor does it cover each of the 187 ships that were in the harbor that day. For manageability sake unnamed yard and service craft and civilian ships are not included, nor are ships that were not actually in Pearl Harbor or directly involved in enemy action. 110 named naval vessels and one Motor Torpedo Boat Squadron are profiled in this book. Many of these ships have already had their individual comprehensive histories written, some others are historical orphans, with nothing but official documents to recognize that they ever existed. This volume's purpose is to help bring to life the stories of these ships and to be a compact single reference source for all the major ships at Pearl Harbor and what happened to them during and after the war. It will hopefully stimulate a curiosity and desire to learn more about one, some, or all of these *"Daughters of Infamy"*.

"What I write about is not war, but the courage of man."

Cornelius Ryan

Author of

The Longest Day
and
A Bridge Too Far

PART I

ONE HUNDRED ELEVEN SURVIVORS

Pacific Ocean

Ward
Antares
Kuroshio

Thornton
Hulbert
Tautog
Dolphin

Rigel
Cummings
Preble

Pruitt
Sicard
Ontario
Grebe
Selby
San Francisco
Honolulu

Tracy
New Orleans
Ramapo
PT Boats

Castor
Sumner

Widgeon

Pelias
PT Boats

Hickam
Field

Narwhal?

Jarvis

Bagley

Shaw
Nagara
Argonne
Sacramento
Helm

Dobbin
Vestal
San
Crssm
Dewey
Pennsylvania

Utility?
Cassin
Downes

Cachalot
Tautog

Ward
Antares
Kuroshio

Condor
Crossbill
Ash

Chang-Ho
Cockatoo
Reedbird
Cinchona~

Alea

Phoenix

Allen
Chew

Oklahoma
West Virginia Maryland
Vestal Tennessee
Arizona
Nevada

Bobolink

California

Avocet

Solace

Dobbin Phelps
Dewey
Hull
Worden

MacDonough

Sotoyomo
Shaw

Ford
Island

Helm

Tangier

Utah
Raleigh

Detroit

East Loch

Setfridge
Case
Blue Tucker
Whitney Reid
Conyngham

Henley
Ralph Talbot
Patterson

Monaghan
Dale
Farragut
Aylwin

Waipio Peninsula

Pearl
City

Trever
Medusa Wasmuth
Curtiss Zane
Perry

Middle
Loch

Gamble
Montgomery
Breese
Ramsay

West
Loch

Pyro

SAMPSON CLASS DESTROYER
DD-66
LAUNCHED: 1916

DECEMBER 7, 1941

By the standards of naval vessels, USS ALLEN was an old lady. She was a 25-year-old World War I era ship and the last of her class in existence. This day she was nested in between the ex USS BALTIMORE, C-3,[1] on her starboard side and USS CHEW, DD-106, to her port. As old and out of place as she may have been, this old lady still had some fight in her.

General quarters was sounded just after the crew saw the first bombs dropped. By 0805 ALLEN's guns were responding to the attack. The #6 three-inch gun hit and brought down an enemy plane that crashed in some nearby hills. The starboard waist .50-caliber gun hit a plane, which exploded in mid-air and crashed between Ford Island and the USS DETROIT, CL-8, berthed at F-13 on the north shore of Ford Island.

This was ALLEN's only enemy engagement of the war and she suffered no damage and no casualties.

THE WAR

While other destroyers, only a year or two younger than ALLEN, where chosen to be refurbished and reborn into new roles and lives, ALLEN was deemed too old to go to war. She served out the war mostly in Hawai'i

---

1   BALTIMORE had been launched in 1888 and was part of Admiral Dewey's fleet that destroyed the Spanish fleet in Manila Bay in 1898. She was decommissioned in 1922 and stricken from the Navy rolls in 1937. She was being used as a floating warehouse at Pearl Harbor.

in anti-submarine patrols, escort duty and playing the enemy target for submarines training to go to war. She also made the occasional trip escorting ships to the west coast of the United States.

Japanese bombers sank the carrier USS YORKTOWN, CV-5, on June 7, 1942 during the battle of Midway. ALLEN was dispatched with other ships to assist in the transport of survivors, transferring 94 members of YORKTOWN's crew from other ships and returning them to Pearl Harbor. ALLEN made one trip to Midway in October of that same year as an escort vessel. She then resumed her regular duties in Hawai'ian waters.

FATE

The de-escalation from a wartime navy to a peacetime navy descended like the flash of a headsmen's axe. Within days of the Japanese surrender, ALLEN received her orders to sail to Philadelphia. Upon her arrival, in October, she was placed out of commission. She sat in reserve for barely a year and on November 1, 1946 her name was struck from the Navy's rolls. She was sold to the Boston Metals Company, of Baltimore, Maryland, for $12,094.25. At the time of her sale ALLEN was the oldest destroyer in the American Navy.

USS Antares

GENERAL STORES SHIP
AKS-3
LAUNCHED: 1919

DECEMBER 7, 1941

The waters off the entrance to Pearl Harbor were very busy on the morning of December 7, 1941. At approximately 0630 ANTARES spotted what it believed to be a submarine conning tower 1500 yards off her starboard quarter. ANTARES had a barge in tow and was waiting to rendezvous with a tug to transfer the towline and then enter the harbor. ANTARES' captain, Commander Lawrence C. Grannis, signaled the USS WARD, on patrol duties outside the harbor entrance, and informed her of the intruder. Several minutes later a PBY Catalina from Patrol Squadron 14 spotted the submarine from the air and dropped smoke floats to mark its position.

Little did the crew of ANTARES know, but they had ringside seats to the first sea battle of World War II between the Empire of Japan and the United States of America. Those on deck watched as WARD came on hard, firing two shots and dropping four depth charges, to expertly sink the mini-sub.

About twenty minutes later, the tugboat USS KEOSANQUA, AT-38, arrived and the two crews set about to transfer the towline. During this process the crew spotted Japanese planes headed for Pearl. The aerial attack had begun inside the harbor, but it soon spilled out onto the open seas when an enemy plane strafed ANTARES, causing insignificant damage and no causalities. The towline transfer continued even under fire, with bombs dropping around both vessels, the captain in his after action reported stated that, *"Men disconnecting the tow and others on exposed stations were calm and steady."* These explosions may very well have been improperly fused antiaircraft ordinance being fired from inside the harbor. At 0835 the transfer was completed and ANTARES departed the area. Originally intending to sail into Pearl Harbor after completion of her mission, Commander Grannis deemed it impractical to sail an unarmed ship smack into the middle of a war. Nor was it safe to sail aimlessly about the waters outside the harbor so ANTARES made for the safety of Honolulu Harbor to the east, where she moored at berth 5-A at 1146.

THE WAR

Like many other ships, ANTARES, underwent modifications after December 7th. She would no longer be an unarmed and defenseless ship, receiving two five-inch guns, four three-inch guns and eight 20-millimeter anti-aircraft machine guns. This lady may not have had teeth, but she at least now had some sharp claws.

After being armed and running some trials, she finally loaded her holds and headed out to war arriving in Pago Pago, Samoa on May 31, 1942. For the next three years ANTARES performed her job as a floating warehouse, following the fleet wherever she was needed to supply any and all ships with whatever was needed to meet the enemy. She easily fell into the routine of the backwaters of war, supplying the fleet for a time, then off to a port for repairs and maintenance then back to the States to resupply and then return to the fleet in the south Pacific to start the cycle anew. Her journeys took her crew to exotic places with exotic names like, Tongatabu, Noumea, Tulagi, Ulithi and Kerama Retto. In March 1943 ANTARES helped salvage the stores ship USS DELPHINUS, AF-24, which had run aground on Garanhua Reef, off New Caledonia.

In May 1945 she was supplying ships in support of operations on Okinawa. Completing this mission she was ordered to Saipan and then on to Pearl Harbor, which she set sail for alone, on June 25, 1945.

Even now, with the war over in Europe and only weeks left of war in the Pacific, ANTARES' captain, Lieutenant Commander N. A. Gansa, USNR, maintained his war footing keeping sharp-eyed lookouts at their stations. It's a good thing that he did. Maybe it was training or experience or just plain common sense, but a lone supply ship with no escorts is a tempting target for marauding submarines. Three days later, around 400 nautical miles north east of Truk, at 1329, the lookouts sighted what appeared to be a periscope at a perilously close one hundred yards away. The eye at the other end of that periscope belonged to, Lt. Cdr. Sugamasa Tetsuaki, the commanding officer of the Japanese submarine, *I-36*. Certainly elated at the sight of an escortless supply ship the Japanese skipper let loose at least one torpedo. Captain Gansa received word of the torpedo in the nick of time and ordered a hard to starboard outmaneuvering the Long Lance torpedo. Lookouts then sighted a "kaitan", a kamikaze torpedo, piloted by Lt. (j.g.) Ikebuchi Nobuo. Against a sub and a manned torpedo the lumbering supply ship would appear to have had little chance.

Gansa immediately commenced a zigzag pattern and ordered her guns to open fire. The #2 three-inch gun found its target scoring a direct hit on the kaitan, which promptly sank. The aft five-inch gun fired on the periscope to the stern where the submarine appeared to be surfacing. Some five-inch rounds from ANTARES and perhaps the sight of the destroyer USS SPROSTON, DD-577, responding to ANTARES' call for help, convinced the sub otherwise. It submerged. ANTARES finally arrived at Pearl Harbor eleven days later on July 9, 1945.

ANTARES made one last trip to the western Pacific, stopping at Ulithi and ending up on Okinawa on the 14th of August, the same day the Japanese surrendered.

FATE

After the war, ANTARES returned to the Far East where she remained for nine months in support of the occupation of both China and Korea, maintaining those duties through April, 1946. In May, she began inactivation chores in San Francisco and then sailed to Mare Island Naval Shipyard, where she was decommissioned on August 2, 1946. On September 25th her name was struck from the Naval Vessel Register. One year later, on September 18, 1947 she was sold to Kaiser and Company to be scrapped.

TENDER
AG-31
BUILT: 1920

DECEMBER 7, 1941

ARGONNE was berthed at the north end of 1010² dock alongside the minesweeper USS TERN, AM-31, when the attack began. Just three minutes into hostilities, ARGONNE's crew was fighting back with three-inch guns and .50 caliber machine guns. Being a tender and lightly armed, the Japanese planes paid little or no attention to her. However, with the newborn war raging in confusion around him, Marine Corps Corporal Alfred Schlag was paying attention to the Japanese planes. Manning one of the .50 caliber machine guns, Schlag took aim at a bomber as it passed by 1010 dock and knocked it down, scoring ARGONNE's first and as it would turn out, only kill of World War II.

ARGONNE received no casualties to her crew and suffered only insignificant minor damage during the attack. Her captain, Commander F. W. O'Connor, reported that his crew was *assisting to get wounded from damaged ships, taking bodies from the water and assisting with repair facilities to full capacity"* during and after the attack.

THE WAR

ARGONNE was the flagship for Admiral William L. Calhoun, Commander, Base Force, Pacific Fleet and remained so, in Pearl Harbor, until the spring when a permanent land headquarters was established.

---

2   Pronounced "Ten-Ten" dock, it is a pier at the Pearl Harbor Navy Yard, so named because it is 1,010 feet long.

Her first mission of the war, in April 1942, was to sail to Canton Island and assist with the salvage of the troopship *President Taylor*, which had run aground, after which ARGONNE returned to Pearl Harbor. She stayed there for two months then returned to Canton Island in July to deliver cargo there and at Suva Harbor, Fiji.

ARGONNE arrived in Noumea, New Caledonia on July 27, 1942. On August 1st, she once more became a flagship when Vice Admiral Robert L. Ghormley, Commander, South Pacific Force and South Pacific Area came on board. Two months later Ghormley was relieved by Vice Admiral William F. "Bull" Halsey, Jr. Halsey kept his command on board until the spring of 1943 when he shifted his command to shore, citing the hopeless inadequacies of the ship for his growing staff and responsibilities.

ARGONNE eventually arrived at Purvis Bay, Florida Island, on August 13th after short trips to Auckland, New Zealand and Espiritu Santo, New Hebrides where she had loaded men from Carrier Aircraft Service Unit 14. USS SELFRIDGE, DD-357, was tended to by ARGONNE during her stay in Purvis Bay, which ended in November 1943. Another stint of tender and salvage duties followed in the Russell Islands until late April, 1944. Assigned to Service Squadron (ServRon) 10, ARGONNE set sail for Majuro Atoll, Marshall Islands where she serviced the fleet until she moved once again in August.

At that time ARGONNE settled in at Seeadler Harbor, Manus Island, in the Admiralty chain. Here again she became a floating headquarters as Captain S. B. Ogden supervised the operations of ServRon 10.

On November 10, 1944, ARGONNE's captain, Commander T. H. Escott was standing outside his cabin talking with his executive officer when, without warning a massive explosion slammed them both to the deck. It took several moments to recover from the shock and get back on their feet. When they did they scanned the harbor to determine what had happened. A quick look made it abundantly clear. USS MOUNT HOOD, AE-11, an ammunition ship, only 1,100 feet away had blown up. It had disintegrated. The damage from the initial explosion included ruptured water and steam pipes, a shattered searchlight and five antennas that had been blown away by the blast. Only seconds later, what was left of MOUNT HOOD literally came raining down upon the harbor and ARGONNE. Pieces of metal fell from the sky like a meteor shower. Over two hundred pieces, some weighing up to 150 pounds crashed down onto the ship. At the end of the day ARGONNE had two men dead, two missing and twelve injured.

The USS MOUNT HOOD explodes in Seeadler Harbor, November 10, 1944.

Repairs were quickly made and in less than a month ARGONNE was once again at work, arriving at Kossol Roads in the Palaus on December 15th. While there ARGONNE was once again a victim of a nearby accident. A Landing Craft Vehicle, Personnel, (LCVP) attempting to dock, carelessly rammed the depth charge racks of a sub-chaser, SC-702, that was moored alongside ARGONNE. The collision dislodged one of the depth charges, which fell into the water and exploded, lifting ARGONNE "several inches" out of the water. Damage was restricted to unsecured gear flying about in forward compartments and no casualties were reported. She was repaired and remained in the Palaus servicing the fleet until she arrived at Leyte in the Philippines on February 15, 1945. She remained there until June 14th when she sailed for the Marshall Islands. She spent the last two months of the war in the Western Pacific servicing ships of the fleet.

FATE

After the surrender ARGONNE continued to serve in the western Pacific supporting occupation forces in Japan for a short time. She returned to the United States after participating in "Magic Carpet" service, the effort to bring service men home as soon as possible. Her last port of call was Mare Island Naval Shipyard where she was decommissioned on July 15, 1946. She was transferred to the Naval Maritime Commission two weeks later and was struck from the Naval Rolls on August 28, 1946. She was finally sold for scrap to the Boston Metals Corporation on August 14, 1950.

Ash

ALOE CLASS NET LAYER
YN-2
LAUNCHED: 1941

DECEMBER 7, 1941

ASH was barely six months old when she arrived at Bishop Point, Hawai'i, August 20, 1941 and began tending to the anti-submarine nets protecting Pearl Harbor. Three quiet months passed before war started there. Like many ships that day, she fired at the enemy but she claimed no hits or kills. She suffered no damage or casualties. The first day of the war was her only day to see action. She never fired another shot in anger.

THE WAR

ASH spent the duration of the war tending the nets at Pearl Harbor. She was commissioned AN-7 on December 20, 1942 and operated at Pearl Harbor until May 11, 1946 when she sailed for San Francisco.

FATE

She was berthed at Mare Island Naval Shipyard in Vallejo, California until November 1, 1946 when she left for Vancouver, Washington where she was placed out of commission on December 13, 1946. ASH was struck from the Navy rolls on September 1, 1962, having been in "reserve" until that time. The Maritime Administration took possession of her and placed her in the National Defense Reserve Fleet, ("mothball fleet"), at Olympia, Washington. Like many of her Pearl Harbor sisters she was eventually sold for scrap, in her case, to the I. D. Logan Company, on May 14, 1971.

USS Avocet

LAPWING CLASS MINE SWEEPER / SEAPLANE TENDER
AVP-4
LAUNCHED: 1918

DECEMBER 7, 1941

AVOCET was tied up at berth F-1 on the southwest side of Ford Island when Japanese bombs started falling only a few hundred yards away. General quarters was sounded, joining the chorus of claxons announcing the same alert on ships throughout the harbor. The responding crew bringing ammunition to the guns were witness to the attack unfolding before them. A Nakajima "Kate" flew in low over the harbor and let loose a torpedo at USS CALIFORNIA, BB-44, only two berths away. As the torpedo hit, rocking the battleship, the "Kate" pulled up and away. AVOCET's starboard gun crew let fly a round striking the torpedo plane which promptly turned into a ball of fire, crashing across the channel near the naval hospital.

As the attack continued her guns fired continuously but scored no more hits. A flight of Kate bombers came into view and dropped their loads, which were probably intended for CALIFORNIA. The bombs all missed their target and fell into the empty berth between AVOCET and CALIFORNIA. All five of the bombs plowed into the muddy bottom of the harbor, but none exploded.

At approximately 0840, USS NEVADA, BB-36 got underway and made a break for the open sea. Her movement garnered great attention from the enemy planes, which made a concerted effort to sink her in the main channel. AVOCET's guns made every effort to cover the battleship's escape as she sailed directly in front of her.

After the last attack was over AVOCET became a little jack-of-all-trades dashing about the harbor. She first received orders to assist in fighting the fires raging onboard CALIFORNIA. After a short twenty minutes there she was sent to aid in beaching NEVADA off Hospital Point and fighting her fires, eventually spending several hours there. The early afternoon found her on the north side of Ford Island providing steam and electricity to the damaged USS RALEIGH, CL-7, were she remained for the rest of the day.

AVOCET survived the attack with no damage and her two causalities were limited to an injured foot, from a dropped ammunition box and another sailor with a wounded forearm from either flying shrapnel or a spent bullet.

THE WAR

AVOCET performed routine duties in and around Hawai'i after the attack and for the first several months of 1942. In May she reported to California for a major refit at the Hunters Point Naval Shipyard in San Francisco.

On July 18th she sailed for the Alaskan waters that would be her major duty station for the duration of the war, arriving at Kodiak Island, Alaska after a brief visit to Seattle. Although originally built as a minesweeper, AVOCET had her classification changed to small seaplane tender before the war and was assigned to Fleet Air Wing 4 in that capacity.

In early September, AVOCET assisted with the salvage and towing of USS CASCO, AVP-12, which had been beached after being torpedoed by *RO-61*, a Japanese submarine, in Nazan Bay, Adak.

Upon completion of a short overhaul at Puget Sound Navy yards she returned to Atka in late January 1943 where she continued her far-flung duties in the northern Pacific. The Lapwing class minesweepers, built after World War I, turned out to be amazingly versatile ships. At 180 feet long they were big enough to do big jobs and at the same time small enough to do little jobs. As one of those Lapwing class ships, AVOCET fit in well at the task of jack of all trades, completing jobs as varied as escorting other naval vessels and civilian ships to transporting materials and personnel and other assignments as needed such as, patrol, survey and rescue missions.

On May 19, 1944, AVOCET had a small set-to with a Japanese Mitsubishi, "Betty" bomber. While on patrol off of Attu Island she was spotted by the "Betty" which commenced a strafing run. AVOCET fired back with three-inch and 20mm guns. The encounter was bloodless on both parts. This was AVOCETs last hostile contact of the war.

FATE

Having survived the war, AVOCET's usefulness was soon over and the twenty-seven year old ship was condemned to uselessness, being sold to the Power Machine Company of Brooklyn, New York where she was used as a hulk. She was scrapped sometime after 1950.

USS Aylwin

FARRAGUT CLASS DESTROYER
DD-355
LAUNCHED: 1934

DECEMBER 7, 1941

Like all battles, Pearl Harbor has its share of certainly interesting, if not amazing stories. One of the most interesting of Pearl Harbor stories is that of the extraordinary baptism under fire of two ensigns. At 0755 on December 7th Lieutenant Commander Robert H. Rogers, captain of the AYLWIN was not on board. In fact, there were no senior officers on board and most of the crew and almost all of the senior petty officers were on shore. At the time of the attack there were only about 50 men on board, just about half the crew. The four officers on board that morning were all ensigns. The junior most of these junior officers were Ensign William K. Reordan, USNR and Ensign Burdick H. Brittin, USNR both of whom had reported on board in November. The senior officers were Ensign Stanley B. Caplan, USNR and Ensign Hugo C. Anderson, USNR. Caplan had a total of eight months experience at sea and Anderson had only seven. When the bombs started falling, Caplan was in command.

Within five minutes of the first bombs falling AYLWIN was firing her guns and firing up her boilers in preparation for getting underway. Below, Ensign Brittin looked out a porthole and saw the UTAH already capsizing. On the bridge Caplan was in command and Anderson was at the helm. The four destroyers nested at buoy X-14 answered the call of Commander

Destroyers Battle Force and sortied heading out the channel north of Ford Island. AYLWIN cut away her anchor chain forward, stern wire and even her mahogany accommodation ladder in order to facilitate her exit. All her guns were blazing as she followed her sister ships down the channel.

With so many ships at such close quarters, firing at enemy planes in what could be called nothing less than a target rich environment, it is difficult to say just which ship was responsible for shooting down which plane. Many ships, including AYLWIN claimed to have shot down a "Val" that then crashed into USS CURTISS, AV-4 that was moored at the south end of Middle Loch. AYLWIN eventually took credit for a total of three planes shot down.

Captain Rogers arrived at Pearl Harbor and saw his ship sailing down the channel and heading out of the harbor. He quickly commandeered a whaleboat and proceeded into the chaos of Pearl Harbor to chase down his ship and board her. The whaleboat carrying Rogers was sighted from the bridge, but under steam, under attack and under orders, Ensign Caplan couldn't stop and board his commanding officer. He proceeded out of the harbor and Rogers returned to shore, (An only slightly fictionalized version of AYLWIN's sortie out of Pearl Harbor appears in the 1961 Otto Preminger film, "In Harm's Way," starring John Wayne and Kirk Douglas.) In notes written the following day, Ensign Brittin said, *"How we succeeded in clearing the channel I will never know, but we did get outside and the marrow in our bones turned to water as we looked back on the smoke and flame that once was Pearl."*[3]

Once outside the harbor AYLWIN received orders to rendezvous with USS ENTERPRISE, CV-6, returning from Wake Island. A small task force was organized to search for the Japanese fleet that had attacked Pearl Harbor. AYLWIN sailed into the night looking for aircraft carriers, looking out for submarines and looking for an enemy to shoot at. She found nothing.

The first day of World War II was certainly a trying day for everyone at Pearl Harbor, but the crew of AYLWIN seemed to do an exceptional

---

3   Air Raid: Pearl Harbor! Recollections of a Day of Infamy, edited by Paul Stilwell, Published by Naval Institute Press, 1981

job. With no senior officers almost no senior enlisted men and only half a crew, those on board fought, sailed and searched for thirty-six hours with no sleep, little food and no relief. Ensigns Caplan and Anderson exhibited extreme courage, leadership and seamanship far beyond what would be expected from men with little experience. Their example was certainly a factor in the performance of the skeleton crew they had.

In his after action report, Captain Rogers had nothing but praise for his officers and men, "*The conduct of the men was magnificent...Every man did more than his job and was eager to fight...Ensign H. C. Anderson, is responsible for much of this vessel's successful operation. He assisted in all important matters and demonstrated remarkable ability as a ship handler. With experience of only seven months at sea he was able to take the ship out under severest conditions...The conduct of Ensign S. Caplan, USNR, who has been at sea a total of eight months in superbly taking command for 36 hours during war operations of the severest type is a most amazing and outstanding achievement...It is recommended that Ensign S. Caplan and Ensign H. C. Anderson, USNR, receive special commendation.*"

THE WAR

The first days of the war found AYLWIN performing anti-submarine duties in the defensive area outside Pearl. She then joined a small task force intended as a diversion, to aid in the defense of Wake Island, but that mission was cancelled. Instead she screened a convoy of evacuees to the States.

As part of Task Force 11, which was en route to raid the Japanese base at Rabaul, New Guinea, during the first week of February, AYLWIN shot down at least one Mitsubishi bomber from a group sent to intercept the task force.

In early May, 1942, AYLWIN was assigned to be one the screening ships of USS LEXINGTON, CV-2, which was part of a combined task force under the command of Rear Admiral Frank Fletcher, south of the Solomon Islands in the Coral Sea. On the morning of the 8th Japanese planes found LEXINGTON's group and attacked. Along with the 150 five-inch shells and 950 rounds of 20mm ammunition fired at the attacking planes by

AYLWIN's guns were several rounds of .45 caliber ammunition fired at the low flying Japanese by Ensign Brittin who drew his sidearm and shot at the enemy. The concentrated efforts of AYLWIN and the other screening vessels could not repel the onslaught of Japanese planes determined to finally sink one of the carriers that they failed to destroy on December 7th. At least two bombs and two torpedoes hit LEXINGTON. Despite valiant efforts on the part of LEXINGTON's damage control parties, the "Lady Lex" could not be saved and had to be scuttled. AYLWIN received survivors on board two days later and returned to Pearl Harbor.

At the end of the month AYLWIN joined the screen for ENTERPRISE and USS HORNET, CV-8, as they headed off to intercept the Japanese fleet that was known to be heading for Midway. The battle commenced on June 4th and both fleets hurled squadrons of airplanes at each other. AYLWIN threw up a lead curtain of protection and this time her charges came through the battle without a scratch, allowing both ENTERPRISE and HORNET to help sink four of the Japanese carriers that had launched the attack on Pearl Harbor.

AYLWIN's duties were shifted from the warm, humid weather of the tropics to the icy cold of Alaska for a month starting in mid-June. Later, she screened the escort carrier USS LONG ISLAND, AVG-1, south to the Solomons in preparation for the invasion of Guadalcanal. She closed out 1942 by sailing to California, having spent the last months of the year in Hawai'i and the South Pacific performing escort, transport and screening duties.

The first nine months of 1943 were once again spent in the frozen north of Alaska, arriving at Dutch Harbor January 13th. For many months she would patrol around the Japanese occupied island of Kiska during the day and fire harassing rounds at the enemy in the night. In May she supported the invasion of Attu, the westernmost of the Aleutians, which was also occupied by the Japanese. In a continuation of the retaking of the Aleutians, three months later in August, Kiska was invaded. After bombarding the island and screening the landing craft AYLWIN along with the rest of the American forces discovered that the Japanese had days earlier, successfully snuck in two cruisers and six destroyers and evacuated the entire Japanese garrison.

After a short stay in California, AYLWIN screened three escort carriers on the way to the New Hebrides and during operations in the Gilbert Islands. She then returned to Pearl Harbor and back again to San Francisco.

1944 must have gone quite quickly for AYLWIN and her crew. In January and February she was assigned to the invasions of Kwajalein and Eniwetok Atolls. Her orders for one of the smaller islands in the Eniwetok campaign was to knock down all the tress on the island, eliminating their use as cover for the enemy. She complied using her main five inch guns and her 40 mm guns to level the foliage. She then began traveling the central and Southwestern Pacific almost continuously for twelve months straight, never staying in any one place for more than a few weeks. She was ordered to Kaua'i, Majuro, Truk, Yap, Hollandia, Rota, and the Marianas. As always for ships as versatile as destroyers she was tasked with multiple missions, including rescuing downed air crews, escorting and screening duties and bombarding enemy positions on Saipan, Tinian and Guam. She crisscrossed the Pacific a half a dozen times and then returned to the states stopping in Bremerton, Washington and San Pedro, California. She then doubled back to Hawai'i then returned to Ulithi.

In December AYLWIN was operating in the Philippine Sea with Task Force 38. All war operations and thoughts of war ceased on the 18th when Typhoon Cobra struck the 3rd Fleet. The only thought in anyone's mind then were thoughts of survival, not survival against an enemy, but survival in the face of nature's fury.

Photo of "Typhoon Cobra" from a ship's radar screen.

AYLWIN's captain, Lt. Cmdr. William Rogers ordered the crew to batten down the hatches and prepare for the storm. The winds and the seas beat the brave ship relentlessly. Wind gusts up to 140 miles per hour were recorded. All through the night AYLWIN was tossed about like a toy in Neptune's bathtub. On numerous occasions she rolled over to 70 degrees and never completely righted herself. The winds tore away her whaleboat and its davits and two crewmen, Machinist Mate 1st Class Sarenski and Lt. E. R. Rendahl, USNR, were washed overboard. The storm wreaked all kinds of havoc on AYLWIN, she lost electrical and steering power, her ventilators failed causing her engine room to be abandoned due to 180 degree heat and the engine room began to flood. AYLWIN survived the typhoon, but three other ships and 790 men did not. She endured a second typhoon four months later in April of 1945, prompting Captain Rogers to write, "with the present sea-keeping and stability characteristics, the Farragut-class destroyers are unable to adequately cope with severe typhoon conditions".

After undergoing repairs at Ulithi AYLWIN picked herself up and went back to war. Marines landed on Iwo Jima on February 19th and on the 21st AYLWIN was there screening transport ships that were landing fresh troops. She then spent the next three days bombarding enemy positions on the island.

In March AYLWIN moved on in preparation for the final major Pacific landing of the war at Okinawa. She was assigned numerous escort duties in support of that operation.

On August 4th she received orders for her last major mission of the war. She was sent to search for survivors of the USS INDIANAPOLIS, CA-35, which had been torpedoed by a Japanese submarine. She searched for two days but found only three bodies. After identifying the remains they were in turn committed to the deep.

FATE

When the Japanese surrendered, AYLWIN was in Apra Harbor in Guam. By the first day of November she no longer existed, at least on paper. It only took the Navy ten short weeks to get her to the states, decommission her and strike her name from the rolls of U. S. Naval vessels. She was barely eleven years old.

She hung around long enough to be stripped of anything useful and then she was sold for $11,041.28 to George H. Nutman, Inc. of Brooklyn, New York. By September of 1948 she was gone.

USS Bagley

BAGLEY CLASS DESTROYER
DD-386
LAUNCHED: 1936

DECEMBER 7, 1941

George J. Sallet was 19 years old and assigned to the #4 five-inch gun on board BAGLEY. His plans for that Sunday morning were to go to the Commissary Store at the nearby submarine base and purchase a new 35mm camera and then go to the Botanical Gardens in downtown Honolulu and take pictures. That, however, is not the way he spent the day. After eating and putting on his dress whites he felt a disturbing vibration through the deck. He quickly ran up a ladder and looked out the hatch. Spent .50 caliber bullet casings from BAGLEY's anti-aircraft guns were already raining down on the deck and he watched as a Japanese plane flew past at eye level and released a torpedo at Battleship Row.

On one of the forward .50 caliber machine guns, Chief Gunner's Mate Harry L. Skinner was already firing at the attacking planes, downing one that crashed near the Officer's Club. BAGLEY was docked at berth B-22 in the Navy Yard in preparation for repairing a damaged bilge keel. The planes had to pass her entire length on their south to north run towards Battleship Row. This allowed the entire firepower of the destroyer to be concentrated on every plane to fly by. The machine gunners on BAGLEY had a field day. Within minutes a second plane was brought down. Moments later, Seaman first class Lowe Peterson - who was not even a machine gunner - manning the #3 .50 caliber fired at a plane causing it to roll and then crash into a crane on the dock. The Japanese gunner on the plane was seen to fall out of the open canopy as it rolled over. In all BAGLEY claimed downing six enemy planes either by herself or in conjunction with fire from other ships.

Orders came thirty-four minutes into the attack for BAGLEY to get underway and exit the harbor. As with other ships that morning, many of BAGLEY's crew were on shore leave including her captain, Lieutenant Commander G. A. Sinclair. Manning the bridge was the senior officer on board, Lieutenant Phillip W. Cann. The destroyer was still hooked up to electrical power from shore and Fireman 2nd Class, Charles Quigley jumped down to the dock and pulled the cables from the still charged power box, receiving second degree burns on his face and arms as a result. On deck and under enemy fire, Chief Boatswain's Mate Robert Bryant almost single handedly made all preparations for getting underway, while Seaman 1st Class Sherman Merry volunteered to single up and cast off the lines. BAGLEY finally got up enough steam to get underway and began to move just as the last enemy planes were heading back to their carriers.

Believing that the south channel out of the harbor might be blocked she took the long way out of the harbor going via the North Channel around Ford Island. This roundabout route afforded the men of the BAGLEY a grand tour of the devastation. OAKLAHOMA, BB-37 had turned turtle with men clinging to her upturned hull. ARIZONA, BB-39, shattered beyond all repair, was a smoking cauldron of death. CALIFORNIA, BB-44, and WEST VIRGINIA, BB-48, had both settled to the shallow bottom of the harbor and were on fire. The flaming, oily waters surrounding them were teeming with the dead, the dying, the injured and the boats trying to save them. As they exited the harbor the last ship they saw was NEVADA, BB-36 the only battleship to get underway during the attack, beached and in flames at Hospital Point. No one on board BAGLEY spoke; they just stood and stared in disbelief.

BAGLEY was ordered to the defensive area outside the harbor to patrol for submarines because her still unrepaired bilge keel would slow her down so she couldn't join the ad-hoc task group that had been formed to search out the enemy fleet. In the evening, crewmen who were off duty requested permission to stay on deck with .30 caliber rifles on the off chance that a Japanese plane would fly by and they might get a chance to shoot at it. They were told to go to bed.

On the morning of the 10th BAGLEY re-entered the harbor after seventy-six hours of continuous duty with no relief. The captain, along with most of his senior officers and senior petty officers, finally came aboard after "missing" the first three days of the war. Reporting on the abilities of "acting captain" Lt. Cann, Captain Sinclair later wrote, *"It is the opinion of the commanding officer that the performance of Lieutenant Cann is highly commendatory and worthy of suitable recognition. His handling of the BAGLEY during the above mentioned period was flawless."* [4]

And George Sallet? Well, he never got his new camera that day, but he did fire over 75 five-inch shells from his #4 gun.

THE WAR

Early January found BAGLEY assigned to several different Task Groups. The first was built around USS SARATOGA, CV-3, near Hawai'i and the second was with USS LEXINGTON, CV-2 in the South Pacific. Into mid 1942 she performed the routine and often mundane duties of a destroyer, including delivering the mail, through out the Pacific.

Her first major action was participating in America's first major offensive of the Pacific War; the invasion of Guadalcanal. During the morning of August 7th she helped in a bombardment of Tulagi and anti-submarine screening missions. In the afternoon her guns helped fight off two aerial attacks. That evening while being serenaded to sleep by gunfire from Guadalcanal members of the crew slept on deck in the tropical heat.

Some ships have the opportunity of making a difference by being in the right place at the right time with the right crew. In BAGLEY's case it

---

4   After action report by Lieutenant Commander G. A. Sinclair, dated December 11, 1941.

was in the First Battle of Savo Island and it made all the difference to the men of USS ASTORIA, CA-34.

Early on the morning of the 8th she was screening the cruiser USS CHICAGO, CA-29 when about 35 enemy planes attacked. The Japanese were met with a barrage of furious anti-aircraft fire and approximately 15 planes were brought down. BAGLEY went to investigate the wreckage of a Mitsubishi G4M "Betty" bomber floating nearby. As they approached they spotted four Japanese crewmen on the port wing. One of the men made a sign as if to surrender. As the ship pulled closer the airman pulled out his pistol, shot his three companions in the head then turned and fired at the BAGLEY inflicting no damage or casualties. Having done his final duty for the Emperor, he turned the gun on himself.

The Japanese were nervous. The battle of Midway had been fought only 2 months earlier and they had been devastated at the loss of four aircraft carriers. The Americans had now invaded Guadalcanal, one of Japan's South Pacific strongholds. The Japanese could not afford to lose it and they were determined to drive the Marines there back into the sea. On the evening of August 8, that duty fell to Vice Admiral Mikawa Gunichi who assembled a small but powerful task force to sail to Guadalcanal and strike a blow so hard that the Americans would be forced to retreat. Mikawa had five heavy cruisers, his flagship *Chokai*, along with *Aoba*, *Kinugasa*, *Kako* and *Furataka*, two light cruisers *Tenryu* and *Yubari* and the destroyer *Yunagi*.

Despite the fact that he knew his small fleet had been detected by American forces, Mikawa moved forward with determination. The trip from Rabaul took time and at about 0100 hours of the 9th the Japanese squadron entered the waters between Guadalcanal and Savo Island. All hell was about to break loose.

South of Savo Island BAGLEY was in a group consisting of the American ships CHICAGO and USS PATTERSON, DD-392, and the Australian heavy cruisers HMAS AUSTRAILIA, D-84, and HMAS CANBERRA, D-33. The droning of a Japanese float plane was heard overhead and the cover of night was ripped away when it dropped flares illuminating the Allied ships below. Mikawa's ships already rounding a point off Savo Island opened fire with both shells and torpedoes. Two torpedoes passed down

BAGLEY's starboard side, barely missing her. One torpedo hit CHICAGO in the bow and two more hit AUSTRALIA amidships. BAGLEY answered back by turning hard to port and fired four torpedoes back at the Japanese but none of them found their intended target. She maneuvered once again to fire another salvo but the Japanese fleet had disappeared into the darkness. With no enemy to shoot at she headed for the designated destroyer rendezvous point. Even though her part in the actual battle was over, her most important work was yet to come.

As she made for her rendezvous a fierce glow appeared before BAGLEY in the darkness. It was ASTORIA. The Japanese had mauled her and she was a blazing wreck with a list to port. The two ships met there in the black shark infested sea, bow to bow. George Sallet heaved a line over to ASTORIA to help transfer wounded. Although the battle was over, the decks of both ships were dangerous places to be. Shells from ASTORIA began to "cook off" and explode throwing hot shrapnel everywhere. One piece of flying debris cut through Sallet's life vest as he worked the line, but luck was with him and the vest was the only casualty.

As injured men began to be passed over to BAGLEY, ASTORIA's captain, William Greenman was on deck. He had been seriously wounded and was bleeding badly. He was giving orders and directing efforts to save his men and ship even as a corpsman fervently worked on his wounds.

A seemingly never-ending parade of wounded were transferred from ASTORIA to BAGLEY; men with gaping wounds and severed limbs were brought aboard. Below decks, the passageways were slippery with blood. Both BAGLEY's and ASTORIA's doctors worked to resurrect lives from shattered bodies. Those wounded who couldn't be accommodated below were placed on deck.

Internal explosions and fire steadily decimated ASTORIA and the list to port increased dramatically. The order was finally given for the crew to abandon ship and hundreds of men jumped over to BAGLEY. Over 400 men were saved that night.

The next day a repair party was sent over to ASTORIA in an attempt to save the cruiser but the gallant lady was too far gone and nothing could be done. The repair party was removed and in the afternoon, ASTORIA saw her last sunlight, joining the ever growing graveyard of ships on the floor of "Ironbottom Sound."[5]

For the next three years, BAGLEY, like so many other destroyers in the Pacific Theater was the "little ship that could," being called on to execute a wide variety of assignments. During that time period she was part of eight different Task Groups, escorted sixteen different convoys, successfully completed eight screening missions, participated in the invasions of Saipan and Okinawa and was engaged in the battles of the Philippine Sea and Leyte Gulf. While screening aircraft carriers in Lingayen Gulf on January 13, 1945 a group of kamikazes attacked the group. A Nakajima Ki-43, "Oscar" fighter aimed for BAGLEY but her gunners brought her down while it was still 1,000 yards away.

BAGLEY was escorting a convoy to Saipan when she got the news that Japan had surrendered. Her crew was rewarded with ten days of rest and recreation.

FATE

On August 31, 1945 BAGLEY hosted Admiral Francis E. M. Whiting as he accepted the surrender of the Japanese garrison on Marcus Island from Rear Admiral Matsubara Masata.

After serving for several months in Japan performing occupation duties BAGLEY was eventually decommissioned back where she started the war, in Pearl Harbor, on June 13, 1946. Her name was struck from the roles of the U. S. Navy on February 25, 1947 and sold for scrap to The Moore Dry Dock Company of Oakland, California on September 8, 1947.

George Sallet served on the BAGLEY for the entire war and many years later served as the commander of the Pearl Harbor Attack Veterans Association.

---

5   The name given by American sailors to that body of water in the Solomon Islands north of Guadalcanal, east of Savo Island and south of Florida Island. So called because of the large number of warships sunk there.

USS Blue

BAGLEY CLASS DESTROYER
DD-387
LAUNCHED: 1937

DECEMBER 7, 1941

On the morning of December 7, 1941 it seems junior officers were running much of the United States' mighty Pacific Fleet. Just as aboard USS AYLWIN, DD-355, the only officers onboard BLUE were four Ensigns: Nathan F. Asher, the "senior" officer, M. I. Moldafsky, J. P. Wolfe and R. S. Scott. The four of them were in the wardroom enjoying the quiet Sunday morning when word came from the bridge that USS UTAH, AG-16, had been torpedoed by Japanese airplanes. General quarters was sounded and BLUE came to life.

Almost immediately her .50 caliber machine guns began chattering away and her five-inch guns boomed at the enemy. Ens. Asher reported to the bridge to take command and ordered all preparations be made for getting underway. Unlike many ships that day, BLUE already had one boiler steaming and a second one was quickly fired up which enabled her to answer the sortie call much faster than other ships. She cast off from berth X-7 firing away as she moved down the channel. Chief Quartermaster J. P. Hammond was on the bridge alongside acting captain Asher who later credited Hammond with *"aiding me considerably in the safe and swift manner in which the BLUE proceeded out."*[6] As she moved down the South Channel her main batteries tore into the swarming planes under the

---

6   After action report by Ensign N. F. Asher, dated December 11, 1941.

direction of Ens. Wolfe, the fire control officer. She hit one plane that through purpose or accident crashed into USS CURTISS, AV-4.[7] A second plane augured into a sugar cane field on the Waipio Peninsula and a third plane, hit by .50-caliber gunfire, went down off the Pan American Airways landing at Pearl City. BLUE was a magnificent sight as she steamed out of the harbor doing 25 knots with all of her guns blazing away at the enemy. BLUE was one of fifteen ships to get underway and exit the harbor before the attack was over.

In war, in the heat of battle, the actions of men are often easy to understand but sometimes hard to explain. Even though Ensign Asher was not the captain of BLUE, she was under his command that morning. As such, his anger and frustration at the entirety of what he was witnessing can be appreciated. A commanding officer can only do so much. He must trust in those serving under him. Even seeing his orders being carried out cannot always relieve the desire for direct personnel action. As BLUE made her run to the sea and planes were diving on her, attempting to kill her, Archer couldn't resist the desire, the need, to do something himself, to help save his ship, to fight back, to do anything! As he stood on the bridge two enemy aircraft dove on BLUE and, without thinking, Asher ripped his binoculars from around his neck and threw them at the planes.

Outside the harbor she preceded to Sector Three of the Defensive Sea Area. At 0950 hours she conducted a depth charge attack on a sonar contact, suspected to be a submarine. She dropped a total of six depth charges and reported a large oil slick and air bubbles. BLUE claimed a definite kill based on these observations though no submarine was actually seen and none was ever recovered from that area.

As USS ST. LOUIS, CL-49, exited the harbor another sonar contact was made. Two depth charges were dropped and an oil slick was reported, though again no kill was confirmed. After this attack BLUE formed up with ST. LOUIS as her screening vessel. For the next 24 hours Ens. Scott did double duty as both the morale officer going from battle station to battle station in order *"to maintain the spirit of the men"*[8] (a job which was

---

7   Several ships, including CURTISS, claimed credit for downing this plane.

8   After action report by Ensign N. F. Asher, dated December 11, 1941.

probably fairly easy) and the "go to officer" who performed all the other officers' duties while they stayed occupied at their battle stations. BLUE stayed on patrol until the evening of the 8th when she returned to Pearl Harbor.

THE WAR

The adrenalin rush of December 7th soon settled into the mundane. For the first two months of the war BLUE was occupied with patrol and convoy duties around the Hawai'ian Islands. In February she was assigned to the USS ENTERPRISE, CV-6, Task Group screening the carrier in her missions that included the attempted relief of Wake Island. For the next months she escorted convoys between Pearl Harbor and San Francisco.

In preparation for the invasion of Guadalcanal, BLUE traveled to Wellington, New Zealand in July 1942. When the Marines landed on Guadalcanal, August 7th, she was there screening the landings and giving fire support. On August 10th she responded to the waters off Savo Island where the Japanese had pummeled an American-Australian fleet the night before in the Battle of Savo Island. She plucked survivors out of the sea from three American cruisers that had been sunk and took aboard sailors from the badly damaged Australian heavy cruiser HMAS CANBERRA, D-33. She then returned to patrolling, screening and escorting duties in support of the ongoing Guadalcanal campaign.

FATE

In the early morning hours of August 22, 1942 Commander Wakabayashi Kazuo, the captain of the Japanese destroyer, *Kawakaze,* took his ship out hunting east of Savo Island. There in the night he detected BLUE and carefully, quietly closed in. When satisfied with her position, *Kawakaze* fired two torpedoes at the American and quickly retired. The TNT laden fish diligently cut their way through the black tropical sea until the unsuspecting prey was found. One torpedo missed. The second slammed into her, killing nine sailors and wounding twenty-one more. The blast ravaged BLUE leaving her dead in the water with two warped propeller shafts, no electrical power and no steering.

With great skill and determination, damage control parties began working to save the wounded ship. With luck it was hoped they could keep her alive until help came. In the morning salvation appeared on the horizon in the form of one of her Pearl Harbor sisters, USS HENLEY, DD-391. HENLEY passed a towline to her in hopes of making Tulagi. For the next two days attempts to tow and resuscitate her went on but it became apparent that the lady was mortally wounded. With no electricity the crew had only hand-operated pumps to work with and no amount of hope or muscle could keep the sea water out. Her stern steadily sank lower into the sea. On the evening of the 23rd the order was given to abandon ship and scuttle her. At 2221 hours BLUE went to her grave. Ironbottom Sound had another victim.

USS Bobolink

LAPWING CLASS MINESWEEPER
AM-20
LAUNCHED: 1918

DECEMBER 7, 1941

The script for every ship in Pearl Harbor that morning was identical. It was just another quiet Sunday morning in Hawai'i with a relaxed schedule for skeleton crews. It was a peaceful day in an idyllic duty station. Then the peace was shattered and men were in momentary shock that was accompanied by disbelief and followed by action.

Commanding officer Lieutenant, (j.g.) J. L. Foley was in his cabin when Signalman 2nd Class J. E. Williams rushed in and said, "Japanese planes are bombing us." Foley immediately ordered general quarters. The crew took to their battle stations and commenced firing.

BOBOLINK was moored adjacent to the coaling docks in a nest with three other minesweepers. In concert with the other commanding officers it was decided that the four ships should separate making themselves smaller targets and affording better fields of fire. This proved to be an excellent strategy as shortly thereafter BOBOLINK or the combined fire of her and the other minesweepers downed a Japanese plane.

Just around 0900, off Waipio Point, BOBOLINK spotted a disturbance in the water, generating mud, which they believed to be a Japanese mini-sub. She blindly fired three rounds in the vicinity of the disturbance, but could not confirm any hits or anything actually in the water. She turned her attention back to the threat from above and continued firing for another forty-five minutes until the last enemy planes vacated the now smoke filled skies over Pearl Harbor.

During the early afternoon BOBOLINK engaged in minesweeping duties off of the entrances to Pearl Harbor and Honolulu Harbor. Close to 1600 she was ordered to report to 1010 dock. Upon arrival there the orders were changed and she was instructed to report to the beached USS NEVADA, BB-36, off of Hospital Point. En route to NEVADA her orders were once again changed. She was diverted to Battleship Row to aid the stricken USS CALIFORNIA, BB-44, that had settled to the bottom as a result of her wounds. The rest of the day was spent pumping water out of the sunken vessel.

THE WAR

Until May 1942 BOBOLINK continued at Pearl Harbor rendering support in the salvage of damaged ships and in her capacity as a minesweeper. She was redesignated AT-131[9] after her conversion to an ocean going tug was completed in June of that year. Her work in Pearl Harbor lasted until September when she was ordered to the Solomon Islands where it soon became evident that her abilities as a tugboat were sorely needed.

BOBOLINK was called into service for that purpose on November 13, 1942 following the Naval Battle of Guadalcanal. The day turned out to be a long one for BOBOLINK. Enemy surface ships heavily damaged the destroyer AARON WARD, DD-483, and BOBOLINK was called in to provide a tow. While setting up the tow, both ships came under fire from the Japanese battleship *Hiei*, but luckily all the shells missed. Around 0630 BOBOLINK took her under tow and delivered her charge to another boat that delivered AARON WARD into Tulagi Harbor. BOBOLINK then returned to Ironbottom Sound to rescue what sailors she could find cast adrift as a result of their ships sinking during the battle. At 0930 she took USS ATLANTA, CL-51, a light cruiser, under tow hoping to get the

---

9   AT being the designation for a Tug.

severely damaged cruiser to a safe port. During the tow both ships came under attack by a lone "Betty" bomber but ATLANTA's guns drove off the plane. ATLANTA was still taking on water and in the early afternoon it was decided that she was too far gone. BOBOLINK released her towline and ATLANTA was scuttled around 1400.

In May of 1943 BOBOLONK towed USS AWAHOU, YAG-24, from Guadalcanal to Espiritu Santo to Efate Island, finally arriving at Auckland, New Zealand after approximately three weeks. On October 1, 1943, Landing Ship, Tank-448, was bombed and seriously damaged by Japanese aircraft. BOBOLINK rendezvoused with the damaged ship and took her under tow. On the 5th the LST sank while being towed. In March 1944 BOBOLINK reported to Long Beach, California for overhaul. As a result she was once again reclassified, this time as ATO-131[10]. She then returned to Pearl Harbor where she served for the duration of the war in the Hawai'ian Islands.

FATE

Shortly after the war BOBOLINK was ordered to Mare Island Naval Shipyard where she remained until she was decommissioned on February 22, 1946. She was sold in October 1946.

---

10   ATO being the designation for, Ocean Going Tug, Old.

USS Breese

WICKES CLASS DESTROYER /
LIGHT MINELAYER
DM-18
LAUNCHED: 1918

DECEMBER 7, 1941

Lt. Horace D. Warden, Medical Corps, the doctor for Mine Division Two, was on deck in civilian clothes waiting for a whale boat to take him ashore. He had been the duty doctor the previous evening and his watch ended at 0800 hours. He was anxious to get to Pearl City so he could drive to Honolulu and have Sunday morning breakfast with his family. Then the first bombs fell on the seaplane hangars of Ford Island.

BREESE was nested with three other destroyers of the division in Middle Loch of Pearl Harbor. The attack was only two minutes old and her .50-caliber machine guns were chattering away with staccato gunfire at the enemy planes. Seven minutes later her three-inch guns were also responding to the threat.

Thirty minutes into the attack BREESE received orders to get underway, but her inboard position in the nest prevented her from doing so. She would have to wait until her sister ships built up enough steam and cleared the berth before she could move. In the meantime she'd have to make do with fighting the war from a stationary position. Her guns kept up a continuous fire. Approximately an hour and twenty minutes into the attack a three-inch shell from BREESE struck a "Val" dive-bomber that had the bad luck to cross the projectile's path. The shell penetrated the fuselage just behind the cockpit causing the plane to break apart in mid-air and explode in flames. The forward portion of the plane crashed onto Waipio Point and the aft section fell into the water.

Just after shooting this plane down, BREESE finally got under way and exited the harbor and proceeded to patrol. At 1115 she dropped two depth charges on a suspected submarine, with negative results. About twenty minutes later a second attack, comprised of five depth charges was made on a sonar contact which "brought up and oil slick and some debris."

By the end of the day BREESE had suffered no damage and Dr. Warden, who had stayed onboard, had treated only three minor casualties; two men injured while loading three-inch shells and one sailor with a laceration on his right hand.

The Executive Officer, Lieutenant A. B. Coxe, Jr., related in his after action report that the *"following landing force equipment was used to augment the anti-aircraft battery; and although its effectiveness is doubtful it served a means of satisfying the offensive spirit of the crew, 3 .330 caliber Lewis machine guns, 3 Browning automatic rifles."*

THE WAR

BREESE was part of the armada sent to the Solomon Islands in preparation for the invasion of Guadalcanal. One of her first assignments came in early August when she was one of the ships sent to help the stricken USS TUCKER, DD-374, which had inadvertently entered an American minefield and been severely damaged. Nothing could be done for her however and TUCKER sank while BREESE helplessly watched.

On May 7, 1943, BREESE along with USS RADFORD, DD-446, and USS PREBLE, DM-20, spent a mere seventeen minutes laying 250 mines in Blackett Strait, just south of Kolombangara Island in the Solomons. This was one of the preferred passages of the Japanese Navy's "Tokyo Express"[11] for resupplying garrisons in those islands. On the evening of the 8th, three Japanese destroyers, *Kuroshio, Kagero* and *Oyashio*, entered the strait from the east and found the surprise that the Americans had left

---

11   Name given by American sailors to the nighttime Japanese naval convoys resupplying garrisons on Guadalcanal and in the Solomon Islands in general.

for them. *Kuroshio* sank immediately as a result of the encounter. *Kagero* and *Oyashio* were so severely damaged that they became sitting ducks for allied airplanes that sank them the next day.

USS BREESE, DM-18, stands by as USS TUCKER, DD-374, splits in two and sinks after hitting a mine.

BREESE spent a great deal of the war in just these kinds of duties, participating in many major operations of the Pacific war, including Iwo Jima and Okinawa.

FATE

After the capitulation BREESE swept for mines in Japanese waters, making them safe once more for peaceful maritime use. As was typical, at the earliest time possible, BREESE was chosen for elimination. She was decommissioned in New York on January 15, 1946 and sold four months later.

USS Cachalot

V-BOAT /
CACHALOT CLASS FLEET SUBMARINE
V-8 / SS-170
LAUNCHED: 1933

DECEMBER 7, 1941

In a way the Japanese attack on Pearl Harbor for CACHALOT wasn't much. American submarines were nowhere on the list of priorities for Japanese aviators. CACHALOT was berthed at 1010 dock undergoing routine maintenance, several hundred yards and a million miles away from the shooting gallery that was Battleship Row. Aside from a few strafing runs, CACHALOT was totally ignored by the Japanese and even though the Japanese got much attention from CACHALOT's guns, neither did any physical damage to the other. Seaman Second Class C.A. Meyers was wounded during one of the strafing runs but as reported by the captain, Lieutenant Commander Waldeman N. Christensen, it was not serious.

THE WAR

CACHALOT performed three war patrols in 1942, none of which was entirely successful. Captain Christensen took her out on her first patrol in early January, mostly to gather information about Japanese activity in the Pacific. She made observations of Wake, Eniwetok, Ponape, Truk, Namonuito and the Hall Islands. She damaged or possibly sank an enemy merchant ship with a torpedo and was bombed and missed by a Japanese plane. In June 1942 CACHALOT was part of the submarine task group searching for the Japanese fleet during the Battle of Midway. Her second war patrol also in the Pacific was a disappointment for she only inflicted minor damage on an empty tanker.

Her last war patrol took her north to the Aleutians under Lieutenant Commander Harry C. Stevenson. On October 10, 1942 she had a minor set-to with a destroyer and large patrol vessel in Vega Bay, Kiska Island. CACHALOT entered the bay and discovered two enemy cargo vessels. After firing two torpedoes at one ship and setting up to fire at the second ship, the destroyer and patrol vessel came after her. One of the ships fired a torpedo at CACHALOT, which missed the sub by a mere 45 feet. Captain Stevenson quickly dove his boat and escaped the attack with no damage.

Being one of the nine experimental V-boats built between the wars it was believed that she wasn't capable of completing long strenuous war patrols. Her poor performance during her three war patrols seemed to confirm that. After returning from her last patrol CACHALOT was ordered to the submarine school at New London, Connecticut where she served as a training ship for the duration of the war.

FATE

The Navy didn't even wait for the war to be over before it ended CACHALOT's career. In June 1945, two months before the atomic bombings of Hiroshima and Nagasaki and three months before Japan's formal surrender, CACHALOT was ordered to report to Philadelphia where she remained until she was sold for scraping in January 1947.

TENNESSEE CLASS BATTLESHIP
BB-44
LAUNCHED: 1919

DECEMBER 7, 1941

Radioman 3rd Class Theodore Mason, a native of Placerville, California, had completed his midwatch duties and was preparing to go to bed. There had been very little radio traffic during the night and he was anxious to hit the rack. He enjoyed a breakfast of pancakes topped off by a last dose of caffeine and nicotine and by 0755 he was ready for bed. Only minutes later he was standing at his battle station high atop the mainmast watching the opening battle of World War Two for the United States unfold before his eyes. Before he even reached his platform the first torpedo had ripped into CALIFORNIA. Five minutes later a "Kate" sent a second torpedo slicing through the water, which found its mark.

The initial offensive action by CALIFORNIA was slow. Few guns of any type had ready ammunition standing by and of those that did, the boxes containing it were locked. Ammunition parties were sent below to gather up the materials needed to fight back. It was a full fifteen minutes before her five-inch anti-aircraft guns began firing, but even this was not enough to protect her.

Despite the two torpedo hits, CALIFORNIA appeared to have luck running with her. Counter flooding, ordered by the senior officer on board, Lieutenant Commander M. N. Little, seemed to be working, decreasing the list that had developed as a result of the gaping holes in her side. An attack by level bombers missed her completely with the bombs falling harmlessly on either side of her and her forward machine guns splashed a dive-bomber. But at 0900 her lucked changed. One of the Japanese armor-piercing bombs penetrated the forward deck and exploded in the second deck below. Fire quickly followed.

Two opposing forces of nature, fire and water, now conspired to destroy CALIFORNIA. Below decks, the crystal blue water of Pearl Harbor flooded in through the two 12 foot wide holes punched through her hull by the torpedoes. There had been no time to properly set Condition Zed, the securing of all hatches to maintain watertight integrity. As a result, water raced unrestricted throughout much of the ship. Above decks, fires began to rage out of control and the waters of Pearl Harbor itself were afire. Oil spewing from the damaged vessels further up Battleship Row had ignited and the flaming slick was inexorably drifting toward CALIFORNIA.

High in the maintop, Radioman Mason had watched the entire attack, his perch giving him a unique, almost detached observation post. Having no weapons and therefore no way to fight back the only thing he could hurl at the enemy was curses. By ten o'clock the attack was over, but not the danger. The burning oil slick had finally reached CALIFORNIA and was threatening to engulf her. She also had a dangerous list and was threat-

USS CALIFORNIA sinking as burning oil from battleship row approaches

ening to capsize. The commanding officer, Captain J. W. Bunkley, who had returned to his ship at about 0915, saw the danger and gave the order to abandon ship. Mason heard the call to abandon ship and with his other shipmates he scrambled down the mast and reluc-tantly jumped into the oily water. Fifteen minutes later when the danger of the fire abated, the abandon ship order was cancelled and he swam back from Ford Island to help save his ship.

As on many ships that day and in that place, CALIFORNIA had its share of heroes. Men like Boatswains Mate 1st Class W. S. Fleming, gun captain of the #4 five-inch gun, who, in spite of being wounded, stayed at his station. Capt. Bunkley later wrote that Fleming, *"by his coolness and example, under fire, instilled confidence in the men about him."*[12]

There was also the ship's Protestant Chaplin, Raymond C. Hohenstein, who helped rescue men from a flooding compartment and later received shrapnel burns and a Purple Heart for his efforts.

There was also Herbert C. Jones, a 23-year-old Ensign, who died from wounds received while leading a party of sailors supplying ammunition to CALIFORNIA's guns. After he fell he refused evacuation fearing his rescuers would die in the attempt. He received the Medal of Honor posthumously.

In the afternoon Radioman Mason left CALIFORNIA for a second time that day after being relieved of his duties in a bucket brigade that was attempting to fight the fires. He was taken by boat to the submarine base where he could clean up. He washed the thick oil off of his body with a kerosene soaked towel. Finally he got into a warm shower. As he luxuriated in the joyous water he started to sing. He sang to celebrate that he was still alive.

THE WAR

The next day the main job began to prevent CALIFORNIA from sinking or capsizing. Multiple ships came to her aid. They came to fight fires. They came to pump out water. But the actions of the enemy and of basic physics had the last word. When morning dawned on Thursday 11th CALIFORNIA was finally sitting on the bottom in the shallow waters just off Ford Island. Her hull was completely underwater and her decks awash, leaving her superstructure the only thing above the water. The small victory was that she did not turn turtle like USS OKLAHOMA, BB-37. This would make raising her much easier.

Salvage operations began almost immediately as CALIFORNIA was deemed to be one of the ships most easily saved. Before she had finished settling, details had already been sent aboard to begin removing

---

12 After action report by Captain J. W. Bunkley, dated December 13, 1941.

her secondary armament. A plan was also soon developed to remove her huge 14-inch guns for the sole purpose of lightening her. This would be needed to prevent her settling further into the soft mud and for making the eventual refloating less strenuous.

A three-part plan was devised for the resurrection of CALIFONIA: raise her, repair her, rebuild her. Once she was raised from berth F-3 at Ford Island, she would undergo such repairs at the Pearl Harbor Navy Yard that would make her seaworthy so she could either be towed or sailed to the Puget Sound Naval Shipyard in Bremerton, Washington where she would be rebuilt.

In February, the cofferdams that were built to allow workers to raise her were all in place. Repairs necessary for refloating were also completed and on February 25, 1942, pumps were turned on and water began to flow out. CALIFORNIA began to rise.

As the ship rose out of the water and work crews entered the ship, the repugnant chore of recovering bodies was required. Corpsmen from the hospital ship USS SOLACE, AH-5, came on board with canvas bags to remove bodies as they were found. Twenty-nine bodies in all were discovered inside the ship and taken away to the Naval Hospital to be identified, if possible, for notification of next of kin.

The first stage finally ended when on March 30, 1942 CALIFORNIA floated free from the silt and mud of the floor of Pearl Harbor. Phase 2 began ten days later when she entered Dry Dock 2 of the Pearl Harbor Navy Yard. The majority of the work done in the dry dock was on repairing or rebuilding engines and generators. On June 7, 1942 she left dry dock but remained in the harbor for another four months while work continued. CALIFORNIA left Pearl Harbor under her own steam on October 10, 1942 and headed east for the Puget Sound Naval Shipyard. The sailors and civilians of Pearl Harbor raised her and gave her new life. The ship builders at Bremerton were now going remake her.

While at Puget Sound, CALIFORNIA was totally rebuilt from the second deck up. The opportunity was taken to completely modernize her, upgrading almost everything on board. When the workers of Bremerton were finished in January 1944, CALIFORNIA was basically a new ship.

On January 31, 1944 the CALIFORNIA departed Bremerton for a shakedown cruise off the coast of its namesake state. In May 1944, under the command of Captain H. P. Burnett, she sailed once more into Pearl Harbor and tied up at Berth F-3, the same berth she was at on December 7, 1941.

The crew of CALIFORNIA was anxious to pay back the Japanese some of what they had gotten on December 7, 1941. They got their wish almost immediately. In the American island hopping strategy of the Pacific war, the next island set for invasion would be Saipan and CALIFORNIA was called on to help. She arrived off Saipan and provided fire support for the invasion on June 15, 1944. The day before the invasion a Japanese coastal battery fired on and hit CALIFORNIA, killing one sailor and injuring nine others. After Saipan, she moved on for similar duties at Guam and Tinian in late July and early August.

The reborn USS CALIFORNIA in her "dazzle" paint scheme on her shakedown cruise after being rebuilt.

In mid September, CALIFORNIA was sailing in formation with USS TENNESSEE, BB-43, near Palau. The ships were steaming in a standard zigzag pattern as a defense against submarine attack, when TENNESSEE had a failure in her steering mechanism. CALIFORNIA did not or could not maneuver out of the way in time and TENNESSEE, unable to steer, rammed CALIFORNIA. After the accident CALIFORNIA sailed to Espiritu Santo for repairs.

When repairs were completed, CALIFORNIA sailed for the Philippines to participate in the invasion of Leyte Island that took place on October

20, 1944. The successful landings gave the Allies a foothold back in the Philippines, which the Japanese could not allow. They sent an enormous fleet separated into three groups to dislodge the landings at Leyte and drive the Americans back. This move was not unexpected and the 7th Fleet Support Force under the command of Rear Admiral Jesse Oldendorf was waiting to meet them.

Oldendorf's force consisted of six battleships, eight cruisers, twenty-eight destroyers and thirty-nine PT Boats. Of the six battleships, five of them had been bombed and resurrected at Pearl Harbor. There was also one cruiser, USS PHOENIX, CL-46, that had been at Pearl Harbor. Unbeknownst to the Americans or the Japanese, the time for retribution had finally arrived. CALIFORNIA and her sisters of Pearl Harbor were about to exact a horrific revenge on the Japanese. The Japanese Southern Force of two battleships, one heavy cruiser and four destroyers commanded by Admiral Nishimura Shoji was terribly outnumbered and about to be out-maneuvered.

During the night of October 24th/25th Oldendorf set his fleet up across the Surigao Strait in three lines: first the PT boats, then the destroyers and then the cruisers and battleships. Nishimura's ships entered the strait in the blackness of the early morning. They were engaged by the PT boats that harassed the Japanese but did no damage. They then met the American destroyers, who like a school of hungry sharks in a feeding frenzy, tore into the Japanese with no mercy. Torpedoes from the destroyers laced the dark tropic ocean. One Japanese battleship, the *Fuso*, took one amidships and immediately exploded and split in two. This was quickly followed by the destruction of two of the enemy destroyers. A third destroyer was damaged so badly it was forced to withdraw and later sank. With typical Japanese fortitude, Nishimura sailed on with the three ships he had left. When he met the American battleships he also met his fate. The CALIFORNIA and her sister battleships fired a total of 285 fourteen and sixteen-inch shells at the three enemy ships from 13 miles away.

Much like the Japanese aircraft at Pearl Harbor, the American destroyers and battleships swarmed the *Yamashiro* mercilessly. Despite this, the valiant ship managed to return fire and keep underway. Literally hundreds of torpedoes and shells engulfed the hapless ship. The *Yamashiro* sank to the bottom of the Pacific and with it went Admiral Nishimura. The Japanese cruiser was later scuttled. The last destroyer was badly damaged and retreated into the night.

The Imperial Japanese Navy lost two battleships, one cruiser, three destroyers and over 4,500 fine sailors that night. The American losses were one PT Boat and 38 sailors killed.

CALIFORNIA's next major assignment was supporting the landings at Lingayen Gulf. On January 6, 1945 she was bombarding the beaches when a kamikaze managed to get through the anti-aircraft defenses and crashed into the mainmast. 44 men were killed and 155 were wounded. Temporary repairs were made and CALIFORNIA stayed on station continuing the shore bombardment. Within weeks she was ordered to return to Puget Sound Naval Shipyard for repair.

CALIFORNIA and her crew made one last trip to the western Pacific in June 1945 where she supported the closing actions on Okinawa.

FATE

CALIFORNIA was steaming off the coast of Luzon when word arrived that Japan had quit, that the war was over. She then spent the next two months in Western Pacific and Japanese waters in support of the occupation of Japan. In mid October she received her orders to return home for the final time. In what can only be called an amazing coincidence, CALIFORNIA sailed into Philadelphia on December 7, 1945, exactly four years to the day since her sinking in Pearl Harbor. This gallant lady who was resurrected from the muddy bottom of Pearl Harbor sailed over 90,000 miles in those four years and exacted a heavy price from the Imperial Japanese Navy for the beating she took in that Hawai'ian paradise four years earlier.

CALIFORNIA's retirement lasted much longer than most of her Pearl Harbor sisters. She spent fourteen years enjoying a well-deserved quiet and peaceful life basking in the sun and in her glory in the "mothball fleet" at the Philadelphia Naval Shipyard. Her time finally came on July 10, 1959 when she was sold to the Bethlehem Steel Company.

USS Case

MAHAN CLASS DESTROYER
DD-370
LAUNCHED: 1935

DECEMBER 7, 1941

USS CASE was sandwiched between two other ships in a nest of five destroyers in East Loch. They were all tied up to the destroyer tender USS WHITNEY, AD-4. CASE was undergoing routine maintenance and receiving all power from WHITNEY. All communications were also through WHITNEY. Essential parts necessary for firing her five-inch guns were on board the tender being repaired. When the attack began CASE was pretty much useless although her .50 caliber guns did fire on Japanese planes that had completed attacks and flew nearby.

In what could only be described as a painfully slow process, it took CASE a full eight hours to get battle ready. Boilers had to be fired up and brought on line, all equipment and weapons that had been dismantled for maintenance had to be put back together and she had to be fully provisioned.

Once underway, CASE was instructed to drop a depth charge on a suspected sunken Japanese submarine between buoys 5 and 7, which she did. At 1900 hours she began circling Ford Island at five knots as protection against further enemy submarine attacks. She continued at this for the rest of the night.

CASE suffered no damage or casualties from enemy action and could perhaps claim a partial kill on one Japanese plane.

THE WAR

Two weeks after the attack CASE helped screen three battleships going to the Puget Sound Naval Shipyards. This was the beginning of five months of escort duty between the west coast and Hawai'i, referred to as the "Pineapple Run." It was during one of these convoys that CASE collided with USS O'BRIEN, DD-441, in a thick fog just off San Francisco. Neither ship suffered major damage.

In late May 1942 CASE was ordered to the Aleutian Islands. While en route she stopped at Midway to drop off a company of Marines. She spent several months in Alaskan waters without much action. On August 7, 1942, CASE took part in the bombardment of Kiska Island. A Japanese tanker was unlucky enough to be in the area at the time and CASE fired on and sank it. CASE remained in the area in support of the American invasion of Adak until late October when she returned to Pearl Harbor.

The remainder of 1942 and early 1943 found CASE mostly in the Solomons and New Hebrides performing standard "jack-of-all-trades" destroyer duties including convoy escort, patrolling, anti-submarine missions off Guadalcanal and shore bombardment. For much of 1943 she was assigned as an escort to USS SARATOGA, CV-3, operating out of Noumea, New Caledonia.

On November 29, 1943, CASE came as close to sinking as a ship can get without actually going under. The enemy this time wasn't the Japanese, but the sea itself. After undergoing a period of overhaul and modernization at Mare Island Naval Shipyard in California, CASE was ordered once again to the Aleutians. Two days after sailing she ran smack into a storm with mountainous seas and hurricane force winds.

The 341 foot long ship was tossed about as easily as a piece of driftwood. Late in the night the angry seas slapped CASE so hard she heeled over to starboard 45 degrees. When this happened a blower intake became submerged and the ocean rushed into the ship from the opening. Once inside, the cascading water soaked the ship's main power distribution panel, which promptly shorted out. All electrical power was gone throughout the vessel and with it, the ability to steer the ship. CASE was now helpless and the thirty-foot waves had their way with her. Bits and pieces of the ship began to be torn away including the ship's whaleboat. More seriously, lifeline stanchions were ripped out of the deck leaving holes that the sea could pour through. And it did, copiously. Berthing spaces below were soon under ten inches of water.

Deep in the interior of the ship electricians were working desperately to once again get power to the steering engine by hooking it up to an emergency generator. All the work was being done in a dark world literally turned on its side. If they failed it was almost assured that they would sink. Every time the ship rolled more water poured in, and the more water that poured in the longer she wallowed almost on her side and the more difficult it became to right herself. At one point she rolled sixty-four degrees to port. CASE was in grave danger of foundering.

For six hours the electricians struggled to regain power. For six hours the ship rolled in an ocean gone wild. For six hours the crew contemplated their deaths. For six hours the steel hull of CASE creaked and groaned and defied the sea's efforts to break her. Finally the electricians headed by Chief Electrician's Mate Harrison Shedd got power to the steering engine and CASE was once again in charge of her own destiny. A course was set for San Francisco, arriving in that city two days later. CASE then spent two weeks at Mare Island repairing the damage inflicted by the storm. Two crewmen were lost in the tempest, presumed washed overboard.

The next year found CASE, as usual, engaged in multiple duties and missions in the Pacific, including screening carriers at the Battle of the Philippines Sea, more popularly known as "The Great Marianas Turkey Shoot" in June 1944. Later in 1944 she participated in the bombardment of Marcus Island and helped support the landings at Leyte in the Philippines.

CASE was assigned as an escort to Cruiser Division 5 for operations at Iwo Jima. In preparation for these operations a large group of ships were berthed at Ulithi Atoll. In the early morning hours of November 20, 1944 CASE was patrolling the Mugai Channel entrance to the atoll anchorage when it spotted what appeared to be a submarine's periscope. It had indeed spotted a periscope but it didn't belong to a submarine, but to a "Kaiten," a manned kamikaze torpedo. CASE rang up full speed and aimed directly at the periscope, intending to ram the Kaiten. Through luck or purpose the Japanese pilot of the Kaiten maneuvered and the destroyer missed its target. CASE came about to try again. This time the Kaiten didn't move and CASE steamed directly over it, striking the Kaiten just behind the conning tower. The destroyer shuddered as it rolled over the piloted torpedo and members of the crew saw it on both port and starboard sides of the ship. That Kaiten sank, but this was a coordinated attack and another Kaiten made it inside the anchorage and sank the oiler USS MISSISSINEWA, AO-59. CASE suffered no damage as a result of ramming the Kaiten.

Just over a month later, on Christmas Eve 1944, CASE joined in on another pre-invasion bombardment of Iwo Jima. During this action a Japanese ship, *Transport No. 8* was spotted running north at high speed. CASE and USS ROE, DD-418 were ordered to pursue and destroy. The enemy vessel had a substantial head start but its top speed was only 22 knots. With their top speed of 37 knots the American destroyers gained on it, but ever so slowly. After two hours the Americans barely closed to within range of their guns and CASE opened fire. With skill and perhaps a little luck one of CASE's rounds found the enemy transport at over 14,000 yards. Damaged and slowing, it was only a matter of time before CASE and ROE caught up with and sank it; which they did.

As if chasing the enemy transport wasn't enough, while CASE was firing on it, one of the lookouts spotted a torpedo heading for CASE and promptly notified the bridge. The ship was maneuvered and the torpedo missed it on the port side. One minute later a second torpedo, obviously fired as part of a spread with the first one, passed by on the starboard side.

There were a large number of survivors in the water and CASE sailed into their midst and dropped lifelines and cargo nets but not one of the survivors took advantage of the efforts to save them.

For the remainder of the war CASE operated in the area of Iwo Jima and Saipan in assignments as varied as search and rescue, anti-submarine patrols and picket duty. She was 60 miles away from Iwo Jima when the Japanese surrendered.

FATE

The end came quickly for CASE. On September 2, 1945 she accepted the surrender of enemy forces on the Bonin Islands. Two weeks later she departed for the United States arriving at Norfolk, Virginia on November 1st. She was decommissioned the following month and sold for scrap on New Years Eve, 1947.

During the war CASE sailed a total of 321,570 miles. In action against the enemy she fired 6,616 five-inch shells, 7,905 40mm rounds and 50,246 20mm rounds. More importantly CASE only lost three crewmembers during the war. All three were washed overboard in rough seas. CASE never lost a man to enemy action.

USS Cassin

MAHAN CLASS DESTROYER
DD-372
LAUNCHED: 1935

DECEMBER 7, 1941

Dry Dock #1 at the Pearl Harbor Navy Yard was full that Sunday morning. CASSIN and her sister ship USS DOWNES, DD-375, were both up on blocks and undergoing maintenance and modernization. Behind them in the dock was the battleship USS PENNSYLVANIA, BB-35. The only weapons operational on her were machine guns so, when the bombs began to drop, CASSIN could do little more then spit back at the Japanese planes.

The first wave of the attack pretty much ignored CASSIN and the Navy Yard. But around 0850 the second wave came in and level bombers and dive-bombers from the aircraft carriers *Zuikaku* and the *Soryu* struck the yards. Two 550-pound bombs hit in rapid succession. Both of them passed all the way through CASSIN detonating only when they hit the concrete floor of the dry dock. The damaged ship began leaking fuel and the explosions set it afire. Dry Dock #1 became an inferno.

Other bombs that hit the yard severed water and power lines making efficient firefighting almost impossible. Thick black smoke generated by the burning oil made it impossible at times to fight the blaze because the fire parties simply couldn't see. The heat generated was intense, at times driving the fire control parties away. On board the ship, munitions became so hot they began to cook off. These explosions further damaged the ship and made quelling the blaze even more difficult. The fire was so hot it melted the warheads on some of the torpedoes. The situation was now so dangerous from the fire and the threat of exploding ordinance, CASSIN's captain, Lieutenant Commander Daniel Shea, ordered the crew to abandon ship.

In an effort to control the fires the dry dock was flooded. This tactic didn't work well. Although it doused the flames burning directly beneath the ship, that were literally cooking it, the burning fuel just floated on top of the water and began to burn the sides of the ship. The dock was flooded and drained twice. When water poured into the shrapnel-riddled hull, CASSIN's position on the blocks shifted and became more precarious. The second time the dock was flooded the highly unstable destroyer came off its blocks, toppled over and came to rest against the DOWNES.

USS CASSIN lays on her starboard side against USS DOWNES in Dry Dock #1, Pearl Harbor, December 7, 1941

The fires on CASSIN were finally brought under control around 1045 hours. Although there were wounded amongst the crew of CASSIN, there were no fatalities. CASSIN herself was limited in her offensive capabilities and claimed no damage to any enemy planes, but twenty-five of her "best gunnery and torpedo personnel" were loaned to USS CUMMINGS, DD-365.

THE WAR

Initial opinions by everyone who saw CASSIN were that she was a total loss. Examination of her disclosed exactly how hot the fires in Dry Dock #1 were. The heat had warped her hull in the middle, raising it up by as much as seventeen inches. Her bow was now 2 feet higher than what it was supposed to be. A combination of massive heat and the forces of water caused her keel to warp. Damage was not confined to what the fires did. The enemy bombs and internal explosions from munitions detonating made her hull look like Swiss cheese. Repairing or patching these holes would be time consuming.

As with many heavily damaged ships at Pearl Harbor, one of the first assignments for CASSIN was the removal of her guns so they could be used elsewhere. This was also needed in order to lighten the ship for refloating, which was of paramount importance because CASSIN and DOWNES were taking up space in a dry dock that was going to be much needed in the rebirth of other ships.

In short order a plan was developed for at least the removal of CASSIN from the dry dock, if not for her final disposition. On January 6, 1942 the first patches were welded onto her hull. On Thursday, February 5, 1942, less than two months after her sinking, Dry Dock #1 was flooded and CASSIN was once gain floated on a more or less even keel, ultimately steadying with a minor 2 degree

The "new" CASSIN at Mare Island in 1943.

list to port. Just less than 2 weeks later, on February 18th, she was finally floated out of the dry dock. The ultimate determination as what to do with CASSIN was finally made on May 25th. She was to have all of her serviceable equipment removed and sent to Mare Island Naval Ship Yard where it would be installed in a new hull being laid down there. The old hull would be scrapped at Pearl Harbor.

By December 1942 all the salvaged equipment had arrived at Mare Island. The shipbuilders there were creating this hybrid ship consisting of a brand new hull and filling it with used machinery. This creation of a new CASSIN went on until February 5, 1944 when she was re-commissioned. CASSIN returned to the Pacific Fleet and to Pearl Harbor on April 22, 1944. Her first assignment was as an escort vessel for convoys to the Marshall Islands which had been captured from the Japanese in January. She remained in this capacity until August. The rest of the war was spent in the western Pacific participating in bombardments of many islands in preparation for invasion. She shelled Aguijan Island, Marcus Island, Tinian and Iwo Jima. She continued around Iwo Jima off and on for the rest of the war.

FATE

Because American prisoners of war were repatriated to the United States by air CASSIN remained in the Iwo Jima area for several months after the end of the war, in order to perform air-sea rescue duties if they were needed. In November, two months after the formal surrender, CASSIN had returned to the Norfolk, Virginia Naval Base where she was decommissioned on December 17, 1945. Two years later, "the ship that wouldn't die," was sold for scrap.

A strong argument can be made that the USS CASSIN, DD-372, that ended the war was not the same vessel that was bombed in Pearl Harbor on December 7th. However, the U.S. Navy considers it the same ship with the same name and same hull number.

USS Castor

CASTOR CLASS GENERAL STORES SHIP
AKS-1
LAUNCHED: 1939

DECEMBER 7, 1941

Some war ships, for various reasons, never fired a shot or effectively got in the fight at Pearl Harbor, but CASTOR - a floating general store - got into action almost as the first bombs began to fall. Berthed at Merry Point, the "Kate" Nakajimas making their torpedo runs on Battleship Row, had to fly directly over CASTOR. Her three-inch anti-aircraft battery and .30 caliber machine guns put up a heavy curtain of fire at the green- painted Japanese planes. Crewmen on deck who were not assigned to gun crews were firing at the enemy with Springfield rifles. Since CASTOR was firing on the planes, they returned the favor with strafing runs. Despite all the firing, no one on board CASTOR was injured and she could only claim a possible kill on one plane.

THE WAR

A general stores ship is the traveling supermarket of the Navy. Although it might carry some munitions and fuel, those jobs are mainly left to ammunition ships and tankers. A general stores ship carries all those things that make living at sea bearable and fighting a war possible. In addition to bombs, bullets, binoculars and boats, a Navy at war also needs, pens, pencils, paper and ping-pong paddles. Stores ships brought fresh fruit and vegetables, ice cream and Coca-Cola, baseballs and beer to other ships and remote bases. A general stores ship would often deliver up to 10 tons of supplies to a destroyer and as much as 120 tons to an aircraft carrier. Many times a technique known as underway replenishment was utilized. This was accomplished by ropes strung from the supply ship to the receiving ship while both were underway and about 30 yards apart.

For the first months of World War II, CASTOR plied the waters between Hawai'i and San Francisco, bringing much needed supplies to Pearl Harbor. For the duration, CASTOR crisscrossed the Pacific delivering its goods and supporting the ships and men that hop scotched their way towards Japan. From 1941 through 1945 she saw New Caledonia, Fiji, New Zealand, Funafuti, Espiritu Santo, the Gilbert Islands, the Marshall Islands, Manus, Ulithi and Okinawa.

CASTOR was in San Francisco undergoing overhaul when the war ended.

FATE

After her overhaul in San Francisco, CASTOR returned to the western Pacific to support occupation forces there. She continued in that role until 1947 when she returned to the City by the Bay, where she was decommissioned and placed in reserve.

CASTOR rested quietly for 3 years. Then the Korean War turned the Cold War hot and she was called back into service. She was home ported at Sasebo, Japan and once again supplied the necessities of life to vessels and men fighting a war. In 1952 CASTOR's home port was changed to Yokosuka, Japan. After hostilities ended in Korea in 1953, she remained there.

After the partition of Vietnam in 1954, CASTOR was called on to help transport those people wishing to leave North Vietnam and move to South Vietnam in what was dubbed "Operation Passage to Freedom." In the 1960s she returned to Sasebo as her home port. From there she supplied the U.S. 7th Fleet in support of operations during the Vietnam War.

CASTOR was decommissioned for the second and last time on October 31, 1968 as a grand old lady who had served her Navy and her country over twenty-nine years and through 3 wars. She was sold for scrap in 1969.

Cheng-Ho

CHINESE JUNK MOTOR YACHT
IX-52
LAUNCHED: 1939

PRE-WAR

Anne Mills Archbold, a wealthy patron of the arts and sciences had CHENG-HO built in Hong Kong originally to conduct botanical expeditions in the South Seas. The ship was well appointed and was equipped with a refrigeration unit and air conditioning. David Fairchild, a botanist from Florida, took her on her first voyage in January 1940. Her second voyage was in 1940-41, to Fiji, under the direction of Otto Degener of the University of Hawai'i. Shortly afterwards Mrs. Archbold sold CHENG-HO to the Navy for one dollar and the Navy took procession in July 1941.

DECEMBER 7, 1941

During the attack CHENG-HO was moored near the mouth of the entrance channel to Pearl Harbor. She was unarmed and could take no offensive action against the enemy. Because of her appearance and being in such an out-of-the-way location it is unlikely that she was attacked or suffered any damage or casualties. There is no after action report from the CHENG-HO, so details of exactly what happened to her are not available.

THE WAR

The CHENG-HO spent the duration of the war attached to the 14th Naval District in Pearl Harbor. She was part of the Hawai'ian Sea Frontier, which was established to conduct patrols in and around the Hawai'ian Islands and perform minor escorting duties. Perhaps because of her appointments and her air conditioning, CHENG-HO ultimately became a floating officers' club for Navy personnel.

FATE

CHENG-HO was struck from the Navy's list of vessels on February 25, 1946 and returned to Mrs. Archbold, her previous owner. She refused the offer and the ship went to Otto Degener. In 1990 she still existed, beached at the harbor of Papeete, Tahiti.

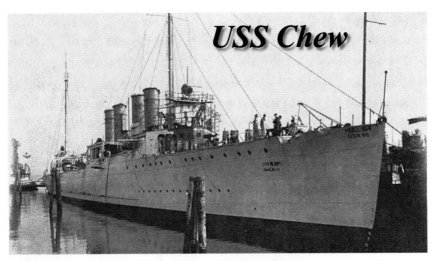

USS Chew

WICKES CLASS DESTROYER
DD-106
LAUNCHED: 1918

DECEMBER 7, 1941

CHEW was moored at berth X-5 alongside USS ALLEN, DD-66, on the northwest side of Ford Island. Her crew responded quickly to the screeching planes and her three-inch gun was firing 8 minutes into the attack and 3 minutes later two of her .50 caliber machine guns joined the chorus. Her position, only several hundred yards away from Battleship Row, gave her gun crew an excellent shot at enemy planes and they took advantage of it. CHEW hit three planes, disintegrating one of them. Her guns put up a continuous wall of fire during the entire attack.

Afterward, CHEW was ordered to patrol in an area southwest of the entrance buoys. Over the next several hours she encountered eight separate sonar contacts, dropping a combined twenty-eight depth charges on them. Although CHEW claimed "evidence" of two kills from her depth charging, there is no confirmation for that claim.

The Japanese planes inflicted no damage and no casualties to CHEW. However two sailors from CHEW were killed while on USS PENNSYLVANIA, BB-38. December 7, 1941 was the only action CHEW saw during the war.

THE WAR

As a World War I "Four Stacker," CHEW was deemed too old to go to war. However, it was felt that she could very capably handle other duties that would free up more modern ships to fight the Japanese. She spent the duration mostly in Hawai'ian waters for local escorts and training with the occasional trip to San Francisco and Seattle screening convoys.

FATE

One week after the Japanese surrendered, CHEW departed Pearl Harbor for the last time and sailed to Philadelphia. She arrived in September and was decommissioned the following month. On October 4, 1946 she was sold to Boston Metal Co. Inc. Baltimore, Maryland for $13,094.25.

Cinchona

ALOE CLASS NET MAINTENANCE VESSEL YN-7 LAUNCHED: 1941

DECEMBER 7, 1941

CINCHONA, along with the other net tenders, was assigned to the section base near the Pearl Harbor entrance channel. She and her sisters operated and maintained the anti-submarine nets that protected it. She was one of the newest ships in the harbor that day having been launched only 5 months earlier. In fact she was so new that she hadn't even been officially commissioned yet. CINCHONA had only arrived in Pearl Harbor 7 weeks before, after her home yard was changed from Mare Island Navy Yard in California. As the Japanese planes swarmed over the harbor her crew manned and fired her three-inch gun and .50 caliber machine guns; she claimed no hits or kills.

THE WAR

Through July of 1942 CINCHONA continued her previously assigned duties in Hawai'ian waters of net maintenance and repairs and salvage operations.

In August she sailed to Midway. Her mission there was to install new nets to protect the docks. When she completed this she returned to Pearl Harbor where she once again resumed her net and salvage duties. A full year after Pearl Harbor, on December 20, 1942 CINCHONA was finally commissioned as a U. S. naval vessel. Another change came for her on January 20, 1944 when her designation was changed from YN-7 indicating her function as a net tender to AN-12 reflecting that she was now a net laying vessel.

On June 15, 1944 the U.S. Marines invaded Saipan in the Mariana Islands. The next day CINCHONA arrived there to begin net and salvage duties. The following day, June 17th, she rendered assistance to LST-84. A flight of Japanese planes attacked the convoy that LST-84 was in and she suffered a hit by an enemy bomb which set her afire. CINCHONA helped extinguish the blaze allowing LST-84 to rejoin the convoy. She returned to Tanapag Harbor on Saipan where she inspected the nets left there by the retreating Japanese. November 1944 found CINCHONA at Guam, which had been invaded 4 months earlier. She was kept busy there not only with her standard net tending duties, but she also assisted in installing moorings and laying a pipeline.

She returned to the United States in late July 1945 and was there when the war ended.

FATE

CINCHONA operated in California, at Long Beach and Mare Island until November 1946 when she reported to Vancouver, Washington to be placed in the Pacific Reserve Fleet, Columbia River Group. CINCHONA rested for many years in the "mothball fleet," eventually residing in the National Defense Reserve Fleet in Suisun Bay, California. She was ultimately sold, in February 1976, to Zidell Explorations, Inc. of Portland, Oregon, at the time, the largest ship breaking company in the country.

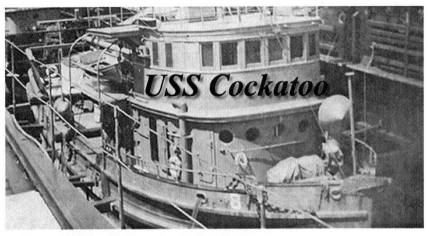

COASTAL MINESWEEPER
AMc-8
LAUNCHED: 1936

DECEMBER 7, 1941

COCKATOO was berthed at the section base near the mouth of the Pearl Harbor channel. Twenty-seven year old Machinist Mate 2nd Class Elbert Lee Brown, a native of Statesville, North Carolina, was on board preparing to raise the flag for morning colors when he heard the first explosions from the harbor two miles away. Within minutes he and the other eleven men on board could see the heavy black smoke ominously rising from Battleship Row. The commanding officer of COCKATOO, J. B. Cook, turned to Brown and said, "Get your rifle." The small minesweeper had begun her life as a fishing boat and was armed only with a single .50 caliber machine gun. Brown disappeared below deck and returned armed with a 12 gauge, double barrel shotgun which he used to fire on low flying Japanese planes.

Knowing that she had limited abilities for either offensive or defensive action and that she soon would be needed to carry out minesweeping duties, COCKATOO, along with other ships at the section base was moved in close to shore to find what little cover they could that was provided by the trees there. Toward the end of the attack a lone bomb came out of the sky splashing into the water only twenty feet away. The expected "whoomph" of an explosion never came. It was a dud.

Four hours after the attack, around 1400, COCKATOO was sent out to sweep for mines off Honolulu Harbor. It then reported to the *S.S. President Coolidge* docked inside Honolulu Harbor and spent the remainder of the day there guarding it. Over the next days Petty Officer Brown and his shipmates stood armed watch over the passenger liner while 2,000 women and children were loaded on to it to be evacuated to the United States.

THE WAR

For the rest of the war COCKATOO operated out of Pearl Harbor in her capacity as a minesweeper. She would journey to Kaua'i, Hawai'i or other islands in the group and spend from one to four days sweeping for mines, playing out her 4,000 feet of cable, keeping the shipping lanes between the islands safe. She would then return to Pearl Harbor while one of the other minesweepers rotated out to perform the same duties. This routine was followed for the next three and a half years. Elbert Brown stayed with COCKATOO for the entire war and promoted to Chief Machinist Mate by the time hostilities ended.

FATE

In March 1946 COCKATOO was placed on the floating dry-dock ARD-8, which was then towed to San Diego from Pearl Harbor. On September 23, 1946, COCKATOO was transferred to the U.S. Maritime Commission for final disposition.

USS Condor

COASTAL MINESWEEPER
AMc-14
LAUNCHED: 1937

DECEMBER 7, 1941

At 0342 on the morning of December 7th, CONDOR was sailing the waters just outside Pearl Harbor on her morning minesweeping duties. The Officer of the Deck was Ensign R. C. McCloy. As he scanned the waters around his vessel he observed an unusual wave off to port. He asked the Quartermaster, B. C. Utterick, to look at the wave to see if he could determine what it was. Looking through binoculars they agreed that it appeared to be caused by either a submarine's periscope or conning tower. USS WARD, DD-139, was patrolling the area and CONDOR sent a message to the destroyer, "Have sighted a submerged submarine on westerly course, speed 9 knots." By the time WARD arrived in the area to investigate, the submarine was nowhere to be found.

With the approach of dawn CONDOR had finished her morning sweeps and headed for home. The anti-submarine nets across the channel into Pearl Harbor were opened at 0458 so that she could pass through. However, CONDOR didn't actually pass through the nets until 0532. The nets then remained open for another forty-five minutes to allow passage of other traffic.

CONDOR tied up back at the section base with the other minesweepers and net tenders. When the attack occurred CONDOR remained there.

THE WAR

CONDOR spent the entire war operating in Hawai'ian waters in her capacity as a minesweeper.

FATE

January, 1946 saw the decommissioning of CONDOR. By July she had been transferred to the Maritime Commission for final disposition.

USS Conyngham

MAHAN CLASS DESTROYER
DD-371
LAUNCHED: 1934

DECEMBER 7, 1941

USS WHITNEY, AD-4, was tending to a nest of five destroyers in East Loch of Pearl Harbor. CONYNGHAM, the most inboard ship of the nest was berthed immediately to the port of WHITNEY and was undergoing routine overhaul. It took almost 13 minutes from the beginning of the attack to get her main five-inch battery in operation. When she did, CONYNGHAM, along with her nestmates, put up a furious curtain of fire. Their location in East Loch afforded them the ability to fire at almost all the attacking planes. As a result, the destroyers in the nest could collectively claim three planes destroyed. CONYNGHAM received only two minor hits from small caliber ammunition and no injuries of any kind to crewmembers. In her action against the Japanese she expended 114 rounds of five-inch ammunition and 2,500 rounds of .50-caliber ammunition. She got underway shortly after 1700 and exited the harbor.

THE WAR

CONYNGHAM served briefly around Hawai'i and as an escort for convoys traveling from the west coast of the United States to the New Hebrides. Her first major action of the war was in June 1942. As part of Destroyer Squadron 6 she was one of the screening destroyers for the USS ENTERPRISE, CV-6, and USS HORNET, CV-8, at the Battle of Midway. On October 26th she was called upon again to screen carriers at the Battle of the Santa Cruz Islands. CONYNGHAM was still under the command of her Pearl Harbor captain, Lieutenant Commander Henry C. Daniel, when she was assigned to Destroyer Division 10 and was part of the screen protecting ENTERPRISE.

On November 11th, while bombarding Japanese positions in the area of Kokumbona on Guadalcanal, CONYNGHAM collided with USS FULLER, AP-14. The ensuing repairs at both Noumea and Pearl Harbor temporarily took her out of action. She returned to the South Pacific three months later arriving at Espiritu Santo on February 4, 1943. During much of that year she engaged in standard destroyer duties of patrol and escort and participated in many shore bombardments.

In September CONYGHAM had an honor conferred on her that is usually reserved for aircraft carriers, battleships or cruisers. She became the flagship for Vice-Admiral Daniel E. Barbey. Barbey was in charge of landing operations for the Seventh Amphibious Force, which was under the command of General Douglas MacArthur.

CONYNGHAM was part of MacArthur's relentless drive to return to the Philippines. As part of that effort she participated in many landings and shore bombardments. After screening the landings on Lae, New Guinea, on September 4, 1943 CONYNGHAM, along with LST-471 and LST-473, and two other destroyers were attacked by Japanese bombers based at Rabaul. Although she received no direct hits, she was damaged by several near misses and one crewman was wounded. CONYNGHAM claimed two enemy planes brought down in the attack. The enemy planes heavily damaged LST-473, which was dead in the water. CONYNGHAM stayed with her until she could be towed to safety.

Five weeks later, on December 14, 1943, she led a force, comprised of both American and Australian ships, that set sail to invade Arawe, New Britain and wrest it and its airstrip from the Japanese. The landings began in the early morning darkness of the 15th. They went well and were only lightly opposed with the exception of "Blue Beach" about 3 miles east of the main landing beach. Expertly concealed enemy guns decimated the troops approaching the shore in 15 rubber boats. In short order 12 of the small assault boats were sunk and the remaining three retreated.

With the main assault successful, most of the ships involved retired. However CONYNGHAM remained in Arawe Harbor in search of any survivors from the "Blue Beach" disaster. Around 0930 over thirty enemy planes approached Arawe to repel the invaders. CONYGNHAM, being the largest ship remaining in the harbor, drew the avid attention of the enemy. Bombers and torpedo planes descended on CONYNGHAM like locusts. It would take a concerted combination of expert anti-aircraft fire and deft ship handling if she was to survive the onslaught. With her propellers churning white water behind her, CONYNGHAM made a dash out of the harbor. Multiple bombs dropped within 150 feet, close enough to shower the decks with water. Every gun onboard pointed skyward to create a lead umbrella that would protect her from the rain of bombs and enemy bullets. As if the bombs weren't enough, torpedo planes unleashed deadly Long Lance torpedoes at the fleeing lady. The quartermaster at the helm with great skill, nimbly maneuvered the ship, avoiding every torpedo fired at her. CONYNGHAM's luck couldn't hold out forever. Deliverance for the beleaguered ship descended from the sky like guardian angels in the form of a flight of American P-38 fighters. The P-38s engaging the Zekes and Vals gave CONYNGHAM the time and space she needed to escape. Through luck or skill, or a combination of both, CONYGNHAM survived the most vicious attacks on her of the war with no damage and no casualties.

CONYNGHAM spent the early months of 1944 being repaired and overhauled in both Australia and San Francisco. She returned to the South Pacific in May and continued with standard destroyer duties at Saipan and the Marianas. In October 1944 the U.S. Army invaded the island of Leyte in the Philippines and CONYNGHAM arrived in Leyte Gulf in November. On the 17th, she once again met the nemesis that had haunted her the entire war: a Japanese plane. Considering her almost miraculous escape from dozens of planes in Arawe Harbor a year earlier, it is amazing that this time a lone enemy plane successfully strafed her deck wounding seventeen men and causing minor structural damage.

On February 1, 1945, around 2300, CONYNGHAM and USS LOUGH, DE-586 engaged what they thought were two enemy patrol boats off Talin Point, Luzon, Philippines. The boats played cat and mouse for about half an hour in the darkness with the two American ships. LOUGH finally found one of them and sank it with a five-inch round. CONYNGHAM quickly followed suit and sank the second boat close to shore, also with a well-placed five-inch shell. It was later discovered that the two boats sunk were American PT Boats, PT-77 and PT-79. Four American sailors were lost, but thirty crewmen of both boats survived and were rescued off the island of Mindoro two days later. The rest of the year CONYNGHAM supported landings on Luzon, Mindanao, Palawan and Borneo.

When the last shots of the war were fired CONYNGHAM was undergoing an overhaul at the American navy base at Subic Bay in the Philippines.

FATE

CONYNGHAM's demise was tied into the dawn of a new age that was born at the end of World War Two. She was just one of many American, Japanese and German ships that were used as part of the American nuclear test program. On June 30, 1946 she was one of the targets for "Test Able" of "Operation Crossroads" at Bikini atoll. After the atomic flash receded and the shock wave dissipated, CONYNGHAM was still afloat.

After surviving the onslaught of a determined enemy and the atomic forces of nature, unleashed by man, CONYNGHAM was sent to her final resting place by U.S. Navy vessels on July 2, 1948 when she was sunk while being used for target practice.

The "Test Able" atomic explosion at Bikini Atoll on June 30, 1946.
USS CONYNGHAM was one of the test ships.

USS Crossbill

COASTAL MINESWEEPER
AMc-9
LAUNCHED: 1937

DECEMBER 7, 1941

CROSSBILL was berthed at the Bishop Point section base near the anti-submarine nets at the mouth of the Pearl Harbor channel. In the early morning hours of December 7, 1941 she was outside the harbor performing regularly scheduled sweeps for mines. When her duties were completed she returned to the section base. Down in the ship's galley preparing breakfast for the crew was 22-year-old cook Ernest Wilkins, working at one of the very few jobs black sailors were allowed in the American navy of World War II.

When the explosions from the harbor began, Wilkins and his crewmates ran on deck to see what was going on. They were quickly ordered back inside. Not only concerned for himself and his shipmates, Wilkins was wondering what was happening to his friends onboard his previous ship. Only a few months before, he had been transferred to CROSSBILL from the USS ARIZONA, BB-39.

CROSSBILL suffered no damage or casualties as a result of the attack.

THE WAR

Assigned to the 14th Naval District, CROSSBILL spent the duration of the war working out of Pearl Harbor in her capacity as a minesweeper. She rotated on a regular basis with the other coastal minesweepers assigned to Pearl Harbor in sweeping the waters around all the Hawai'ian Islands. She also engaged in patrol duties and search and rescue missions.

FATE

CROSSBILL remained attached to the 14th Naval District until March 1947 when she was decommissioned and turned over to the Maritime Commission for disposal.

USS Cummings

MAHAN CLASS DESTROYER
DD-365
LAUNCHED: 1935

DECEMBER 7, 1941

CUMMINGS was sitting in the Pearl Harbor Navy Yard getting a new radar system. The installation of the modified foremast for it was about sixty percent complete. When the buzz of torpedo planes and the whump of exploding bombs shattered the stillness on that Sunday morning, unlike many other ships in the harbor, almost all of CUMMINGS compliment of 158 officers and crew were onboard. Her aft .50 caliber machine guns were firing within minutes. Her forward machine guns had been disassembled, but were quickly put back together and joined the fray.

The gunners onboard her must have felt like they were in a hornet's nest. The Navy Yards are centrally located in Pearl Harbor and enemy planes swarmed all around. It was a target-rich environment. The men scored hits on many planes and the crew of gun #4 claimed a kill on a horizontal bomber when it blew off its wing.

The second wave of enemy planes arrived just after 0900 and the Navy Yards came under attack. Enemy dive-bombers were met with fierce fire from CUMMINGS and the other ships in the yards. Although she took no direct hits, bombs dropped both forward and astern of her causing superficial damage from fragments. Three crewman suffered minor injuries from shrapnel due to these hits.

At 1040 CUMMINGS' captain, Lieutenant Commander George D. Cooper had his ship underway and headed out of the harbor to hunt for enemy submarines. A first sonar contact at 1127 was met with three depth charges but there was no evidence to confirm a hit or a kill. Twelve minutes later another contact was greeted with two more depth charges. Despite the sighting of "splotches of oil" there, again, was no confirmation of a hit or kill.

THE WAR

For the first nine months of the war CUMMINGS escorted convoys to the west coast and then to the South Pacific after which she reported to San Francisco for an overhaul. She returned to southern waters again as an escort vessel, but then headed for Guadalcanal to perform patrol and escort duties. She remained there until May 1943. In fact, through December 1943 CUMMINGS' life was a routine of mostly escort duties punctuated with the occasional overhaul. These missions took her as far north as Adak, Alaska and south all the way to Auckland, New Zealand and to places like the Fiji Islands, the New Hebrides and the Solomon Islands. Early 1944 found CUMMINGS supporting operations in the Marshall Islands, Ceylon, Sumatra and Java. She even participated in joint exercises with the British navy.

In July 1944 CUMMINGS was one of the escorting vessels for the cruiser USS BALTIMORE, CA-68. However, this time CUMMINGS wasn't screening the vessel because she was part of a task force or participating in an invasion or bombarding an island. This time she was screening BALTIMORE solely because of the special cargo the cruiser carried: Franklin Delano Roosevelt, the President of the United States. The president departed San Francisco on July 21st for Pearl Harbor where he met with General Douglas MacArthur and Admiral Chester Nimitz to review and discuss the conduct of the war in the Pacific. He then traveled to Adak in the Aleutian Islands to inspect new bases there and finally to Juneau, Alaska.

At the completion of the President's tour, CUMMINGS was given the honor of transporting Mr. Roosevelt back to the United States. She departed Alaska on August 8 with the Commander-in-Chief on board and arrived in Seattle, Washington on August 12th. While at the Puget Sound Navy Yard, the President broadcast a nationwide radio address from the deck of CUMMINGS.

In late October 1944 CUMMINGS had a small role in exacting the final revenge on the Imperial Japanese Navy for the attack on Pearl Harbor. As a member of Task Force 38 she took part in the Battle of Cape Engaño, which was an engagement in the larger Battle of Leyte Gulf. As a member of Destroyer Squadron 4, CUMMINGS screened the aircraft carriers hunting down the Japanese fleet in Philippine waters. The flagship of that fleet was the *Zuikaku,* which was the last surviving aircraft carrier of the six in the Pearl Harbor attack force. On the morning of the 25th 180 American planes pounced on the Japanese fleet. The Americans quickly decimated the small flight of 30 Japanese planes protecting the enemy ships. When they finished that appetizer they dug into the main course. The pilots were relentless and merciless. By the evening three Japanese carriers had been sunk including, *Zuikaku.* The battleships ARIZONA, OKLAHOMA, UTAH and their dead crewmen that still slept eternally inside their wrecked hulks on the bottom of Pearl Harbor had finally and irrevocably been avenged.

Intense naval and air corps bombardments were required to soften up the heavily entrenched defenders of Iwo Jima. Even though the invasion didn't take place until February 1945, CUMMINGS first reported there in November 1944 to aid with this vital mission. She returned more than once over the next months for the same purpose. CUMMINGS was there once again to provide support fire when the Marines finally went ashore on February 19, 1945. She remained in the Iwo Jima theater of operations for the remainder of the war conducting escorts and providing air-sea rescue coverage.

During the waning days of the war, in the summer of 1945, a stop at Saipan garnered CUMMINGS something it didn't expect: a stowaway. While returning to the ship from Saipan, a mongrel dog, whose previous owners were the former Japanese occupiers of the island, was discovered aboard the ship. The dog was reluctant to return to the island so the sailors adopted him, naming him "Gizmo." It was immediately apparent that the dog only responded to commands given in Japanese, so he was quickly indoctrinated into the English language. Gizmo got his sea legs after some early bouts of seasickness. Despite the fact that he never got used to the claxon announcing general quarters or the boom of the main five-inch guns, Gizmo became the ships mascot and stayed with CUMMINGS through the end of the war.

FATE

A week after the Japanese signed the capitulation on the deck of the USS MISSOURI, BB-63, in Tokyo Bay, CUMMINGS was providing support for the occupation of Haha Jima. After returning to Iwo Jima she received her orders to sail home, arriving at Norfolk, Virginia in September after her long journey through war. On that last voyage home CUMMINGS stopped at Tampa, Florida, where the Tampa Morning Tribune did a story on their mascot, Gizmo.

The veteran ship avoided immediate sentencing to the scrap pile, but the reprieve was short-lived. After being decommissioned in December 1945 she was sold in July of 1947 to the Boston Metals Company of Baltimore, Maryland for the sum of $20,838.37.

USS Curtiss

CURTISS CLASS SEAPLANE TENDER
AV-4
LAUNCHED: 1940

DECEMBER 7, 1941

CURTISS was the lone ship at berth X-22 in Pearl Harbor. Located at the mouth of Middle Loch, just south of the Pearl City peninsula and just north of Ford Island. This berth put the huge, 527-foot long, tender out in the open. She was just an enormous target in the middle of the harbor. So when the first planes attacked the ships moored on the north side of Ford Island, CURTISS was a target so tempting it couldn't be ignored. Planes started strafing her almost immediately. And the immediate response given to CURTISS' gun crews was to _"fire individually on any target making an offensive approach_[13]_"_, which, of course was all of them.

In the middle of the harbor and in the midst of all the chaos were Lt. Iwasa Naoji and Petty Officer 1st Class Sasaki Naokichi in a submarine. It was the only one of five Japanese mini-subs to penetrate the anti-submarine defenses and may have been in the harbor for as long as two hours, waiting for the attack to begin and to make their move. They stealthily made their way up the main channel on the west side of Ford Island looking for a target. For whatever reason, Lt. Iwasa focused on CURTISS.

---

13   USS CURTISS, official After Action Report.

At 0836, forty-one minutes into the attack, Iwasa's periscope was spotted seven hundred yards off the starboard quarter. This information was relayed to the bridge and the main batteries were ordered to open fire on the deadly intruder. The number 2 and 3 main guns both fired and both missed. Almost simultaneously the mini-sub partially surfaced exposing the conning tower and the bow. Whether this was done deliberately or by accident is unknown, but the now exposed submarine became a clearer target. At this time Lt. Iwasa literally took his best shot and launched a torpedo up Middle Loch. What his intended target was is unknown. It could have been CURTISS or any one of the eight destroyers that were nested there. The torpedo missed all targets and exploded when it hit a pier at Pearl City. Ensign G. K. Nicodemus and his crew of CURTISS' No. 3 gun finally got the range and put at least one five-inch shell through the enemy's conning tower. CURTISS ceased fire and the crew watched as the destroyer, USS MONAGHAN, DD-354, administered the coup de grâce by ramming the crippled submarine, sailing over it and then dropping two depth charges on the sub as it passed underneath her stern.

A little more than twenty minutes later at approximately 0905, a Japanese "Val" was shot down and crashed into CURTISS' No. 1 crane.[14] The plane exploded on impact with the crane and showered the boat deck with flaming aviation fuel. The fire forced the evacu-

Wreckage of the "Val" that crashed onto the deck of CURTISS

ation of the nearby No. 3 gun and Ens. Nicodemus organized his gun

---

14 CURTISS along with two other ships claim to have shot down this plane. Numerous ships and guns that morning were shooting at the same planes. In many cases, it is impossible to credit a specific ship for shooting down a specific plane. Since American ships claim to have shot down more than the 29 planes actually lost by the Japanese, it is clear that some planes were brought down by the fire of multiple ships with each ship then claiming an individual kill.

crew into a firefighting team to aid in quelling the flames. Once the fire was under control, Nicodemus gathered his gun crew together, returned to the No. 3 gun and rejoined the battle.

Seaman First Class R. R. Beiszcz and Seaman First Class J. A. D'Amelio remained on the boat deck to continue fighting the fire despite being strafed by enemy planes.

No sooner had CURTISS recovered from the crashed Val and the resulting fire than a flight of bombers attacked. Four bombs fell. Three missed. The fourth hit the boat deck, the same location as the fire started by the Val. The bomb penetrated several decks and exploded deep inside the ship. The blast ripped into decks and bulkheads, starting new fires and destroying entire compartments, including the radio room.

Four sailors were inside the radio compartment when the bomb struck, Radioman 1st Class R. E. Jones and Radiomen 2nd Class J. G. Raines, D. B. Orwick and B. Schlect. The compartment was an instant inferno. Jones and Raines discovered that their shipmates were now trapped beneath heavy equipment that had been tossed about like toys and crashed onto them. They first lifted a transmitter off of Orwick's legs and carried him to safety. They then returned to save Schlect, but the heat, smoke and the situation itself were too much. Jones and Raines made several attempts to rescue him, each time being forced to retreat. In the end there was nothing they could do to save him.

Fire control parties were busy throughout the ship including one headed by Ensign R. C. Kelly, who despite being injured, competently directed his men in bringing the fires under control and aided in saving his wounded shipmates.

The aft engine room had been evacuated due to smoke from the fires and ruptured steam lines caused by the explosion. In order to remove the water that had begun to fill the compartment, Chief Water Tender J. H. Mosher, Chief Machinist Mate F. Beach and Machinist Mate 1st Class S. F. Safranski reentered the steam filled, smoke choked engine room to start pumps clearing the water.

All of CURTISS' fatalities were as a result of the bomb hit or the ensuing fires, which killed twenty sailors.

While hell was being battled below decks another battle still raged above. Planes continued to flock toward CURTISS whose overworked gun crews gallantly defended the tender against all comers. All told, CURTISS claimed shooting down 6 enemy planes, one as close as 1,500 feet.

Based on the actions of his crew, the CURTISS' commanding officer, Captain Henry S. Kendall, like many other COs that day, made the following, somewhat dry and understated comment in the closing paragraph of his After Action Report, *"The conduct of the officers and crew was that traditionally expected of naval personnel."* Kendall pointed out that sailors of the U. S. Navy are expected to be courageous and on December 7, 1941 at Pearl Harbor, Territory of Hawai'i, the men of CURTISS were that and so much more.

Pearl Harbor, December 7, 1941. USS CURTISS burns from a bomb hit and an enemy plane that crashed into her.

THE WAR

Temporary repairs of her damage were done at Pearl followed by more repairs at San Diego. A short five weeks later on January 13, 1942, she was back in Pearl Harbor and ready to go to war. CURTISS sailed to the South Pacific bringing much needed men and materials. She then reported to Espiritu Santo to support seaplanes, destroyers and small craft during the Solomon Islands campaign.

In November 1942 she arrived at Funafuti in the Ellice Islands to act as the flagship for the Commander Air, Central Pacific. She served as the flagship following his command throughout the Pacific to Tarawa, Kwajalein, Eniwetok, Saipan and ending in Guam in February 1945.

Receiving routine repairs and maintenance in San Francisco, CURTISS sailed to Okinawa to serve as the flagship for the Commander, Fleet Air Wing 1 in May 1945. It was at this time that fate played a very cruel joke on the crew of CURTISS. Since the day the war started at Pearl Harbor CURTISS had suffered no damage or casualties at the hands of the enemy. Now, only weeks after the surrender of Germany and the end of the war in Europe and only weeks before Japan's surrender in the Pacific, CURTISS' luck ran out.

It happened on June 21, 1945. Early in the evening, just at dusk, without any warning, a lone kamikaze appeared out of the gloom and flew into her starboard side near the bow. The plane and the 1,000-pound bomb it carried penetrated deep into the hapless ship's interior. The resulting explosion killed 35 and wounded 21 sailors. Once again just as on December 7th, CURTISS' highly trained damage control parties responded to the devastation, quickly conquering the fires.

CURTISS returned to the Mare Island Naval Shipyard for repairs, which is where she was when the Japanese surrendered.

FATE

Unlike many of her Pearl Harbor sister ships, CURTISS had a very active and diverse post World War II life. Initially she operated in the far western Pacific seeing duty in Okinawa and China. In 1947 she returned to the United States to be outfitted with scientific apparatus for the Atomic Energy Commission. Then in 1949 she sailed to frigid Alaskan waters to help evaluate cold weather equipment.

At the outset of the Korean War CURTISS returned to the Far East and was assigned duty as a tender for two squadrons of PBM Mariner flying boats and an Australian squadron of Sunderland flying boats.

Her gradual transformation into a hybrid naval/research vessel continued when she underwent further changes to accommodate more scientific instrumentation in 1951. She then sailed to Eniwetok where she served as flagship for the atomic tests of "Operation Greenhouse." CURTISS returned to Eniwetok in 1952 where she repeated the same function for the "Operation Ivy" tests that witnessed the first detonation of a hydrogen bomb. She participated in "Operation Castle" in 1954 and "Operation Redwing" in 1956, more hydrogen bomb tests, also at Eniwetok.

In connection with the International Geophysical Year in 1956, CURTISS sailed for the Antarctic to participate in "Operation Deep Freeze II," America's effort to build a permanent station at the South Pole. She operated in these waters through early 1957 when she returned to San Diego to undergo repairs for ice damage.

She was finally placed in reserve in September 1957 after serving her country continually for over seventeen years in both war and peace. Her end came in February 1972 when she was sold for scrap.

USS Dale

FARRAGUT CLASS DESTROYER
DD-353
LAUNCHED: 1935

DECEMBER 7, 1941

Like millions of Americans, sailor John Cruce was starting his Sunday morning with a cup of coffee and the newspaper. Quietly, near the #5 gun on deck he perused the *Honolulu Advertiser.* Also on deck and absorbed in a newspaper was Ernest Schnabel who was doing the crossword puzzle. The sound of planes disturbed his concentration and he looked up to see two planes flying by no higher than the ships mast.

Just as on her sister ship USS AYLWIN, DD-355, the captain of DALE was not on board that morning. Also, as on AYLWIN, the acting commanding officer was an Ensign, in this case Ens. F. M. Radel. It was Radel who saw the attack begin and gave the command to sound general quarters and to make all preparations for getting underway. Very soon DALE was firing her aft .50-caliber machine guns and five-inch gun. Her place in the nest of four destroyers severely restricted her field of fire and aircraft that otherwise could have been fired on were left unchallenged. However, one plane making an attack run on the USS RALIEGH, CL-7, came under fire by all the ships in the nest and crashed into the harbor.

Twenty-five minutes into the attack DALE was underway and proceeded to back out of her berth in the nest. As she did, an enemy torpedo, perhaps intended for RALIEGH, passed underneath her bow.

Clear of the nest and out in the open DALE increased speed to 25 knots and headed out of the harbor. The destroyer's movement didn't seem to interest the Japanese who totally ignored her, that is, until she approached the mouth of the channel. Even a ship of her size would block access into and out of the harbor if she was sunk there and the Japanese knew this all to well. Suddenly DALE was the center of attention for the enemy pilots. Planes filled the sky above and dropped bombs all around her and planes that weren't dropping bombs were strafing her. Geysers of water sprang up all around DALE as the bombs splashed into the channel. Luck was with her, however, and they all missed. Even those bombs that were close had no effect because they exploded only after being enveloped by the soft mud at the bottom of the harbor, absorbing most of the blast.

Of all the images one could conjure up from Pearl Harbor, one of the most incongruous occurred on board DALE as she made her run out of the harbor. In order to protect the crew from dangerous flying splinters caused by bomb or bullet hits, a boatswain's mate was tossing anything on deck made of wood overboard. He soon got to the wooden locker that contained one of the most desired items on board; ice cream. When it was seen that he was about to jettison the cabinet he was stopped. The lock was quickly disposed of and the cold delicacy was hastily handed out to anyone and everyone. So with bombs dropping all around them and bullets whizzing by their heads, the men of USS DALE manned their guns and sailed into World War II eating ice cream.

Just as the ship cleared the entrance channel Ensign Radel employed a somewhat unorthodox maneuver. Seeing a flight of three dive bombers making a run towards DALE from behind, he stopped the port engine and ordered the wheel hard a port causing the nimble little destroyer to turn sharply to the left. This abrupt turn caused the enemy planes to overshoot the ship. It also allowed DALE's guns to fully come to bare on the planes as they passed along the starboard side of the ship. When they did, DALE'S guns blew the first plane in the formation out of the sky. The other two planes turned around to make a second run on her, but the .50-caliber greeting they received from DALE's guns gave them other ideas and they retired quickly.

Once outside the harbor DALE commenced anti-submarine patrol. During this time DALE encountered several sampans flying white flags heading for the safety of Honolulu Harbor and officers were hard pressed to prevent their gunners from firing upon them. Shortly after 1100, DALE formed up with USS WORDEN, DD-352, and another ship to investigate reports of Japanese transport ships off Barbers Point. The reports turned out to be false and DALE then screened four cruisers that had sortied to form an ad-hoc task force to look for the Japanese fleet that was presumed to be near by or approaching.

Unfortunately, DALE's port engine soon developed serious problems and the ship was forced to abandon her place in the task force. Onboard repairs were made during the night but they proved to be insufficient to allow her to rejoin to the task force. She did, however, return to continue patrol duties outside of the harbor.

THE WAR

In March, 1942 DALE was screening two of the prime targets that the Japanese missed at Pearl Harbor, carriers LEXINGTON, CV-2, and YORKTOWN, CV-5. They were on their way to New Guinea to participate in one of the first American offensive strikes of the war. Aircraft from those carriers hit Japanese airfields at Lae and Salamaua.

In the middle of 1942 DALE screened convoys bringing in supplies in preparation for the invasion of Guadalcanal. On August 7th she supported the landings there and continued in the Solomons through September.

The Japanese had captured and occupied Attu and Kiska islands in the Aleutians in June 1942. This was the only American territory occupied by an enemy in World War II. DALE was called to those icy waters in January, 1943 where she was a member of the occupation forces on Amchitka Island. On March 26, 1943 DALE took part in the Battle of the Komandorski Islands. The Japanese had sent a convoy of three ships to resupply their Alaskan garrisons. This convoy was escorted by four cruisers and four destroyers. They were met by a smaller American force consisting of two cruisers and four destroyers. When the two enemies met in the frigid ocean the running sea battle that ensued lasted three and a half hours. DALE, captained by Commander Anthony Rorschach, provided smokescreen coverage for the small flotilla and also managed to fire 728 rounds of five-inch ammunition at the Japanese. Despite being outnumbered and outgunned, the lesser American force beat back the Japanese and prevented the resupply from occurring. After this defeat, the Japanese abandoned surface resupply efforts in the Aleutians and went exclusively to submarines.

DALE crisscrossed the Pacific numerous times over the next two years. As an artillery platform and screening and escort vessel she took part in actions at Wake, the Gilberts, Kwajalein, Eniwetok, Majuro, Palau, Saipan, Guam, Yap, Ulithi, Iwo Jima and Okinawa.

FATE

DALE was already sailing home when the Japanese delegates were signing the instrument of surrender on board USS MISSOURI, BB-63 in Tokyo Bay. She arrived in New York harbor on September 25, 1945. Three weeks later she was decommissioned. Just over a year later she was sold; her service to her country finished, her life over.

OMAHA CLASS LIGHT CRUISER
CL-8
LAUNCHED: 1922

DECEMBER 7, 1941

John Millner, from McAllen, Texas was a radio operator on board DETROIT and was at his duty station below decks when the first bombs began to fall on Ford Island. He immediately jumped up and looked out of a porthole. What he saw was the first of the enemy planes dropping torpedoes from only 15 feet above the water. Of the first four torpedoes in the water, two hit USS UTAH, AG-16, one hit USS RALIEGH, CL-7 both berthed aft of DETROIT. The fourth torpedo passed beneath DETROIT's stern, impacting harmlessly into Ford Island. General quarters was sounded and World War II started for DETROIT.

Making the ship watertight was required during general quarters in order to eliminate or diminish the possibilities of flooding or sinking during an attack. To meet these conditions all portholes were secured. Millner's battle station was below decks so with their window on the war gone he and his fellows could no longer see the battle, they could only hear it. They were now blind men on a battlefield and could only imagine the devastation that was occurring in the world outside of their steel enclosure. The deck shuddered below their feet with every explosion. With every bomb that dropped or torpedo that hit anywhere near, their bones vibrated in harmony with the metal bulkheads surrounding them.

At least those above decks could see what they were facing, could take offensive or defensive or protective action based on their observations. The men inside could only wait and hope and wonder. Minutes into the attack a massive shock wave rocked DETROIT liked an earthquake bouncing the men inside about like dolls. It was the ARIZONA, BB-39, exploding more than a half a mile away. At the same time bombs dropped all around DETROIT, all coming very close, but none hitting.

DETROIT got underway at 1230 hours. By some fluke of luck she emerged from the carnage that was Pearl Harbor totally unscathed. The worse she got was a shower of muddy water from near misses by bombs. Injuries to her crew were limited to two men with very minor wounds.

Forming up with other vessels that sortied from the harbor she sailed to the west of Oah'u in order to meet the invasion force presumed to be advancing. If it proved to be a phantom, then they would search out the Japanese carriers that launched the attack. DETROIT remained at sea for three days, returning to Pearl on the 10th. On December 19th she escorted the passenger liner *S.S. President Coolidge* and the U.S. Army Transport ship *Scott*, loaded with women, children and 125 wounded to San Francisco, arriving there on Christmas Day.

THE WAR

On March 3, 1942 the fleet submarine USS TROUT, SS-202, pulled into Pearl Harbor with a cargo of just over six tons of gold, thirteen tons of silver coins and a large amount of paper securities. This fortune belonged to the government of the Philippines and to banks, businesses and individuals. It had been removed from Corregidor so it would not fall into Japanese hands. This treasure was transferred to DETROIT who then sailed to San Francisco. It was deposited at the U.S. Mint for safekeeping until the war was over and it could be returned to its owners.

After escorting several convoys to the South Pacific, DETROIT reported in November 1942 to the frozen seas off the Aleutian Islands. There she served for the majority of the war. The mission there was to prevent further occupations by the Japanese, interdict the enemy forces already there and eventually eliminate the enemy presence on American land.

DETROIT took offensive action in April 1943 when she bombarded Holtz Bay and Chicago Harbor on the Japanese occupied island of Attu. The invasion, which followed in May, was supported by DETROIT. The same pattern was repeated in August when she pounded Kiska with shells and covered the landings there on the 15th. The landing was unopposed because the enemy had spirited the garrison off the island. The Japanese were no longer in Alaska.

DETROIT stayed in the North Pacific through the middle of 1944. After a short stay in the States for repairs she was assigned as the flagship to the South East Pacific Fleet. She patrolled the waters off the coast of South America until December.

In 1945 DETROIT was assigned the job of flagship for Replenishment Group, 5th Fleet, a position she held until the end of the war.

FATE

On September 2, 1945 USS DETROIT was present in Tokyo Bay to witness the formal surrender of the Japanese.

For a few months she supported the occupation of the Japanese homeland. She then took up duties as a transport, bringing Japanese back to the home islands from Pacific outposts and afterwards bringing Americans back home.

John Millner, the radioman who was on board at Pearl Harbor, served the entire war on board DETROIT. After the war he worked for 35 years for the Boeing Aircraft Company.

DETROIT was in Pearl Harbor at the beginning and she was in Tokyo Bay at the end; one of only two ships that could make that claim, the other being the battleship USS WEST VIRGINIA, BB-48. The fact that she had come full circle and perhaps could tell a tale or two about her journey from her birth in 1922, through the hell of December 7, 1941 and finally to the triumph and peace of 1945 Tokyo Bay, didn't seem to matter much to the decision makers. The United States was having a yard sale, selling items for pennies on the dollar. They hung out a sign that said, "Everything Must Go!" And, go it did.

On January 11, 1946, in Philadelphia, the city where American Independence was born, USS DETROIT, a ship that fought to keep that independence alive and viable, was decommissioned. Six weeks later she was sold for scrap.

To close out the surrender ceremonies in Tokyo Bay, 450 carrier-based airplanes flew over in a show of the industrial might and the fearsome power that Japan had called down upon itself. The battleship on the left is USS MISSOURI. The cruiser on the right is USS DETROIT.

USS Dewey

FARRAGUT CLASS DESTROYER
DD-349
LAUNCHED: 1934

DECEMBER 7, 1941

All ships, especially naval vessels, are very high maintenance. They are in constant need of repair and upkeep if they are to perform at their best. On December 7th, Destroyer Division One, which included DEWEY, was berthed in a nest of five ships alongside USS DOBBIN, AD-3, a destroyer tender. These ships were undergoing repair and overhaul in the middle of Pearl Harbor about 400 yards east of Ford Island.

Frank Kucklick, a machinist mate and a few other sailors were in a small boat heading for Sunday mass at the Catholic Chapel on shore when the Japanese planes appeared in the sky. On board DEWEY, general quarters was sounded just after Gunner's Mate 2nd Class G. E. Osborn saw UTAH, AG-16, take a torpedo and immediately begin to capsize. Within minutes, all of DEWEY's guns were firing back at the enemy planes. The gun crews kept up constant fire throughout the attack. The forward guns, however, were blocked by the masts and superstructure of the ships in the nest and could only fire at planes not blocked by these obstacles. Even the bridge crew drew automatic rifles and fired on the low flying planes. Kucklick and his crewmates in the shore boat, not wanting to be caught in the middle of the harbor, turned and headed for the nearest shelter, which was Ford Island.

As the attack was drawing to a close around 0945, the major targets of battleships and airfields being exhausted, the enemy planes finally got around to attacking targets of opportunity, Destroyer Division One being one of them. Bombs dropped all around DEWEY, one as close as 75 feet, but none hit or did any damage.

The commanding officer of DEWEY, Lieutenant Commander August J. Detzer, Jr. reported that combined fire of the division brought down two enemy attackers. There was no damage to the ship and no reported injuries to any of the crew. Detzer got his ship underway at 1505 and stood out of the harbor. Frank Kucklick, who spent the entire battle on Ford Island, was assigned to a burial detail until his ship returned.

THE WAR

DEWEY's first mission of the war came only a week after the Pearl Harbor attack when she was assigned to Task Force 11 which was being sent to Wake Island to relieve the Marines there. The relief never made it however. Wake Island fell on December 23 and the dejected Task Force returned to Pearl Harbor.

Her next foray, in February 1942, was also with Task Force 11, this time for a strike at Rabaul, New Guinea. En route the task force was spotted by Japanese observation planes and the mission was called off. The enemy then sent bombers to attack the group but they were driven off.

In May, Task Force 11, built around the carrier USS LEXINGTON, CV-2, was once again sent on a mission and this time nothing was called off or cancelled. DEWEY, as one of the screening vessels, was about to participate in the first major sea battle of the Pacific War. The Japanese had implemented a plan to capture Port Moresby on the island of New Guinea and use it as a forward base to harass the allies and as a first line of defense when the inevitable allied counter-offensive began. To accomplish this the Imperial Japanese Navy's 4th Fleet was sent in. The Americans and Japanese met in the Battle of the Coral Sea, which was the first naval battle in history in which the enemy fleets never saw each other. It was a battle fought strictly by naval aircraft from carriers.

Late in the morning of May 8th, the second day of the battle, 14 enemy torpedo planes in two groups, attacked LEXINGTON simultaneously from both sides. DEWEY and the other screening destroyers put up concentrated anti-aircraft fire but despite this, a pair of torpedoes found LEXINGTON's port side. Immediately after the torpedo plane attack 19 dive-bombers targeted LEXINGTON. DEWEY and the other destroyers delivered massive anti-aircraft fire. It wasn't enough and LEXINGTON was hit, this time by two bombs which penetrated the flight deck. Although fires from these hits were initially controlled, massive secondary explosions devastated the carrier and the crew was ordered to abandon ship. At 1430 DEWEY was ordered to the carrier's stern to search for survivors, eventually rescuing 112 of LEXINGTON's men. The carrier was ordered scuttled and five American torpedoes sent her to her final resting place in the depths of the Southwest Pacific Ocean.

DEWEY provided support for the landings at Guadalcanal on August 7, 1942. She bombarded the island and also provided anti-aircraft fire. Japanese planes attacked the ships providing support for the invasion the next day around 1200. Twenty-six planes attacked but only nine got through. One of those planes put a torpedo into the side of USS JARVIS, DD-393, killing 14 sailors. DEWEY came in and towed JARVIS to safety. Shortly after assisting JARVIS, DEWEY came to the aid of the transport, USS GEORGE F. ELLIOT, AP-13. A Japanese bomber that had been shot down crashed into ELLIOT amidships causing a serious fire. DEWY once again broke out the tow line and began to pull the blazing ship to safety. The fires on board could not be controlled and it soon became apparent that ELLIOT wasn't going to make it. DEWEY abandoned the tow and rescued 40 crewmen off ELLIOT.

After a three month overhaul period in the United States, DEWEY was sent to Alaska two days after Christmas. Two weeks later, USS WORDEN, DD-352, was pushed onto an outcropping of submerged rocks by a powerful current in Constantine Harbor, Amchitka Island, while protecting the landing of U.S. Army troops. The rocks ripped open her hull below the water line and WORDEN lost all power. DEWEY passed a tow cable over to WORDEN and attempted to pull the ship free. The grip of the rocks was too great and as DEWEY pulled the strain on the cable exceeded its strength and the line parted. A storm moved in and the seas began to swell and toss the powerless ship towards more rocks. The WORDEN's captain, Commander William Pogue, ordered abandon ship and DEWEY came in to supervise the rescue. During these efforts the waves began to tear WORDEN apart and swept 14 sailors to their deaths.

USS DEWEY, (foreground) supervises the rescue of crewmen off of USS WORDEN, DD-352, which had run aground in Constantine Harbor, Amchitka Island, Alaska, January 12, 1943.

DEWEY completed her duties in Alaska in 1943 by participating in the landings on Attu in May and Kiska in August. By the beginning of 1944 DEWEY had returned to the Central Pacific. Throughout the first part of the year she participated in actions at Eniwetok, Palau, Tinian, Saipan and Guam, returning to Puget Sound Naval Shipyard for an overhaul in early August.

In September 1944 DEWEY was assigned to the Third Fleet and was with them when the entire fleet was mercilessly mauled by Typhoon Cobra on December 18th. The storm hit with crushing wind gusts of up to 140 miles an hour and a formidable sea with 50 to 60 foot waves. Even with a displacement of over 1,700 tons and a length of 341 feet, DEWEY was a plaything to the ruthless tempest. The force of the storm sprung a hatch on deck, allowing seawater to pour below decks onto the main electrical distribution board which promptly shorted out, leaving the hapless ship with no electrical power. The ship had been rolling heavily through out the storm but now DEWEY rolled over to seventy-eight degrees. Almost on her side, the ocean entered the bridge and filled it with water up to the helmsmen's arms. For almost a full minute the ship and the sea fought each other to see if DEWEY would roll completely over and sink or right herself and perhaps, live a little longer. Slowly, almost leisurely, DEWEY came back up. The storm had ripped her forward smokestack off making the vessel less top heavy and reducing its profile, catching less wind. Lcdr. Charles Calhoun, Jr., captain of DEWEY, and her crew weathered the storm and sailed for Ulithi to repair their ship and contemplate their near-death experience.

Repairs to DEWEY were complete by the beginning of February and she set sail for her last battle; Iwo Jima. Two days before the landings took place DEWEY once again came to the aid of another ship. There was an explosion in a forward paint locker onboard the oiler USS PATUXENT, AO-4. The burning vessel carried highly volatile aviation fuel and DEWEY and the other ships that came in to help fight the fire did so at great risk to themselves. For three long hours the inferno raged until it was finally brought under control.

DEWEY spent the last few months of the war screening oilers that were refueling ships in operation for the invasion of Okinawa.

FATE

DEWEY headed for home in late August and pulled into the Brooklyn Navy Yard on September 25, 1945. She was decommissioned less than a month later and sold five days before Christmas 1946.

USS Dobbin

DESTROYER TENDER
AD-3
LAUNCHED: 1921

DECEMBER 7, 1941

DOBBIN was moored at buoy X-2 on the northeast end of Ford Island providing services, such as water and electricity, to the five ships of Destroyer Squadron One that were nested with her. On that December morning, Tennessee native Chuck Bailey, a 20-year-old Machinist Mate 2nd Class, was asleep on her fantail. Bailey had spent a portion of the early morning hours on board the USS ARIZONA, BB-39, visiting with friends that he had been in boot camp with. It was after 0330 when he finally set up his cot on deck and was lulled asleep by the tropical night air. World War II was the alarm clock to which Chuck Bailey awoke.

When the attack began, DOBBIN and her crew went into an intense multi-tasking role. First and foremost was, of course, defense. All guns opened fire on any enemy planes within range. Ira Schab, a 21-year-old sailor, who had been preparing to attend church services on board, helped man additional weapons to fight the enemy. Four .50 caliber machine guns and thirteen .30 caliber machines guns were brought on deck and joined the battle.

Secondly, all of her boats were put in the water to assist wherever they could in rescuing sailors from the harbor. On board one of them was 16-year-old sailor Jim Harris. A year earlier Harris had lied to a Navy recruiter, telling him that he was 19, in order to enlist. The boy who had become a sailor suddenly had to become a man in the space of a few hours. He spent the morning plucking injured men out of the harbor. At one point he reached over the side of the launch and grabbed the arm of a sailor who had been severely burned. The man's skin came off in Harris' hands. The sailor then sank beneath the waves.

Thirdly, all assistance possible was given to the five destroyers berthed alongside DOBBIN, including the transfer of ammunition, in order to get them up and running as soon as possible.

Although DOBBIN suffered no direct hits from enemy bombs, shrapnel from a near miss decimated the #4 anti-aircraft gun on the boat deck killing three men. The sailor in charge of the gun crew, H. A. Simpson, retained his composure, got a new crew together, and continued fighting.

By the end of the day all of the destroyers under the care of DOBBIN were underway and ready for war.

THE WAR

After spending the first few months of the war in Pearl Harbor, DOBBIN was sent to Sydney, Australia where she spent the next year servicing ships of the Pacific Fleet. In June 1943 she set sail for Milne Bay, New Guinea arriving there in September. She remained there for almost a year and a half, leaving for the Philippines in February 1945, which is where she was when the war ended.

FATE

DOBBIN left the Philippines in November and returned to San Diego on December 7, 1945, four years to the day after her baptism by fire in Pearl Harbor. One year later she was transferred to the Maritime Commission, which placed her in the reserve fleet in Olympia, Washington. Her retirement there lasted only three and a half years. She was sold for scrap to the Ziedell Shipwrecking Company of Portland, Oregon in May 1950.

USS Dolphin

V-BOAT /
DOLPHIN CLASS FLEET SUBMARINE
V-7 / SS-169
LAUNCHED: 1932

DECEMBER 7, 1941

The Executive Officer of DOLPHIN, Lieutenant Bernard Clarey, was at home, having breakfast with his wife and infant son. Their house was only a short drive from Pearl Harbor and Clarey was scheduled to report for duty at 0900. Shortly before 0800 Clarey noticed smoke coming from Hickam Field, which was some distance from the house. No sound was heard, but Clarey noticed numerous planes flying over the base and small puffs of black smoke in the sky indicating anti-aircraft fire. Clarey hopped into his car and drove to Pearl Harbor.

A similar scene was playing itself out on the opposite side of the island in the little community of Kaimuki, just north of Diamond Head. Petty Officer First Class Jim Peirano was taking his one-year-old son Grant on a Sunday morning outing to the grocery store. With the exception of the droning of a large number of planes in the air it was quiet. When they returned home Peirano turned his radio on and discovered just why there were so many planes in the air. The announcer said that all military personnel were to return to their stations at once. Peirano quickly changed into his dress white uniform and grabbed a cab to the submarine base.

On his way to the base, Lieutenant Clarey could see the terrible vista unfold before his eyes. Battleship Row was already ablaze and black, evil smoke was spreading over the harbor. When he arrived at the dock DOLPHIN was already in the thick of the fighting. All anti-aircraft machine guns were manned and being fired at Japanese planes that came within range. In addition to that, rifles had been handed out and sailors on deck were also firing on the enemy. One of those sailors was Jim Peirano who fired at the Japanese with a Browning Automatic Rifle. The enemy pilots flew so low he could see their faces and the scarves wrapped around their necks.

By the end of the attack, DOLPHIN claimed one kill. She suffered no damage or casualties because the Japanese never attacked the sub base.

THE WAR

Just days before the attack, DOLPHIN had returned from the second of two pre-war defensive patrols to Wake and Midway islands. She hadn't had an overhaul in six months and was in serious need of one. She wasn't going to get it. For the two weeks following the attack her crew got almost no sleep as they prepared their boat[15] for war.

In the late morning of Christmas Eve 1941, DOLPHIN passed out of Pearl Harbor on her first war patrol. Her mission was to simply gather intelligence of Japanese activities in the East Marshall Islands. Although the mission was completed and good information was gathered, the patrol was severely hampered by numerous and almost constant mechanical problems, not the least of which were leaks so severe that at times DOLPHIN could not submerge – a significant handicap for a submarine. Another issue that dogged the mission was the inability to communicate with superiors due to several radio deficiencies.

After returning from patrol, the captain, Lieutenant Commander Gordon Rainer, complained loudly about the condition of the boat and its negative effects on his ability to properly carry out his mission and the

---

15 During World War II, the only U.S. Navy warships that could correctly be referred to as a "boat" were submarines and Motor Torpedo Boats, all others were "ships".

enormous burden it placed on his crew. Over thirty mechanical defects ranging from the galley refrigerator to the engines were listed in his report. DOLPHIN spent the next several months in the Navy Yard for overhaul.

DOLPHIN left Pearl Harbor in May 1942 when she participated as a search vessel during the Battle of Midway. After the battle, she remained there for a month, then left for her second war patrol. DOLPHIN stayed out for 68 days, two weeks longer than a normal war patrol. She fared much better than on her first patrol but mechanical failures still persisted. When she returned to Pearl Harbor she was deemed fit for war duty despite her age.

Her third war patrol was to the Kuril Islands north of Japan for reconnaissance. The mission was extraordinarily uneventful and on December 5, 1942 at 1215, DOLPHIN returned to Pearl Harbor from her third and, as it turned out, last war patrol. Despite the fact that she had fewer mechanical problems on this mission than on her previous two, the Navy decided that DOLPHIN could serve better in other duties.

For the rest of the war DOLPHIN was used as a training vessel, first at Pearl Harbor, then in the States at the submarine school at New London, Connecticut.

FATE

Within five weeks of the signing of the surrender, DOLPHIN was at the Portsmouth Navy Yard in New Hampshire, where she had been built thirteen years earlier. There she was decommissioned in October 1945 and sold for scrap ten months later in August 1946.

*   *   *   *

Lieutenant Bernard Clarey, the executive officer of DOLPHIN on December 7, 1941 stayed in the submarine service for the entire war. He was in the Navy for 39 years retiring in 1973. Rising to the rank of Admiral he was the Commander-in-Chief of the Pacific Fleet when he retired. He died in Honolulu in 1996.

Petty Officer First Class Jim Peirano also remained in the Navy after the war. He was promoted through the ranks during his 24-year career, and was a Lieutenant Commander when he retired in 1960. He was the captain of USS COUCAL, ASR-8, a submarine rescue vessel. He died in Laguna Woods, California in 2009.

USS Downes

MAHAN CLASS DESTROYER
DD-375
LAUNCHED: 1936

DECEMBER 7, 1941

DOWNES was sharing Dry Dock #1 in the Pearl Harbor Navy Yard with her sister destroyer USS CASSIN, DD-372, and the Flagship of the Pacific Fleet, the battleship USS PENNSYLVANIA, BB-38. Lieutenant (jg) J. D. Parker was both the duty officer and the senior officer on board. His duties that Sunday morning were really nothing more than that of a caretaker. Not one weapon onboard was in battle-ready condition. None of the .50 caliber machine guns were mounted and the five-inch main guns all had their breech plugs removed for alterations. Because she was in dry dock, much of her ready ammunition had been transferred to the ammunition depot. What ordinance was on board was below decks in the magazines. DOWNES was not ready for war.

The crew responded quickly to the sound of the claxon calling general quarters. Lt. Parker ordered all weapons assembled. While some bluejackets jumped to that chore, others turned to below, belting up .50 caliber ammunition. Still others started a line to pass five-inch ammunition up to the main guns. All of this was being done in the dark, as the power that was being supplied from the yard was lost soon after the raid began. Despite the challenges, the .50 caliber machine guns were mounted and firing within fifteen minutes.

Below, in the engineering spaces, Chief Machinist Mate Charles Johnston and Chief Electrician's Mate James Raidy struggled in the darkness to bring power to DOWNES. Thirteen minutes after the loss of power, the two chiefs succeeded in getting the emergency diesel generator up and running. Suddenly, DOWNES became alive again. Suddenly, she had a chance.

The crew had succeeded in reinstalling the breech in the #3 five-inch gun shortly after electricity surged through the ship again. When he was informed of this, Lt. Parker asked Lieutenant Commander Daniel Shea, captain of the CASSIN, for permission to test fire the No. 3 gun. There was serious concern that firing the big five-incher might knock the destroyer off the blocks she was sitting on in the dry dock. Shea gave the go-ahead and DOWNES fired. There was a split second of uncertainty as the concussion vibrated through the ship, but the tin can remained solidly on the blocks. Satisfied, Parker gave the order to engage the enemy.

The second wave of Japanese planes arrived. Unlike the first wave that practically ignored the ships in the Navy Yard, this wave took more interest in them. Both horizontal and dive bombers were overhead. The machine guns engaged the "Vals" diving on the dry dock and the five-inch main battery targeted the "Kates" flying at 10,000 feet altitude.

DOWNES fired one shell from the No. 3 five-inch gun. As it turned out it would be the only shell fired at the enemy from her main battery. Almost simultaneously a "Val" dropped a bomb that impacted the concrete dry dock floor between CASSIN and DOWNES. The explosion ripped open DOWNES' diesel tank spilling fuel. Almost instantly Dry Dock #1 was ablaze. Fire control parties immediately turned hoses on the flames but the water only spread the fire.

The stern of the vessel was engulfed in flames inside and out. Down in the engineering spaces, Chief Johnston and his men fought fires until the flames were out of control. He then ordered his men out. On deck, the stern was surrounded by fire, yet the two aft machine guns, under the supervision of Ensign R. L. Stewart, were still manned and firing. Only when the heat went beyond endurance did he order his men to abandon their posts. When Stewart jumped to safety he broke his foot. Fireman

2nd Class Edward T. Kwolik was fighting the inferno aft. In the midst of smoke and flame he spotted the men from engineering coming out the hatch. Flames surrounded the hatch and despite being ordered to leave the area, Kwolik played his stream of water on the hatch, which allowed the sailors to escape unharmed. Chief Johnston and his men began fighting fires again as soon as they escaped engineering. At one point Chief Raidy's clothes caught fire and Johnston knocked him down and rolled him on the deck to extinguish the flames.

The stern had been afire for close to a half hour and in spite of heroic firefighting efforts it was clear that further actions were useless. Lt. Parker ordered the stern of the ship abandoned. Less than ten minutes later, after surveying his ship's condition, Parker ordered DOWNES abandoned. No sooner was that order given than another bomb exploded in the dry dock and soon the entire ship was on fire. Parker made valiant efforts to ensure that those who were still alive had gotten off the ship, but the flames ultimately compelled him off the ship too. He left just in the nick of time. A final bomb found its mark and hit DOWNES, totally obliterating the bridge.

Now that the ship had been abandoned, the crew found other things to do. Once on the walkway surrounding the dry dock, Parker led the efforts to fight the fires incinerating his ship. Ensign Stewart, ignoring his broken foot, commandeered a car and began an ad hoc ambulance service, rushing wounded to hospital. Two Gunner's Mates, Michael G. Odietus and Curtis P. Schulze, took it upon themselves to high tail it to the Marine armory. After helping to hand out weapons and ammunition there, they were issued two Browning Automatic Rifles and ammunition. They returned to Dry Dock #1 with the B.A.R.s to protect their shipmates from Japanese planes that were strafing the dock.

The fires on DOWNES were now intense. The paint itself on the ship was burning. Soon the heat generated was searing. On deck the warhead of the torpedo in the #3 tube exploded, punching a hole in the deck and showering pieces of hot metal on the deck of PENNSYLVANIA over 100 yards away. Five-inch shells that had been brought on deck for the main battery began to cook off. One of these shells exploded and the flying shrapnel struck Lt. Parker in the head. He received medical attention and, with a bandaged head, returned to once again take control of firefighting at the dry dock. For a time the exploding rounds forced evacuation of the firefighters. The dry dock was flooded in order to aid in fighting the fires but the water only succeeded in causing CASSIN to come off her keel blocks and slam against DOWNES.

Despite all efforts, DOWNES was severely damaged by the fires and twelve crewmen were killed. In his after action report, the captain, Lieutenant Commander William Thayer had nothing but praise for his crew and Lt. (jg) Parker, *"Lieutenant Parker…displayed leadership, good judgment, resourcefulness, coolness, and courage to the highest degree. His handling of the emergency under the most trying conditions was above reproach…The ship was lost, but the Commanding Officer has naught but praise for the officers and…crew who fought under such unfortunate circumstances. They did their utmost…against almost insurmountable odds…Their primary concern…was to get the guns in action, and their biggest regret was that they couldn't meet the enemy in a fair fight at sea. I am proud to have commanded the USS DOWNES".*

THE WAR

DOWNES was written off as a total loss almost immediately. After the dry dock was drained the true extent of her damage was revealed. Her hull was like Swiss cheese, holed from shrapnel and exploding ordinance. 243 holes were counted just on her port side. The seams between some hull plates were split by as much as four feet. The intense heat from the fires had warped her bow upward by just over three feet. Her aft smokestack had collapsed onto the dry dock floor.

An inventory of her interior spaces painted a somewhat brighter picture. Equipment inside the destroyer, like boilers and other heavy machinery, was discovered to be either undamaged or salvageable.

DOWNES needed to be removed from the dry dock as soon as possible as it was much needed to work on ships that it was felt could be saved. Removal of ammunition and guns began within days while simultaneously plans were made to patch her hull so she could be floated out of the dry dock. By January 23rd work was well underway with almost her entire superstructure removed. On February 6th Dry Dock #1 was flooded and a watertight DOWNES was floated out and taken over to 1010 dock.

Debate continued into May 1942 as to what the final disposition should be for the crippled destroyer. Should she be scrapped or rebuilt? If she were rebuilt should it be done at Pearl Harbor or at some shipyard back in the States? The Bureau of Ships finally decided in late May that a new hull was to be laid down at Mare Island in California and that all salvageable equipment was to be removed from the "old" DOWNES and be installed in the "new" DOWNES.

A new hull was already laid down and waiting when the guts of the old DOWNES started to arrive at Mare Island. Construction went on for over a year and was completed in November 1943. Seaworthiness trials were run through the beginning of the new year. On March 8, 1944 she left San Francisco, escorting a convoy to Pearl Harbor. From there she continued on to Majuro, in the Marshall Islands. She remained in the Marshalls for several months, blockading Wotje and then patrolling off Eniwetok.

In late July, DOWNES covered the invasion of Tinian in the North Mariana Islands. She followed this up by shelling the Japanese garrison on Aguijan Island only a few miles south of Tinian. In October she sailed to Marcus Island to shell and harass the Japanese outpost there.

After a short overhaul period at Pearl Harbor at the end of 1944, DOWNES returned to the Pacific front in March 1945. There she remained for the last five months of the war conducting patrol and training missions around the Marianas and Iwo Jima.

The new DOWNES on a shakedown cruise in San Francisco bay, December 8, 1943.

FATE

DOWNES and her crew were back in the United States just a month after the surrender was signed, arriving at Norfolk, Virginia on November 5, 1945. Two years later, in November 1947, she was sold for scrap.

USS Farragut

FARRAGUT CLASS DESTROYER
DD-348
LAUNCHED: 1934

DECEMBER 7, 1941

On Saturday night, December 6th, Harold White and a couple of friends had liberty in Honolulu. Like any sailors out on the town the first order of business was a bar. There, over a few drinks, they decided to hit the tattoo parlors when they were finished and get new tattoos. True to their word, around 2200, as they returned to FARRGUT on the liberty boat White had a fresh tattoo of a crane on his left arm.

The following morning he sat on the edge of his bunk admiring his new artwork when all hell broke loose. He ran to his battle station when the claxon sounded and made it on deck in time to see the former battleship, UTAH, AG-16, begin to turn turtle, victim to the first torpedoes loosed on the American fleet. White bounded up the ladder to his .50 caliber machine gun beneath the bridge. As he did, an enemy plane strafed the ship leaving bullet holes in the stack.

FARRAGUT got underway from her nest just under an hour after the attack began. She was under the command of Ensign James A. Benham, a 24-year-old native of New York City. The calm, cool-headedness and seamanship displayed by the young Princeton graduate that day ultimately earned him a Bronze Star. The destroyer was ordered to exit the harbor and stop for nothing, so she sailed by the inferno of Battleship Row and past the sailors swimming in the oil covered water and headed down the main channel. Both her main batteries and anti-aircraft weapons fired at the enemy as she sortied. Just as she was about to make it to the open sea one of her .50 caliber guns brought down a dive-bomber that made the mistake of getting within range.

Throughout the fleet, many officers and sailors could not get to their assigned ships that very hectic morning. Those that couldn't, got on any ship they could in hopes of doing battle or eventually catching up with their own ships or both. Thus it was with the men of FARRAGUT. The captain, Lieutenant Commander George P. Hunter sailed out of Pearl commanding the destroyer HULL, DD-350, as ordered by the commander of Destroyer Flotilla One. Another FARRRAGUT officer Lieutenant D. J. Wagner accompanied him on HULL. Two FARRAGUT Ensigns, Hodapp and Bonnvillian, went out on USS CHEW, DD-106. For two days Hodapp stood watches on CHEW in civilian clothes because all his uniforms were on FARRAGUT. Another FARRAGUT Ensign, G. A. Manning, went out on USS DEWEY, DD-349.

FARRAGUT returned to Pearl Harbor on Tuesday the 9th after waiting for two days to repulse the imminent, but fictional, Japanese invasion. She sailed into the harbor with no casualties and only a few bullet holes as damage.

THE WAR

Through March 1942 FARRAGUT was a regular on the "Pineapple run" from Hawai'i to San Francisco escorting convoys. She was part of the fleet that met and beat back the Japanese at the Battle of the Coral Sea in May, where she suffered some minor damage due to "friendly fire."

In August she was in the Solomons where she shelled the landing beaches at Guadalcanal. FARRAGUT lingered in the area, patrolling for several days after the invasion. She then received orders to sail as part of the screen for the aircraft carrier SARATOGA, CV-3. This Task Group and two others were sent out to intercept the Japanese attempts to reinforce Guadalcanal. They met the Japanese Navy on August 24th and 25th in the Battle of the Eastern Solomons.

On the first day of the battle, eight "Kate" torpedo planes were spotted coming in to attack SARATOGA. FARRAGUT, as part of the screen, began firing at them at a distance with her five-inch main batteries. Harold White was at his battle station manning a 20mm Oerlikon anti-aircraft gun. When the enemy was within range of his gun he opened fire. One "Kate" strafed FARRAGUT as it passed on its way to the aircraft carrier. One of the enemy's 7.7mm bullets struck White just above his left eye and it exited his head just behind his left ear. Another half inch to the left and the bullet would have missed him completely. Another half inch to the right and it would have killed him. As it was, the bullet severely fractured the left side of his skull. He was taken below for medical aid and was eventually taken to Brisbane, Australia for treatment. FARRAGUT and SARATOGA survived the encounter with the Japanese who withdrew, failing to land their reinforcements.

FARRAGUT continued in the South Pacific escorting convoys. Three weeks after he was admitted to the hospital in Brisbane, Harold White was released to return to the United States. White refused repatriation back home and insisted on returning to FARRAGUT. He returned to his ship and resumed his duties as a signalman. The headaches he suffered as a result of his injuries he kept to himself, lest he be separated from his ship.

After a period of overhaul in early 1943 FARRAGUT was bound for the frozen north as she joined the campaign in the Aleutians. She stayed in Alaska from April through September 1943. She participated in the invasions of both Attu and Kiska. When her duties were completed there she gratefully returned to the sunny climate in California for overhaul.

The first half of 1944 was very busy for FARRAGUT. She marched across the Pacific covering the landings at Kwajalein in January, Eniwetok in February and Guam in July. After Guam she once again returned to the States for overhaul, this time to Puget Sound. Harold White's head injury became extremely troublesome for him so he was hospitalized and eventually received a medical discharge. When his ship returned to the western Pacific, she returned without him. Once back in the war zone, she aided in the liberation of the Philippines, covering the landings at Mindoro in November 1944.

The rest of the war was spent mainly screening aircraft carriers in operations surrounding Iwo Jima and Okinawa and escorting convoys.

FATE

FARRAGUT left Saipan on August 21, 1945, seven days after the Japanese announced their surrender. Two months and two days later she was decommissioned in the Brooklyn Navy Yard. Twenty-two months, later, in August 1947, she was sold for scrap.

USS Gamble

WICKES CLASS DESTROYER /
LIGHT MINELAYER
DD-123 / DM-15
LAUNCHED: 1918

DECEMBER 7, 1941

Along with the other ships of Mine Division Two, GAMBLE was berthed in Middle Loch off the Pearl City peninsula. Within ten minutes of the first enemy bombs falling, above decks every gun on GAMBLE was firing back at the enemy and below decks all preparations were being made to get underway.

The combined fire of the four ships of Mine Division Two brought down a probable five Japanese airplanes, with GAMBLE claiming at least one kill. With the exception of one vessel, all ships of the division exited the harbor during the attack and under enemy fire.

GAMBLE got underway and left her berth at 0930, but had difficulty getting out of the harbor. Japanese planes concentrating their attack on the harbor channel - probably in an attempt to sink the battleship USS NEVADA, BB-36 - caused GAMBLE to stay her sortie and she anchored temporarily astern of the repair ship USS MEDUSA, AR-1. Ten minutes later she was underway again and, sixteen minutes after that, she was out of the harbor and beginning anti-submarine patrols.

Shortly after noon, a sonar contact was made on a suspected enemy submarine and GAMBLE dropped three depth charges with negative results. Four and a half hours later she had a near-disastrous encounter with another submarine. At 1631 GAMBLE sighted a submarine surfacing in her patrol area. Already at battle stations and anxious for some retribution she fired her four inch gun at the vessel but missed. Before a second round could be unleashed the submarine identified herself as an American vessel, USS THRESHER, SS-200, and then quickly resubmerged.

By the early evening GAMBLE had joined up with USS ENTERPRISE, CV-6, to shield her from any enemy attacks as she returned to Pearl Harbor from Wake Island. For GAMBLE, the first day of the war was over.

THE WAR

Hawai'ian waters were home to GAMBLE through February 1942 when she sailed south. There she laid mines off of Tutuila Island in Samoa, then in Fiji. After being redirected north to escort convoys during the Battle of Midway, she returned south to lay more mines near the island of Espiritu Santo in the New Hebrides. By August GAMBLE was part of the vast armada of ships involved in America's first invasion of Japanese-held territory at Guadalcanal.

Lieutenant Commander Nakai Makoto was the captain of the Japanese submarine *I-123* patrolling near Savo Island in the Solomons. Early on August 29, American planes spotted *I-123* and Nakai radioed to his base that his ship was being pursued. GAMBLE's lookouts spotted the sub's conning tower and went after it. *I-123* dove but GAMBLE chased the sub down. She made one depth charge run and then laid down a second pattern but the sub was still untouched. GAMBLE and her crew were dogged in their determination to sink the sub and the attack continued for just over three hours. Beneath the waves Nakai shot off another radio message. This one informed his superiors that he was under heavy depth charge attack. It was the last message *I-123* ever sent. GAMBLE relentlessly continued the attack and soon she spotted a huge air bubble break the surface followed by debris and an oil slick, all evidence of the submarine's demise.

Despite a grueling but successful attack on the sub, the day was not yet over for GAMBLE. As she set her course for Guadalcanal, she passed the small island of Nura. Once again the sharp-eyed lookouts spotted something unusual: four men on the beach, waving wildly. GAMBLE anchored off the islet and sent her whaleboat to investigate. What the sailors found was the crew of a TBM Avenger torpedo bomber off of the aircraft carrier USS SARATOGA, CV-3. The Avenger had gotten the short end of an engagement with a Japanese fighter and the pilot ditched near Nura. The plane's crew was loaded into the whaleboat and delivered safely onboard GAMBLE.

Amazingly enough, after sinking an enemy submarine and rescuing four downed aviators, GAMBLE still had one more job to do. During the rescue, Admiral Halsey instructed GAMBLE to sweep Lengo Channel, on the north coast of Guadalcanal, clear of possible enemy mines. After pointing out that they were a minelayer and not a minesweeper, the order was repeated to sweep Lengo Channel. The skipper of GAMBLE, Lieutenant Commander Stephen Tackney, devised a way to comply with the instructions even though his ship was not equipped with minesweeping gear. If he couldn't sweep the channel with cables and paravanes then he would sweep it with the eyes of his men. He ordered all available men on deck in the hopes that almost 100 pairs of eyes would spot any mines that may be present. He then rang up 20 knots on the engines and proceeded to traverse the channel. The trip was tense but Tackney brought his ship and crew safely to an anchorage off Henderson Field and reported Lengo Channel free of mines.

August 29, 1942: an amazing day of accomplishments for USS GAMBLE.

Throughout the rest of the war GAMBLE continued to exhibit her abilities and those of her crew. She did everything from transport Marines to salvage grounded ships. And she laid mines. She sowed the ocean with mines from Alaska to the South Pacific; her mine laying efforts being partially responsible for the destruction of at least three ships of the Imperial Japanese Navy.

FATE

February 1945 brought GAMBLE to Iwo Jima to participate in the invasion of that Japanese stronghold. On the day she arrived, the 17th, she participated in a softening up barrage, shelling enemy positions on the island. One of her shells made a direct hit on a Japanese ammunition dump that exploded in a pyrotechnic extravaganza.

The following day enemy aircraft bombed GAMBLE. She was hit by two 250-pound bombs that holed her hull, killing five sailors outright. The blue Pacific waters rushed into the stricken lady, flooding her. She was soon dead in the water. The gallant efforts that were made to keep her afloat paid off. She was still alive the next day and a relay of ships towed her to Saipan for repairs. Several months passed before it was finally decided to write her off as a loss. In July she was towed to a location off Guam and scuttled.

GAMBLE was the last Pearl Harbor survivor that was lost due to enemy action.

USS Grebe

LAPWING CLASS MINESWEEPER
AM-43
LAUNCHED: 1918

DECEMBER 7, 1941

If a common denominator can be found in the experiences of every sailor in Pearl Harbor that Sunday morning it would be how extraordinarily ordinary it all began; just another Sunday. No portent revealed itself, and why should it? It was a Sunday like the last one and as far as anyone knew it was going to be a Sunday, just like the next one.

For 25-year-old Bob Ohnemus that was certainly his state of mind. GREBE was in the Navy Yard undergoing a major overhaul. Her three-inch guns had been dismantled and her engines were cold. There was really nothing to do. However the South Dakota native and a friend of his had a small business going. They were charging their crewmates fifty cents each to do their laundry. The two of them were on the dock with hoses and bundles of their dirty clothes and those of twenty-five other sailors.

At the sound of the first bomb going off, Ohnemus thought the magazine on another ship had blown up. But then other explosions followed and the previously empty blue sky was now filled with the black silhouettes of Japanese warplanes.

The only weapons available to the crew were rifles and pistols, so they stood on the deck and fired at the enemy planes with those; no big anti-aircraft guns, no heavy caliber machine guns, just rifles and pistols. The sailors on GREBE met the foe with a few small arms backed by a lot of guts. The David and Goliath scenario played itself out to the end, when the crew of GREBE shot down one enemy plane.

THE WAR

Through the fall of 1942 GREBE operated out of Pearl Harbor, towing fuel oil barges to Johnston and Palmyra Islands. GREBE had her mission and designation changed to that of an ocean going tugboat, AT-134, on June 1, 1942. In that capacity she sailed for the South Pacific in November 1942 where she would meet her fate.

FATE

Within weeks of arriving in the South Pacific, in December 1942, GREBE was dispatched to Vuata Vatoa in the Fiji Islands. The liberty ship *Thomas A. Edison* had run aground and needed to be rescued. On December 6, 1942, while attempting to pull the liberty ship free, GREBE herself became grounded on the rocky shoals off of Vuata Vatoa. For almost a month both GREBE and *Edison* remained on the rocks, unable to be freed. During the night of January 1, 1943 a typhoon ravaged the island splitting the *Edison* in two and sinking GREBE. Both ships were gone.

USS Helena

ST. LOUIS CLASS LIGHT CRUISER
CL-50
LAUNCHED: 1927

DECEMBER 7, 1941

On that quiet Sunday morning HELENA was berthed at 1010 dock, inboard of the USS OGLALA, CM-4, which was tied up to HELENA's starboard side. At 0757, Seaman 1st Class C. A. Flood, on watch on the signal bridge, notified the Officer of the Deck, Ensign W. W. Jones that the planes he saw flying overhead were Japanese. Flood had recently returned from duty in Asia and had seen Japanese planes before. The planes began their attack and bombs started dropping on the seaplane base on Ford Island. Ensign Jones immediately got on the ship's public address system and announced, "Japanese planes bombing Ford Island! Man all battle stations, break out service ammunition!"

A plane flew low over the dock and strafed HELENA, but as few crew were on deck nothing came of it. The crew had come alive and rushed to man all battle stations. About one and a half minutes later, a Nakajima B5N2 "Kate" torpedo plane, aimed at HELENA and released its modified torpedo approximately 500 yards away. The torpedo passed underneath OGLALA and struck HELENA eighteen feet below the waterline. The explosion flooded several boiler rooms, fifteen fuel tanks and put the ship's turbo generator out of commission, but the engineering department quickly brought other generators online allowing HELENA to use her guns. Within four minutes of the initial sighting, HELENA's guns were barking back at the Japanese.

The crew in all aspects was superb that day. Unlike some other ships HELENA maintained her watertight security and the damage control parties isolated the wounds caused by the torpedo strike, both actions saving the ship from sinking. Fire control parties throughout the ship quickly extinguished the many fires that broke out. On deck expertly manned guns protected her from attack. HELENA's gunners claimed seven enemy planes shot down that morning, but there were losses on both sides. Two men on deck were killed as a result of bomb splinters and either splinters or bullets wounded seven others. All told HELENA lost 34 men, the majority of which died from the initial torpedo impact.

In his after action report for December 7th, HELENA's Commanding Officer, Captain Robert H. English said of his crew, *"Not a single instance of faltering on any task as noted; on the other hand, many men performed tasks other than their regular ones with skill and dispatch. Had not a single order been issued – and very few had to be, in fact, – it is believed that every job would have been carried out by someone who saw the need for the task. This reveals the intelligent discipline that is standard throughout the ship. The orders that were necessary to issue were those that required timing, and they were carried out fully, quickly, and well."*

THE WAR

HELENA initiated repairs at Pearl Harbor, but soon steamed to Mare Island Naval Shipyard, in Vallejo, California. There she had a new SG radar system installed and heavy modifications were made to her superstructure to reduce her silhouette.

She was assigned to Espiritu Santo where she joined in the first amphibious landing of the war at Guadalcanal. After the initial landings, HELENA joined the task group built around the aircraft carrier USS WASP, CV-7. The group was attacked on September 15, 1942 while delivering troops from the 7th Marine Regiment to Guadalcanal as reinforcements. This time the Japanese succeeded at what they failed to do at Pearl Harbor; they sank an aircraft carrier. Three torpedoes of a six torpedo spread slammed into WASP. A fourth torpedo from the same spread narrowly missed HELENA astern. The fifth torpedo struck USS

O'BRIEN, DD-415, and USS NORTH CAROLINA, BB-55, was struck by the sixth.

Almost instantly WASP was ablaze, the intense fires fed by burning aviation fuel, spilled from damaged planes onboard. In short order it became apparent that WASP was doomed and the order to abandon ship was given. HELENA came along side with other vessels and took on board 400 officers and men of the sinking carrier and brought them to Espiritu Santo.

The battle for Guadalcanal was fierce. The Japanese did not want the first domino of its Pacific fortress to fall. The Imperial Japanese Navy was pressed into duty. Sometimes they bombarded Henderson Field at night to destroy the American air presence and other times attempted midnight runs to transport reinforcements to its dwindling garrison.

On September 15, 1942, HELENA was a member of Task Force 64, commanded by Rear Admiral Norman Scott, on a mission to deny the Japanese access to Guadalcanal. At 2332 hours, HELENA's new radar detected the Japanese force approaching from 33 miles away. With this much lead time Scott was able to maneuver his fleet into a position that allowed him the ability to employ the classic naval strategy of "crossing the T." By bringing his ships in at an angle perpendicular to the enemy, all guns of his ships could come to bear while the enemy could only use its forward guns.

HELENA began the engagement and opened fire at 2346 hours. The battle raged, there on the dark waters off of Guadalcanal, for thirty-five minutes with HELENA and the other U.S. ships firing shells and torpedoes at the enemy and the Japanese making a good account of themselves despite being surprised and out maneuvered. When the guns went silent HELENA had helped to sink the heavy cruiser *Furataka* and the destroyer *Fubuki*. The Americans lost USS DUNCAN, DD-485. HELENA came through the engagement without a scratch.

On the night of October 20th, while plying the waters between its home base of Espiritu Santo and San Cristobal HELENA dodged another bullet. Two torpedoes sliced through the water toward HELENA. It was only the sharp eyes and quick actions of Lt. Sam Leiman that prevented disaster. Leiman spotted the oncoming torpedoes and ordered the ship hard to starboard causing the high explosive fish to miss the target.

On November 11th, HELENA participated in escorting a convoy of transports to Guadalcanal. The next afternoon, as the transports were unloading men and equipment, word was received that Japanese planes were approaching. HELENA and the other escort ships maneuvered to form an anti-aircraft screen around the transports. The attack came in two waves and lasted less than ten minutes. When it was over the enemy had been forced to retire and the Japanese had eight fewer airplanes, HELENA reportedly bringing down four of them.

The Japanese were tenacious. Even at this late date, three months after the initial landings on Guadalcanal, they were putting enormous effort into dislodging the American foothold in the Pacific. Later that same night reports came from coast watchers that a large Japanese naval force was coming down "The Slot"[16]. The American fleet sortied to meet the approaching danger. In the early morning hours of November 13th, the two fleets met in the crowded waters off Guadalcanal. It was described by an officer on board USS MONSSEN, DD-436, as "a barroom brawl after the lights had been shot out".

The Japanese force consisted of 2 battleships, 8 cruisers and 16 destroyers, while the Americans had 2 battleships, 5 cruisers (including HELENA), and 12 destroyers. The two opposing forces were well aware of each other's presence and proceeded to maneuver in the pitch blackness in attempts to gain strategic position. As a result both fleets became hopelessly intermingled. Just before 0200 hours two Japanese ships turned on their massive spotlights and the chaos began. All the ships began firing, some at a range of only a mile. In the first exchange HELENA and others ships fired on the destroyer *Atkatsuki* and sank her within the first few minutes of the battle. The confused position of the ships, along with the close quarters, caused several American ships to fire on each other. One result was the death of Admiral Scott on board USS ATLANTA, CL-51. Heavy cruiser SAN FRANCISCO, CA-38, came under fire by four enemy vessels killing Rear Admiral Daniel J. Callahan, one of the task group commanders. HELENA came on her in an attempt to shield her. The

16 The colloquial term for New Georgia Sound, the narrow waters running northwest to southeast through the middle of the Solomon Islands.

destroyer *Amatsukaze* spotted the crippled SAN FRANCISCO and came in for an attack in an attempt to finish her off. In her haste to sink the heavy cruiser, *Amatsukaze* failed to spot HELENA coming to the rescue. HELENA unleashed her batteries of 6-inch guns and riddled the destroyer with a massive broadside. *Amatsukaze* was heavily damaged, but did not sink. She retired behind a smoke screen. HELENA was unable to pursue as she then came under attack by three other enemy ships.

The melee in the dark lasted thirty-two minutes. With the deaths of Admirals Callahan and Scott, Captain Gilbert Hoover of the HELENA was now the senior officer of the fleet and he ordered a cease fire at 0226 hours. Both fleets retired from the scene licking their wounds. HELENA survived this major engagement with only one killed, nine wounded and minor damage to her superstructure.

After the battle, the remaining ships headed toward Espiritu Santo. In the late morning of the 13th, USS JUNEAU, CL-52, was torpedoed, split in half and sank in less than half a minute. Capt. Hoover did not want to risk HELENA in obviously dangerous waters and thinking there were few, if any, survivors, ordered all ships to continue. He did signal a nearby B-17 of the JUNEAU's sinking. There were, in fact, over one hundred survivors adrift at sea. Almost all of whom died due to inadequate rescue attempts. As a result of his actions, or lack thereof, Capt. Hoover was relived of command by Admiral Halsey. Hoover was later exonerated by the Navy and was awarded the Navy Cross for his command of HELENA during the battle.

Throughout early 1943 HELENA continued to support the effort to keep and garrison Guadalcanal and preventing the enemy from retaking it. This effort included bombardment of the Japanese airstrips at Munda on New Georgia and Vila Stanmore on the southern coast of Kolombangara. In February one of her float planes assisted in sinking a Japanese submarine. Overhaul in Sydney, Australia followed and she returned to Espiritu Santo in March where the focus continued to be the defense of Guadalcanal.

FATE

In support of the campaign for New Georgia Island, HELENA found herself off the coast of Kolombangara, in Kula Gulf on July 5, 1943. Once again word had been received that the Tokyo Express, this time consisting of ten destroyers, was making a run down The Slot with troops to be landed on Kolombangara. HELENA and six other ships were stationed to meet them.

Shortly before 0200 on the 6th, the two task groups met in battle. HELENA commenced a rapid and continuous fire with her fifteen 6-inch guns, firing hundreds of rounds in the first minutes of the engagement. Unfortunately, the muzzle flashes from her own fire created an almost perfect and constant silhouette for the enemy to zero in on.

Approximately seven minutes into the battle HELENA was struck by a torpedo. A minute later another torpedo hit and then a third torpedo found its mark. The strikes broke the gallant lady in two, with her bow and stern both pointing up into the night sky forming a V. The stern rapidly sank, but the bow stayed afloat.

Many of the crew made it to lifeboats and rafts in the sea while others clung to the bow and some just floated in the ink black ocean. After the battle two destroyers returned to search for survivors and pulled over 450 sailors out of the water, carrying them back to Tulagi. HELENA's commanding officer, Captain C. P. Cecil, using boats and rafts led 88 men to a near-by island where they were rescued the following day. For the 200 men that stayed with the severed, but buoyant bow, a different adventure lay ahead. A Navy B-24 Liberator dropped life rafts to the group, which then set out for Kolombangara, but wind and currents prevented them from making landfall. Two more days passed before they managed to make it to Vella Lavella where natives and a coast watcher cared for them and radioed Guadalcanal of their location. On July 16th, ten days after being shipwrecked the last of HELENA's crew was rescued. Amazingly, of her 900-man compliment, 732 men survived her sinking.

USS Helm

BAGLEY CLASS DESTROYER
DD-388
LAUNCHED: 1937

DECEMBER 7, 1941

The two Carrolls were on the bridge, the man proudly showing the boy the workings of his command. The captain of HELM, Lieutenant Commander Chester E. Carroll, was a U.S. Army veteran of World War I. After that war he became a 1924 graduate of the United States Naval Academy at Annapolis. HELM was somewhat unique in Pearl Harbor that Sunday morning because she had her captain and entire crew on board. In fact, she had one extra person on board: a guest that morning was Chester T. Carroll, the captain's 13-year-old son. HELM had a minor chore to take care of and the elder Carroll thought he'd take advantage of the quiet Sunday morning to show his son a U. S. Navy destroyer at work. Young Chester was about to get the show of a lifetime.

Lcdr. Carroll pulled his ship away from berth X-7 in East Loch at 0726. The ship's destination was the deperming buoys at the opposite end of the harbor in West Loch. A huge steel object like a ship develops its own electromagnetic signature as it interacts with the Earth's magnetic field. This signature makes it vulnerable to mines and plays havoc with compasses. Deperming is a process that helps reduce a ship's magnetic signature.

HELM rounded Ford Island and headed down the main channel. Halfway down she began a hard turn to starboard at the entrance to West

Loch. Just about then, at 0755, the first enemy planes were sighted over the harbor and the first bombs were seen dropping on Ford Island.

Two responsibilities became immediately apparent to Lt. Cmdr. Carroll: the safety of his ship and his son. His son came first. He had young Chester put on a helmet and placed in a life jacket. He then had him sent down to the captain's cabin to wait out the attack in relative safety. Carroll's second order was to put his ship in full reverse to get his ship pointed back down the main channel. He wanted to get his ship out of the mousetrap of the harbor.

Two hours earlier, Hirano Takashi had taken off from the deck of the Japanese aircraft carrier *Akagi*, in his Mitsubishi A6M2 "Zero." His mission was to escort the dive-bombers to Pearl Harbor. This mission was complete and he was now free to attack targets of opportunity. The target he spotted was HELM, making her run for the open sea down the main channel. He put his "Zero" into a dive and began a strafing run on the escaping destroyer.

On board HELM was Gunner's Mate 2nd Class W. C. Huff. He was manning the port side aft .50 caliber machine gun. Huff saw the "Zero" coming his way and opened fire with a devastating stream of lead. Bullets and plane intersected. Hirano's plane crashed into Building 52 at Fort Kamehameha.

A few minutes later HELM passed out of the mouth of the channel and into the open sea, becoming the first ship to exit Pearl Harbor after the attack began. Almost immediately, the conning tower of a mini-sub was spotted, apparently hung up on Tripod Reef, just west of the harbor entrance. Carroll ordered his main guns to open fire on the sub. There were no direct hits, but two close misses.

Inside the submarine were the commanding officer, Ensign Sakamaki Kazuo and his single crewman Petty Officer 2nd Class Inagaki Kiyoshi. Their sub had been recalcitrant all morning, possibly due to gyroscope problems. They had been just outside the harbor entrance since 0700 and couldn't manage to get into the channel. Now they were hung up on a reef and couldn't get off. Their savior, oddly enough, came in the form of HELM. The two close misses from the destroyer jarred the sub loose from the reef. It then disappeared beneath the waves. The shaking also rattled the occupants and Sakamaki was knocked out.[17]

After escaping from the harbor and firing on the mini-sub, HELM found herself all alone. So she took it upon herself to fire on stray enemy planes and commenced searching for other submarines. It was another forty minutes before other ships made it out of the harbor to join her.

Just about 0915 a "Val" dive-bomber was spotted coming after HELM. Machine gunners fired on it and the captain ordered up evasive maneuvers. The enemy pilot was undaunted and fearlessly came on letting loose two bombs. The bombs straddled the bow of the destroyer. The concussion partially buckled hull plates and caused flooding in forward compartments. The bombs also induced a whole laundry list of minor electrical and mechanical problems. None of the damage totally disabled HELM, but her ills gave the crew a challenge.

One more chore was left Lt. Cmdr. Carroll and that was to get his son safely off the ship before he sailed off to war. A Coast Guard vessel was contacted and met HELM off of Waikiki beach. The two ships ran parallel to each other and a boatswain's chair was strung between the two. Young Chester was retrieved from his father's cabin, brought on deck and put in the chair. The transfer went smoothly. Chester's presence onboard HELM put his father and him in the history books as the only father/son shipmates of Pearl Harbor.

THE WAR

January 1942 found HELM making a run south to Howland and Baker Islands to evacuate six civilians from those two desolate equatorial rocks.

After the sinking of the oiler NEOSHO, A0-23, during the Battle of the Coral Sea in May 1942, HELM, was dispatched to search for survivors. She departed Noumea on the 13th. NEOSHO had been scuttled on the 11th and 128 survivors rescued. There were still 68 men unaccounted

---

17 Sakamaki's sub drifted for the rest of the day and eventually grounded miles away from Pearl Harbor on the beach off Bellows Field on the eastern side of O'ahu. After a failed attempt to scuttle the sub, Inagaki drowned and, exhausted, Sakamaki washed ashore. He was captured, becoming the first Japanese prisoner of the war.

for who were known to have escaped the damaged vessel on life rafts. HELM arrived at the search area on the 15th and searched all day, finding nothing. The following day HELM discovered a partially sunken life raft and whaleboat, but no survivors. At 2000 HELM sighted a life raft and recovered four NESHO sailors, the only four survivors of the missing 68.

In August 1942 HELM participated in the invasion of the Solomon Islands. HELM was part of the force that took Tulagi on Florida Island north of Guadalcanal. She screened the landings in the morning. Later in the day the Japanese sent planes in to repulse the incursion; HELM shot down two "Betty" bombers.

Two days later, in the early morning hours of the 9th, HELM was involved in the disaster that was the Battle of Savo Island, where the combined American-Australian fleet lost four heavy cruisers. HELM fired its main guns and went off in the darkness in pursuit of enemy ships but found none. When she returned it was to pick up survivors from the sunken ships and return them to Guadalcanal.

HELM slogged through the campaign in the Pacific in 1943 escorting convoys, screening landings and shelling enemy strongholds. In November 1943 she levied a 400-shell bombardment against Gasmata, New Guinea in preparation for removing the Japanese garrison there. In early 1944, HELM returned to the United States for the first time in two years to undergo a long-needed overhaul at Mare Island. After a two month stay HELM returned to the Pacific in May 1944.

She soon resumed her routine of support and rescue missions. In fact HELM became somewhat adept at rescuing downed American pilots. In June 1944, at the Battle of the Philippine Sea, later known as the "Great Mariana's Turkey Shoot," HELM pulled many American pilots out of the ocean. Upon returning the aviators to their respective aircraft carriers, grateful captains rewarded the destroyer with gallons of ice cream. If saving a castaway pilot wasn't enough incentive, the ice cream certainly added to it.

In conjunction with the American return to the Philippines, HELM was providing a screen for ships in the Leyte area in October 1944. On the 28th, just around noon, HELM made a sonar contact. She revved up her engines and made several depth charge attacks on the presumed Japanese submarine. The second attack produced an oil slick. The destroyer USS GRIDLEY, DD-380, came in to assist. Between the two destroyers a total of seven depth charge attacks were made. More oil and a large air bubble broke the surface, indicating the death of the submarine. Confirmation of a kill was obtained when boats from HELM ventured out and saw debris that included human remains.[18]

During the first week of 1945, the U. S. Navy bombarded targets on Luzon in preparation for upcoming landings. For days the Japanese threw wave after wave of kamikazes at the gathering armada. On the 5th, three separate enemy air attacks rained down on the fleet. The pilots of the Divine Wind were indiscriminate, attacking any and all ships, including HELM. The tiny tin can fought for her life. Ordinance - both large and small - shot up to the sky seeking the enemy that fell from it. One plane struck HELM a glancing blow in her upper superstructure, leaving only minor damage. HELM remained in Lingayen Gulf supporting the landings there until January 19th.

In February she headed for Iwo Jima in the company of a vast number of ships that would pepper the island with bombs and artillery as a prelude to the invasion. Once again the kamikaze was the bane of the Navy. On the 21st two struck and sank the escort aircraft carrier BISMARK SEA, CVE-95. HELM, along with several other destroyers, pulled hundreds of sailors out of the sea and returned them to safety.

Amid heavy anti-aircraft fire, a kamikaze attacks HELM in Lingayen Gulf, January 5, 1945.

---

18   The victim of this attack may have been *I-46* or *I-54*. Japanese records show that both subs were operating in this area and both turned up missing at the same time.

The closing months of the war followed rapidly and HELM was kept busy. She underwent repairs in the Philippines and then did a quick turn around heading back north for Okinawa. There she conducted pre-invasion shelling, covered the landings and then screened the invasion force and supply ships.

In her final invasion of the war, HELM reported to the island of Borneo in July where, only weeks before the dropping of the atomic bombs on Japan, she covered the invasion of Balikpapan by the Australian army.

FATE

Originally scheduled as a target for the Operation Crossroads Atomic tests, HELM was saved from that particular end. Instead she followed so many of her Pearl Harbor sisters and was consigned to the scrap heap. She was sold to the Moore Dry Dock Company of Oakland, California in 1947.

Throughout the war HELM was considered lucky. From the dawn at Pearl Harbor to kamikaze attacks in 1945, HELM never lost one man or suffered even one causality from enemy action.

*   *   *   *   *

Chester E. Carroll received a Bronze Star for service as the commanding officer of HELM at Pearl Harbor and Guadalcanal. He also received a Silver Star for his World War II service after he left HELM. He retired from the Navy in 1954 as a Rear Admiral and passed away in 1987. His son Chester T. Carroll served in the Navy during the Korean War and passed away in 2000.

USS Henley

BAGLEY CLASS DESTROYER
DD-391
LAUNCHED: 1937

DECEMBER 7, 1941

Seaman First Class Jack Carson was lying below decks in his bunk waiting for the sound of morning colors at 0800. The young man from Oregon had the boat duty and after the raising of the flag he would be busy ferrying sailors to and from the ship for the rest of the morning. At about 0750 instead of hearing the "Call to Quarters" over the loudspeakers he heard "General Quarters." The Petty Officer of the Watch mistakenly pulled the wrong lever. In response to the general quarters call, the crew reported to their battle stations and were milling around them as the word was passed that the battle stations call was in error.

The crew started to return to the normal routine of their Sunday morning. Carson, jolted from his happy bunk, returned to his quarters to get ready for his boat duties when he heard the general quarters alarm for the second time in the space of five minutes. This time it was the right call.

Many of the crew were still at or near their battle stations when the first enemy planes flew in over the harbor and they saw the first torpedoes dropped. The ship, already roused, was swift to respond and guns were blazing in short order. Carson reported to his battle station as the powder loader in the #4 five-inch gun. Unfortunately, of the twenty men assigned to battle stations in this gun, only six were on board. As a result, many of the shells fired were not properly fused to explode at altitude where the

Japanese planes were. They simply flew through the air and exploded upon landing miles away, some of them in Honolulu.

Below decks, in the engineering spaces, Chief Machinist's Mate W. H. Fiddler was busy getting the ship ready to sortie. He and his men had the destroyer ready in just over half an hour and at 0830 HENLEY made her run out of the harbor. She built up speed in the North Channel and turned to port past Ford Island to head down the main channel toward the mouth of the harbor. HENLEY was under the command of Lieutenant Francis E. Fleck and expertly piloting the ship was Chief Quartermaster M. O. Nelson. The captain, Commander Robert H. Smith and the executive officer, Lieutenant H. G. Corey, were not on board at the time of the attack.

As she passed Hospital Point, an enemy plane dove on her making a strafing run. Deadly trails of bullets danced all around the tin can. Manning the #2 machine gun was Gunner's Mate 3rd Class D. J. Seely. The Japanese plane came from behind HENLEY firing its 7.7 mm machine guns and Seely met it shot for shot with his .50 caliber. In the end Seely's bullets did more damage than the Japanese pilot's. The enemy plane, with smoke and flames trailing behind, crashed in the water.

Once outside the harbor, HENLEY commenced patrolling. It wasn't long before she picked up a sonar contact. Lt. Fleck brought the ship around and dropped two depth charges on the suspected submarine. The contact was lost and there were no outward signs that the sub was hit or damaged.

By the time Commander Smith and Lieutenant Corey arrived at Pearl Harbor their ship was gone, so they hitched a ride on the destroyer minesweeper, USS TREVER, DMS-16. TREVER eventually caught up with HENLEY on the open sea. HENLY streamed a raft on a rope aft to TREVER. When the raft was alongside TREVER, Smith and Corey got into the raft, which was then pulled back to HENLEY. The captain and exec finally set foot on deck at 1216.

HENLEY stayed out for three days, returning to Pearl Harbor on Wednesday the 10th. She suffered no casualties among her crew and her physical damage was limited to three bullet holes in a shield and some ricochet marks on the deck.

THE WAR

In February, HENLEY escorted the destroyer USS SHAW, DD-373, to Mare Island to repair the severe damage she received on December 7th. While there HENLEY underwent minor alterations, extending her stay by a week. When she left San Francisco Bay she formed up as a screen for a convoy of about ten ships heading for Pearl. While still in sight of the American coast she made a sonar contact and dropped a pattern of depth charges but no hits or kills were indicated.

In May, the Japanese Navy collided with the United States Navy in one of the first major naval engagements of the war in the Coral Sea. Two American victims of that clash were the oiler USS NEOSHO, AO-23, and the destroyer USS SIMS, DD- 409. In an action against enemy planes on May 7, 1942 SIMS was sunk and NEOSHO severely damaged. On the 11th HENLEY was dispatched to the crippled oiler to render assistance and pick up survivors.

When HENLEY arrived on scene she was greeted with the sight of a heavily listing NEOSHO struggling to stay afloat and life rafts filled with burned, maimed and exhausted survivors. The entire crew of the destroyer was engaged in helping in one of two things, dealing with survivors or scuttling NEOSHO. Neither was easy.

Below decks Jack Carson was helping with survivors. He was bathing one man with severe burns in a tub of ice water. In the middle of the bath the sailor died. Carson had never seen a man die before. Above decks HENLY was attempting to scuttle NEOSHO. Two torpedoes were fired at the oiler but she wouldn't go down. Then over 140 five-inch rounds were fired into her before she finally succumbed. HENLEY delivered the survivors to Brisbane, Australia.

Remaining in the waters around Australia, HENLEY toiled there until August 1942 when she headed for the invasion of Guadalcanal. On the 7th she screened landing forces and helped to repel attacking Japanese planes, helping to shoot down two "Betty" bombers.

Two weeks later, HENLEY was on a night patrol with the destroyer USS BLUE, DD-387, near Savo Island. During the mid-watch, about 0330, BLUE registered a radar contact. Both ships commenced searches for the presumed enemy but were unsuccessful and the contact was lost. A half hour later radar picked up another contact, this time by both ships. The moonless night proved to be daunting, the curtain of blackness could not be pulled back and no identification could be made of the ship in the darkness. Its identity could soon be inferred when the phosphorescent wakes of two high-speed torpedoes came at BLUE. Trailing behind, HENLEY could do nothing but watch as one torpedo struck her Pearl Harbor sister bringing her to a halt.

HENLEY raced to the aid of the crippled destroyer. As the early morning light broke on the horizon HENLEY took BLUE under tow. The damaged stern of BLUE created an enormous drag and the towline parted twice. The incredibly difficult tow lasted until the late hours of the 22nd when the two ships eventually neared Tulagi. Based on the damage to BLUE and an expected attack by the Japanese, the decision was made to scuttle BLUE. HENLEY took on board the doomed destroyer's crew and then, with much regret, sent BLUE to the depths of Ironbottom Sound.

After Guadalcanal, HENLEY returned to duties in Australia conducting anti-submarine patrols and convoy escorting duties. In September 1943 she was involved in the efforts to dislodge the enemy from New Guinea.

In the pre-dawn hours of September 22, 1943 HENLY and other destroyers escorted and protected Australian troops landing at Finschhafen on the northeast coast of New Guinea. The allied ships bombarded the beaches and jungles which allowed the Aussies to be well entrenched by 0930.

Around noon, the enemy sent an aerial armada to remove the invaders. For the next thirty minutes both the sky and sea were a tempest of bombs, bullets and torpedoes. Under the direction of observers on board ships, the Army Air Force engaged the attacking Japanese. Destroyers also blasted the swarming planes that got past the American fighters. Between the Army and the Navy almost fifty enemy planes were brought down. HENLEY came through the battle without a scratch.

FATE

On October 3, 1943 HENLEY along with two other destroyers, USS REID, DD-369, and USS SMITH, DD-378, were on anti-submarine patrol off the New Guinea coast. Despite the fact that all three ships had sonar, none of them detected the Japanese submarine *RO-108* submerged almost directly in front of them.

At 1812, Lieutenant Commander Arai Atsushi, the captain of *RO-108*, introduced himself to the captain of HENLEY, Commander Carleton Adams, by means of a well placed spread of torpedoes. The lookouts on HENLEY spotted the torpedoes and Adams gave a firm command for hard left rudder. The destroyer quickly responded to the helm and one torpedo passed in front of the bow and a second passed astern. Unfortunately a third torpedo hit dead amidships exploding in the #1 fireroom.

Jack Carson was on deck when the TNT laden fish struck. The shock was so strong that he would have gone overboard had he not grabbed onto something stationary. The ship started to list and sink almost immediately. Within four minutes the sea was even with the main deck. Carson saw a life raft float by and he simply stepped onto it, hardly getting his feet wet. Other crewman followed Adams' order to abandon ship and the sea was soon full of sailors and life rafts. Adams himself, in the best tradition of the sea, was the last man off HENLEY. A quarter of an hour after being hit, she was gone, taking fifteen men with her.

REID and SMITH went after the submarine but *RO-108* escaped. The two tin cans then returned and picked up the survivors of HENLEY; 18 officers and 255 sailors.

Hoga

WOBAN CLASS YARD TUG
YT-146
LAUNCHED: 1940

DECEMBER 7, 1941

Most tugs assigned to Pearl Harbor called the Yard Craft Dock at the Navy Yards their home. That is where HOGA was that Sunday morning. With the exception of the boat's cook, all ten of the other members of her crew were on board, including Tugmaster Chief Boatswains Mate Joseph B. McManus and Assistant Tugmaster Robert Brown. McManus was in his cabin shaving when he heard the roar of bombs exploding. Looking out his porthole he could see USS OKLAHOMA, BB-37, already hit and listing on Battleship Row.

The orders HOGA received were pretty straightforward. She was to get underway and assist wherever she could. In ten minutes she was moving out into the harbor and headed toward

HOGA fights the fires on the forecastle of NEVEDA, near Hospital Point.

Battleship Row. On the way she pulled two sailors out of the water. She made her way to the repair ship USS VESTAL, AR-4 which had been moored next to USS ARIZONA, BB-39 when the battleship blew up.

HOGA pulled VESTAL away from the fires engulfing the doomed battle-ship. With that done she reversed course and headed to 1010 dock to assist the minelayer, USS OGLALA, CM-4. OGLALA was threatening to cap-size and pin the cruiser USS HELENA, CL-50 against the dock. HOGA pulled OGLALA away so HELENA could get free.

On that Sunday morning, in the midst of chaos, there was always something else to do. Next HOGA went to help USS NEVADA, BB-36. She was the only battleship to get underway that morning, but the severe pasting she received from the Japanese prevented her from exiting the harbor.

She grounded herself in order not to block the narrow channel. HOGA assisted NEVADA in beaching herself and then along with other ships helped fight the fires on board her. HOGA actually tied herself to NEVADA's port bow to help in her firefighting efforts which took over and hour.

With other boats now assisting NEVADA, HOGA returned to battleship row where every ship was aflame. There, thick black smoke mingled with intense heat and orange flames. The waters of the harbor itself were on fire with burning oil. HOGA's firefighting abilities were much needed there. When she arrived, she fought fires on USS MARYLAND, BB-46, USS TENNESSEE, BB-43 and ARIZONA. HOGA got to ARIZONA late Sunday at around 1600 hours and stayed fighting the fires emanating from the battleship until 1300 hours on Tuesday afternoon.

For his efforts on that Sunday morning, McManus received a letter of commendation from Admiral Chester A. Nimitz, which read in part, *"For*

For almost 2 days HOGA valiantly fought the fires onboard ARIZONA

distinguished service in line of your profession as Commanding Officer of the Navy Yard Tug HOGA, and efficient action and disregard of your own personal safe-ty during the attack... When another ship was disabled and appeared to be out of control, with serious fires on the fore part of that ship, you moored your tug to her bow and assisted materially in ex-

tinguishing the fires. When it was determined that the damaged ship should be beached, as there was serious danger of her sinking in the channel, you assisted in the beaching operations in an outstanding manner. Furthermore, each member of the crew of the HOGA functioned in a most efficient manner and exhibited commendable disregard of personal danger throughout the operations."

THE WAR

For the first weeks of the war HOGA performed varied functions including recovering bodies from the harbor and clearing the waters of flotsam and jetsam. She engaged in duties revolving around the multiple salvage efforts in the harbor and of course operated in her basic function as a yard tug for the duration of the war.

FATE

HOGA continued in her vital role as a Pearl Harbor tug until 1948 when she was put on temporary loan to the city of Oakland, California which used her as a fireboat in the port. The "temporary" loan lasted for over forty-five years, until 1994 when she was returned to the Navy.

During her long career in Oakland, HOGA, which had been renamed *City of Oakland*, fought ship, warehouse and pier fires. She also served as a rescue vessel pulling accident victims out of the cold waters of San Francisco Bay. She was the host vessel to then President Jimmy Carter when he toured the port in 1980 and she greeted Queen Elizabeth II on a visit in 1984. The ship was declared a National Historic Landmark in 1989.

After her return to the U. S. Navy, HOGA was placed in reserve in the "mothball fleet", in Suisun Bay, at the extreme northeast arm of San Francisco Bay. In 2005 the Navy donated HOGA to the Arkansas Inland Maritime Museum at North Little Rock. As of 2011 HOGA was still in Suisun Bay awaiting transport to Arkansas.

USS Honolulu

BROOKLYN CLASS LIGHT CRUISER
CL-48
LAUNCHED: 1937

DECEMBER 7, 1941

Reveille is at 0600, time to rise and shine and hit the deck. There wasn't much work to do when your ship was in the Navy Yard as HONOLULU was that morning. Most of the activity onboard in that early hour centered around one of three things: eating, getting ready for church call, or sprucing up for a day on the town.

Bill Speer was a 23-year-old Yeoman 2nd Class from Kentucky. He was the Executive Officer's clerk and his living space was also his workspace. He had just finished a shower and was standing there somewhat damp in his skivvies[19] preparing for liberty. Robert Sellers, a Seaman 2nd Class, was assigned to the galley. Breakfast was just completing and he was preparing to clean up. Gunner's Mate Jiles Riggs had just finished breakfast and was lying on his bunk relaxing.

The first bombs and torpedoes hitting Ford Island and Battleship Row sent massive shock waves through the tranquil waters of the harbor and caused HONOLULU to shudder at her dock. Bill Speer was a well-trained and highly disciplined sailor. When general quarters sounded he took off like a shot for his battle station, without pausing to put his uniform on. He arrived on the Communication Bridge in his skivvies.

Sellers abandoned his cleaning chores and reported to his battle station on the shell deck of the #2 main turret. His job as a "talker" was

---

19   Navy terminology or slang for underwear, t-shirt and/or shorts.

to receive orders over headphones and communicate them to the rest of the gun crew.

Riggs sprang out of his bunk and raced topside. His battle station was one of the four .50 caliber machine guns on the bridge. When he arrived there the ready ammunition box was locked. He grabbed a screwdriver, jammed it into the hasp on the box, and yanked hard. The hasp snapped. He dove into the box and pulled out four belts with fifty rounds each and handed them out to the other gunners. In moments all the machine guns were loaded and they opened fire. With a firing rate of over 600 rounds per minute, the fifty rounds in each gun didn't last long and they were soon reduced to observers of the attack until more ammunition was available.

Also silent were the main guns on HONOLULU. The big six-inch guns were useless against the fast moving, low flying Japanese planes. In the #2 turret the entire crew was ordered to stand down and report to other duties, with the exception of the talker, Sellers, who was ordered to remain at his station. He was soon all alone with nothing to keep him company except a copy of that Sunday morning's newspaper comic page. The sounds of the attack going on outside distracted him to such an extent that he gave up looking at the paper.

A "Val" dropped a 250 pound armor-piercing bomb, but it missed the cruiser and hit the concrete pier next to it. The bomb passed completely through the pier and detonated in the water beneath the dock. The concussion punched a depression into the hull causing minor leakage and resulting electrical short circuits.

When the attack was completed Bill Speer reported back to his quarters and put his uniform on. He had spent the entire morning on the bridge in his underwear. No one had ever given Robert Sellers permission to leave his battle station in the #2 turret. He stayed there obediently waiting for instructions. By noon he decided he'd waited long enough. He hung up his headset and came out on deck and looked around. Pearl Harbor was much different from the last time he had seen it four hours before.

THE WAR

The minor hull damage to HONOLULU was quickly repaired at Pearl Harbor and the cruiser was soon conducting convoy escorts to San Francisco and Australia. In June she sailed north to Alaska for a four month stay in the Aleutians. There she shelled enemy positions on Kiska and covered the American landings on Adak. With that done, she turned her bow south and headed for overhaul at Mare Island. When that was complete she escorted a convoy to Noumea and ultimately arrived in the Solomons in November.

Shortly after her arrival she was involved in the Battle of Tassafaronga, conducted just before midnight on November 30, 1942, in the dark waters off Guadalcanal. Of the five American cruisers that engaged the enemy that night, HONOLULU was the only one to come out of it unscathed.

HONOLULU continued conducting regular patrols in The Slot looking for the Tokyo Express. On July 6, 1943, just after 0100 she found it in Kula Gulf off the island of Kolombangara. A force of ten Japanese destroyers were attempting to reinforce positions in the Northern Solomons. The two opponents maneuvered for position and didn't start firing until just before 0200. The battle raged for twenty-one minutes with the American ships firing an average of one shell every two seconds. One enemy destroyer was sunk outright. In typical fashion the Japanese fired a school of TNT laden steel fish at the Americans. One American cruiser, USS HELENA, CL-50, fell victim and was sunk. HONOLULU missed being hit by sheer luck when she made a turn and a torpedo passed down her port side.

Seven days later they met again. Just after 0100 on July 13th, west of Kolombangara, an Allied column of three cruisers (one of them from New Zealand) and ten destroyers encountered a smaller enemy force of one cruiser, five destroyers and four transports. In a rare use of radar by the Japanese, they detected the Allies first. Following their standard operation, they fired a wall of torpedoes at the Allies. The enemy cruiser *Jintsu*, turned on her powerful searchlight to illuminate the American column. This also gave the Allied ships a very good target to shoot at, which they did. *Jintsu* was smashed by at least ten shells fired by HONOLULU and the other cruisers. The enemy cruiser was taken out of the action and later sank.

The Japanese launched more torpedoes and they soon took their toll. One American destroyer was badly damaged and had to be scuttled and all three cruisers were hit.

HONOLULU took one torpedo in the bow and one in the stern. The stern torpedo turned out to be a dud. It simply punched a two foot wide hole in the hull and then dropped back into the sea. The one in the bow, however, was a different story. It struck low on the starboard side some thirty-six feet from the bow. The explosion took out supporting frames for the forward section of the ship and the bow collapsed, folding down into the ocean.

All parties withdrew to assess the damage. Although there were injuries as a result of the torpedo strike, there were no deaths. HONOLULU made it back to Tulagi for repairs.

HONOLULU in Tulagi with eighty feet of her bow folded down into the sea from a torpedo hit off Kolombangara.

The road to recovery began at Tulagi. The path next lead to Espiritu Santo and then to Pearl Harbor, where a new bow was installed. And finally to Mare Island for overhaul and refit. She left the United States for Pearl Harbor on November 17, 1943.

In late 1943 and early 1944, HONOLULU was engaged in operations around Bougainville and New Ireland north of the Solomons. She continued in her support by bombarding Saipan, Guam and the Palau Islands throughout the rest of 1944.

In October she was part of the fleet engaged in the liberation of the Philippines. She shelled Leyte and then screened the landings there on the 20th. At 1600 HONOLULU was laying off the coast waiting for call fire assignments. She barely had any speed on, just loitering in the area. A lone torpedo plane came from Leyte and headed straight for HONOLULU. Due to her lack of headway she couldn't maneuver out of the way.

All ships in the area took the plane under fire, including HONOLULU. Lady Luck smiled that day on the Japanese pilot and not on HONOLULU. The plane was able to drop its torpedo and escape. The torpedo found its way to the cruiser's port quarter. It detonated, ripping a huge hole in her side killing 65 men. To make matters worse, while attempting to shoot down the enemy plane, friendly fire struck HONOLULU and killed five more men. HONOLULU headed for home. She wouldn't return to the war.

HONOLULU pulled into Norfolk, Virginia on December 20, 1944. There she would undergo repairs for nine months. When completed, she found a new and easier life as a training ship on the East Coast. She performed this duty until the end of the war.

FATE

HONOLULU was decommissioned in Philadelphia in February 1947 and then sent to the Reserve Fleet there. She remained in reserve until late 1959 when she was sold to the Bethlehem Steel Company. The brave cruiser was scrapped at a facility at Sparrow Point, Maryland in August 1960.

USS Hulbert

CLEMSON CLASS DESTROYER / SEAPLANE TENDER
DD-342 / AVD-6
LAUNCHED: 1919

DECEMBER 7, 1941

Ensign Robert L. Eichorn was the deck officer that morning. The old destroyer had been converted to a seaplane tender and was tied up at the submarine base. When Eichorn saw the attack commence he and Carpenter's Mate 2nd Class Andrew S. Rose readied the .50-caliber anti-aircraft batteries. Moments later, Ship's Cook 3rd Class William J. Morris arrived at his battle station and manned the guns; he promptly brought down a "Kate" torpedo plane. The men of HULBERT kept up continuous fire for the next two hours, defending themselves and their fleet. At approximately 0820, the combined fire of HULBERT and one or more other ships brought down a bomber.

In the aftermath of the raid, the captain of HULBERT, Lieutenant Commander J. M. Lane, reported no damage or injuries.

THE WAR

HULBERT sailed for the Hawai'ian island of Hilo two days after the attack. There she was to establish an advanced base for patrol planes. On Christmas Day HULBERT sailed out to repair a seaplane, which had landed in mid-ocean. When the repairs were completed the plane couldn't take off due to heavy seas and HULBERT had to tow the plane. The Japanese submarine

I-1 spotted HULBERT moored in the bay at Hilo during the afternoon of December 30th. Just three weeks earlier *I-1* was one of the submarines in the Pearl Harbor attack fleet and under Commander Ankyu Eitaro, had waited to sink ships escaping from the harbor but no targets came his way. Today Eitaro surfaced his submarine after darkness fell and fired ten shells at HULBERT. The converted destroyer and some coastal batteries returned fire but missed the target. HULBERT incurred no damage and no casualties. *I-1* slipped into the night unharmed. The encounter was a bloodless draw.

HULBERT reported for duty in Alaska in June 1942. Her main function there was to service the PBY Catalinas making up VP-43, a patrol squadron. She also performed other functions as needed such as landing Marines on Seguam Island in August and rendering assistance to USS CASCO, AVP-12, after she had been torpedoed. After a short stay in San Francisco for maintenance, she returned to Alaska where she tended patrol bombers.

On December 17, 1942 HULBERT was transiting Kupreanof Strait near Kodiak Island en route to the US Naval Section Base at Sand Point. Lookouts posted on HULBERT had notified the bridge of the presence of the 60-foot civilian mail boat, *Phyllis S.*, also in the strait. Despite this knowledge, at 1433 hours HULBERT rammed the *Phyllis S.* amidships and cut her in two. The crew of HULBERT made valiant efforts to rescue the passengers and crew. Almost immediately a cable was passed and attached to the severed bow of the *Phyllis S.* in order to keep it afloat. Lieutenant Robert L. Eichorn, who had been the deck officer on December 7, 1941, and Apprentice Seaman Theodore Stouder dove into the frigid ocean, following the cable under water into the partially submerged bow. Fighting the numbing effects of the ice-cold sea, Eichorn and Stouder searched for victims or survivors, but found none. Two passengers, Mary Paakhanen and her granddaughter Helen Agik were killed in the collision. The resulting inquiry found that the Officer of the Deck, Lieutenant (j.g.) Richard B. Redmayne and the commanding officer, Lieutenant Robert B. Crowell should be court-martialed for "culpable inefficiency in the performance of their duties.[20]"

---

20 Lieutenant (j.g.) Redmayne received a reprimand for his part in the incident. A search of the National Archives reveals no record of reprimand or court-martial for Lieutenant Crowell. A graduate of Annapolis, class of 1934, Crowell retired from the Navy as a full Commander.

In June 1943 HULBERT was the victim of a strong North Pacific storm, which grounded the boat on the shores of Massacre Bay on the island of Attu. The severity of the damage necessitated a visit to Seattle, Washington for significant repairs.

At this time something unusual happened to HULBERT. Many ships start their life out as one thing and end up another. In HULBERT's case she started out life as a destroyer and was then converted and reclassified as a seaplane tender. To be reclassified again is not unusual. Many navy vessels underwent several incarnations being reclassified many times almost always being downgraded. What was unusual about HULBERT's reclassification was that she was upgraded back to a destroyer, becoming DD-342 once again.

For the rest of the war HULBERT acted as a screening vessel for aircraft carriers and a target ship for training pilots.

FATE

As HULBERT was on her way to Philadelphia, her final port of call, she was given one last mission; to escort aircraft carrier USS RANGER, CV-4 through the Panama Canal. She completed that task and sailed into the City of Brotherly Love on October 17, 1945. Decommissioning quickly followed in November. She was sold to Ship Shape, Incorporated of Philadelphia for scrapping in October 1946 for $13,338.00.

USS Hull

FARRAGUT CLASS DESTROYER
DD-350
LAUNCHED: 1934

DECEMBER 7, 1941

It was not unusual in the Navy of the 1940s to have brothers serving side by side on the same ship. For example, there were 37 sets of brothers on USS ARIZONA, BB-39. HULL had its own set of brothers, the Goens boys, Robert and David.[21] Robert was a cook and that morning was in the galley serving a breakfast of bacon and eggs to his crewmates. When the raid began, Robert and David reported to and manned a .50 caliber machine gun and together took on the enemy side by side.

The Goens brothers, however, were not the first to fire on the Japanese planes from HULL. The sailor standing the gangway watch spotted the aircraft as the attack began. As two of the planes flew past the destroyer's bow, at a distance of only 50 yards, he drew his .45 caliber pistol and fired at them. No official records mark weather he hit them or not. By 0812 all main batteries and machine guns onboard HULL were firing including three Browning Automatic Rifles.

HULL was nested alongside other destroyers being overhauled by the tender DOBBIN, AD-3. As was standard, DOBBIN was supplying all power to the destroyers but at the outset of the attack she cut power. HULL and the other ships had to pass ammunition, load and aim their main five-

---

21   After the deaths of the five Sullivan brothers in the sinking of USS JUNEAU, CL-52, in November 1942, the Navy endeavored to prevent siblings from serving together.

inch guns by hand. Despite this hindrance, the men on HULL managed to fire 200 five-inch rounds at the attacking planes. HULL claimed to have seriously damaged or shot down at least four enemy planes while suffering no damage or casualties herself.

In his after action report, Lieutenant Commander Richard Stout, captain of HULL, pointed out that *"Any vessel or any nest of vessels that could maintain a volume of fire suffered little or no damage. Time and again attacks…directed at this nest of ships…were successfully driven off."*[22] His was not the only report that described attacking Japanese planes veering off or totally avoiding any ship or nest of ships that put up even a moderate defense.

THE WAR

The first major action in the war for HULL was the invasion of Guadalcanal on August 7, 1942. The following day she helped repulse aerial counterattacks by the Japanese, splashing three enemy planes in the process.

In the first months of 1943 she went in for overhaul at Mare Island Navy Yard near San Francisco. There, 20-year-old Pat Douhan a native Californian, fresh out of boot camp and eight weeks of sonar school in San Diego joined her. After provisioning she sailed for the Aleutians in April. Shortly after arriving, HULL was assigned anti-submarine screening to USS NEVADA, BB-36, one of her Pearl Harbor sisters. As they prepared for the invasion of Attu, NEVADA had a man overboard. HULL, trailing behind the battleship, attempted to pluck the bluejacket from the icy waters, but the sailor missed the lifeline thrown to him. By the time the destroyer came round for a second attempt the frigid waters had done their worst and the only thing recovered from the sea was a frozen body. HULL remained in Alaskan waters only a short time. She stayed just long enough to supply shore bombardment prior to the landings on Kiska. She then sailed for Pearl Harbor.

After a short stay at Pearl she participated in raids on Japanese-held Wake Island. In November 1943, she was part of a battle group that included the escort carrier USS LISCOME BAY, CVE-56. On the 24th,

---

22 From after action report dated December 9, 1941.

while operating near Makin Island in the Gilberts, LISCOME BAY was torpedoed by the Japanese submarine *I-175*. The carrier exploded in a brilliant pyrotechnic exhibition and sank, taking 644 of her crew down with her. Among those lost was Doris Miller, the black cook who received the Navy Cross for his bravery on board the battleship USS WEST VIGINIA, BB-48, at Pearl Harbor on December 7, 1941. HULL picked up some of the 272 survivors of the disaster.

To deny the enemy the benefit of cover prior to an invasion HULL would lay off an island and bombard it. The destroyer would pull in to less than a thousand yards from the beach, open fire with her five-inch guns and then run parallel to the island, shelling, until not a tree was left standing. For the next year HULL plied the waters of the Pacific shelling islands and providing protection for the fleet at places like Kwajalein, Eniwetok, Majuro, Saipan and Guam. In August 1944 she returned to the United States for overhaul. Three months later, in November she once again set sail for the West Pacific to participate in the liberation of the Philippines.

FATE

December 18, 1944 HULL was part of Task Force 38 operating off the Philippine island of Luzon. Notice had been received that a typhoon was coming. The previous day the seas had become noticeably rough, halting all operations. Task Force 38 soon found itself in the center of the storm, designated Typhoon Cobra.

What occurred on the bridge of HULL during the morning of December 18th is the stuff that books and movies are made of. The captain, Lieutenant Commander James A. Marks, had significant differences with his officers and crew as to how the ship should be handled in the tempest. Marks gave few, if any, orders and those that he did give, seemed to put the ship in even more peril. The ship was doing so badly under the command of Marks that several of the crew even spoke to the Executive Officer about relieving the captain in order to save the ship. Pat Douhan, the young sonarman, was on the bridge most of the night. The sight of the captain cowering in a corner of the bridge did not inspire any confidence in him. Even though things looked grim, Douhan thought they'd make it through.

Throughout the morning the unstable ship continuously rolled heavily. She inclined up to sixty and seventy degrees. Her bow would plow headlong into waves as much as eighty feet tall and her stern would lift totally out of the water exposing screws and a rudder trying to grip into nothing but thin air. Around 0800 Douhan was relieved from his watch. The design of the FARRAGUT class destroyers was such that there was no way to get from the forward part of the ship to the aft with out going out on deck. Douhan headed for the aft deckhouse and would have been washed overboard had he not grabbed onto the torpedo tubes amidships.

At about 1000 a lookout on the bridge wing was washed overboard. A short while later a Chief Boatswain's Mate recommended to Marks that the ship's whaleboat be cut away, lest it break loose and cause damage or even death. Marks forcefully denied the request. In fulfillment of the Chief's prophecy, the boat eventually did break free from its davits and careened wildly down the deck striking at least a dozen sailors killing some of them outright and knocking others overboard.

Just around noon, Marks gave what many on the bridge believed to be an ill-advised order to turn the ship in a way that brought HULL into the trough of a wave. From that moment on HULL was doomed. The ship rolled so heavily to starboard that seawater poured directly down her stack. There was soon hip-deep water in the engineering spaces. Every time she rolled, more water stowed away on board to the tune of almost one ton per cubic yard. Finally the sea rolled her. The dial of the ship's inclinometer stopped at seventy-two degrees because that was the angle at which, theoretically, the ship could not recover. When the hand on the meter hit that mark the ship continued to roll until she lay on her side at ninety degrees. After that the over 100 miles per hour wind kept her down.

Seeing the end was at hand, many crewmen who had not already been washed into the angry green sea, jumped in. The conditions were such that the waves pounded against the ship like a hammer against an anvil. Many of those in the water were caught in between and were literally beaten to death against the hull of their ship.

Those men on the bridge made it out onto the port wing and later recalled that they suddenly found themselves adrift in the water when the ship just dropped from beneath them into the depths.

The water held many dangers. Debris and men littered the ocean and the waves slammed them all into each other. The ocean threw them into the air and then drove them down beneath the surface. It tried to crush them and drown them all at the same time. It was the ultimate sailor's nightmare; floating like a cork, alone in the center of a raging typhoon, relying only on a kapok lifejacket and the capricious will of the gods for salvation. Most of the men could do nothing but wait to die or be saved.

Sonarman Pat Douhan, like most of his shipmates, drifted alone for hours, learning how to survive the torrents that buffeted them. They learned the rhythm of the insane waves that drove them to depths that made their eardrums feel like they would burst. First came the swell, then the wave, then take a deep breath, then the tons of ocean that pushed them deep, then the uplift of the lifejacket that brought them back to the surface, then a few seconds respite before the cycle began anew: swell, wave, breath, water, uplift; swell, wave, breath, water, uplift. For the crew of HULL this is how many of them spent the first twelve hours alone in the ocean.

The next morning broke with hope. The sun appeared and the seas were becoming calmer every minute. Sailors who were alone drifted by others and became pairs. Pairs drifted into other pairs and became clusters of six or eight which found other clusters which became groups of fifteen or twenty. But hope soon turned to despair as searching ships and planes were spotted but none stopped to rescue. Then the marauders came. Not the Japanese - the sharks. The eating machines plowed into the groups tearing men in half. Sailors swam for their lives, splitting up in a panic and finding themselves alone again. After two days, some men went insane from drinking salt water, some just died from exhaustion, others gave up hope and waited for the sea to take them. Hope was ultimately rewarded and five different vessels eventually pulled sixty-two HULL crewmen from the waters of the Pacific, including Pat Douhan and the captain, James Marks.

Pat Douhan, along with other survivors, was delivered to a Pearl Harbor sister, the hospital ship USS SOLACE, AH-5. Douhan arrived on Christmas Eve and was soothed by the sound of the nurses singing Christmas carols. There he was treated for exhaustion and exposure.

A court of inquiry was formed by order of Admiral Chester Nimitz to investigate the loss of HULL and two other destroyers in the typhoon. The court convened on December 26, 1944 on board the destroyer tender, USS CASCADE, AD-16, at Ulithi Atoll. The court ultimately exonerated Marks, stating that he may not have been experienced enough to have competently handled his ship in such extreme conditions and therefore could not be blamed for her loss or the deaths of the 202 officers and men that went down with her. No surviving officer or crewman who testified to the court said anything negative about the captain or his conduct. However, unofficially, officers and crew who were on the bridge during the storm blamed Marks' inept seamanship for, at the very least, contributing to the loss of HULL and their shipmates. Other contributing factors were not enough fuel or water ballast on board, the ship's original low-slung deck design and the addition of equipment onto her superstructure making her top heavy.

USS Jarvis

BAGLEY CLASS DESTROYER
DD-393
LAUNCHED: 1937

DECEMBER 7, 1941

When the Navy isn't at war it's training for war, and training was the order of the day for the Pacific Fleet at Hawai'i. JARVIS had returned on Thursday, December 4th, from training exercises off Mau'i. She berthed at the Navy yard and was undergoing routine maintenance.

The after action reports written by the senior officer on board, Lieutenant J.C. Ford, and three Ensigns, W.F. Greene, R.V. Fleege and J.A. Chiles all attest to the cool, calm and well-trained actions of the crew on the first day of war. A soon as general quarters was sounded, all officers and men reported to their battle stations. Within ten minutes all guns on JARVIS were firing. Many of the crew sprang to their jobs without orders and others saw jobs that needed to be done and did them also without orders. Lieutenant Ford later reported, *"My job of coordinating the ship's effort was made easy by all hands."* [23]

The machine gunners fired on all enemy planes they saw, whether they were in range or not. Lieutenant Ford saw this but allowed his men to shoot at the out-of-range planes anyway, feeling that it boosted the crew's morale. Fire from JARVIS was continual throughout the raid and the destroyer claimed four enemy planes downed and others damaged. Some sailors suffered minor ear damage because they never had time to put in hearing

---

23 After action report dated, December 12, 1944 by Lt. J.C Ford.

protection. During the battle, Seaman 1st Class Lelon Lantrip was hit in the thigh by a bullet fragment, but he, *"bound up the wound and remained at his station passing ammunition to the guns aft."* [24]

The men of JARVIS were not any braver than any other crew in the harbor that day, but their actions were inspiring enough that all four officers mentioned it in some way in their reports;

"There was no sign of cowardice or fear, and the natural nervousness of the part of some individuals disappeared as soon as fire was opened." Lieutenant J. C. Ford

"The conduct of the crew in their first shooting engagement was exemplary. It is difficult to single out any one man…No man flinched or hesitated at any time in the performance of his duties…The ship can fight." [25] Ensign W. F. Greene

"My highest respect goes to the enlisted men who even though destruction seemed imminent performed with no more excitement than is noted at a regular scheduled practice. Every man on board did his best…" [26] Ensign Ralph V. Fleege

"All of our men carried out their duties with utmost dispatch and vigor and showed great initiative in performing their duties…I am extremely proud and consider it an honor and privilege to be a member of such a ships (sic) company as we had aboard this ship Sunday." [27] Ensign J. A. Chiles

The captain of JARVIS, Commander James Topper, gave the final word as to the quality of his crew in his report, *"From my personal investigation after coming on board I found all action taken was timely and correct. Plans were being expeditiously carried out to get ship underway. Firing had ceased but all guns were manned ready for action. Morale was at highest pitch. Action taken appeared to be well thought out and deliberate. The action(s) of all on board were commendable."* [28]

There is undoubtedly a biased pride exhibited by these officers for their crew, but men in battle take cues from each other. It only takes one

---

24   After action report dated, December 12, 1944 by Ens. W.F. Greene.
25   After action report dated, December 12, 1944 by Ens. W.F. Greene.
26   After action report dated, December 12, 1944 by Ens. Ralph V. Fleege.
27   After action report dated, December 12, 1944 by Ens. J. A. Chiles.
28   After action report dated, December 12, 1944 by Commander James Topper

man on a battlefield to turn and run to start a rout. By the same token, one man binding his wounded leg and staying at his post can set an example and inspire others to do the same. Both cowardice and courage are contagious.

At 1018, just a little more than thirty minutes after the end of the attack, JARVIS stood out of the harbor toward the open sea to begin her war career.

THE WAR

Late January 1942, JARVIS was part of a Task Force 11 en route to make a strike on Wake Island. On the morning of the 23rd, the oiler USS NECHES, AO-5, sank when the Japanese submarine *I-72* put two torpedoes into her. Fifty-seven crew went down with the tanker, but JARVIS pulled 182 survivors out of the ocean.

Through the middle of 1942 JARVIS escorted convoys to San Francisco, Fiji and Noumea. She settled in protecting convoys in and around Australia and New Zealand. In August she was sent to Guadalcanal.

On the 7th she provided fire support and screened the initial landings. The following day the Japanese sent planes to dislodge the nascent invasion. About forty planes attacked the ships supporting the Marines on shore. The anti-aircraft fire was brutal, stopping many of the planes, but some got through. One plane launched its torpedo toward JARVIS and blasted a fifty-foot gash into her starboard side, killing fourteen and wounding another seven. The destroyer went dead in the water. She was critically, but not mortally, wounded. The destroyer was towed to nearby Tulagi in order to be examined.

It was determined that she could sail under her own power back to Australia where she could be repaired by her Pearl Harbor sister, the destroyer tender USS DOBBIN, AD-3. Preparations were made for JARVIS to set sail. As often happens in war, communications seem to break down just when they are the most critical. The destroyer's radio was not working, which may be the reason she didn't wait for an escort. At any rate, the captain, Lieutenant Commander William Graham headed out just past midnight on the 9th.

He headed south across Sealark Sound, (soon to be known as Ironbottom Sound), toward Savo Island. Commander Graham had no way of knowing he was going to sail his ship smack through the middle of a vicious surface action, the Battle of Savo Island.

Around 0130, eight Japanese ships engaged in a running gun and torpedo battle with twenty-three American ships. JARVIS was like a blind man wandering through a barroom brawl. Whether or not the destroyer was totally oblivious to what was going on around her is unknown because her radios were still out. She was deaf and dumb, she couldn't send and she couldn't receive. Both American and Japanese vessels spotted an unidentified ship wandering through the battle. The Japanese heavy cruiser *Furutaka* sailed as close as 1,200 yards from JARVIS and launched a pattern of torpedoes at her, all of them missing. The American heavy cruiser, USS CHICAGO, CA-29, may have fired on JARVIS also.

There were two more sightings of JARVIS by American forces on the 9th. At about 0300 the destroyer USS BLUE, DD-387, a Pearl Harbor sister, saw her. Once BLUE identified JARVIS as an American ship BLUE turned around and headed back toward Savo Island. Shortly after sunrise an American plane from the carrier SARATOGA, CV-3, spotted JARVIS southeast of Guadalcanal. She was down by the head, crawling along at eight knots and leaving a very noticeable oil slick in the water.

Only the crew of JARVIS knew what was happening on board the destroyer. Whether her wounds from the day before had gotten worse or if she had been hit again during the night was unknown. There had been absolutely no communication from her since she left Tulagi.

FATE

The Japanese believed that a light cruiser that had been heavily damaged in the previous nights action was wandering around wounded. They sent thirty-one planes out to find her and finish her off. They succeeded. Their only mistake was that it wasn't a cruiser - it was JARVIS.

Before she left Tulagi, anything and everything above deck that wasn't needed to get to Australia was dumped, that included boats and life rafts. At around 1300 the enemy planes arrived. Crawling at eight knots and down by the head JARVIS was no match at all for thirty-one swarming planes. The attack broke the gallant lady in half and she sank taking her entire crew of 247 men with her.

Although JARVIS was only an innocent bystander in the Battle of Savo Island, she became the last victim.

USS Keosanqua

ALLEGHENY CLASS FLEET TUG
AT-38
LAUNCHED: 1920

DECEMBER 7, 1941

KEOSANQUA sailed lazily out of the Pearl Harbor channel that Sunday morning on an extremely routine mission. She was to meet USS ANTARES, AG-10, which was arriving from Palmyra Island south of Hawai'i, with a 500 ton steel barge in tow. KEOSANQUA was to relieve ANTARES and take over the tow.

At 0715, KEOSANQUA met ANTARES and came alongside the barge. The switchover was in progress when, at 0755, explosions were heard coming from the harbor. Five minutes later Japanese planes strafed the two ships. With unbelievable coolness, both crews continued their duties on the exposed deck while under fire. At 0805 KEOSANQUA had loaded her machine guns and opened fire on the attacking planes. It took another half hour before the tow exchange was completed and KEOSANQUA took control of the barge. Both ships then headed for Honolulu Harbor, as all traffic into Pearl Harbor had been stopped.

THE WAR

A sailor onboard KESANQUA, Warren Verhoff, later recalled that for several days after the attack, as the ship worked in the harbor, horribly maimed bodies were recovered from the water as they floated to the surface.

For two years KEOSANQUA operated in Pearl Harbor aiding in salvage operations and in her basic duties as a tug. In December 1943 she sailed west for the war. After several stops she finally settled in at Eniwetok in April 1944 where she remained until the end of the war.

FATE

KEOSANQUA stayed at Eniwetok until late November 1945 when she sailed to San Francisco. She continued in her duties as a tug on the west coast until she went to Seattle where she was decommissioned in May 1946. She was sold in 1948 to Pacific Coyle Navigation, Vancouver, British Columbia and renamed *Edward J. Coyle*. She was renamed once again as *Commodore Strait* in 1960 and worked under that name until 1968 when she was scrapped.

USS MacDonough

FARRAGUT CLASS DESTROYER
DD-351
LAUNCHED: 1934

DECEMBER 7, 1941

Frank Kluska's life in the Navy was pretty good. He had enlisted in his native Pennsylvania two years earlier in 1939 and had only eleven months left in his tour of duty. As the man in charge of the ship's laundry he earned, over and above his base pay of $54.00 per month, an extra dollar a month for every one of his shipmates that sent their laundry to him. So, he was making as much if not more than a petty officer. On top of this, his access to the beauty and joys of shore leave were for the most part, his for the asking. All he need do, which he did often, is tell the Officer of the Deck that he needed to go ashore for "laundry supplies" and permission was granted. Yes, life in Pearl Harbor was good.

This Sunday morning he had just finished breakfast and was on the quarterdeck drinking coffee and talking with a Chief Gunner's Mate when he saw four planes drop low out of the sky and release torpedoes into the harbor. His immediate thought was how unusual it was to hold torpedo practice in the harbor. But then the torpedoes exploded against the hull of the converted battleship USS UTAH, AG-16, sending geysers of water two hundred feet into the air. Then the red "meatballs" on the underside of the wings became apparent and Kluska knew war had started.

He immediately ran to sound general quarters. With that complete he normally would have reported to his battle station, which was as captain of one of the five-inch guns. But since the five-inch gun was being overhauled and therefore inoperable, he instead headed for one of the .50-caliber machine guns just under the bridge wing. When the ready ammunition at the gun was expended Kluska had to run below decks to hand load more belts and then run them back up to the gun and start again.

There was the only one officer on board MACDONOUGH that Sunday morning, Ensign R. W. Clark, and he was in command. MACDONOUGH was alongside the destroyer tender USS DOBBIN, AD-3, with four other ships of Destroyer Division One and she was cold. Nothing was running or supplying power internally on MACDONOGH; DOBBIN was supplying all power and electricity to the destroyer. Clark coolly and systematically brought his ship back to life. He also insured she was defended, organizing human chains to pass ordinance hand-to-hand from the magazines to the guns. Because there was no power, all the guns - including the big five-inch batteries - had to be loaded, moved and aimed by hand. Clark oversaw all of this from the bridge and like a captain on a 19th century wooden frigate, he used a megaphone to shout his orders over the shot and shell of battle.

At the end of the day Clark stated that he believed MACDONOUGH might have shot down two enemy planes. He also stated in his after-action report, *"I have the greatest pride and admiration for every member of the crew. All hands were calm, and determined...."*[29]

The captain of MACDONOUGH, Lieutenant Commander John M. McIsaac, arrived on board just as the attack was ending. By that time Ensign Clark had the ship ready for action and McIsaac took her down the channel and joined the cruiser USS DETROIT, CL-8, outside the harbor. She stayed out on patrol for the next three days.

THE WAR

Upon her return to Pearl, ships still smoldering on Battleship Row greeted MACDONOUGH. As they passed the devastated USS ARIZONA, BB-39, the crew manned the rails and rendered a hand salute. The destroyer docked, resupplied and four hours later sailed back out. Before she sailed,

---

29   From the after action report of Ensign R.W. Clark dated December 12, 1941.

however, all hands were ordered to write home. They were instructed to give no information other than that they were healthy and uninjured.

The first months of the war for MACDONOUGH were spent patrolling around the Hawai'ian Islands and escorting convoys to the west coast of the United States. Mid 1942 found her in that large group of vessels heading for Guadalcanal where she provided support for the invasion on August 7th.

Several weeks later on the 31st she was screening the carrier USS SARATOGA, CV-3. At 0746, two events occurred simultaneously on MACDONOUGH. First, there was a sonar contact indicating a submerged object dead ahead. Second, lookouts spotted a periscope less than 100 feet from the bow.

The next sixty seconds were very busy for both the Americans and the Japanese. MACDONOUGH raised signal flags announcing an enemy submarine had been sighted. Just as those flags were raised, the submarine, *I-26*, launched a spread of six torpedoes against SARATOGA. The captain of MACDONOUGH, Lieutenant Commander Earle V. Dennett, radioed notification of the torpedoes headed for the carrier. Captain DeWitt C. Ramsey of SARATOGA ordered up evasive maneuvers. MACDONOUGH released two depth charges that dropped harmlessly into the water because, in the rush, no depth settings were dialed in on them. Following the splashes of the depth charges the screeching sound of metal against metal reverberated throughout the ship as MACDONOUGH's hull sideswiped the submerged enemy submarine.

MACDONOUGH, along with two other destroyers, mounted an attack against *I-26*, but the sub slipped away unharmed. The SARATOGA was hit by one torpedo suffering minor damage and no fatalities.

After a short period of overhaul at Mare Island, MACDONOUGH sailed north for the Aleutian Islands in April 1943. One month later in May, her stay was over. While there, she collided with one of her Pearl Harbor sisters, the minelayer USS SICARD, DM-21. This necessitated a return to Mare Island for repairs where she stayed until September.

Between repairs, trial runs, and practice maneuvers MACDONOUGH didn't get back into the war until February 1944. On the 16th the

Japanese submarine *RO-40* was spotted on sonar near Kwajalein when she approached a convoy that was being screened by MACDONOUGH. Now being captained by Commander John W. Ramey, MACDONOUGH and two other destroyers executed an attack and dropped depth charges on the contact. The quick and decisive action by the three destroyers brought an end to *RO-40*. A week later she participated in the bombardment of Perry Island, at Eniwetok Atoll.

Two months later, at the end of April, MACDONOUGH was operating with a task force engaged in an offensive against the Japanese base on Truk. Early in the morning of the 30th, MACDONOUGH made a radar contact at 12,000 yards. Commander Ramey then plotted an intercept course. When the distance to the target closed to within 1,800 yards it suddenly disappeared from the radar screen but it almost immediately appeared on sonar, clearly indicating that the target was an enemy submarine. Ramey advanced his ship over the target and dropped a pattern of depth charges. Another attack followed by the destroyer USS STEPHEN POTTER, DD-538, which also dropped depth charges. MACDONOUGH then completed the "hat trick" with a third depth charge attack. Debris and oil soon bubbled to the surface. The Imperial Japanese Navy had lost a second submarine, *RO-45*, to the skill of MACDONOUGH and her crew.

The duration of the war for MADONOUGH was a hodgepodge of destroyer duties. She escorted and screened against submarines, shelled islands and patrolled. She sailed to the Philippines, Okinawa and Guam, having no further major engagements with the enemy.

FATE

Despite being only twelve years old, MACDONOUGH was very rapidly consigned to the scrap heap. The eight FARRAGUT class destroyers were deemed to be too unstable in rough weather. Two of them, USS HULL, DD-350 and USS MONAGHAN, DD-354, capsized and sank in the great storm of December 1944, Typhoon Cobra, and a third ship USS AYLWIN, DD-355, almost sank in that same storm and came close to sinking again in another storm.

MACDONOUGH was sent to New York harbor where she was decommissioned in October 1945, barely seven weeks after the surrender was signed in Tokyo Bay. She was sold just over a year later in December 1946 to a scrap dealer in Brooklyn, New York, George H. Nutman. At the time, the value of the steel in a FARRAGUT class destroyer was deemed to be $4,000.00.

Manuwai

HARBOR FERRYBOAT
YFB-16
LAUNCHED: 1927

DECEMBER 7, 1941

MANAWAI was owned and operated by the United States Navy, but she was never a commissioned naval vessel. She was what is known as being "in service." At the time of the attack she was moored at the ferry landing in Southeast Loch. She had no weapons and there is no account of her actions, if any, during the attack. A logical presumption can be made that after the attack she resumed her duties as a ferry or perhaps was pressed into service in some other capacity.

THE WAR

Ferry service between Naval Air Station Ford Island and the Pearl Harbor Naval Base was provided by MANUWAI for the entire war. The distance from the Pearl Harbor ferry landing to the Ford Island landing was just over one mile, for a round trip distance of two miles. While battleships and aircraft carriers and cruisers were sailing tens of thousands of miles around the world bringing the battle to the enemy, MANUWAI also traveled tens of thousands of miles; the only difference being that MANUWAI did all hers in one mile increments and never left Pearl Harbor. She was also occasionally pressed into service as a tugboat. MANUWAI is the ship that reminds us that every vessel served a purpose during the war. Wherever there was a job to be done, some ship and some crew did it whether they sailed from Pearl Harbor to Tokyo Bay or from boredom to tedium and back again.

FATE

MANUWAI continued her duties as a ferry until the last day of February 1949 when she was placed out of service. She was kept in the Pacific Reserve Fleet, Pearl Harbor Group until she was struck from the register of naval ships on September 17, 1954.

Marin

NET TENDER
YN-53
LAUNCHED: 1941

DECEMBER 7, 1941

As with all the net tenders, MARIN was at the Station Base adjacent to the anti-submarine nets at the mouth of the Pearl Harbor channel when the attack began. There are no records that indicate that she suffered any damage or causalities as a result of the attack and nothing to indicate that she inflicted any damage or causalities on the enemy.

THE WAR

MARIN was a member of that small cadre of boats that spent the duration of the war doing the day-to-day drudgework that makes a navy and a harbor run. She remained at her post in Pearl Harbor tending the nets at the mouth of the channel for the duration of the war. The work she did was not flashy or newsworthy but it was essential.

FATE

With her war service complete, MARIN sailed to San Diego where she was struck from the Navy rolls in July 1946. She was sent to the Maritime Commission for final disposition in March 1947.

USS Maryland

COLORADO CLASS BATTLESHIP
BB-46
LAUNCHED: 1920

DECEMBER 7, 1941

On this Sunday morning the battleship MARYLAND led a charmed life. Of all the dreadnaughts on Battleship Row she suffered the least damage. She also sailed away with the fewest deaths - one officer and two enlisted men - and only thirteen wounded.

Pearl Harbor, Territory of Hawai'i, was a long way from Missouri, particularly in 1941. Seaman 1st Class Leslie V. Short was going to bridge that gap this lazy Sunday morning by writing some letters and Christmas cards home. He pulled his six-foot, two-inch frame into a tranquil spot on the superstructure near a machine gun and let the cool breezes wash over him as he began writing.

Earl Havlin Selover at 24-years of age was already an old salt having been in the Navy for seven years. He had advanced rapidly in that time. When he joined the Navy he was already a qualified ham radio operator. It didn't take the Navy long to get him to radio school and in seven years, not only was he a Chief Petty Officer, but he was also the Chief Radioman on MARYLAND. He was a newlywed, too. He and his wife of six months, Ella Mae, had a nice apartment near Waikiki Beach. Selover was home for the weekend and all set to enjoy Sunday with his bride.

Down in the galley eating breakfast was Signalman 1st Class Fletcher A. Manning. The only thing on his mind was finding a place to sleep once he finished breakfast. He'd been up all night, but he hadn't been standing a watch. He had been engaged in an age-old Naval tradition, an all-night poker game, in his office space on the Signal Bridge. The game had just broken up at 0700.

One of the youngest "men" on board MARYLAND that morning, in fact one of the youngest "men" in uniform at Pearl Harbor that day, was 16-year-old Raymond Crane[30]. He was in the engineering spaces awaiting his relief, which was to come at 0800. He was anxious to get over to the battleship USS OKLAHOMA, BB-37, berthed outboard of MARYLAND. The chaplain onboard MARYLAND was Protestant and being Catholic, Crane wanted to attend the mass said by the Catholic chaplain on OKLAHOMA.

Just about 0755 an officer came down a ladder and told Crane that there were Japanese planes outside. Crane went over to a porthole, and, looking outside, did indeed see Japanese planes bombing the Naval Air Station on Ford Island. He immediately reported to his battle station in the engine room.

Up in the superstructure the roar of explosions disturbed Leslie Short as he wrote his letters. He easily spotted the red "Rising Sun" against the light gray fuselage of the "Val" dive-bombers attacking Ford Island. The cards and letters were forgotten. Without hesitation or instruction he broke out ammunition from the ready boxes and loaded the .50 caliber machine gun next to him.

In a report submitted by the skipper of MARYLAND, Captain Donald C. Godwin, Short related what happened next in his own words. *"I...opened fire on two torpedo planes coming in from the east which had just dropped two torpedoes. Flames and smoke burst from the first plane I aimed at, and it veered off to the left falling toward the hospital. I think I also hit the second plane which I aimed at immediately after shooting at the first one but by then I was so busy that I cannot say for sure."*[31]

---

30 With a lie and a forged birth certificate, both sworn to by his older brother, Crane joined the Navy when he was 15.

31 Report on meritorious action by Captain Donald C. Godwin, dated December 11, 1941.

At Waikiki, the sound of neighbors banging on his front door rudely awakened Earl Selover from his tropical slumber. They told him of the attack and he told them to go back to their party. It took some convincing but Selover turned on his radio and heard the news. He quickly put on his uniform, kissed Ella Mae good-bye, and headed for Pearl Harbor.

Seaman Manning had finished breakfast and returned to the Signal Bridge. He was just hunting for a quiet place to lie down and sleep when the attack began. The first thing he did was to quickly pick up the cards and clean up any other evidence of the previous night's poker game. Only then did he begin receiving and sending signals from his battle station.

Manning's battle station was high in the superstructure where the attack unfolded before him. He could see everything. Young Raymond Crane's battle station was deep inside MARYLAND, many decks below one of the main fourteen-inch turrets. He could see nothing. In the engine room, his job, along with another sailor with him, was to monitor bearings on the massive propeller shaft and ensure that they didn't overheat when the ship was underway. Once locked into their watertight compartment all they had to do was monitor the bearings, wait to be relieved and listen to the battle going on outside.

Like a big sister, OKLAHOMA protected MARYLAND, not by any overt act, but simply by being there. With OKLAHOMA on her port side and Ford Island on her starboard, MARYLAND was immune from the aerial torpedoes that devastated OKLAHOMA. The only danger for her was from above.

Fuchida Mitsuo was high above Pearl Harbor in his "Kate" bomber. Only minutes earlier, as the commander of the attack, he had ordered the now famous code, "Tora, Tora, Tora," to be sent back to the Japanese fleet, indicating that they had achieved total surprise. Now he was on his bombing run, heading for Battleship Row. As he made his approach his plane shuddered as it was struck by anti-aircraft fire, but he pressed on. In his sight he spotted two battleships berthed side by side. He put the inboard ship in his crosshairs and dropped his two bombs. Through a peephole in the bottom of the plane he followed their long downward journey and saw them strike MARYLAND.[32]

The two hits that MARYLAND took were painful to be sure, but in the grand scheme of things they were relatively insignificant. No damage was done that hindered her ability to fight or her seaworthiness.

Manning, in his position on the Signal Bridge, saw the Admiral's flag run down the yard arm on the battleship CALIFORNIA, BB-44, berthed forward of MARYLAND. He believed this was done to prevent the enemy from specifically targeting flagships. He realized that MARYLAND also flew an Admiral's flag, that of Admiral Walter S. Anderson, Commander of Battleship Division Four. Manning climbed the cage mast himself to bring it down hoping to save his ship from further damage. Only later, after monitoring signal traffic at his post did he realize that the flag was removed from CALIFORNIA because that Admiral had removed his command from CALIFORNIA as a result of the severe damage on that ship. Manning then ran Admiral Anderson's flag back up the mast, hoping that no one had noticed that a lowly Signalman 1st Class had removed the Admiral's flag on his own initiative and without proper authority. He never heard anything about his decision.

MARYLAND was also spared further damage by two of her other sisters, the battleships WEST VIRGINIA, BB-48, and ARIZONA, BB-39. They had both suffered catastrophic damage and were producing copious amounts of thick, black smoke. The prevailing wind blew that smoke over her and significantly obscured MARYLAND from further bombing attacks.

Throughout the attack, Manning and the other sailors on the Signal Bridge coordinated the messages and orders MARYLAND received from the Pearl Harbor control tower, other ships, and other commands. These messages included damage and casualty reports and, in an amazing demonstration of "life goes on" even in the middle of a war, they received transfer orders for an officer on board.

When Earl Selover finally arrived at Pearl Harbor, the second wave was still bombing and strafing. He hitched a ride on a boat that was bringing

---

32 Fuchida knew MARYLAND well; in 1924, as a midshipman, he toured the battleship in San Francisco.

men out to their ships. As they crossed the harbor so many bullets were hitting the water that the mini-geysers that erupted made it look like a rainstorm. He saw the upturned hull of OKLAHOMA and first thought it was MARYLAND until a gust of wind cleared the black smoke and he saw his ship still afloat. The boat brought him to CALIFORNIA. Selover then had to cross her to Ford Island, walk down to where MARYLAND was berthed and then do a balancing act across a pipeline to get aboard. He reported to his radio shack just as the raid was ending.

Captain Godwin reported that he believed that his ship's gunners had brought down seven enemy planes, of which four could definitely be confirmed. For 16-year-old Raymond Crane and his shipmate the muffled sounds of the raging storm outside of MARYLAND died down and they waited for the ship to get underway, for new orders, or to be relieved.

With the very long night and day over, Fletcher Manning was ready to collapse. He got no sleep the night before because of the poker game. The Japanese never let him have his nap. And now, after the sun had set and the adrenaline had run its course, all he wanted to do was sleep. A glance to port gave him pause. There, an arm's length away was the overturned hull of OKLAHOMA. Already rescue parties were working to free those men trapped inside her when she capsized. Manning did not want that to happen to him if the Japanese returned during the night. Instead of returning to his quarters below decks he found a quiet corner in a compartment in the superstructure. There he lay down on the hard deck and slept like a baby.

THE WAR

MARYLAND, with her minimal damage and casualties, was able to go on the next morning in a somewhat normal routine. At 0800, twenty-four hours after the attack began, morning colors occurred on the fantail just like any other day. The national ensign went up the flagpole as the MARYLAND band played the Star-Spangled Banner. Today however, with WEST VIRGINIA and ARIZONA still burning only yards away, and with unprecedented death and destruction surrounding them, the song and the flag took on new meaning to all those who witnessed the ceremony. As if to add emphasis to the resolve now felt, when the national anthem ended the band immediately broke into another song – Anchors Away. Cheers erupted from all corners of the harbor.

Deep inside the engineering section of MARYLAND, an officer heading a work detail heard a metallic banging on a hatch in the deck beneath him. He bent down and opened the hatch. To his surprise he found, looking up at him, the face of Raymond Crane. He asked Crane and the sailor with him how long they had been down there. Crane responded that they had been locked in since the bombing had begun that morning. The officer replied that the bombing had begun and ended yesterday morning and that they had been in there for over a day.

Not much work was required to get MARYLAND ready for sea. Thirteen days after the attack, on Saturday the 20th, just before 1600, MARYLAND set out for the Puget Sound Navy Yard in Washington. She arrived there on December 30th and stayed for two months. As little repair work was needed, most of that time was spent upgrading and modernizing the twenty-one year old battlewagon.

The first year of the war was spent training and escorting convoys. It wasn't until late 1943, the end of the second year of the war, that MARYLAND finally got into action. In November she was sent to Tarawa Atoll. There she fell into the routine that all American battleships did of supporting invasions with their massive and very accurate main batteries.

MARYLAND followed up Tarawa with Kwajalein Atoll in January 1944 and Saipan in June. On the 22nd, after being on station for several days, taking out two coastal batteries and providing coverage for the landings, MARYLAND and her sailors were at rest. The sun was about to go down and the crew was relaxing, gathered in small groups on the deck, playing cards or just passing on the latest "scuttlebutt."[33]

Japanese pilots often utilized the tactic of flying alone, at dusk, coming in low, skimming mere feet above the surface of the ocean or hugging the contours of an island. On this evening that's exactly what happened. A "Betty" twin engine bomber carrying aerial torpedoes arrived in just those

---

33 Originally a water barrel on a sailing ship, now, a water fountain, in Navy slang it is the latest rumor or gossip.

circumstances and no one spotted it until it was way too late. Not one shot was fired in defense by MARYLAND. The plane came in unchallenged and fired its torpedo almost as if it were a practice run. The torpedo headed for the bow. The crew that was gathered there jumped up and ran aft just as fast as they could. At 1952 the TNT fish slammed home on the port bow, sending a geyser of water a hundred feet into the air. The impact also tossed the men on deck into the air like bowling pins.

The battleship sailed to Eniwetok for a quick inspection of the damage and then set off for the repair yards at Pearl Harbor, arriving there July 10th. She stayed there until the end of August.

In September she traveled to the island of Peleliu. Between the 12th and the 15th she fired 814 sixteen-inch shells[34] on that tiny island in preparation for and in support of the Marine assault that began on the morning of the 15th. On the 14th alone she shelled the island for twelve hours straight.

MARYLAND dutifully moved on, and in October was in the Philippines for the landings there at Leyte on the 20th. On the 25th she, along with other of her sister battlewagons from Pearl Harbor, met an enemy force in the Surigao Strait and decimated them.

All Allied navies were beset by kamikazes at this point of the war. Japan was willing to sacrifice planes and that most precious of commodities, men, in a vain effort to stem what was by now an inevitable tsunami of force that would soon swamp the militarists of that island nation.

On the 27th MARYLAND expended a total of 3,400 rounds of five-inch, 40mm and 20mm ammunition to shoot down, with other ships of her task group, eleven attacking enemy planes.[35] Two days later at 1813 a kamikaze slipped through the air defenses and hit MARYLAND between Turrets #1 and #2. The bomb it carried exploded on the second deck. Thirty-one sailors died. Neither the damage nor the deaths hindered the battleship and she stayed on station.

---

34 USS MARYLAND deck log entries September 12-15, 1944.
35 USS MARYLAND deck log entry November 27, 1944.

Photo taken the instant a Japanese kamikaze hit MARYLAND at 1813, on November 29, 1944, off the Philippines.

On December 9th, after a short stay at Manus Island, MARYLAND sailed for Pearl Harbor for repairs. She remained there for sea trials through March 1945. In late March she was assigned to the bombardment of Okinawa. On the 25th she began pounding that island with her sixteen-inch guns.

Every day after that, the guns of MARYLAND spoke, to either hit enemy positions on Okinawa, or to protect herself from enemy aerial attack. On the 6th of April alone she shot down five enemy planes. The next day the odds once again caught up with the "Fighting Mary" and she was, for the second time, hit by a kamikaze. This time the plane hit turret #3 at 1848. By 2030 all the fires from the suicide plane were out. As before neither the damage nor the fifty-three casualties she suffered stopped MARYLAND. She fought on. Another Japanese plane was shot down on the 12th. That would be the last kill of the war for MARYLAND. Two days later she headed for home. On May 7, 1945 at 1332, she anchored at Puget Sound Navy Yard. The war was over for MARYLAND.

FATE

MARYLAND was a participant in Operation Magic Carpet, bringing thousands of American soldiers, airmen, and Marines home after the war. With those duties complete she returned to Puget Sound Navy Yard in April 1946 and was decommissioned and placed in the "mothball fleet" in April 1947. She was sold to the Learner Company of Oakland, California, as scrap in 1959.

MEDUSA CLASS REPAIR SHIP
AR-1
LAUNCHED: 1923

DECEMBER 7, 1941

For most sailors at Pearl Harbor, the shock and surprise of the Japanese attack was momentary. Rumors of war had been in the air for some time and although all hoped it wouldn't come, most knew it would. So when Lieutenant Commander John Miller heard the first bombs fall on Ford Island and he rushed to his battle station he knew immediately what to do. He passed the magazine keys to the Gunner's Mate on duty and ordered ammunition to be broken out and passed to the guns. In ten minutes the three-inch guns on MEDUSA were responding to the raid and continued to fire for the duration of the attack. Miller saw four planes shot down in the Middle Loch area where MEDUSA was moored and credited his gunners with bringing down two of them.

James Murphey was assigned as a loader on a five-inch gun. He arrived as his battle station but was told to take cover. The five-inch gun would remain silent. So Murphey and his crew watched the battle unfold from a porthole below decks.

About thirty minutes into the attack, MEDUSA along with every other ship in the area sighted the periscope of a midget submarine in the harbor 1000 yards off her starboard quarter. Miller ordered all guns with a clear shot to open fire. As they did, the mini-sub fired a torpedo, which missed CURTISS, AV-4, the probable target, and struck a pier. The sub changed course despite several apparent hits on the conning tower by MEDUSA and other ships. The sub then fired another torpedo, this time at USS MONAGHAN, DD-354, which was heading straight for it but this torpedo also missed, passing the destroyer closely but harmlessly, on the starboard side. MEDUSA ceased firing at the sub for fear of hitting MONAGHAN, which was making an attack run on it. MONAGHAN rammed the submarine, passing directly over it and then dropped two depth charges. The sub disappeared.

Below deck, James Murphey and his gun crew were following their orders to stay under cover. Murphey was chain-smoking his way through a pack of cigarettes as he helplessly watched his ship fire on the mini-sub and other crewman armed with Browning Automatic Rifles shoot at enemy planes.

During the second wave of the attack, ships in the area became targets. One bomb struck the nearby CURTISS and four bombs fell around MEDUSA but missed. Two of these severely rocked the ship exploding in the water only twenty-five feet off her starboard bow.

The attack waned and MEDUSA set about to assist in any way it could. Repair parties were sent to the light cruiser RALEIGH, CL-7, which was listing due to a torpedo strike and rescue parties were dispatched to the former battleship, UTAH, AG-16, which had capsized in the opening minutes of the attack. Twenty-one Springfield rifles and 40,000 rounds of .50-caliber ammunition were given to a unit of soldiers from Ft. Shafter patrolling nearby Pearl City. When three civilians were spotted on the shore taking photographs of the ships in the area, MEDUSA sent an armed patrol over and arrested them, turning them over to the Army detachment.

MEDUSA suffered no damage at all in the attack and only one minor casualty.

THE WAR

MEDUSA spent close to 16 months in Pearl Harbor after the beginning of the war. She was one of the armada of ships that was invaluable in helping to resuscitate the fleet. In the days immediately after the attack she sent welders and divers to OKLAHOMA, BB-37, to help release trapped men. Over the next months she put the full weight of her men and facilities into repairing her sister ships.

The United States Navy had never before built a ship from the keel up specifically as a repair ship until MEDUSA and her vast workshops were desperately needed at Pearl. She was outfitted with anything that could possibly be useful in repairing and maintaining ships at sea. She had an onboard foundry and blacksmith, electrical, plumbing, carpentry, sheet metal and machine shops with lathes and equipment for milling, slotting and boring. There were facilities for repairing optical gear like binoculars and periscopes. She even had a laundry, a bakery, refrigeration units and a motion picture lab. MEDUSA could take on almost any job that a Navy Yard could.

In the aftermath of the attack, MEDUSA employed her prodigious talents in the resurrection of the fleet. She aided many ships, particularly the battleships USS NEVADA, BB-36, and USS TENNESSEE, BB-43. Her optical shop was extremely busy repairing rangefinders and other equipment used by gun crews for targeting the enemy.

In April 1943, MEDUSA finally left Pearl Harbor behind and headed for the forward areas of the war to repair and maintain the ships that were fighting it. She arrived at Havannah Harbor at Efate in the New Hebrides and stayed there for almost a year. Within days of her arrival she was hip deep in work. In one week-long period in her first month there, she performed 258 separate jobs. Not all of these jobs were done on other ships either. Some were done on shore, as when she helped fix some equipment at one of the recreation facilities. Records show that on April 30th there were 60 of her crew laboring throughout the fleet on 9 separate work details.

In July 1943 MEDUSA made a short trip to Espiritu Santo where her facilities and the skills of her crew were urgently needed. One of her Pearl Harbor sisters, the light cruiser USS HONOLULU, CL-48, had been torpedoed and her bow was badly damaged. MEDUSA reported there and in 11 days fashioned a temporary bow to enable HONOLULU to get back to the states for more complete repair.

The repair ship herself needed repairs in late May 1944 when she grounded on Buna Shoal off New Guinea. It took three days to pull

MEDUSA off the reef. She then sailed to Sydney, Australia to have her hull patched up. Seaworthy once again, she returned to her duties ministering to the fleet.

In July 1945 MEDUSA moved to Manus in the Admiralty Islands, which is where she was when the war ended.

The USS HONOLULU in a 1941 photo, with her original bow, (top) and her temporary, shortened bow (bottom), installed by USS MEDUSA, (the top photo is reversed for comparison purposes).

FATE

After a three month stay in Manila, MEDUSA reported to San Diego in December 1945 where she undertook the job of preparing other naval vessels for deactivation. She continued in this function until it was her turn in the spring of 1946. She was rather unceremoniously towed to Bremerton, Washington where she was decommissioned in November of that year. After everything of possible use or value was removed from her, she was sold to the Zeidell Shipwrecking Company of Portland, Oregon, which scrapped her in 1951.

USS Monaghan

FARRAGUT CLASS DESTROYER
DD-354
LAUNCHED: 1933

DECEMBER 7, 1941

Shortly after 0100 Lieutenant Iwasa Naoji, of the Imperial Japanese Navy, along with his lone crewman, Petty Officer 1st Class Sasaki Naokichi, launched their midget submarine from the deck of its mother sub, *I-22*. They were nine miles from the entrance to Pearl Harbor. Their mission was to infiltrate the security defenses of the harbor and fire their two torpedoes at American Naval ships there. Theirs was the only mini-sub confirmed to have accomplished this mission.

Just before 0800, the captain of MONAGHAN, Lieutenant Commander William P. Burford, received orders to join USS WARD, DD-139, on anti-submarine patrol duties outside the harbor entrance. Preparations were already underway to comply with that order when the aerial attack began. As a result, MONAGHAN had a full head of steam up within a half hour and left her nest of destroyers at 0827.

Sailing down the North Channel, Burford saw signal flags on the seaplane tender, USS CURTISS, AV-4, indicating the presence of a submarine inside the harbor. It didn't take long to confirm that, as several ships flanking the North Channel were observed to be firing on the exposed conning tower of the sub in question.

Inside the midget sub, Lieutenant Iwasa was sizing up the enemy after his arduous seven-hour trek. He had managed to penetrate the harbor and remained unseen until he was off the northwestern corner of Ford Island. There he came under intense fire. He then fired one torpedo, apparently at CURTISS, but the "fish" missed its mark and struck a pier at Pearl City.

What followed was an intense, dangerous and courageous game of chicken on the part of both commanding officers. MONAGHAN was sailing west down the North Channel and the mini-sub was heading east. When Burford recognized this situation he made the immediate decision to ram the intruder and accordingly ordered up flank speed. Iwasa saw the 1,300 ton, 341 foot long, destroyer bearing down on his much smaller 46 ton, 78 foot craft, at an increasing speed. To the Japanese commander the solution must have seemed quite evident: sink the MONAGHAN.

By now at least four ships were firing upon the mini-sub including MONAGHAN. The advancing destroyer let fly a five-inch shell from her #2 gun that missed and, like a skipping stone, ricocheted off the water. The shock waves of near misses rocked the tiny sub, but Iwasa was undeterred and pressed on. MONAGHAN initially spotted the sub at a distance of 1,000 yards. As the destroyer's engines rapidly increased revolutions to her flank speed of 36 knots, the gap between the two adversaries closed just as quickly.

One of the most difficult shots in naval warfare is a straight on "bow shot." The target vessel presents its most narrow profile to the attacking sub and this is exactly the situation Iwasa was faced with. The longer he waited the better chance he had of hitting the oncoming destroyer, because even though the profile was narrow, it was getting bigger the closer she got. Once the torpedo left the submarine there would be nothing more for Iwasa and Sasaki to do; the torpedoes were the only offensive weapons available to them.

The two ships continued their head-on approach and neither one of them blinked. More than a minute passed, allowing ample time for each captain to contemplate what was about to happen. Iwasa had to hit the destroyer with his torpedo or the onrushing juggernaut would certainly plow into his tiny submarine. Burford knew that as the distance closed the Japanese sub's chances of killing him with the bow shot improved geometrically.

The time finally arrived. The two enemy ships were no more than 100 yards apart when Iwasa fired. As the torpedo exited the tube at 44 knots, it "porpoised" out of the water twice before its propeller got a solid grip sending it speeding toward MONAGHAN. Almost immediately after the launch of the torpedo one of the other American ships firing on the sub hit it squarely in the conning tower instantly killing the brave Iwasa. The "Long Lance" torpedo raced through the azure water of Pearl Harbor and passed down the starboard side of MONAGHAN missing the destroyer by 75 feet.

When the submarine, because of its proximity, could no longer be seen from the bridge an announcement went over the destroyer's loudspeaker to prepare for an imminent ramming. MONAGHAN struck the submarine and rolled right over it with barely a perceptible shock. The bow and conning tower of the sub slid along the length of the starboard side of the destroyer. Just as it passed from underneath the hull two depth charges were dropped from the stern racks. MONAGHAN had its first kill of the war.

Burford had little time to contemplate his victory. He immediately ordered full back on his engines in order to check the high speed of his ship. The engines couldn't slow the ship fast enough and she struck a glancing blow to a derrick moored just off Beckoning Point and ran aground. Within minutes Burford had his ship free and heading out to sea with only very minor damage.

The hulk of the mini-sub sunk by MONAGHAN after its recovery from the harbor.

THE WAR

The first months of the war held the promise of action for MONAGHAN. She was part of the relief fleet for Wake Island and she participated in the

Battles of the Coral Sea and Midway, but the relief of Wake was called off and she was only in the periphery at Coral Sea.

On June 5, 1943, the second day of the Battle of Midway she was ordered to the side of the heavily damaged carrier, USS YORKTOWN, CV-5. Her assignment was to render any assistance she could in saving or protecting the flattop. The following day, with the carrier under tow and repair parties on board, it appeared as if she was going to be saved. MONAGHAN and other destroyers were screening her. But once again a Japanese submarine was about to play a role in the life of MONAGHAN.

In the very early morning hours of the 6th, the distressed YORKTOWN was spotted by the Japanese submarine *I-168*, captained by Commander Tanabe Yahachi. After an extremely slow and cautious nine-hour approach that took him inside the destroyer screen, Tanabe fired four fish at YORKTOWN at a range of 1,900 yards. One torpedo sank the destroyer USS HAMMANN, DD-412, two others struck the carrier and the forth passed just astern of the flattop. MONAGHAN and two other destroyers immediately reacted and began to hunt down the submarine. Over the next several hours they dropped a total of sixty depth charges, seriously damaging *I-168*, but the submarine got away.

The following month MONAGHAN was in the Aleutians, but the stay was short-lived. On July 27th, while conducting operations off Kiska Island in heavy fog, she collided with the minesweeper USS LONG, DMS-12. The resulting damage ultimately brought her to Mare Island in California for repairs. She returned to the Pacific in November and in March 1943 she was back in the Aleutians.

On the 27th MONAGHAN, along with two cruisers and three other destroyers, was involved in a four-hour long donnybrook with an enemy group consisting of four cruisers and four destroyers. Known as the Battle of the Komandorski Islands, when it was over the casualties on both sides totaled three badly damaged cruisers and two wounded destroyers. MONAGHAN came through unscathed. The battle was a draw, but marked the beginning of the end of the Japanese in the Aleutians.

About three weeks later, on June 21st, while conducting patrols off Kiska Island, her radar picked up a target approximately 14,000 yards away. Heavy fog prevented lookouts from visually identifying the ghost ship. MONAGHAN closed on the unseen vessel and about 1930, when she was 2,000 yards away, the destroyer opened fire using only her radar for fire control. In an amazing demonstration of the new technology of radar controlled fire, MONOAGHAN, although unknown to her at the time, hit her target. Two five-inch shells smashed into the conning tower of the Japanese submarine *I-7* killing all the senior officers on board. MONAGHAN disengaged at this time.

At 0035 on the morning of June 23rd MONAGHAN was once again in contact with an unknown target. This time it was darkness that prevented the destroyer from seeing her contact. The engagement was almost an exact replay of the events of two nights before. Her radar picked up a target at 14,000 yards and once again she opened fire after closing in to 2,300 yards. Once again her shells penetrated the conning tower of the same Japanese submarine, *I-7*. And as before, the officer in command of the sub was severely wounded and the Engineering Officer was killed. A running gun battle ensued in the darkness, with MONAGHAN and her radar-directed gunfire devastating the submarine while the harried Japanese fired blindly in the darkness causing no damage. The destroyer's fire was so accurate that at one point the submarine lookouts thought they were under attack by three destroyers. MONAGHAN delivered at least four more hits on the sub. The Japanese boat, although crippled, could still maneuver and headed in close to shore. MONAGHAN, fearing the treacherous rocks near the coast, did not follow and broke off her attack. It turned out to be a wise decision too, because forty minutes later the Japanese boat grounded. A call for help was sent out and the Japanese evacuated the remaining forty-three crewmen. The next day Japanese divers scuttled the *I-7* in sixty feet of water.[36]

For the next year MONAGHAN was used almost exclusively as an escort for various ships throughout the Pacific. She escorted carriers and battleships to and from operations and occasionally participated in shore bombardment duties. She made her way toward Japan with the rest of

---

36 In September U.S. Navy divers entered the submerged hulk of *I-7* and removed a considerable amount of intelligence documents.

the fleet in actions at Tarawa, Kwajalein, Eniwetok, Palau, Saipan and Guam.

FATE

In December 1944 the American Navy was deeply involved in the liberation of the Philippines and MONAGHAN was there. In mid-month she was operating as an escort for oilers assigned to refueling operations for the fleet. In the morning hours of December 18th several destroyers, including MONAGHAN, were running low on fuel. She attempted refueling, however the weather became increasingly nasty and the seas became very rough with waves reaching twenty to twenty-five feet. Efforts to take on more fuel were abandoned as the conditions steadily became worse. The seas were the result of a typhoon in the area and the fleet was ordered to sail away from the developing storm. But the gods are capricious and man is imperfect and the fleet actually sailed into the heart of the storm that was to be named Typhoon Cobra.

Water Tender 2nd Class Joseph McCrane was below decks in the engineering section. He had been ordered to take on water ballast. The ballast had been dumped earlier in order to take on the expected fuel. Since the fuel wasn't taken on, the ship was now too light and the seawater was needed to make the ship heavier. Fireman 1st Class Evan Fenn had completed his watch and went to the galley to get breakfast. Neither sailor could complete their tasks as the seas had now become so rough that doing even the simplest things was becoming near impossible.

The waves steadily grew larger. Sailors on deck, in the trough of a wave saw nothing but an angry wall of green water and when they looked up at the top of the wave they saw another ship thirty feet above them. If you dared step out on deck you had to be tied with lifelines for fear of being washed overboard. The morning wore on and with it came winds that increased in speed to fifty, seventy, one hundred miles an hour with gusts up to one hundred forty. The waves churned by these winds grew to a monstrous sixty feet.

McCrane and close to forty other sailors sought refuge in the aft five-inch gun mount. It provided shelter from the storm and it was above deck.

Nobody wanted to be below. Fenn was below in his quarters trying to ride the typhoon out in his rack. Every time the ship rolled his mattress would fly out from under him and he would grab it and shove it back beneath him. At about 1100 the lights went out and he figured it was time to get above. He grabbed his life jacket and made for the passageway.

In the gun mount McCrane and his fellow bluejackets were praying, loudly, as if they had to shout for the Almighty to hear their pleas above the storm. A huge wave hit the ship and she rolled to starboard. She began to right herself, but before she could fully come up another wave hit her, this time rolling her more than before. This happened at least six more times; each time MONAGHAN rolled further until after one wave she was over at least seventy degrees. Then came the last wave. The giant smashed down on the little destroyer and rolled her completely over onto her starboard side. The men inside the gun mount knew it was the end. With great effort they forced open the hatch and scrambled out into the tempest.

Just as she rolled on her side, Fenn managed to make it on deck where he was quickly washed overboard along with all the sailors bailing out of the gun mount. By some miracle both Fenn and McCrane found themselves and others clinging to a lone life raft. The last any of them saw of MONAGHAN she was wallowing in the angry ocean on her starboard side. None actually saw her sink, but the survivors all later testified that she must certainly have sunk within seconds of their escape. For hours they could only hold on to the raft because the seas were too wild to allow the sailors to climb in. Even after the seas calmed down enough to do that, giant waves regularly capsized the raft. Those bluejackets who held on tightly enough had to right it and those that were thrown off into the insane seas had to swim back. This went on for almost a full day.

Only thirteen men made it to the raft. For the next three days, one by one, sailors were lost to injury and delirium. Two sailors swam to another raft that floated by. They were never seen again. One sailor just swam away and never returned. Two more days passed like that, with the wounded dying and the delirious going insane. Ships and planes would pass by and the men would yell and wave theirs arms but the still heavy seas made the tiny raft almost invisible.

After three days the men began to believe they would all soon be among the dead. McCrane was the healthiest on board and did his best to aid the others. Fenn had been tossed out of the raft so many times that the skin on his legs was literally rubbed off from climbing back into it.

Salvation finally appeared on the morning of the third day when they were spotted by search planes. Shortly thereafter the destroyer USS BROWN, DD-546, appeared on the horizon and was soon taking the castaways on board. BROWN sailed with the rescued men to Ulithi where she delivered the survivors to their Pearl Harbor sister, the hospital ship USS SOLACE, AH-5.

Of the 263 men assigned to MONAGHAN only six returned from the sea.

WICKES CLASS DESTROYER / LIGHT MINESWEEPER
DM-17
LAUNCHED: 1918

DECEMBER 7, 1941

MONTGOMERY was nested with the other ships of Mine Division Two in Middle Loch at the north end of Pearl Harbor just off of the Pearl City peninsula. She and her crew were in the thick of the fighting almost immediately. Machine guns were manned and enemy planes were engaged as they flew over the ship after making their bombing or torpedo runs.

In his After Action Report Lieutenant Commander Richard A. Guthrie, the captain of MONTGOMERY, claimed that the ships of Mine Division Two, either jointly or singly shot down at least five enemy planes, all of which crashed in or near Middle Loch.

At one point during the attack, Guthrie received word that two Japanese airmen were in the water near Pearl City, swimming by the wreckage of their airplane. He dispatched the ship's whaleboat to look into the situation. When the whaleboat arrived at the scene they found the enemy pilot in the water. The crew motioned to the pilot, indicating they wanted him to get in the boat. Instead of complying, the Japanese reached inside his leather jacket. Thinking that he was reaching for a gun, Seaman 1st Class D.F. Calkins promptly shot him. The pilot sank into the water.

Shortly after the attack was over MONTGOMERY was ordered out of the harbor and within an hour she was conducting anti-submarine patrols off the harbor entrance. At around 1500, MONTGOMERY made a sonar contact and dropped eight depth charges on it, but no kill was confirmed. She stayed on continuous patrol for six days, returning to Pearl Harbor on the morning of the 13th.

THE WAR

MONTGOMERY spent the first four months of the war in and around the Hawai'ian Islands escorting convoys and conducting anti-submarine patrols. In April 1942 she left Hawai'i to begin the war in earnest. She laid mines as far north as the Aleutians and south in the Solomons. While laying mines off of Guadalcanal on a dark August night in 1943, MONTOGOMERY collided with her Pearl Harbor sister USS PREBLE, DM-20. The collision took off twenty feet of MONTGOMERY's bow. She underwent temporary repairs that enabled her to make it back to San Francisco for more complete work in a naval yard.

After her repairs were completed she returned to the Pacific where she laid mines around Kwajalein and performed escort and anti-submarine duties in the march across the sea toward Tokyo. In October 1944 she participated in the invasion of the small atoll of Ngulu, south of Ulithi in the Caroline Islands. On the 15th she bombarded the atoll as part of the invasion. Two days later, on the evening of the 17th, she was anchored off of Ngulu when the watch spotted a Japanese mine floating off to port. A wind came up and swung the vessel on her anchor chain, driving the MONTGOMERY into the mine. The resulting explosion caused considerable damage and killed four sailors. The destroyer USS ELLET, DD-398, came to the aid of MONTGOMERY with water pumps to help keep her afloat. When the ship was stabilized ELLET took her under tow to Ulithi.

FATE

It took until January 1945 for MONTGOMERY to be able to make it back to America on her own. Once she arrived in San Francisco, a close inspection soon revealed that she wasn't worth repairing and her decommissioning was recommended. That occurred in April 1945 and she was sold for scrap in March 1946.

Motor Torpedo Boat Squadron #1

77' ELCO MOTOR TORPEDO BOATS
PT's 20, 21, 22, 23, 24, 25, 26, 27, 28, 29, 30 and 42
LAUNCHED: 1941

DECEMBER 7, 1941

Motor Torpedo Squadron #1 was in Pearl Harbor awaiting transport to the Philippines. Half the squadron was being prepared to leave. PT's 27, 29, 30 and 42 were already loaded onboard USS RAMAPO, AO-12, in preparation for shipment. The 26 and 28 boats were on the dock waiting to be hoisted aboard RAMAPO. The rest of the boats were moored at berth S-13 in Magazine Loch near a covered barge, YR-20, which acted as the boat tender.

As the crews ate breakfast on board the barge Ensign N. E. Ball, the Squadron duty officer, spotted planes swarming in the skies above the harbor and recognized their markings as Japanese just as the first bombs fell. All crews scrambled to the .50 caliber machine guns on the boats. On board PT-23, Gunner's Mate 1st Class Joy van Zyll de Jong and Torpedoman 1st Class George B. Huffman each tumbled into the turrets and immediately commenced firing. In short order two enemy torpedo planes were brought down by their fire. Of all the claims made that day by numerous ships throughout the harbor, as to being the first to fire and/or the first to bring down an enemy plane, it is most likely that these two men, on board one of the smallest fighting vessels in the Navy, were actually the first to fire on the enemy in Pearl Harbor and the first to claim kills.

The crews of the boats onboard RAMAPO also began firing. These men however had an obstacle to overcome. Because they were being transported, their engines could not be started and couldn't power the hydraulic system of the boats turrets. But the men adapted and overcame. They simply cut the hydraulic lines and two men manually turned the turret left or right while a third man fired the .50 caliber machine gun.

When the squadron commander, Lieutenant Commander William C. Specht, arrived in the waning moments of the attack he received orders to take the squadron out and patrol the mouth of the channel for submarines. The boats quickly got under way. Specht divided the squadron into two groups of three with one group just inside the mouth of the harbor and the other group just outside.

Lt. Cdr. Specht, in PT-24, sighted what was believed to be a submarine periscope about six miles out. The 24 boat along with a destroyer charged full speed to where the periscope was sighted but could now find nothing. The squadron stayed out until 2200 and reported back to Pearl Harbor.

None of the boats suffered any damage and no crewmen were injured. The boats fired a combined total of over 4,000 rounds of .50 caliber ammunition during the attack.

THE WAR

The plan to send the squadron to the Philippines was changed after the attack and the boats already loaded on RAMAPO were removed. In May 1942 the squadron was sent to Midway instead. The boats were not transported, but rather they sailed there under there own power. The 1,385-mile, 4-day voyage was the longest made by American PT boats up to that time. The first day out, PT-23 turned back to Pearl Harbor with a broken crankshaft. Along the way

PTs 28 and 29 escort USS HORNET, CV-2 into Pearl Harbor on its return from the Doolittle Raid, April 1942.

PT-25 developed engine trouble and had to be towed to Midway. The squadron arrived there on May 29th.

On June 4th the PTs met the enemy as they attacked Midway. The boats anchored in the lagoon fired at the enemy planes making bombing and strafing runs. The 21 and 22 boats splashed a "Zero." As enemy planes attempted to attack other vessels in the lagoon the intense fire put up by the PTs drove them off. When the attack was over some boats picked up pilots that had been shot down in the lagoon. At 1930 the entire squadron was sent out to search for crippled enemy ships and sink them if possible, but none were found.

The squadron was split up in July 1942. PTs 21, 23 25 and 26 were sent to the Pacific island of Palmyra. In November 1942 these four boats were involved in the rescue of Eddie Rickenbacker, the American World War One flying ace. Rickenbacker was on a mission for the Secretary of War when the B-17 he was flying in crashed. After three weeks adrift in a raft the survivors were discovered and Rickenbacker was ferried back to safety on PT-26.

PTs 22, 24, 27 and 28 were sent to the far north for duty in the Aleutians. The boats didn't fair well in the harsh conditions of the Alaskan waters. Add to that the fact that there were no facilities there to service the boats and they soon were in a bad state. During a storm the 24 boat rammed the 22 boat damaging both vessels. For a week the four boats struggled with rough seas, ice, dragging anchors and running aground. PT 24 and 27 survived the storm.

FATE

None of the boats of the squadron survived the war as PT boats. PT 22 and PT 28 were both destroyed as a result of the storm in Dora Harbor, Unimak, Alaska in January 1943. Five of the boats were reclassified as small boats and assigned to duties other than combat. PTs 23, 25 and 26 were reclassified in October 1943 and the 24 and 27 boats in December 1944. The remaining five boats of the squadron were all stricken from the Navy's rolls as being obsolete; PT-21 in October 1943, PT-30 in March 1944 and the 20, 29 and 42 boats in December 1944.

USS *Mugford*

BAGLEY CLASS DESTROYER
DD-389
LAUNCHED: 1936

DECEMBER 7, 1941

Considering where MUGFORD was and the condition she was in on that Sunday morning, one wouldn't expect much from her. At Berth No. 6 in the Navy Yard, her fuel tanks were practically dry and the machinery that powered her had been disassembled. In the midst of a scheduled overhaul she would appear to have been a sitting duck. MUGFORD and her crew were full of surprises, however.

Within minutes of the beginning of the attack, MUGFORD was filling her empty fuel tanks, reassembling her engines and firing her anti-aircraft guns. Just about twelve minutes into the raid, a Japanese "Kate" launched a torpedo at the minelayer, USS OGLALA, CM-4, berthed nearby at 1010 dock. When the plane banked left after dropping its torpedo, its exposed underbelly presented itself to the gunners onboard MUGFORD and they took full advantage, making the plane their first kill of the day and of the war, but not her last. Only minutes later, the second plane to fall at the hands of MUGFORD met its end. Another "Kate," making a torpedo run on Battleship Row, crossed the destroyer's stern, flying a mere twenty feet above the water. Her .50-caliber machine guns found the predator and riddled it with bullets. The plane crashed on Ford Island without dropping its torpedo – without killing more American sailors. The crew of MUGFORD shot down one more enemy plane that morning for a total of three.

Bullets were not the only things being shot that morning. On MUGFORD, as on other ships, a vast amount of pictures were being shot. The attack lasted just under two hours, giving many photographers, both professional and amateur, ample time to load their cameras and capture, on film, history as it happened. MUGFORD had a "designated Camera Officer" who was instructed by the captain Lieutenant Commander Edward Young, to photographically record the attack. Young also had the assistance of a somewhat strange serendipity. A crewman had been on liberty in Honolulu, and as any good tourist, he had his camera with him. In his case it was an amateur 8-millimeter movie camera that he kept stored in a locker on shore. When news of the attack spread, along with orders for all military personnel to report to their duty stations, he made it back to MUGFORD, camera in hand. Bringing a camera on board was a breach of security and was immediately brought to the captain's attention. Not being one to miss an opportunity, Young ordered the sailor to also photograph the attack. Between the two ad-hoc photographers, when the attack was over Young had in his possession two rolls of 8 mm movie film and four rolls of 35mm still negative film recording the first battle of World War II for the United States.

All during the enemy onslaught, the preparations for getting underway continued. By 1005 her engines were back together and her boilers were lit. Two hours later her tanks contained 115,000 gallons of fuel and at 1214 she got underway and exited the harbor.

At the end of the day MUGFORD was undamaged and her crew suffered no fatalities and only minor injuries. She had fired 280 five-inch shells and 5,000 rounds of .50-caliber ammunition.

THE WAR

The first months of the war found MUGFORD escorting convoys to Australia. In August 1942 she was, like many of her Pearl Harbor sisters, part of that mighty armada that made the first thrust against Japan at Guadalcanal.

The Marines landed on Guadalcanal just after 0900 on the morning of August 7, 1942. In the afternoon, the Japanese counterattacked from the sky, sending over thirty bombers from their massive base at Rabaul to strike at the impudent Americans who dared to stand against His Imperial Majesty's empire. Just before 1500, MUGFORD was in the midst of a fight for her life. The destroyer's gunners downed two attacking bombers. Bombs from other planes dropped in the ocean around MUGFORD sending geysers of water soaring into the sky. One bomb, however, struck home, penetrating her superstructure and killing 17 sailors. Courageous efforts beat back the ensuing fires, and the little tin can continued on.

Two days later MUGFORD plucked from the ocean over 400 survivors of the cruisers USS VINCENNES, CA-44, and USS ASTORIA, CA-34, which had been sunk by the Japanese in the Battle of Savo Island. This was not the last time MUGFORD would fish helpless castaways from the sea.

In the early morning hours of May 14, 1943, off the coast of Australia, the Japanese submarine *I-177* torpedoed the Australian hospital ship AHS CENTAUR. The captain of the enemy vessel was Lieutenant Commander Nakagawa Hajime.[37] The hospital ship went down in three minutes taking 268 people with her. The ship sank so fast that no distress signal was sent out nor were lifeboats properly deployed. The next afternoon the survivors were spotted floating in the sea by an Australian scout plane that just happened to fly over them. The nearest allied ship was contacted and directed to the area. It was MUGFORD.

By the time MUGFORD arrived on the scene the survivors had been in the water for 36 hours and had drifted twenty miles from where their ship had sunk. The destroyer found them scattered across an area two miles wide, some clustered in groups and some floating alone. All were clinging to floating debris. For an hour and twenty minutes, Commander Howard Corey, the captain of MUGFORD, guided his ship and crew in their humanitarian efforts. They plucked a total of 64 souls from the water. Corey continued searching into the night but picked up no more survivors. Around midnight MUGFORD delivered her charges to Brisbane.

---

37 After the war Nakagawa denied sinking CENTAUR, but plead guilty to other war crimes and was sentenced to four years in prison.

Through the rest of 1943 and into 1944, MUGFORD was on call to perform whatever duties were needed in the march across the Pacific. In the course of her patrol, escort and bombardment duties, she also managed to destroy many enemy airplanes. October 1944 brought her to the Battle of Leyte Gulf where she helped to escort aircraft carriers that had been damaged by kamikaze strikes.

On December 5, 1944, while patrolling the Surigao Strait in the Philippines she came to the defense of some amphibious craft under aerial attack. Japanese bombers and fighters harassed Allied operations in the area all day and MUGFORD and other destroyers met them head on all day. In the late afternoon another flight of enemy planes arrived but this time they were kamikazes. One of them, a "Val", chose MUGFORD as its target. Despite heavy anti-aircraft fire sent up against it, the Imperial marauder made it through and crashed into her port side. Aviation fuel spewed from the mangled plane and was ignited by the bomb it carried. The impact, explosion and following inferno killed ten and severely burned sixteen others. Even as fire control parties battled the flames, MUGFORD, fought on.

She sailed to San Pedro Bay, the Philippines for repairs. A month later she was sent to Mare Island for an extensive overhaul. In March 1945 she returned to the Pacific where the last months of the war passed quietly for her.

FATE

She spent the first months of the post-war period bringing Allied prisoners of war out of Japan to freedom. In November she returned to San Diego to prepare for her next assignment: MUGFORD was chosen to participate in the next phase of the development of atomic weapons.

In San Diego she was stripped of any and all equipment still useful or valuable. When that task was completed, MUGFORD sailed for Bikini Atoll in the Marshall Islands. She was one of the twelve destroyer target vessels of the total 92 ships used for the two atomic bomb tests of Operation Crossroads.

The detonation of the test "Able" atomic bomb in Bikini Lagoon on July 1, 1946.

The first test, "Able," occurred on July 1, 1946. "Able" was an airburst detonated 520 feet above the target fleet. The second test, "Baker," took place on July 25th, just over three weeks later. That test was a submerged detonation with the device 90 feet below the surface of the lagoon.

After both tests MUGFORD was still afloat, but she was highly radioactive. She then became the subject of decontamination experiments. When those were complete she was towed to the island of Kwajalein where she was sunk on March 22, 1948.

V- BOAT / FLEET SUBMARINE
SS-167
LAUNCHED: 1928

DECEMBER 7, 1941

The crew of NARWHAL had ample opportunity to fire at enemy planes once the attack began because no enemy action was taken against the sub base at all. Her four anti-aircraft machine guns were in action within minutes of the beginning of the raid. Manning the aft .50-caliber was a young sailor, Allen L. Commens. From NARWHAL's berth at one of the sub base piers, Commens and her other gunners fired at every plane that was in range and took credit for helping to splash two Japanese aircraft. When one of them crashed in the water nearby, Commens could feel the heat from the flames until the wreck sank. As the attack continued, Commens and his gun crew let other NARWHAL sailors take turns at the .50-caliber to shoot at enemy planes.

NARWHAL at the sub base during the attack, as sailors look across South East Loch at fires in the Navy Yard

NARWHAL received no damage and suffered no casualties in the attack.

THE WAR

NARWHAL was originally built as a "V-Boat," an experiment in submarine construction and tactics. She was intended to be a big, long range, "submarine cruiser." Because of that, she was much larger than previous American submarines and even larger than the later workhorse of the American submarine fleet, the GATO class submarine. She was a monstrous 371 feet long, longer even than contemporary destroyers, and she displaced 3,900 tons, compared with the GATO submarines, which were 311 feet long displacing 2,400 tons. Further evidence of her unique conception was her deck armament. Where typical World War Two destroyers had four or five-inch guns and submarines had one three-inch deck gun NARWHAL had two huge six-inch guns one each mounted just fore and aft of the conning tower, the largest guns ever mounted on an American submarine. Unfortunately, her size also made her slower and less responsive to the helm.

Less than two months after the attack, NARWHAL left Pearl Harbor on her first war patrol. The mission was primarily for gathering information on enemy activities but she sank her first ship, a cargo vessel, during this trip. Her second patrol quickly followed when she participated in the Battle of Midway as a scout ship. On her third war patrol she claimed three more enemy vessels in the Kurile Islands north of the Japanese mainland.

Upon return from her third war patrol she reported to Mare Island Naval Shipyard for some modifications. Portions of compartments fore and aft were gutted in order to make room for bunks and other facilities needed to accommodate 100 fully equipped soldiers. Once these modifications were complete she headed south to San Diego along with her sister ship USS NAUTILAS, SS-168 where they picked up the 7th Army Infantry Scout Company. Together they sailed to Alaska where the scouts were deposited at Massacre Bay on Attu Island for preliminary actions in the recapture of the island from the Japanese.

In June 1943, three American submarines entered the Sea of Japan for the first time during the war to hunt enemy shipping in its own backyard. In July, after completing their mission the three subs were ready to leave. To facilitate their exit, NARWHAL was called upon to help. The escaping subs were going to traverse the Etorofu Strait in the Kurile Islands. NARWHAL was chosen to go to Matsuwa Island north of the strait and using her 6-inch guns shell Japanese positions there. The idea was for NARWHAL to raise as much hell as she could, drawing the enemy's attention in hopes the Imperial Japanese Navy wouldn't see the other subs leaving. On July 15th, after waiting several days for extremely foggy conditions to improve NARWHAL began shelling the enemy airfield on Matsuwa.

William B. Azbell was transferred to NARWHAL from NAUTILAS during the Mare Island modifications. His job on board was to adjust the throttles on the engines, but his battle station was on one of the 6-inch deck guns. He reported to the deck to help load and handle the 102-pound six-inch shells and the 55-pound powder bags that launched them on the eight-mile journey toward their targets.

NARWHAL commenced firing at 2020. The fire was slow but accurate. On deck Azbell while loading the gun was steadying himself against a lifeline, which suddenly parted, throwing him toward the icy Japanese waters. Only luck and a stronger secondary lifeline saved Azbell from a cold and hazardous dunking.

Using the hangars as an aiming point, Azbell and the gun crew zeroed in on the airfield and fires could soon be seen on shore as a result of the barrage. Although it took some time, the enemy shore batteries began to return fire. Not accurate at first, the Japanese shells whistled overhead but began to find the range with several shells splashing dead ahead of the sub. Only twelve minutes after they started, the guns were secured and NARWHAL dove. The mission was a success as the other three subs exited the Sea of Japan unseen and unmolested.

On September 11, 1943 during her sixth war patrol, NARWHAL sank a small freighter near the isolated South Pacific island of Nauru. Within minutes of firing her two torpedoes at about 0810, an escort vessel set upon NARWHAL and dropped at least a dozen depth charges on her. Commander Frank Latta, her skipper, rigged for depth charge attack and silent running. He then took her down to 320 feet, which was 20 feet below her tested depth limit. NARWHAL took a beating and began to flood, making it difficult to keep her in a stable upright position. In a few more minutes at least three enemy vessels were hunting her. For an hour and a half NARWHAL could hear her stalkers circling, looking for her. At 0944 six final depth charges, of a total of 38, were dropped on NARWHAL. Battered but not beaten from her encounter with the enemy sub hunters NARWHAL slipped away.

While in Brisbane, Australia further modifications were made that would dictate her missions for the rest of the war. Bunks in both forward and aft crew quarters were removed and NARWHAL suffered, in the eyes of her crew, the indignity of being converted to an underwater cargo ship. Azbell and his fellow sailors felt that running supplies was an insane use for their boat and it was extremely depressing for young sailors wanting to do battle with the enemy. But as they soon discovered, there are many ways to fight an enemy.

NARWHAL became the major lifeline to courageous Filipino and American guerillas fighting the Japanese in the Philippines. On her seventh war patrol - her first support mission to the Philippines - she loaded up 92 tons of ammunition, supplies and covert personnel and headed for the island of Mindoro. Among her passengers was Lieutenant Commander Charles Parsons who was the Navy's "man in the Philippines." He went on numerous secret missions on several different submarines throughout the Philippines, delivering supplies, passing information and gathering intelligence. At 0308, on November 13, 1943 Parsons and his party departed NARWHAL in a rubber boat in Puluan Bay off Mindoro. Captain Latta then submerged his vessel and dodged local shipping for the next fourteen hours. At 1738 Latta resurfaced and picked up Parsons and his team. NARWHAL departed the area and less than an hour later at a new location she was unloading supplies and men to the guerillas under the cover of darkness.

Two days later on the 15th, Azbell was down in the engine room when he felt a shudder. NARWHAL had run aground in a shallow channel while approaching a wharf in the Philippine town of Nasipit. He, along with the rest of the crew, was called on deck to assist with remedying the situation. A combination of skilled manipulation of ballast and engines coupled with a majority of the crew running back and forth on the deck rocked the submarine free. Azbell returned to the engine room only to be summoned about an hour later by a shipmate who told him that if he wanted to see something unbelievable he'd better come topside. Azbell arrived on deck just as NARWHAL was pulling up to the dock at Nasipit, where he saw, greeting them, a fully uniformed band of Filipinos playing "Anchors Aweigh;" so much for secret missions.

Thirty-two evacuees, among them 8 women, 2 children and a baby, replaced the supplies that were off loaded. They were all suffering from malnutrition and vitamin deficiency. These problems were soon rectified with the help of NARWHAL's cooks and medical staff.

The next eight missions were more of the same. Following repairs and refits in Australia, NARWHAL would load up with cargo, ammunition and personnel to be delivered to the guerillas scattered throughout the Philippines. She would deliver her cargo and pick up evacuees. In between she would gather intelligence, shell enemy shore facilities and occasionally torpedo enemy vessels. All the while she endured intermittent depth charging by lucky or skilled Japanese sub chasers.

Although her crew never developed a liking for this type of stealthy, cloak and dagger kind of warfare, NARWHAL performed a vital service in the Philippines. In her one year of service there, NARWHAL traveled over 75,000 miles, delivered more than 550 tons of supplies to the American and Filipino guerillas and rescued over 200 evacuees, many of whom were women and children, including one woman who was seven months pregnant. Eighty-one American prisoners of war were also rescued and brought to safety.

By the end of 1944 NARWHAL was a seagoing jalopy. Every war patrol brought on a new set of mechanical challenges for her skipper and crew. Her engines were constantly breaking down at sea and were put right with jury-rigged solutions. For some of her last patrols she was haunted by a mysterious oil leak that left a shimmering slick behind her wherever she sailed, making her dangerously visible to the enemy.

FATE

By the completion of her last war patrol in November 1944, it was evident that NARWHAL had seen better days and had done her duty over a very hard seventeen-year life span. Beside her secret duties in the Philippines she was credited with sinking six enemy ships over the course of the war. In January 1945 she set sail for the Philadelphia Navy Yard where she was decommissioned and stricken from the Navy rolls in the spring of that year. She was subsequently sold for scrap.

NARWHAL's unique six-inch deck guns were saved from the scrap pile, however. They were removed and now stand sentinel outside Morton Hall at Submarine Base New London, in Groton Connecticut.

CIMARRON CLASS OILER
AO-23
LAUNCHED: 1939

DECEMBER 7, 1941

On Saturday, December 6, 1941, just shortly before midnight, Commander John S. Phillips, berthed his ship, NEOSHO, on the south side of Ford Island. Once she was settled in she began pumping her cargo of highly volatile aviation gasoline into the storage tanks for the Naval Air Station. This process continued all through the night and at 0755 the next morning had just been completed.

When general quarters was sounded, 19 year old Bill Leu, a Fireman 3rd Class, reported to his battle station at the forward three-inch gun. Leu and the rest of the gun crew received orders to fire at will at any enemy planes that came within range. Since NEOSHO was berthed smack in the middle of Battleship Row, finding targets was not going to be difficult. What was going to be difficult was hitting a low flying, fast moving plane with a three-inch gun.

Berthed forward of NEOSHO was CALIFORNIA, BB-44, and aft of her were the rest of the battlewagons, MARYLAND, BB-46, and OKLAHOMA, BB-37, being directly behind her. Being surrounded by primary targets for the Japanese was like being in the eye of a hurricane. Disaster and carnage encircled her. Torpedoes and bombs set upon the capital ships but she was disregarded. She was in a hornet's nest without being stung. NEOSHO in her berth was blocking MARYLAND. Phillips ordered all lines cut and at 0842 proceeded to back away from the pier in order to make an unobstructed path for MARYLAND. She barely cleared the already capsized OKLAHOMA as she continued to sail backwards into the South Channel. All the time her guns blazed at the attacking planes while the enemy still totally ignored her.

Once in the channel, she came between Battleship Row and the planes attacking from the south. Heavy fire from NEOSHO's guns caused several "Kates" making torpedo runs on the battleships to veer off without dropping their fish. It was at about this time that NEOSHO's gunners hit a plane that they believed crashed out of their sight.

Commander Phillips now steered his 553-foot long tanker toward Merry Point Landing near the submarine base at the south end of the harbor. The second wave of the attack was still underway as NEOSHO made her way across the harbor. The Japanese never targeted NEOSHO, but a number of bombs were near misses, which shook the ship. At 0930 she tied up at the Merry Point Landing. Amazingly, after being moored on Battleship

This photo taken from Ford Island shows NEOSHO, distant right, in the middle of Pearl Harbor after escaping the destruction on Battleship Row.

Row at the beginning of the raid and then sailing across a harbor that was rife with torpedoes, bombs and strafing planes NEOSHO at the end of the day was completely undamaged.

THE WAR

Three days after the start of the war, NEOSHO went out to refuel the ships that had been sent in the futile search for the Japanese fleet. For the next months NEOSHO followed the fleet refueling the ships at sea as needed.

She would then return to Pearl Harbor, replenish and head back out to sea. This continued until early May when she joined the task force that was waiting to repel the imminent Japanese invasion of New Guinea.

On May 6, 1942 NEOSHO refueled the aircraft carrier YORKTOWN, CV-5 and the cruiser ASTORIA, CA-34. When this was completed she retired under the escort of the destroyer SIMS, DD-409. NEOSHO was to lay low under the watchful eye of her escort and be on call to refuel the ships of the task force as needed.

That evening Bill Leu and his shipmates were told to take freshwater showers and to put on clean dungarees. Where the norm is salt-water showers a freshwater shower at sea is almost unheard of. The crew was then informed that if they were wounded, infection would be less likely if they and their clothes were as clean as possible. With this sudden emphasis on cleanliness and wounds, they figured something bad was about to happen.

FATE

The following morning at around 0730, NEOSHO and SIMS were spotted by Japanese search planes which mistook the oiler for an aircraft carrier. The Imperial Japanese Navy jumped on the chance to take out a flattop with a lone destroyer as an escort.

Over sixty enemy planes in three waves came hunting the two ships. After Pearl Harbor, NEOSHO was fitted with 8 twenty-millimeter anti-aircraft guns. She was going to need them today. Both ships put up an enormous amount of anti-aircraft fire; enough to keep the attackers at bay for a while. In fact, the first two waves did no damage. NEOSHO's gun crews brought down three dive-bombers. One crew got a bomber in its sights as the plane dove on NEOSHO. The plane got closer and closer but the crew held their fire until it was almost at point blank range. Only then did they shoot, hitting the enemy plane, which disintegrated.

Below decks Bill Leu was in the Number One magazine. Unlike Pearl Harbor where he was above deck and could see the battle raging around him, this time he could only listen and feel the battle. Over his headphones he could hear other crewmen calling out the location of enemy planes. He could also feel the vibrations in his body as the concussion of near misses pulsed through the deck and bulkhead. He could also tell when one of the bombs found its target. The ship would jump and he could tell she'd been hit. Leu felt his ship, the only ship he'd ever served on, get hit seven times that morning. The NEOSHO severely damaged an enemy plane that then deliberately crashed into the aft superstructure.

Damage parties were swarming throughout NEOSHO trying to save the ship. Heading one of those parties was Chief Watertender Oscar Verner Peterson who had already been severely injured. Down in the bowels of NEOSHO Peterson and his party struggled to make the ship watertight and, as much as possible to contain the fires raging on the ship. Injuries decimated his team and Peterson continued on with the men he had left, but it was Peterson himself who closed valves in fiery compartments to maintain watertight integrity. His efforts cost him dearly as he incurred severe burns.

When the planes left and the battle was over NEOSHO was heavily damaged and on fire, but she was in far better shape than her escort. The destroyer SIMS had been sunk with the loss of 237 men. There were only 15 survivors. NEOSHO had 20 dead.

The oiler began to list so badly that the starboard rails were underwater. Afraid that his ship might capsize and sink at any minute, Commander Phillips gave the order to abandon ship. Life rafts, whaleboats and men went into the sea. Some of the men who jumped in drowned and some of the life rafts eventually drifted away and they and the men on them were never seen again.

The following morning a minor miracle was revealed to Phillips and his crew: NEOSHO was still afloat. The efforts of Chief Peterson had paid off and possibly prevented the ship from sinking. Phillips and his crew re-boarded the ship even though its deck was canted at an extremely precarious thirty-degree angle. For the next three days the oil-soaked crew stayed aboard the crippled NEOSHO. A PBY Catalina flew over the drifting wreck on the 10th and radioed for help, which arrived the following day in the form of USS HENLEY, DD-391.

Bill Leu survived the battle and abandoning ship. He, along with the 123 other survivors of both NEOSHO and SIMS, were passed over to

HENLEY where medical services were given to the injured. Several days later, as a result of his severe burns, Chief Peterson lost his life, but his actions earned him the gratitude of his shipmates and a Medal of Honor.

It was determined that NEOSHO was a total loss and there was nothing left to do but scuttle her. Reluctantly HENLEY fired two torpedoes at the oiler to finish her off. The first torpedo was a dud. The second one failed to do enough damage to sink her. NEOSHO just refused to die. Not wanting to use any more torpedoes, HENLEY's skipper ordered the main batteries to administer the coup de grâce. Even at point blank range it took 146 five-inch shells to finally end her life.

Only those who have served on board a ship, particularly a naval vessel or a warship in time of conflict can ever really understand the relationship between a ship and her crew. Like any relationship, bonds become stronger and closer the more hardship and trials you go through together. It is true for the camaraderie of the crew and perhaps even more so for the love of the ship. Out in the vastness of the ocean your ship, no matter how big it is, can seem very tiny indeed and in time of peril your entire world is that ship and your life depends on her. She is your mother. The close quarters create a personal and intimate environment, which cannot be avoided, and your crewmates become your brothers.

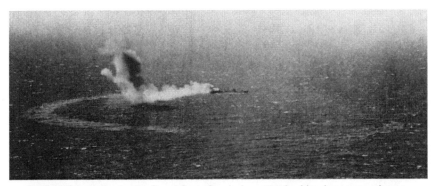

NEOSHO burning in the Coral Sea after being attacked by Japanese planes.

It should not be a surprise then that as the crew of NEOSHO stood on the deck of HENLEY and watched their gallant and valiant ship slipping beneath the waves, these grown men, these sailors against the sea and an enemy, had waves of emotion wash over them. It didn't matter that she wasn't a sleek cruiser or bold battleship or a mountainous aircraft carrier. She was just an oiler, a tanker that transported gas from place to place and quenched the thirst of dry ships. But she was their mother and their home and they would never see her again and she was taking their brothers with her. The men of NEOSHO watched the Pacific swallow her and they cried. They cried for the loss of their crewmates. They cried for the loss of their ship.

USS Nevada

NEVADA CLASS BATTLESHIP
BB-36
LAUNCHED: 1914

DECEMBER 7, 1941

Edward D. Taussig was born in 1847, graduated from the United States Naval Academy at Annapolis in 1867 and died in 1921. He was the captain of a gunboat during the Spanish-American War and retired a Rear Admiral. Joseph K. Taussig was his son. He was born in 1877, graduated from Annapolis in 1899 and died in 1947. He also fought in the Spanish-American War. In World War I he was in command of the first Destroyer Division to report to Europe. His son was Joseph K. Taussig, Junior. He was born in 1920 and was a graduate from Annapolis in the class of 1941.

On this day, Ensign Taussig, who had the good looks of a Hollywood matinee idol, was the Officer of the Deck, (OOD). His regular assigned duty was as the junior gunnery officer in command of the starboard anti-aircraft guns. As OOD his first job of the day was to supervise the raising of the flag on the fantail. After that he would man the gangway and oversee the release of men going on Sunday liberty.

The appearance of Japanese planes disturbed the solemnity of the observance of morning colors. As war broke out around him Taussig raced to his battle station in the starboard anti-aircraft director, five decks up in the superstructure. His job was to coordinate anti-aircraft fire against the attacking planes. NEVADA responded splendidly. Four of her .50 caliber machine guns were already manned when the attack began and the rest of her batteries were manned and firing within minutes. This rapid response almost assuredly had a direct effect on her lack of torpedo damage. In the early moments of the attack a lone torpedo struck the battleship's port bow. In that same time period the .50 calibers and the five-inch guns of NEVADA literally blew out of the sky two "Kate" torpedo planes before they could let loose their torpedoes on her.

On the machine gun platform of the forward mast, Marine Gunnery Sergeant Charles E. Douglas and the men under his command were also doing excellent work. They shot down or helped to shoot down at least three more enemy planes.

In the heart of the battle, NEVADA and her crew were the subject of bombing and strafing runs. Only minutes into the raid a single round from a Japanese machine gun struck Ens. Taussig. The hot metal hit him with amazing force. The blast mangled his left leg to such an extent that his left foot, still attached to his leg, was flung upwards and came to rest underneath his left armpit. Sailors under his command saw his severe injuries and offered to take him to safety and medical aid. Taussig refused and continued directing anti-aircraft fire from his position.

On the forward gun platform Gunnery Sergeant Douglas had his own problems. A bomb hit had knocked out the pumps that supplied water to his water-cooled .50 caliber machine guns. Fires were raging around the superstructure beneath him and making the situation very hot indeed.

In the military, the immediate carrying out of orders is something that is so ingrained into personnel it comes as naturally as breathing. It isn't second nature; it is first nature. If you are ordered to "Man that gun!" you man the gun. If you are ordered to "Save that life!" you save that life. That is, unless, a war has just started and the orders you receive contradict your best judgment and what you know to be right.

Boatswain's Mate 1st Class Robert Norman literally went through fire to get to Ens. Taussig at the gun director. Norman's uniform caught on fire on his way there. Once there he arranged for a cot to be brought to the wounded, but still fighting, Ensign. Norman had a tremendous concern for Taussig's well-being and survivability if his wounds went untreated. He told the young Ensign that he was going to get him to medical care. At that time Taussig gave him a direct order to leave him alone. Norman with great reluctance told the ensign that he was not going to obey that particular order. Fires below their station prevented the removal of Taussig by conventional means. Norman rigged the ensign's cot with ropes and got him lowered to the boat deck below, all the while enemy bullets pinged around him on the steel deck.

On the .50 caliber gun platform, Gunnery Sergeant Douglas and his men were ordered to abandon their battle station due to the fire beneath them and their impaired weapons. The Gunnery Sergeant ignored that order. Douglas and his men continued to fire their guns. They fired them in the face of the flames that rose and licked at the deck they stood on. And they fired them until the guns overheated from lack of water and froze up. Then and only then did Douglas and his men leave their post.

By this time the USS ARIZONA, BB-39, berthed directly in front of NEVADA, had blown up and the flaming oil it discharged was threatening NEVADA. High in the wheelhouse was Chief Quartermaster Robert Sedberry, who had already signaled the engine room to fire up the boilers and prepare for getting underway. Tugboats that would normally assist the huge battlewagon out of her berth were unavailable, so Sedberry had to do it alone. He had been in the Navy for seventeen years, all of them spent on NEVADA. There wasn't a sailor or officer on board who knew the ship better than he did. With the magic of some magnificent engine orders, rudder movement, and line handling Sedberry got the 583-foot long giant away from the quays, away from the burning battleships and out into the south channel.

As NEVADA headed down the South Channel and sought the safety of the open sea, every eye in Pearl Harbor fixed on her. This bold act of defiance gave hope to every beleaguered American sailor who saw it - and they all saw it. As NEVADA made her sortie, cheers could be heard from every ship in the harbor. It was as if, there in that moment, NEVADA encapsulated the one-hour-old war for everyone there: an initial blow followed by determined resourcefulness. On fire, smoking, slightly down by the head and with guns blazing, she was a glorious and inspiring sight. Everyone that witnessed it would remember that scene till the end of their days.

From several thousand feet up, the Japanese also spotted NEVADA making her run. Planes of the second wave were just arriving and the moving battleship was an inviting and very obvious target. The pilots realized that their chance to bottle up the harbor was at hand. Sinking her in the South Channel would certainly cause serious problems for the remaining American fleet. However, if they could sink her in the entrance channel, Pearl Harbor would be at a standstill for weeks, perhaps even months.

Chief Sedberry now had to perform some intricate and difficult helmsmenship. Sticking out into the middle of the South Channel was a dredge with a pipeline attached that snaked back to Ford Island. This left only a narrow bit of channel available for Sedberry to maneuver through, which he did, exhibiting superb seamanship.

NEVADA, center, makes her run for freedom down the South Channel. The dredge pipeline that she had to dodge runs through the middle of the photo and the minesweeper, AVOCET, is at the Ford Island pier in the foreground.

The dive-bombers of the Japanese second wave had their way with NEVADA. Previously hit by at least two bombs before her sortie, they hit her now with at least four more. The battleship also had to run a gauntlet of countless near misses that damaged her hull below the waterline. On board, the anti-aircraft crews kept up a steady defensive fire, possibly downing another three planes. Between the bombs and the strafing, the majority of casualties suffered by NEVADA were above deck by those anti-aircraft crews. In a testament to their determination and character, the guns on NEVADA were never silenced. Every time a sailor fell, dead or wounded, another stepped up to take his place. From the first bomb to the last, NEVADA never stopped shooting.

The harbor control tower saw that NEVADA was badly wounded and ordered her to beach herself in order not to block the channel. Chief Sedberry nosed the great ship over and grounded her at Hospital Point near the turn into the main channel. It was later deemed necessary to move NEVADA from there and two tugboats pushed her across the channel to the waters just off the cane fields of Waipio Peninsula. There she slowly settled on the shallow bottom, burning and filling with water.

By the time Captain Francis W. Scanland got on board the battle was over. He reported 50 dead and 109 wounded. He also stated that, *"The damage, while considerable, should be capable of speedy repairs once the ship is afloat and alongside a dock in the Navy Yard."*

Ensign Taussig spent the entire war in hospitals. In April 1946 his left leg was amputated at the knee. Three days later he was placed back on active duty. For his inspirational actions as gunnery officer while severely wounded he was awarded the Navy Cross.

THE WAR

The fires continued to burn through Monday. The Navy wasted no time. Literally, before the smoke cleared, the first team reported aboard to inspect her damage and make recommendations on her salvage. With cleaning up, patching up, and pumping out, NEVADA was slowly resurrected. She remained off Waipio Point for two months and was moved to Dry Dock #2 in the Navy Yard on February 18, 1942. There she underwent the minimum repairs needed to get her back to the States. In April she left Pearl Harbor for Puget Sound Navy Yard in Washington. Her rebuild and modernization took place there through October. When completed her appearance had been drastically altered.

After a shakedown cruise and training along the coast of California she headed for her first post repair mission in the frozen Aleutians in the North Pacific. There she blasted enemy positions during the May 1943 landings on the island of Attu. After a short one-month stay she headed for more modernization, this time to the East Coast at the huge naval base at Norfolk, Virginia.

Her further modernization completed, NEVADA was assigned to the Atlantic fleet and began escorting convoys to Europe. These duties continued until early 1944 when she was sent to England to prepare for Operation Overlord, the invasion of France.

NEVADA, here off Utah Beach on June 6, 1944, was the only Pearl Harbor ship to be in the Normandy invasion.

In the early morning hours of June 6, 1944 NEVADA unleashed the power of her fourteen-inch guns on the German defenses off Utah Beach. Some of her targets were as far inland as seven miles. When the landings began her guns protected the landing craft as they approached the beach. When she fired her main batteries, the soldiers in the Higgins boats cheered.

Two months later NEVADA participated in Operation Dragoon, the invasion of Southern France. Here she fired over 5,000 rounds and helped to destroy the fortress on the Isle Saint Mandrier in the Port of Toulon. On August 23rd NEVADA, along with other ships, took part in a six and a half hour long slugfest with the guns on Saint Mandrier. The fortress finally fell on the 28th.

After the two invasions in France, NEVADA was reassigned to the Pacific Fleet. She returned there in time for the invasion of Iwo Jima in February 1945. She followed that up by taking part in the invasion of Okinawa. American ships there were subjected to almost daily attack by Japanese kamikaze planes.

On March 27, 1945, Les Coe, a sailor who had been on NEVADA continually since before Pearl Harbor, was at his battle station high in the superstructure. Like most days before, the kamikazes came, one heading directly for NEVADA. The screening ships and NEVADA put up a wall of anti-aircraft fire, but this one plane was undeterred. It was heading straight for Coe and he knew his time had come. His eyes locked onto the plane as it came closer and closer still. When a mere 600 feet away the anti-aircraft fire took effect and one of the attacker's wings was blown off, sending it into a crazy spin. The plane plowed forward and missed Coe's position by fifteen feet. It hit behind him near turret #3 damaging the fourteen-inch guns and killing eleven.

NEVADA sailed to Pearl Harbor for repairs then returned to the Pacific for the closing months of the war.

FATE

After some minor occupation duties in Japan, NEVADA returned to Pearl Harbor where she was prepared for her next and final mission. She was the ship chosen as the main target, "ground zero," for the Operation Crossroads atomic bomb tests. That very special place required a very special paint job. In order to give the bombardier a clear and distinct target she was painted a very un-Navy red-orange.

On July 1, 1946 a B-29 Superfortress named *Dave's Dream* dropped an atomic bomb with a 23 kiloton yield over the target fleet. The bomb detonated 520 feet above sea level. NEVADA, as it turned out, was not ground zero. The bomb was off target by almost half a mile. Still, NEVADA suffered some damage. On July 24th the second test, "Baker" was completed when another bomb was detonated beneath the surface of Bikini Lagoon. NEVADA survived that blast too. The atomic battleship was returned to Pearl Harbor to study what effects both the blasts and the radiation had on her.

Her useful life was deemed complete two years later and she was taken out for target practice. Once again NEVADA was the target. This time the shooters did not miss. However NEVADA stubbornly refused to sink. In an ironic act it was American airplanes firing torpedoes that finally sank her, something Japanese torpedoes tried to do seven years earlier. The gallant and tired lady went down some sixty miles south west of O'ahu on July 31, 1948.

*　　　　*　　　　*　　　　*　　　　*

Joseph Taussig retired from the Navy in 1954. When he retired at age 34, he was the youngest Captain in the Navy. He continued serving his country and saving lives by working at the Pentagon as the Assistant Deputy Undersecretary of the Navy for Safety and Survivability. He passed away in 1999. Both his son and grandson carried on the Taussig family tradition and graduated from the United States Naval Academy.

Robert Norman, the Boatswain's Mate that helped to save Taussig's life stayed in the Navy also and retired as a Captain in 1973 after 36½ years of service. Captain Taussig never felt Norman had received proper recognition for coming through fire and dodging enemy bullets in order to save his life. Based largely on a letter-writing campaign from the well-respected Taussig, Robert Norman was awarded the Silver Star for his actions. On April 8, 1998, at the age of 79, fifty-seven years after Pearl Harbor, Norman received his medal in a ceremony at the Naval Academy at Annapolis.

USS New Orleans

NEW ORLEANS CLASS HEAVY CRUISER
CA-32
LAUNCHED: 1933

DECEMBER 7, 1941

Of the seven cruisers that were in Pearl Harbor that Sunday morning, four of them were in the Navy Yard undergoing some form of overhaul or modification. NEW ORLEANS was at Berth 16 having her engines repaired. All power was being supplied from the dock.

At the beginning of the raid, rifles and pistols were issued to some crewmen who stood on the fantail and fired at the green colored "Kates" making their torpedo runs on Battleship row. The enemy planes were at eye level of the sailors and not more than a few hundred feet away.

Below decks, Fire Controlman 2nd Class Arthur J. Morsch hadn't even been to breakfast when he heard the explosions outside the ship. He answered the call to general quarters and quickly ran up the ladder to the boat deck. When he arrived he was greeted with the sight of a Japanese plane flying by and dropping a bomb. It then circled around and commenced a strafing run on NEW ORLEANS. Morsch stood there transfixed by the sight. He saw the flash of gunfire from the plane and he heard the bullets hitting the metal deck beneath his feet. When the plane zoomed past he came alive and headed for his battle station as a pointer for the ship's main eight-inch guns. Since the big guns were useless in this situation he was sent back below to help hand carry five-inch shells to the secondary guns.

Fifteen minutes into the attack, all the anti-aircraft guns on NEW ORLEANS were firing. A group of "Val" dive-bombers came at the yard and the ships docked there. All the ships fired back and clearly hit some of the planes. The ferocity of the anti-aircraft fire drove most of the planes off to seek weaker prey. A few planes dropped their bombs. One of them hit the water near NEW ORLEANS and exploded, peppering the ship with shrapnel.

Shortly after the onset of the raid, all power stopped from the dock and the interior spaces became black, metal caverns. Electrically powered machinery, including the ammunition hoists, came to a stop. All work was done by hand and illuminated by flashlight. To get ordinance to the guns above deck, human chains were formed and the shells were passed from man to man up the line.

The ship's chaplain, Lieutenant (jg) Howell M. Forgy, was at his battle station in sickbay. Seeing the labors of the men and feeling his calling, he felt that some spiritual help and encouragement was needed. So he walked down the passageway patting the sailors on the back saying as he went, "Praise the Lord and pass the ammunition."[38] It seemed to help.

Although her guns damaged enemy aircraft, the captain, Commander James G. Atkins, claimed no kills in his after action report. He also noted that other than the minor holes in the hull from bomb fragments and a severed fuel line on deck, there was no damage to the ship nor were there any casualties.

THE WAR

Only days after the attack, the engines in NEW ORLEANS were running once again. She escorted a convoy to Johnston Atoll and Palmyra Island south of Hawai'i. Once that mission was completed she sailed east to Mare Island for more thorough work on her power plant. By February 1942 she was back in Pearl Harbor and commenced convoy escort duties to Australia.

---

38 The story of Chaplin Forgy eventually made its way to songwriter Frank Loesser who, in 1942, wrote the song *Praise the Lord and Pass the Ammunition*. The tune became an American anthem for the war and a number one hit for bandleader Kay Kyser in 1943.

In early May NEW ORLEANS was assigned to the attack group of Task Force 17, which had been given the mission of stopping further Japanese expansion. The enemy intended to extend its reach in the South Pacific by taking Tulagi in the Solomon Islands and Port Moresby on New Guinea. On May 2nd the Japanese successfully landed on Tulagi.

On May 7th, the Battle of the Coral Sea was joined between the two opposing fleets in the first major sea engagement of the Pacific war. It was also the first sea battle primarily fought between aircraft carriers and ships that never actually saw each other. NEW ORLEANS, in what proved to be a learning experience, provided anti-aircraft support for the aircraft carrier, USS LEXINGTON, CV-2.

The following day, Friday May 8th, the Japanese put in an all-out effort to sink LEXINGTON. Carriers had been the priority targets for the Japanese at Pearl Harbor and there had been none present so they were anxious to finally get one. At 0930, NEW ORLEANS received word of inbound enemy aircraft. Every ten to fifteen minutes, updates on the progress of the Japanese aerial armada came in via radio. Finally at 1114 the planes arrived and commenced their attack on LEXINGTON. All other ships were ignored. LEXINGTON was their target. Every gun onboard the cruiser leapt into action to protect the carrier. They continued firing without stopping for the next twenty minutes.

Like hungry locusts, dive-bombers and torpedo planes descended on the carrier. So many planes flew past NEW ORLEANS that central fire control was almost impossible and most batteries fired on their own volition as targets entered their field of fire.

The Japanese efforts were too intense, too dedicated to their goal and no amount of anti-aircraft fire was going to save LEXINGTON. Two torpedoes and two bombs had hit the carrier, crippling her. She was scuttled by the end of the day. Even though LEXINGTON was lost, the Imperial Japanese Navy and the twelve transports filled with invasion troops were turned back. Port Moresby was saved.

NEW ORLEANS played an integral part in rescuing almost 600 hundred sailors from LEXINGTON. The cruiser sent her boats close enough to the flaming carrier that the danger from flying debris was very real.

The preceding carrier-to-carrier battle, fought with soaring planes was something totally new to warfare. Commander Atkins wrote a multi-page after action report with detailed comments and recommendations on tactics and operations for this new way to fight a war at sea. He noted a large amount of friendly fire that threatened his vessel. He discussed everything from differentiating enemy from friendly planes and maintaining adequate quantities of anti-aircraft ammunition, to better and more intense anti-aircraft training for gunners and keeping closer distances between the carrier and screening vessels.

The following month, NEW ORLEANS screened another aircraft carrier, USS ENTERPRISE, CV-6, at the Battle of Midway. The cruiser was more successful at her screening duties this time, as ENTERPRISE came through the struggle virtually untouched.

On November 30, 1942, the United States Navy met the Imperial Japanese Navy during a night action on the waters between Guadalcanal and Savo Island. This was the fourth time in as many months that this happened. In the Battle of Tassafaronga an inferior enemy force once again mauled a superior American force.

The scenario here was not much different from prior ones. The Tokyo Express, this time consisting of eight destroyers, was on its way to resupply Japanese forces on Guadalcanal. An American force of five cruisers and four destroyers intercepted it. The Americans detected the enemy ships on radar at 2314. They opened fire with torpedoes at 2320 and with guns one minute later. The guns put one of the Japanese destroyers out of the battle almost immediately. All the American torpedoes failed to hit anything. After that the Japanese responded.

The enemy destroyers set loose on the American column a total of 44 torpedoes in the space of about ten minutes. Before the last Japanese torpedo was fired, the first ones started to hit. At 2327 two of them slammed into the cruiser USS MINNEAPOLIS, CA-36. One blew her bow off and took her out of the fight. Seconds later another hit NEW ORLEANS in the bow, which folded back and was ripped off the hull by the force of her momentum through the ocean. Two American cruisers were now out of action. Minutes later, the third victim of the Japanese torpedoes, the cruiser USS PENSACOLA, CA-24, was hit amidships. Finally the cruiser USS NORTHHAMPTON, CA-26, was hit on the port side by two more torpedoes. She sank several hours later.

NEW ORLEANS crawled back to Tulagi at reduced speed. She lost 183 men in the attack. Her forward 150 feet, fully one quarter of the ship's length, was now at the bottom of Ironbottom Sound. After emergency repairs were made she sailed for Australia where temporary repairs were performed that would allow her to sail to America. She spent over three months in Sydney before leaving for Puget Sound Naval Yard in March 1943. Once in

NEW ORLEANS in Tulagi harbor the day after she lost her bow to an enemy torpedo at the Battle of Tassafaronga.

Washington she underwent a stem-to-stern overhaul. She didn't return to the war until August 1943.

The remainder of 1943 and all of 1944 was spent slogging across the Pacific from invasion to invasion and from bombardment to bombardment. She participated in the invasions of Hollandia, Guam and Mindoro, and shelled Satawan, Saipan and Tinian.

On Saturday, April 22, 1944 NEW ORLEANS was screening the carrier USS YORKTOWNN, CV-10, then conducting operations against Wakde Island off New Guinea. At 0516 a TBF-Avenger Torpedo plane piloted by Ensign Owen H. Ramey that had taken off from YORKTOWN crashed into the foremast of NEW ORLEANS. The plane was ripped open and rained fuel down on the cruiser. The Avenger plunged into the ocean with no survivors. NEW ORLEANS suffered one killed and one wounded.

In January 1945 she sailed to Mare Island for overhaul. She returned to the Pacific via Pearl Harbor in April. She then sailed to Ulithi and then on to Okinawa. There she provided call fire as needed. She was in Subic Bay, the Philippines, when the Japanese surrendered.

FATE

After some occupation duties in Japan, Korea and China, NEW ORLEANS made two round trips from the Pacific theater to the United States with returning veterans. After that she was sent to the Philadelphia Navy Yard arriving in March 1946. She was decommissioned there on February 10, 1947. NEW ORLEANS was held in reserve for over twelve years. In 1959 she was sold for scrap to the Boston Metals Company of Baltimore, Maryland.

*   *   *   *   *

In the fast-moving world of warfare, advancement can occur at a whirlwind pace. On December 7, 1941, Arthur J. Morsch had been in the Navy four years. He was a Fire Controlman 2nd Class, an enlisted man. When he retired from the Navy sixteen years later, after twenty years service, he was a Rear Admiral. He then spent another twenty years in government service retiring as a Magistrate from the Federal Court System. He passed away in February 2011.

Nihoa

HARBOR FERRYBOAT
YFB-17
LAUNCHED: 1941

DECEMBER 7, 1941

Of all the Pearl Harbor ships, NIHOA is unique in that she was actually built right there at the Pearl Harbor Navy Yard. She was also the youngest ship there. Her keel was laid down in April of 1941 and she was delivered to the Navy on November 7, 1941, exactly one month before the Japanese attack.

NIHOA was in the center of the harbor when the attack began. She managed to dodge all the bombs, bullets and torpedoes and dock safely.

THE WAR

Like her sister ferry, MANUWAI, NIHOA and her crew of five spent the entire war carrying people and vehicles from the Navy base to Ford Island.

FATE

NIHOA ended her Navy career in the same place that it started: Pearl Harbor. Very few naval vessels have the life that NIHOA did. Most are built then move on to travels across oceans, if not across the world. They often times perform tasks that they weren't necessarily designed for. But NIHOA was built for a specific purpose and performed that service in her own little world for her entire twenty-year career.

NIHOA was stricken from the Navy roles in April 1961 and later sold to a private party.

Nokomis

FLEET TUG
YT-142
LAUNCHED: 1939

DECEMBER 7, 1941

Just like her sister tugs in Pearl Harbor, NOKOMIS was an "in service" craft owned and operated by the U. S. Navy. She was never a commissioned vessel and therefore did not have the designation of a "United States Ship", (USS).

She was berthed at the Yard Craft Dock in the Navy Yard when the attack began. Venturing out into the harbor she rescued sailors from the burning waters of the harbor and moved from ship to ship fighting fires. She found her way to Hospital Point and joined with the

NOKOMIS just off Ford Island, fights the oil fires around USS CALIFORNIA on the morning of December 7, 1941.

tug HOGA in helping to beach USS NEVADA, BB-36 and prevent her from sinking in the main channel.

THE WAR

Like many other yard craft, NOKOMIS spent the entire war at Pearl Harbor. There she served the ever-growing number of warships that passed through on their way to pushing the Japanese off of their Pacific strongholds and back to their home islands.

FATE

NOKOMIS remained at Pearl Harbor for thirty years after the end of the war. She was turned over to the Defense Reutilization and Marketing Service who in turn sold her to the Crowley Maritime Corporation in September 1974. Renamed *Sea Serpent,* she plied the waters of San Francisco Bay for another twenty years. In a strange coincidence, NOKOMIS once again teamed up with HOGA, which was on loan to the city of Oakland, California just across the bay. In 1984, piers 30 and 32 on the San Francisco waterfront caught fire and an enormous conflagration followed. The two Pearl Harbor sisters joined together once again to fight the fire. She was abandoned in 1994 and left a derelict. She was acquired in 2002 by a private organization with the intention of restoring her. Those efforts failed and NOKOMIS was demolished in Alameda, California in August 2010.

USS Oglala

MINELAYER
CM-4
LAUNCHED: 1907

DECEMBER 7, 1941

Don Rodenberger had joined the Navy in 1939, not to see the world, but, in order to learn music. So it was with great satisfaction that the 21 year-old went to sleep two years later, on the evening of December 6, 1941. The crewmen of USS SACRAMENTO, PG-19, just recently returned from China, put on a show that evening for fellow sailors and Rodenberger played his brand new saxophone in the orchestra. Because the show kept him up later than usual he was given the privilege of sleeping in late.

His alarm clock that Sunday morning was a Japanese torpedo that literally tossed him out of bed. One of the first torpedoes dropped by the enemy that day was aimed right at OGLALA. However, several days before, OGLALA had unloaded all of her mines at the ammunition dock in West Loch. As a result she was riding very high in the water and the torpedo passed under her and hit USS HELENA, CL-50, which was inboard of her at their 1010 dock berths. Even though it was HELENA that was hit, the resulting underwater shock wave ruptured OGLALA's hull. The warm blue waters of Pearl Harbor rushed into the ship.

Only minutes later a Japanese bomb missed both OGLALA and HELENA and fell in the narrow eight-foot gap between the two of them. The bomb detonated in almost the exact same place as the torpedo only increasing the previously inflicted damage. Within a very short time OGLALA began to list to port. The fire room and the engine room were flooding rapidly. Without them, there was no power onboard and without power the pumps couldn't work and without pumps the flooding couldn't be stopped. OGLALA was going to sink.

The capsized USS OGLALA along 1010 dock shortly after the conclusion of the attack.

Harold Burns, a 19 year-old Fireman 1st Class, made his way to the dock still not quite understanding exactly what was going on. The situation soon became abundantly clear to him. He looked up to see a plane with the red Japanese "meatball" on the underside of the wing coming straight at him, strafing the dock. Burns dove for what limited cover there was. As he did he could see the pilot's face, smiling.

The decision was quickly made to move OGLALA and tie her up directly to 1010 dock. Doing that would, at the same time, free up HELENA, which was trapped between the dock and OGLALA. Two tugs were brought in and towed OGLALA astern of the cruiser and she was made fast to the pier. By this time however, nothing could be done to save her. The laws of physics slowly took over and inch-by-inch, degree-by-degree the minesweeper heeled to port. The order to abandon ship was given.

Right before 1000, just as the last Japanese planes cleared the skies over the harbor, OGLALA came to rest on her port side along 1010 dock. When she went down she took Don Rodenberger's new saxophone with her.

THE WAR

Most of OGLALA's crew were soon dispersed throughout the fleet. Harold Burns was assigned to the destroyer USS MUGFORD, DD-389. A few others, like Don Rodenberger, remained to help with her salvage.

Like other ships that had been sunk that day, OGLALA was initially written off as a total loss. Later review convinced the Navy that she could be raised, repaired and reborn. The early months of 1942 were spent preparing for her resurrection. Parts of her fell under the welder's torch, sealing hatches and closing cracks in the hull. Other parts of her, like her superstructure, came under cutting torches in order to make her refloating easier.

In early April 1942, after two attempts, OGLALA was righted. She was still mostly underwater, but at least she wasn't on her side anymore. The next three months were occupied with the plans and work needed to ready her for refloating. Close to 2000 hours of dive time were expended in the preparation. Enormous wooden cofferdams were constructed and attached to her to aid in raising her. Finally on June 23rd the pumps were turned on and she slowly rose to the surface. Once raised, Don Rodenberger ventured below decks in search of his saxophone. He found it. It was in need of repair, too.

Still not watertight, pumps were kept running to keep her afloat. Unfortunately, on the 25th, one of the pumps malfunctioned and OGLALA sank once again. She was refloated four days later and unbelievably, sank again when a cofferdam failed allowing water to rush in. She was raised one last time and finally brought into Pearl Harbor's Dry Dock #2. The rest of 1942 was spent making OGLALA seaworthy enough to make the voyage back to the United States.

Work was completed on her and, in December 1942, she set sail under her own power for California in order to continue her repairs. There she was reincarnated once again. OGLALA was originally built as MASSACHUSETTS in 1907. Purchased by the Navy in 1917 she was renamed USS SHAWMUT in 1918 and converted to an Aviation Tender after World War I. She then was converted to a minelayer in 1920 and finally renamed OGLALA in 1928. The 1943 – 44 rebuild converted her again, this time to an Internal Combustion Engine Repair Ship, ARG-1. She was recommissioned in February 1944.

She was one of the last of the Pearl Harbor ships that had been sunk to return to the fleet. In April 1944, OGLALA made her way to New Guinea to ply her new trade of repairing internal combustion engines. She stayed there until December when she sailed to Leyte in the Philippines, which is where she was when the war ended.

FATE

OGLALA stayed in the Pacific for a few more months and returned to California in early 1946. She was decommissioned February 11th of that year. The next day she was stricken from the Navy rolls and turned over to the Maritime Commission which sold her in 1965.

Young Harold Burns, the sailor who was strafed on the dock on December 7th and then sent to the destroyer MUGFORD, was later transferred to the vehicle landing ship, USS OZARK, LSV-2. As a result, Burns became a member of that rather exclusive club of people who were there at the beginning of the war in Pearl Harbor and who witnessed the end. OZARK and Burns were present in Tokyo Bay on September 2, 1945 when the Japanese signed the surrender.

Scrapping USS OGLALA at Joffe Brothers Shipbreaking Yard, Richmond, California in December 1965

*　　　　*　　　　*　　　　*　　　　*

Don Rodenberger, who learned to play music in the Navy, continued to do so after the war. He had the saxophone that he recovered from OGLALA repaired. He played it in different bands until the year 2000 when he stopped playing because of a stroke.

USS Ontario

SONOMA CLASS TUG
AT-13
LAUNCHED: 1912

DECEMBER 7, 1941

Small ships, like tugboats, often have only one officer assigned to them. Duties on other ships that would normally be assigned to junior officers are given to senior enlisted men. That is why, when the Japanese raid commenced, the Executive Officer in command of ONTARIO was Chief Boatswains Mate J. C. Hale.

ONTARIO was in a tough spot that Sunday morning. Her main battery, a single three-inch gun, had been removed as part of the overhaul she was undergoing at Berth 18 in the Repair Basin. She was one of the last coal burning ships in the Navy and was being converted to burn oil. Her engine had also been disabled. So ONTARIO couldn't run and she couldn't hide. The only thing she could do was sit there. However, she did have on board one .30-caliber Lewis machine gun, twelve Springfield rifles and six .45 caliber Colt automatic pistols. Oh yes, she also had some very brave and determined sailors to stand behind those weapons.

As Japanese planes were screaming overhead, Chief Hale issued the small arms to his deck crew and sent others to get ammunition from the minelayer, USS SICARD, DM-21, which was berthed next to them. There were no helmets on board. Those crewmen not engaging the enemy were ordered below decks to wait out the attack in order to avoid injury from bullets and flying shrapnel.

ONTARIO was certainly an interesting, if not inspiring, sight. Helmetless sailors, standing totally exposed on deck, firing a lone, light machine gun, a dozen rifles and a few handguns at a determined enemy, who was dropping bombs all around them. I'm sure if you asked, none of them would use adjectives like brave or courageous to describe themselves or their actions that morning on the deck of the tug. However, E. C. Mayer, the commanding officer did. In his After Action Report, Mayer stated, *"Those who manned the small arms and remained exposed, firing upon low flying aircraft, exhibited willing personal bravery."*

THE WAR

ONTARIO remained in the Navy Yard until her conversion was complete. She was then assigned to Pearl Harbor as a yard tug and stayed there until late 1943 performing basic yard duties and towing target sleds and wrangling practice torpedoes.

In 1943, ONTARIO headed further out into the Pacific Ocean to support the fleet. Her jobs were varied. She performed simple jobs like laying buoys in harbors or marking channels, and more standard jobs that involved moving or towing other ships and barges. She often towed large barges of up to 10,000 tons made of concrete and manhandled battleships at anchor. In October 1944 she towed USS MONTGOMERY, DMS-17, to Ulithi after the minesweeper ironically struck a mine. Due to her age, these heavier jobs put a strain on her hull and she would often have to put a man over the side to weld cracks that appeared in her outer plates. In July 1945 ONTARIO was involved in the search for USS INDIANAPOLIS, CA-35, which had been sunk by a Japanese submarine after delivering the Hiroshima atomic bomb to Tinian.

FATE

In August 1945, ONTARIO made her way via Eniwetok, Pearl Harbor, and San Diego to her final assignment in Long Beach, California where she worked as a yard tug. She remained there until she was decommissioned in June 1946. She was sold in 1947 to a man in California.

Osceola

HARBOR TUG
YT-129
LAUNCHED: 1938

DECEMBER 7, 1941

OSCEOLA was docked at the yard craft pier in the Navy Yard and certainly accompanied the other tugboats and yard craft in assisting in any way she could with saving the men and ships of Pearl Harbor during and after the attack.

THE WAR

OSCEOLA spent the entire war at Pearl Harbor, performing the all too necessary but very unglamorous task of a harbor tug. It was her job to skillfully push and pull massive aircraft carriers and battleships into and out of their berths in the harbor. Her services as a towing vessel and fire fighting ship were used as needed.

FATE

Unlike the vast majority of her Pearl Harbor sisters, OSCEOLA was not rushed off to the scrap yard after the war. In fact she spent her entire lifetime at Pearl Harbor, reporting in 1938 and remaining there, diligently performing her duties for 35 years, until she was sold in 1973 to be scrapped.

USS Patterson

BAGLEY CLASS DESTROYER
DD-392
LAUNCHED: 1937

DECEMBER 7, 1941

Breakfast was over. Below decks in the main galley Clarence Cleaver was lazily cleaning the mess hall. Just before 0800 three events took place in rapid succession - very distinct heavy vibrations accompanied by muffled explosions were felt and heard through the hull of the ship. Secondly, general quarters was sounded over the ship's speakers followed quickly by the third event, the announcement over the PA that this was no drill.

Cleaver dropped what he was doing and dashed to his battle station, the fire control director above the bridge, high in the superstructure. When he arrived he discovered that someone else had beaten him to it so he stepped out onto the open wing to observe the attack. He saw planes flying so close to him he found himself looking for something to throw at them. But below him, in the No. 2 five-inch gun, they certainly had something to throw. Cleaver looked just as the gun fired and he saw the shell sail out of the barrel and score a direct hit on an enemy plane, which immediately disintegrated, falling into the harbor in pieces. According to Lieutenant Albert White, the senior officer in command, anti-aircraft fire put up by PATTERSON was *"vigorous and spirited."*[39]

PATTERSON was underway and headed out of the harbor less then an hour after the attack began and while it still raged. As she raced down the channel, enemy bombs fell around her and the other ships that

---

39   USS Patterson after action report dated December 12, 1941.

were making a sortie out of the watery inferno that was the harbor. Also following the destroyer was a launch going full speed that carried the captain of PATTERSON, Lieutenant Commander Frank R. Walker and other crewmembers. Walker wouldn't give up the chase. The small launch pursued the destroyer. At about 0930, two miles out into the open ocean, Walker caught up with his ship, boarded her, and took command.

PATTERSON remained on patrol around O'ahu for the rest of the night. She did not encounter any further enemy contact and she returned to Pearl the next day, with no damage and no casualties.

THE WAR

On December 28, 1941, one day after returning from the abortive attempt at relieving Wake Island - PATTERSON rescued 19 men from a merchant ship that had been sunk just southwest of Hawai'i by a Japanese submarine eleven days earlier.

February 1942 found PATTERSON in the task force engaging the enemy at Rabaul, New Guinea. A large flight of enemy bombers attacked the task force, littering the ocean with bombs. PATTERSON commenced an intense zigzag course to avoid the destruction from the sky. Although her actions spared her any direct hits, one near miss injured Charlie Faught, a cook, and another caused her rudder to jam. This left PATTERSON steaming in a circle. The rest of the task force moved on. Captain Walker ordered the ship halted in mid-ocean, and a team of divers was put over the side. Repairs were made on the spot. She got underway and rejoined the task force about four hours later.

The Battles of the Coral Sea and Midway were defensive, counters against further Japanese expansion. The Solomons were chosen as the spot where the Allies were to begin the offensive against Japan. Seventy-five ships and an enormous amount of men and material went directly into participating or supporting the invasion of Japanese held Guadalcanal. This was the enemy's southernmost stronghold that was being prepared as a base of operation for further expansion and as a forward outpost for protecting its large base at Rabaul. Here in the Solomons, it was the Allies turn to strike.

The first day of the invasion, August 7, 1942, PATTERSON was already in the thick of things. In the morning she escorted Marines to the beaches then retired to screen the fleet from submarine and air attack and provide artillery support as needed.

The following day the Japanese sent out numerous aerial attacks to repulse the invading Marines, the transports bringing them, and the ships supporting them. The gunners on PATTERSON splashed four enemy planes. At one point a downed enemy aircraft was seen floating in the sea near the destroyer. Captain Walker sent a boat out to pick up the Japanese pilot who was standing on the wing of his plane. As the boat approached the enemy flyer pulled out a pistol and began to fire at his well-meaning rescuers. Walker ordered the boat to return and instructed one of the 20mm anti-aircraft batteries to sink the plane and the pilot. They did.

The Imperial Japanese Navy had superior skills and tactics in fighting nighttime naval battles. This was proved in the early morning hours of August 9, 1942 when a Japanese force that was outnumbered two to one decimated a joint American-Australian force in the black waters between Guadalcanal and Savo Island, all in the space of about thirty-seven minutes.

PATTERSON spotted the oncoming enemy ships first and put out a frantic radio call to the rest of the Allied ships. In the opening seconds of the battle the Australian heavy cruiser HMAS CANBERRA, D-33, was laid waste by enemy fire. Twenty-four shells hit the Australian within two minutes. On board PATTERSON, Captain Walker ordered the attack. The destroyer heeled to port, fired star shells and opened up with her main five-inch battery. He also ordered torpedoes to be fired, but engulfed in the proverbial "fog of war", that order wasn't heard. The Japanese responded to PATTERSON with deadly accurate fire, hitting the tin can in both the No. 3 and No. 4 guns and setting the ship ablaze. Ten sailors were killed and eight others wounded.

Damage control parties soon had the fires out. PATTERSON was ordered to report to the burning and listing CANBERRA to render aid. When she arrived on scene, another vessel was spotted approaching through the darkness. PATTERSON asked the ship to identify herself, but when no answer was received, the destroyer opened fire. The ghost ship returned fire and for a minute another surface duel raged. Luckily, in the flashes of blazing guns, Captain Walker recognized, in the silhouette of the intruder, the American heavy cruiser, USS CHICAGO, CA-39. Emergency recognition signals quickly ended the exchange.

PATTERSON was soon next to CANBERRA helping to fight fires and take on wounded. By dawn it was apparent that the cruiser could not be saved and she was ordered scuttled. PATTERSON left the area and took the survivors to safety on Guadalcanal.

In May 1943 PATTERSON was escorting the *SS Fingal*, a merchant ship, on a run off the east coast of Australia when the cargo vessel was torpedoed by the Japanese submarine *I-180*. Two torpedoes devastated the ship and it sank in less than sixty seconds, taking twelve of her thirty-one-man crew with her. PATTERSON dropped a pattern of depth charges with no apparent effect. She then departed the area, not knowing that there were nineteen survivors of *Fingal* still behind her. When a plane from the Royal Australian Air Force notified the destroyer of men adrift in the water, she turned around and picked them up, delivering them to the port city of Newcastle, New South Wales.

Screening convoys was one of the main functions of the destroyer. Protecting unarmed or lightly armed merchant and cargo vessels was an extreme burden carried by the tiny tin cans of the Navy. On August 25, 1943 PATTERSON demonstrated her abilities in this area superbly. PATTERSON was now captained by Lieutenant Commander Albert White, the same man who, as a Lieutenant, took command of her on December 7, 1941 and met the enemy on the first day of the war in the Pacific.

At approximately 1900, while escorting a convoy from the New Hebrides to the Solomons, PATTERSON detected a distinct "blip" on her radar screen. When she approached the location indicated on the radar, the blip disappeared. However, suddenly there was now a target on the sonar. This was clear evidence of a surfaced submarine that had gone under. PATTERSON closed in and quickly dispensed a pattern of depth charges. For the next three hours the destroyer systematically hunted the submarine dropping depth charges whenever she believed she had found it. Finally, just before 2200, after dropping a pattern of charges, a rumble was detected from the ocean depths and there was no longer a responding "ping" from the sonar search. Japanese records show that two subs, *I-25*[40] and *RO-35* were both lost that night in that area. One of them had met its end at the hands of PATTERSON.

Just over a month later, PATTERSON and other ships were attempting to interdict Japanese barges landing reinforcements in the New Georgia Islands in the Solomons. In the darkness of the night on September 29th-30th, USS McCALLA, DD-488, had a major steering malfunction and accidentally rammed PATTERSON, almost taking off her bow. The collision killed three and injured ten sailors on PATTERSON. As the destroyer ever so slowly crawled back to port, the tenuous strands of steel keeping her bow attached severed. The disembodied bow was left behind floating in the ocean like a cork. She made her way to Espiritu Santo, where a temporary bow was attached. This allowed PATTERSON to sail to Mare Island Naval Shipyard in California for more permanent repairs. When she arrived there, the Mare Island magicians already had a replacement bow manufactured and waiting. The new bow was put in place, and in early 1944 PATTERSON was ready to return to war.

The Navy, like an advancing tsunami, gathered speed in the retaking of the Pacific. New campaigns and invasions seemed to occur on a weekly basis. In June, PATTERSON was at Saipan bombarding that island prior to the invasion. On invasion day she escorted landing craft to the beaches and following that, she provided anti-aircraft fire. Following action at Saipan, PATTERSON engaged the enemy almost continuously for the next four months at the Battle of the Philippine Sea, Tinian, Iwo Jima, Yap, Palau and Okinawa.

In October 1944 the Japanese began employing with full force and great effectiveness their newest weapon, the kamikaze. The Japanese knew they could not hold on much longer, and part of their strategy was to raise the cost in human life to the Americans to such a level that they would negotiate peace terms. The kamikaze was used to help meet that end.

---

40 *I-25* was part of the enemy submarine task force that participated in the Pearl Harbor attack two years earlier.

For the last agonizing months of the war PATTERSON battled this force more than any other. During the Battle of Leyte Gulf, she fought off kamikazes that rained from the sky, damaging the aircraft carriers USS BELLEAU WOOD, CVL-24, and USS FRANKLIN, CV-13. She rescued sailors from both vessels. During the invasion of Mindoro Island in the Philippines, in mid December, her major role was defending carriers against the "divine wind" blowing fiercely from Japan.

In the first week of January 1945 she once again rescued sailors from kamikazed aircraft carriers, this time the USS OMMONEY BAY, CVE-79, and USS MANILA BAY, CVE-61 and the destroyer escort, USS STAFFORD, DE-411. A week later she claimed credit for splashing a kamikaze diving on another carrier, USS SALAMAUA, CVE-96.

The invasion of Iwo Jima was the beginning of the last act of the Pacific war. On February 21, 1945, two days after the initial landings, two kamikazes hit the escort carrier USS BISMARK SEA, CVE-95. This was enough to sink the 500-foot long behemoth. PATTERSON once again came to the rescue, saving 106 bluejackets from the carrier.

The Naval Battle of Okinawa was witness to no fewer than seven major kamikaze attacks during the two-month long battle. On the second evening of battle a flight of kamikazes attacked the escort carrier USS LUNGA POINT, CVE-94. PATTERSON was one of the ships screening the convoy and, along with the other escorts, sent up a wall of lead to greet the suicidal predators. PATTERSON killed one of the kamikazes for sure and was credited with a probable kill on a second. This was the destroyer's last enemy encounter of the war.

FATE

In late August 1945, PATTERSON received word that she would be reporting to the west coast of the United States for an overhaul. En route to that destination her orders were changed and she was now to report to New York for decommissioning. She arrived there on October 11th. After several weeks of work that removed valuable and still useable material, she was towed to the Brooklyn Navy Yard to await her fate.

If there is any doubt as to how sailors who have been to war feel about their ship keep in mind the following: when PATTERSON was nearing her end, tied up to a pier on the East River in New York, being slowly dismantled before scrapping, Chief Water Tender Raymond J. J. Russell of Union City, Tennessee, who had been aboard her ever since the attack at Pearl Harbor, had this to say about his old ship, "...if she's going to be turned into razor blades, she'll make good razor blades—the best."[41]

On August 18, 1947, PATTERSON was sold to the Northern Metals Company and was made into the best razor blades ever.

---

41   Source http://usspatterson.tk-jk.net/theend.htm, from an unnamed newspaper article dated, October 22, 1946.

USS Pelias

SUBMARINE TENDER
AS-14
LAUNCHED: 1939

DECEMBER 7, 1941

Commander William Wakefield was the only captain PELIAS had ever known. She had been in Pearl Harbor for only fifteen days. As the tender for Submarine Squadron Six she was berthed at the Submarine Base in Magazine Loch in the southeast corner of Pearl Harbor. The flight path of the Japanese torpedo planes making their runs on Battleship Row took them within 100 yards of PELIAS' guns. Even though she was only lightly armed, her crew made the best of them. The tender may have scored a kill in conjunction with the fire from other ships at the submarine base and possibly damaged another.

In his after action report Cmdr. Wakefield reported no damage to his vessel and no injuries to his crew.

THE WAR

PELIAS remained in Pearl Harbor servicing submarines until May 1942 when she made a short trip to San Francisco for re-provisioning. She then made her way to Freemantle, Australia where the main submarine base for the Southwest Pacific was. There she stayed for almost two years, leaving in May 1944. During this time she serviced 59 submarines, by repairing damage, refitting new equipment and performing needed maintenance.

After a brief overhaul for herself in the States, PELIAS reported to Midway in January 1945, where she again serviced submarines. Her stay there was short and she left in May for San Diego. While there she helped prepare the boats of Submarine Squadron 45 for decommissioning. This is where she was when the war ended.

FATE

PELIAS was taken out of active service in September 1946. She remained in reserve for 24 years and was finally decommissioned in June 1970. Three years later, in October 1973 she was sold for scrapping.

USS Pennsylvania

PENNSYLVANIA CLASS BATTLESHIP
BB-38
LAUNCHED: 1915

DECEMBER 7, 1941

PENNSYLVANIA was the flagship of the Pacific Fleet. She was the home and headquarters for the Commander in Chief, Pacific Fleet, (CINCPAC), who, on December 7, 1941 was Admiral Husband E. Kimmel. Normally PENNSYLVANIA would be berthed on Battleship Row. When he worked on board and not in his office at the submarine base, Kimmel preferred not to have to take a boat out to the ship. So, since his becoming CINCPAC in February 1941, PENNSYLVANIA was tied up at 1010 Dock. However, on this particular Sunday morning, the great flagship was neither place. She was sitting in Dry Dock #1 and had been for several days. Three of her massive twelve foot, seven inch diameter propellers had been removed and were lying on the dry dock floor along with their shafts. She was undergoing routine maintenance and cleaning.

Standing at the top of the gangway guarding the battleship that morning was Marine Private 1st Class Roy Capps. Just three days earlier, on Thursday the 3rd, Capps reported aboard after being reassigned from another unit at Pearl Harbor. He had been assigned a battle station at one of the five-inch guns and after settling in over the next few days he was standing his first regular duty this morning. Being a Sunday morning in dry dock he had little to do but stand there and gaze at the tropical Hawai'ian sky. The rifle he held was loaded with the standard five rounds.

Also on deck that Sunday morning was another Marine, Corporal Roscoe Taylor. His regular job was that of driver to Admiral Kimmel, but today he was part of the detail preparing to raise the flag on the fantail.

It didn't take long for either of the Marines to figure out what was happening when the Japanese planes began to fly over. Taylor unholstered his .45 caliber Colt pistol and began firing at the low flying planes as they flashed by. Capps stood at the top of the gangway waiting to be relieved so he could report to his battle station, a five-inch gun with the other Marines, but no relief arrived. He stayed at his post. He didn't fire his rifle, figuring his five rounds would be like slapping an elephant with a fly swatter.

PENNSYLVANIA opened fire almost immediately with all her guns except the 14-inch main batteries. Her large caliber five-inch and three-inch anti-aircraft guns fired 650 rounds and 350 rounds respectively during the hour and fifty-minute attack. However it was her .50 caliber gun crews that performed prodigiously. The eight .50 caliber machine guns fired a massive total of 60,000 rounds, meaning they blasted away at a rate of more than one round per second for the entire attack. Despite this enormous amount of fire, Captain Charles M. Cooke, Jr. made no claims for downing any planes in his after action report.

Pvt. Capps finally left his post when a sailor was wounded nearby. He and a bluejacket carried him to a first aid station. Cpl. Taylor made it down to his battle station, the No. 7 five-inch gun that was manned by the Marine detachment on board.

The second wave of enemy planes arrived at Pearl Harbor just before 0900 and targeted the Navy Yard. Multiple bombs fell in and around Dry Dock #1. USS CASSIN, DD-372, and USS DOWNES, DD-375, two destroyers berthed in the dry dock forward of PENNSYLVANIA, were both hit and were soon on fire. One bomb hit PENNSYLVANIA just behind the No. 7 five-inch gun. It penetrated the main deck and exploded in the deck below. Roscoe Taylor was in the passageway near the No. 7 gun. The blast slammed him against the bulkhead and knocked him out. When he came to, he discovered his fellow Marines who had been manning the gun dead. Dazed and injured he found another detail of men distributing ammunition and joined them.

The dry dock was flooded in an attempt to douse the flames. However, the fires fed by fuel oil only floated on the surface scorching the battleship. Explosions from the destroyers forward splattered burning debris on PENNSYLVANIA also causing fires. The crew and civilian yard workers brought all these under control.

When the attack was over PENNSYLVANIA had 16 dead and 48 wounded.

THE WAR

Although bloodied in the attack PENNSYLVANIA was far from beaten. Her damage was considered superficial and work began on her immediately since she was, conveniently, already in the dry dock. Her propellers and shafts were quickly reinstalled and repairs were begun on the bomb damage.

Less than two weeks after the attack, on the afternoon of Saturday the 20th, PENNSYLVANIA sailed out of Pearl Harbor for the West Coast. She passed under the graceful lines of the Golden Gate Bridge and entered San Francisco Bay on the 29th. There she underwent repairs at the Mare Island Naval Shipyard. She took part in training off the California coast with another short stay at Mare Island for modernization through the end of March 1942.

For the rest of the war PENNSYLVANIA prowled the Pacific laying waste to enemy men and material with her fourteen-inch guns. She began in the Aleutians in April 1942 and ended with a bombardment of Wake Island on August 1, 1945. In between she fired a total of 134,659 rounds of all types of ammunition at the enemy, downing at least five planes, destroying a concentration of Japanese tanks in the Philippines and providing cover for almost a dozen landings. She was also one of five surviving Pearl Harbor battleships that helped to obliterate the Japanese fleet at the Battle of Surigao Strait, in October 1944.

Along the way the enemy took several opportunities to try and sink PENNSYLVANIA. On May 12, 1942, while off Attu in the Aleutians the Japanese submarine *I-31* fired at least one torpedo at the battleship. A PBY Catalina flying boat spotted the torpedo's wake and radioed a warning to

PENNSYLVANIA. The battleship made evasive maneuvers and the fish passed by harmlessly astern. Two days later the scenario played out again when torpedo wakes were spotted heading for the battleship. They also missed.

In her last action of the war, PENNSYLVANIA was at Buckner Bay, Okinawa preparing to support operations there. On Sunday, August 12, 1945, at 2045, a Japanese torpedo plane somehow managed to fly in undetected. The pilot let loose his single torpedo which hit PENNSYLVANIA in the stern. Twenty men were killed and ten wounded.

Two days after the torpedo hit, August 14, 1945, the Japanese surrendered and the war ended. On that day a 19-year-old ensign from the American Mid-West, named John W. Carson, reported on board PENNSYLVANIA. Carson was a graduate of the V-12[42] program at Columbia University and had only recently been commissioned. His first assignment, as the most junior ensign on board, was to supervise the detail removing the bodies of the sailors killed in the torpedo attack.

FATE

PENNSYLVANIA stayed in Buckner Bay for two weeks making the minimum repairs needed to be made seaworthy. On the 18th of August two tugboats began towing her to Guam. There she was repaired in a floating dry dock so she could then travel under her own power back to the United States.

En route to the States, the #3 propeller shaft broke and had to be cut free by divers. The shaft and its propeller sank to the bottom of the Pacific. PENNSYLVANIA finally arrived at the Puget Sound Naval Yard on October 24, 1945. Her World War II voyage of 146,052 miles was over.

Her service to her country was, however, not yet done. PENNSYLVANIA was over thirty years old and, especially after the beating she took in the last few months, she was tired and deemed not worthy for repair. She was suitable for one mission. She was chosen to be a target vessel for the atomic bomb tests at Bikini. There, in July 1946, she was subjected to both the airburst test "Able" and the submerged

---

42 The V-12 program at colleges and universities trained men to become commissioned naval officers.

detonation test "Baker." She survived both blasts. After she was examined for damage and radioactivity she was towed to Kwajalein Atoll in the Marshall Islands were she was scuttled on February 10, 1948.

Highly radioactive after two atomic bomb blasts, PENNSYLVANIA is scuttled off Kwajalein February 10, 1948.

*　　　　*　　　　*　　　　*　　　　*

Both Roscoe Taylor and Roy Capps stayed in the Marine Corps. Taylor was wounded in Korea, retired in 1959 and passed away in 1998. Capps survived the fighting on Okinawa and was wounded twenty years later in Vietnam. He retired as a Master Gunnery Sergeant and passed away in 2006.

Ensign Carson spent three years in the Navy and was discharged in 1946. Better known as "Johnny" Carson he went on to an extraordinary career in television, hosting the *Tonight Show* from 1962 to 1992 and becoming an American icon in the process.

CLEMSON CLASS DESTROYER
MINESWEEPER
DMS-17
LAUNCHED: 1921

DECEMBER 7, 1941

Ensign George Gill Ball came from a military family. His father, who died when George was 5, was an Army officer. His great uncle, R. H. Jackson, was a retired Rear Admiral[43] who encouraged him to attend the U.S. Naval Academy at Annapolis, which he did. After his graduation his first assignment was to PERRY and since June he had been the ship's Engineering Officer. On this Sunday morning he was enjoying a pleasant breakfast with his mother and stepfather, Colonel R. M. Bathurst, who by coincidence, was stationed at Schofield Barracks only a few miles away from Pearl Harbor. When the Japanese began their preemptive strike on the Army Air Corps planes at nearby Wheeler Field, Ensign Ball jumped into his car and drove hell-bent for his ship at Pearl Harbor. En route, he became a target of opportunity for a Japanese pilot who dove his plane on Ball's car and strafed him.

Unlike many ships in Pearl Harbor that day, PERRY had ready ammunition available at all of her anti-aircraft guns. Within a minute

---

43 R.H. Jackson was awarded the Navy Cross during his 43 years of service and had retired to Pearl City on the north shore of Pearl Harbor. Admiral Jackson watched the attack from his front porch and, although not required to do so, wrote a detailed report of his observations and sent it to the Commander-in-Chief of the U.S. Fleet.

of the beginning of the attack all of these guns, six .50-caliber and two .30-caliber machine guns were firing back at the enemy.

Just a short while into the battle a Japanese plane made a strafing run on PERRY and the three other ships of Mine Division Four with which she was nested. Fire Controlman 3rd Class J.C. Cole was the gun captain of the #3 .50-caliber machine gun. A bullet from that enemy plane hit Cole in the neck wounding the young sailor. Another 3rd Class Fire Controlman, G.A. Christian saw his shipmate go down and without hesitation rushed to take his place at the .50-caliber while the injured Cole was taken to sick bay for treatment.

At approximately 0830 PERRY, along with almost every other ship in the Middle Loch area of the harbor spotted the conning tower of a Japanese mini-sub in the main channel as it rounded the northwest corner of Ford Island. PERRY fired two four-inch rounds from her main battery at the sub. She missed with the first shot but claimed a hit with the second shell.[44] She then ceased firing for fear of hitting USS MONAGHAN, DD-354, as MONAGHAN was making an attack run on the sub.

Ensign Ball arrived at the Pearl City landing after his harrowing run to Pearl Harbor and took a boat out to PERRY. Once on board he took command and sortied the minesweeper out of the harbor. In the open ocean he screened one of the cruisers that had made it out of the harbor and also commenced sweeping for mines outside the harbor entrance. Under combat conditions Ball retained command of PERRY for the next four hours, until her captain, Lieutenant Commander Lermond Miller, reported on board.

Of Ensign Ball, Captain Miller later said, *"His action[s] were those of an officer of far greater experience…Ball's conduct deserves the utmost praise. His readiness was due in my opinion, first, to a fine background and second to the training received by him from my predecessor Lieutenant Commander R.E. Elliott, USN, in ship handling and in accepting responsibility. I am proud to*

---

44 Since multiple vessels were firing at this same target at the same time it is almost impossible to determine which ship hit the sub.

have him on board."[45] The Navy was in agreement with Miller's assessment and awarded Ball a Bronze Star for his actions that day.

PERRY suffered no material damage other than to antenna and rigging, most likely from her own guns or other friendly fire. Despite the location of the wound to Fire Controlman Cole, it was not serious. The bullet was removed from his neck at the Pearl Harbor Naval Hospital and he was returned to duty.

THE WAR

For the first few months of the war, PERRY was assigned to various jobs in and around the Hawai'ian Islands. On January 11, 1942 she was providing screening coverage for the aircraft carrier USS SARATOGA, CV-3, several hundred miles south west of O'ahu. The Japanese submarine *I-6*, which had been part of the Pearl Harbor attack fleet, was still lurking in Hawai'ian waters awaiting this exact opportunity: the chance to sink an American aircraft carrier that had escaped destruction on December 7th. Lieutenant Commander Inaba Michimune fired three torpedoes at SARATOGA from three miles away. On board PERRY, the lookouts spotted one of the torpedoes heading straight for them. However, by the time they spotted it, the torpedo was too close to evade. The crew stood by for the explosion and shudder that would come when the torpedo hit. Agonizing seconds ticked by. No explosion or shudder came. The telltale trail of the torpedo passed directly beneath PERRY and reappeared on the other side. PERRY escaped disaster by a few feet. One of the torpedoes did find its intended mark and hit SARATOGA amidships. The carrier managed to limp back to Pearl Harbor for repairs.

A minesweepers job is an inherently dangerous one plying the ocean to try and detect and destroy the very thing that has been put there to destroy it. During the war PERRY spent much of her time doing just what it was designed for. She swept for mines all across the Pacific, in the Aleutians, at Kwajalein in the Marshalls, the Solomons and Saipan.

---

45   After action report dated December 22, 1941, by Lieutenant Commander L. H. Miller

Her routine often involved escorting a convoy to a new island, then upon arrival, sweeping for mines. She would then join in the bombardment of the island in preparation for invasion, followed by escorting landing craft to the invasion beaches and then screening duties for the invasion fleet afterwards. This scenario was repeated many times during her life in the Pacific. In September 1944 she was called on to repeat it again.

FATE

The invasion of Peleliu in the Palau Islands brought PERRY to its furthest point west in the Pacific. She arrived on September 12, 1944 and immediately began sweeping operations. Shortly after 0800 her port sweep gear encountered an enemy mine that blew up. The damaged gear was reeled in and replaced, and her sweep continued for the rest of the day. The following morning, the 13th, PERRY once again commenced sweeping operations. These took her within 700 yards of Anguar, the island just southwest of Peleliu. They were so close in fact, that Japanese soldiers on shore were firing at her with small arms.

Just after 1400 the cat and mouse contest between PERRY and enemy mines came to a conclusion, and PERRY lost. The minesweeper brushed against a mine on her starboard side and the mine erupted with a dev-

astating blast, holing PERRY amidships. Almost immediately a second explosion occurred when one of her damaged boilers blew up. Eight sailors were killed. In short order PERRY took on a very dangerous 30-degree list. The captain, Commander William N. Lindsay, ordered abandon ship, a ship he had taken command of only ten days earlier.

PERRY listing heavily to starboard after hitting a mine.

Repair parties were kept on board in the faint hope that the flooding could be controlled and perhaps the ship saved.

Just 200 yards astern of PERRY was her Pearl Harbor sister USS PREBLE, DM-20 who now came to aid those who had abandoned ship. Those sailors in the water were in a tough position. The current was carrying them toward the Japanese held island and they had to struggle to prevent that. There was also the very real danger that PERRY could drift into another mine, setting off an explosion, whose concussion might kill every sailor in the water. As PREBLE advanced she could see many mines in the area just six feet below the water and she had to perform a delicate dance around them in order to save herself and the men in the water.

For over an hour PREBLE fished grateful sailors out of the ocean. Eventually it became apparent that PERRY could not be saved and the repair parties also left the ship. At 1605 PERRY turned turtle and two minutes later she sank in 240 feet of water. All of the remaining 146 men were rescued.

*   *   *   *   *

George Ball, the young Ensign who expertly commanded PERRY on December 7, 1941, spent 30 years in the Navy, retiring in 1972 as a Captain. In 1956 he became the commanding officer of another destroyer. It was a Gearing class destroyer built in 1945, named USS PERRY, DD-844.

USS Phelps

PORTER CLASS DESTROYER
DD-360
LAUNCHED: 1935

DECEMBER 7, 1941

PHELPS pulled into Pearl Harbor on December 3rd having just completed practice maneuvers. The crew was looking forward to two big upcoming events. First and foremost was liberty and blowing off some steam in the bars of Hotel Street in downtown Honolulu. The second one, although not nearly as much fun, was the time honored "Change of Command" ceremony that was to take place on Saturday the 6th. At that time Lieutenant Commander Edward Louis Beck would relieve Commander Walfrid Nyquist as captain of PHELPS. Both events took place without a hitch.

The excitement and pomp of the Change of Command ceremony on Saturday gave way to the quiet and routine of Sunday. The new captain, like most others in the fleet, was not on board. In command was Lieutenant Bruce E. S. Trippensee, the ship's engineering officer. He was supervising the extremely average maintenance and service being provided to PHELPS by the destroyer tender, USS DOBBIN, AD-3. As a result of the maintenance, PHELPS was a "cold ship," meaning all of her boilers were shut down and cold. DOBBIN was providing all electrical power.

On deck, just before 0800, a group of sailors with liberty cards in hand were waiting for the word that would allow them to board the launch taking them to shore. In that happy group was Seaman 1st Class Frank Chebetar, a native New Yorker, who had been on board PHELPS since January. He was a cook striker[46] who had already been up for hours. It was his job to report to the galley and break out for the cooks everything needed to prepare the morning meal for the crew. With his work accomplished and part of his $21.00 per month pay in his pocket, he was anxious to get to Honolulu.

When the attack began and general quarters sounded, Chebetar reported to his battle station at the aft 1.1-inch anti-aircraft gun. He scanned the sky as he ran toward the stern and quickly observed that everywhere he looked there were enemy planes. Arriving at his gun he discovered that the breech had been disassembled as part of the overhaul. It had to be put back together before the gun crew could shoot back at the enemy. Although Chebetar did this quickly, the gun didn't get into action until the raid was twenty minutes old.

Lt. Trippensee immediately ordered the boilers fired up and electrical power turned on. Down in the engine room, Electrician's Mate Dean Griffith started the diesel generators as ordered by Trippensee. Once the generators were on line Griffith reported on deck where he helped disconnect the huge four-inch diameter power cables that were providing power to PHELPS from DOBBIN. He muled the heavy cables across the deck and went below to deal with the connections. As he came back up the hatch one of the destroyers tied up to PHELPS let fly a five-inch round at the enemy. The concussion threw Griffith down the hatch, but the driven sailor picked himself up, unharmed, and continued his duties.

At the forward 1.1-inch anti-aircraft gun, Gunner's Mate John Lawhon was also coming up a hatch as he brought ammunition from the forward magazine to his gun. The adjacent destroyer fired another round, this time the concussion blasted Lawhon but it didn't knock him down. He also pressed on undeterred. The crew on Lawhon's gun engaged a plane flying directly in front of them. Lawhon saw their rounds hitting the aircraft and it crashed in a sugarcane field.

---

46 A "striker" is a sailor who is being apprenticed to learn a specific occupation or "rating."

Just before 0930, while the attack was still going on, PHELPS got underway. Fearing he might run down sailors adrift in the water, Lt. Trippensee slowly moved out of the harbor. He ordered crewman not engaging the enemy to man the rails and throw life jackets to any sailors they saw in the water and report them to the bridge.

The roar of hostile planes continued to engulf PHELPS as she moved down the channel and past the beached and burning battleship NEVADA, BB-36. Frank Chebetar was still manning the aft anti-aircraft gun. He had been shooting almost continuously for nearly two hours, stopping only in the short intervals between running out of ammunition and being reloaded. Now, just as PHELPS escaped the holocaust, a Japanese plane presented itself in his sights. As he and his ship exited the harbor, Chebetar shot the attacker down.

Once out on the open sea the destroyer joined up with the light cruiser ST. LOUIS, CL-49, in searching out the enemy. Multiple times depth charge attacks were made on suspected enemy submarines but no kills were confirmed.

PHELPS returned to Pearl Harbor the following day just as the sun was setting. Lt. Trippensee had commanded her for over 33 continuous hours under the severest of combat conditions. When he finally turned PHELPS back over to her new captain, Commander Beck, she was in perfect condition, with no damage inflicted by the enemy and no casualties.

THE WAR

For the bloodied American Pacific Fleet, the first major engagement against the Japanese was at the Battle of the Coral Sea. The Allies' intention was to repulse any further advances of the Japanese in the Pacific. PHELPS, along with other survivors of Pearl Harbor, met the enemy again. The confrontation took place one month short of the enemy's six-month goal of keeping what they hoped would be a neutralized and demoralized American fleet out of their way in the Pacific. This was also the battle that gave proof to the new naval strategy that made battleships obsolete and the aircraft carrier the dominant force of the sea. There wasn't a battleship within a hundred miles of the clash, and had they been there, they would have been used only as targets as the Coral Sea was the first naval battle in history in which the opposing fleets never set eyes on each other.

When the battle was over the Japanese had been turned back from their major objective of Port Moresby, New Guinea. The victory, however, was costly. The carrier USS LEXINGTON, CV-2, was critically damaged by several bomb and torpedo hits. Despite the heroic efforts of her crew, LEXINGTON was a listing, blazing wreck. PHELPS was sent in to assist in removing the crew.

As she moved in, John Lawhon sat in the forward five-inch battery looking through his sighting periscope at the drama of the burning carrier. Just like the words of the Star Spangled Banner, Lawhon spotted the American flag, waving through the smoke high atop the carrier's mast. LEXINGTON was being torn apart by internal explosions as bombs cooked off. Lawhon was gazing at the proud ensign when one of these explosions ripped through the carrier, severing the lanyard causing the flag to flutter into the flames.

Just before 1900 Lieutenant Commander Beck received orders to close in on the dying carrier and put her out of her misery. With the crew evacuated, PHELPS took aim and put five torpedoes into the carrier. About an hour later the great green closed in over her and the "Lady Lex" was gone.

A month later, PHELPS was at the pivotal Battle of Midway. Her job here was as a screening vessel in the Task Force built around the carriers USS ENTERPRISE, CV-6, and USS HORNET, CV-8. Two months later, in August 1942, she was part of the support force for the landings at Guadalcanal. After a very busy first year of war, PHELPS returned to the west coast for a much-needed overhaul at Mare Island Naval Shipyard.

The first evening back home PHELPS was anchored beneath the San Francisco-Oakland Bay Bridge. Lawhon was taking the air on deck when he realized something was very different. Above him he could hear the rumble of cars and trains crossing the bridge. Looking around he could see the blackness of the bay surrounded by a circle of lights from the cities of Oakland and San Francisco. In the world of war the night is a time of secrecy, stealth and safety and anything making noise or illuminated becomes a target and invites death and destruction. With the exception of the flashes of guns and lightning, it had been almost a year since he had seen lights at night. He realized how lucky all Americans were that unlike the peoples of Europe, Asia and the Pacific Islands the war wasn't being played out in their front yard.

The extended overhaul was completed in December 1942, and PHELPS returned to the Pacific – but this time it was the North Pacific, to the Aleutian Islands. In May 1943 PHELPS was one of the lead ships in the invasion of Attu. Now under the command of Lieutenant Commander John Edwards, she escorted, through thick fog, a team of Aleut scouts to the landing beaches and then returned escorting the main force in landing barges. When the landings were complete, PHELPS' mission changed to one of firing her main batteries to aid the advance of the Army. She fired so many rounds, that within the next two days, she had almost exhausted her entire supply of five-inch shells. A week later she came under attack by enemy planes but her fierce curtain of anti-aircraft fire drove the marauders off. The invasion of Kiska occurred three months later, in August, and once again PHELPS was there.

After her adventures in Alaska, PHELPS returned to the more balmy climes of the South Pacific. On February 16, 1944 she was part of the Eniwetok Expeditionary Group. In the fading light of the late afternoon, a sonar contact brought the ship to battle stations. Lieutenant Commander David Martineau, the skipper of PHELPS, hunted down the suspected submarine and dropped 13 depth charges. The small 900-ton minesweeper, USS SAGE, AM-111, also dropped a pattern of depth charges. After the two attacks the sonar screen went blank and sometime later an oil slick appeared. The combined efforts of the two vessels had sunk the Japanese submarine *RO-40* that was only four days into its first war patrol.

In the five months from February through June 1944, she was involved in actions at Kwajalein, Eniwetok, Palau and Saipan. On the morning of June 19th, PHELPS was called upon to silence a shore battery on Saipan. The destroyer opened fire on the coordinates that must have been pretty close to right on, because the enemy battery objected strenuously and returned fire. PHELPS found herself in a large caliber duel. The winner, in this case, was the Japanese shore battery. Two enemy shells struck PHELPS, killing one sailor and wounding 15 others.

She reported to the nearby repair ship USS PHAON, ARB-3, to be mended. While being tended to alongside PHAON she also replaced her stores of ammunition. In a further demonstration of the skills of her captain and crew, while being repaired and loading ammunition, she was called upon to provide a shore bombardment. She accomplished this without halting the other two operations. During this bombardment PHELPS fired 958 rounds of five-inch ammunition.

In August 1944, PHELPS was ordered to the East coast of the United States for overhaul. In November she was assigned to convoy duty in the Atlantic. Over the next seven months she made four trips to North Africa and the Mediterranean. Her last voyage of the war ended in New York harbor in June 1945.

FATE

The end came rapidly for PHELPS. Five short months later she was decommissioned. She was sold for scrap a year and a half after that to the Northern Metals Company in Philadelphia, Pennsylvania.

*   *   *   *   *

PHELPS was certainly a unique and rich training ground. Lieutenant Bruce Trippensee, who commanded PHELPS through the first thirty-three hours of the war, was promoted to Lieutenant Commander and, at that rank, became the first captain of the destroyer USS CAPPS, DD-550, in June 1943.

In what may be some kind of record, each of the six men that captained PHELPS during the war stayed in the Navy and each one eventually became an admiral. All of them achieved the rank of Rear Admiral. Commander Bledsoe rose higher still eventually promoting to Vice Admiral.

Many years after the war, Frank Chebetar became the President of his local chapter of the Pearl Harbor Survivors Association, in Virginia. Dean Griffith retired from the Navy in 1960 as a Chief Petty Officer.

BROOKLYN CLASS LIGHT CRUISER
CL-46
LAUNCHED: 1938

DECEMBER 7, 1941

Milton Kraut wanted to be in the Navy very badly. So badly, in fact, that he asked his father to sign the papers to allow him to join when he was only 17. His father refused. Young Milton had to wait. He did get to join in July 1940 after he turned 18. He went to boot camp at Great Lakes, Michigan. Twelve weeks later he was on his way to Mare Island Naval Shipyard in California. There he joined PHOENIX, which was undergoing overhaul.

A year and a half later, Milton and PHOENIX were in Hawai'i where two week training cruises were a way of life. The latest in this never-ending cycle finished on Friday December 5th when PHOENIX sailed back into Pearl Harbor. Liberty parties for the weekend were slightly larger than usual, as Friday had been payday and the sailors of the Pacific Fleet had money to burn. Kraut was in his quarters preparing for a day in Honolulu when a shipmate came running in yelling something about being bombed.

PHOENIX was berthed all by herself at the southern end of East Loch near McGrew Point. This and the fact that light cruisers were low on the priority list for Japanese pilots may account for the fact that she was totally ignored by the enemy and suffered virtually no damage, (the claim of a single bullet hole in one of her smokestacks is very probably true). She did fire at planes that came within range but she claimed no significant hits and no kills.

PHOENIX got underway at 1010 after the attack was over, and headed out of the harbor. She didn't get far before Captain Herman Fischer received orders not to sortie and to return PHOENIX to her berth. At 1030, orders were once again received to sortie. The cruiser got underway and proceeded out the North Channel. Only minutes later she was told again to return to her berth. Before she got back to the buoy, those orders were countermanded and PHOENIX was ordered to exit the harbor. She finally sailed out of the harbor via the South Channel and headed out to open sea.

The passage through the harbor was not pleasant. The stench of burning human flesh permeated the atmosphere. Dead bodies floated in the oil-covered water. Rescue details with blowtorches were already on the upturned hull of USS OKLAHOMA, BB-37, attempting to cut out men trapped inside. As she passed the beached and battered battleship USS NEVADA, BB-36, the crew of that ship paused from fighting fires long enough to cheer PHOENIX on.

Because of her total lack of casualties or damage on December 7th, members of her crew took to calling PHOENIX the "Luckiest Ship in the Navy".

PHOENIX sorties from Pearl Harbor, passing the burning ships of Battleship Row, at 1040 on December 7th.

THE WAR

After returning to Pearl Harbor from the unsuccessful search for the Japanese fleet, PHOENIX was put on convoy duty. She escorted the first convoy from Hawai'i to the West Coast and then returned to Hawai'i with another. She then escorted a convoy of troops from San Francisco to Melbourne, Australia. Moving farther west PHOENIX escorted convoys in the Indian Ocean. She remained in that theater until July 1943 when, in a rare move for a vessel assigned to the Pacific Fleet, she sailed to the Philadelphia Navy Yard for reconditioning.

After completion of work in Philadelphia, PHOENIX was pressed into political duties ferrying Secretary of State Cordell Hull to a meeting in Casablanca. With the summit completed, PHOENIX returned Hull to the United States and then sailed once more to the Pacific. She arrived at Espiritu Santo in December.

Throughout 1944 PHOENIX participated in a half dozen landing and bombardment operations. She saw much action on New Guinea, at Cape Gloucester, Madang, Alexishafen and Milne Bay.

In June as part of Task Force 75, PHOENIX was involved in the invasion of Biak Island that lies just off the northern coast of New Guinea. On June 4th the Japanese launched an aerial counterattack against allied ships. Two fighter-bombers specifically targeted PHOENIX. Her anti-aircraft batteries fired on the intruders but failed to shoot them down. They did cause the enemy bombs to miss their target. One of these was a near miss that killed one sailor and injured four others with shrapnel. The cruiser also suffered minor hull damage from the bomb. The evening of the 5th another attack ensued from torpedo planes. PHOENIX managed to escape unharmed from this encounter. Four nights later a unit of enemy destroyers were chased off by PHOENIX and other allied ships.

The curtain was beginning to close on the Japanese at the end of 1944. The steady push of the allies across the Pacific was slowly choking the enemy. This was all part of General Douglas MacArthur's drive to fulfill his pledge to return to the Philippines. On October 20, 1944 when the landings were made on the island of Leyte, PHOENIX was there providing shore bombardment.

Five days later she was involved in the Battle of Surigao Strait. The Imperial Japanese Navy was pressed to repulse the invasion of the Philippines by Allied forces. They created a large flotilla divided into Northern and Southern forces. American Rear Admiral Jesse Oldendorf was in command of the ships sent to meet the enemy Southern Force that was advancing northward through the Surigao Strait.

Just before 2300 on October 24th the first offensive action against the enemy fleet was taken by a picket line of PT boats. The plywood vessels fired torpedoes at the enemy damaging at least one. The Japanese pressed on. Around 0300 on the 25th it was the destroyers' turn to take on the enemy. The American tin cans so ravaged the battleship *Fuso* that it withdrew and later sank. They also damaged another battleship, *Yamishiro* and sank two destroyers

By the time the enemy fleet arrived at the next line of Allied ships - the cruisers - they were pretty beat up. At 0353 the cruisers opened fire. PHOENIX concentrated her fire on the crippled *Yamishiro*. The cruiser fired her main batteries, pumping out salvos of three six-inch shells every fifteen seconds. *Yamishiro* responded, firing her huge fourteen-inch guns at PHOENIX. The "Luckiest Ship in the Navy" retained her luck as the massive enemy shells fell short. Twenty-six minutes later *Yamishiro* capsized, the victim of a ruthless barrage of shells from PHOENIX, other cruisers and battleships and torpedoes from destroyers. The Japanese fleet lost two battleships and three destroyers, the other enemy ships retreated, broken and battered.

Over the next months PHOENIX continued in the Leyte area, surviving several bombing and kamikaze attacks. She also covered other landings in the Philippines at Cebu and Mindoro and bombarded Corregidor.

PHOENIX was en route to Pearl Harbor for overhaul when the Japanese surrendered.

FATE

PHOENIX was decommissioned in Philadelphia in July 1946. She was sold to Argentina in 1951 for 7.8 million dollars. She was originally renamed 17 DE OCTOBRE. After the coup d' état that overthrew Juan Peron her name was changed again, this time to GENERAL BELGRANO.

In April 1982, Argentina invaded the Falkland Islands, a British possession, in the South Atlantic, citing a claim of ownership going back to the 1800s. For several weeks, the navies of the two belligerents danced around each other. The British sent an invasion force to the islands. GENERAL BELGRANO and the Argentine navy were prepared to stop it.

On May 2nd the British nuclear submarine HMS CONQUERER, S-48, sighted the GENERAL BELGRANO south of the Falklands. The submarine fired three torpedoes at the Argentine cruiser just before 1600. One missed, but two found their mark. One hit forward, ripping off the bow. The second blew a hole in her port side. The 805 pounds of high explosives devastated the ship. It exploded in the aft engineering compartments and the blast vented upward through crew spaces and exited by punching a sixty-five foot hole in the main deck.

The ship began listing and twenty minutes after the torpedo struck, Captain Hector Bonzo gave the order to abandon ship. The crew deployed their life rafts into the wild and cold South Atlantic. Shortly after that, GENERAL BELGRANO/PHOENIX went to the bottom of the Atlantic. 323 men were killed in the attack. 770 men were rescued by Argentine and Chilean ships.

During World War II, PHOENIX lost only two men to enemy action. In her second life "The Luckiest Ship in the Navy" finally ran out of luck.

USS Preble

CLEMSON CLASS DESTROYER / LIGHT MINELAYER
DM-20
LAUNCHED: 1920

DECEMBER 7, 1941

PREBLE was undergoing overhaul at Berth 15 in the Navy Yard that Sunday morning. As with most ships in that place and in that circumstance she was without power, ammunition or guns. General Quarters was sounded when the attack began and helmets and gas masks were issued to the crew. The commanding officer, Lieutenant Commander Harry Darlington Johnston, sent members of the crew to the ship berthed adjacent to them, USS CUMMINGS, DD-365, to assist with ammunition and aid their gun crews.

By the end of the day the crew had reassembled the guns on board PREBLE. She suffered no casualties or damage as a result of the Japanese attack.

THE WAR

In early January 1942, 22-year-old Louisiana native Theo Rabb sailed into Pearl Harbor on board a troop ship. He had joined the Navy three days after the attack and following a highly accelerated boot camp in San Diego, less than a month later he was in Hawai'i. Rabb was assigned to PREBLE. He was barely on board when she was sent out to patrol the Hawai'ian Islands for enemy submarines. Although she made depth charge attack runs on suspected subs, no kills were ever confirmed.

When she was laid down at Bath Iron Works in Maine in 1919 it was as a destroyer. But like many ships of her type and age the Navy found other uses for her. In 1937 she was converted to a light minelayer and in April 1942 she set about her new mission for the first time in war.

Along with other ships of Mine Division One she set sail for French Frigate Shoals, northwest of Hawai'i, where she helped lay a minefield. Several months later PREBLE accomplished the same task near Kodiak, Alaska. Throughout the war PREBLE traversed the Pacific laying mines in and around the Marshall Islands and off Guadalcanal, the Shortland Islands, and in Ferguson Passage, all in the Solomons.

In February 1943 mines laid by PREBLE and other ships sank the Japanese destroyer *Makigumo* off Guadalcanal. Later that same year in May she and two other ships laid a minefield in Blackett Strait to harass and interdict the "Tokyo Express" supplying Guadalcanal. These mines sank another enemy destroyer, *Kuroshio* and damaged two others so badly that American planes were able to sink them the next day.

On May 24, 1943, only weeks after the successful mining of Blackett Strait, PREBLE came to the rescue of American sailors. In the early morning hours Lieutenant Commander Harada Hakue, commanding the Japanese submarine *I-17*, put a torpedo into the tanker STANVAC MANILA that promptly began to sink. The tanker was carrying six PT Boats that were lashed to the deck. Eight hours later, shortly after noon, when the STANVAC MANILA finally slipped beneath the surface, four of the boats were floated off their brackets on deck. Less than an hour later, PREBLE arrived on scene rescuing 85 sailors and taking three of the PT Boats in tow, delivering them all safely to Noumea, New Caledonia.

PREBLE continued laying and sweeping mines and providing escorts and invasion support duties throughout 1944. In 1945, after an overhaul in the United States, she returned to Pearl Harbor and was then redesignated AG-99, a miscellaneous auxiliary vessel. PREBLE finished out the war, escorting and screening aircraft carriers involved in the final major invasion of the war at Okinawa.

Over the course of the war PREBLE was credited with sinking 8 enemy vessels.

FATE

On the fourth anniversary of the attack on Pearl Harbor, December 7, 1945, PREBLE was decommissioned at the Norfolk Naval Shipyard in Virginia. Ten months later she was sold for scrap to Luria Brothers of Philadelphia, Pennsylvania.

USS Pruitt

CLEMSON CLASS DESTROYER /
LIGHT MINELAYER
DM-22
LAUNCHED: 1920

DECEMBER 7, 1941

If destroyers and their related hybrid sisters, like minelayers and minesweepers, were on the priority target list of the Imperial Japanese Navy at all, they must have been at the very bottom. With the exception of three destroyers that were severely damaged, almost by accident, not one of the other 39 destroyers or mine vessels in Pearl Harbor that morning suffered anything but minor damage, none of which had any effect on their later ability to fight.

And so it was for PRUITT. Berthed in the Navy yard for overhaul all her main guns were inoperable at the time of the attack. However, the men of PRUITT fought back anyway. As soon as the attack commenced the small arms locker was opened and handguns, Springfield rifles, Browning Automatic Rifles and .30 caliber machine guns were handed out to the crew, along with helmets and gas masks.

While under fire by the enemy, other members of the crew not engaged in shooting at low-flying planes were forming fire-fighting parties, working on the docks to reinstall the ship's three-inch guns, or assisting on board other ships with their guns and ammunition.

Although PRUITT came out of the battle unscathed, she lost one crewman, Radioman 3rd Class G.R. Keith. Keith was killed while assisting on board the battleship USS PENNSYLVANIA, BB-38.

THE WAR

For the first weeks of the war PRUITT remained in the Pearl Harbor Navy Yards completing her overhaul. She was then assigned to basic patrol and mine laying duties in the Hawai'ian Sea Frontier. In June 1942 she was sent back to the States and then shortly after she was off to the frigid waters of the Aleutians. For the rest of the year PRUITT performed various functions in a large triangle across the Pacific that took her from the Aleutians to Hawai'i to the American West Coast.

May 1943 found her once again in the Aleutians where she performed possibly her most critical mission of the war. The Army had been planning to remove the Japanese from Attu Island ever since the enemy captured the American territory six months earlier in October 1942.

The invasion force arrived in late April 1943, but a storm was battering the island so they waited for better weather. The invasion was postponed until May 9 and postponed again until May 11, both times due to bad weather and incredibly heavy fog. Finally on the 11th the invasion force was in place and H-Hour was designated as 0740. The landing was to take place at the rather ominously named location of Massacre Bay. H-Hour came and went but no invasion began. An intensely thick fog was hugging the coast of Attu and no ship or landing craft could see the island, let alone the beach.

With the invasion in jeopardy, a way had to be found to make it

USS PRUITT leads the invasion of Attu Island through the fog, May 11, 1943

happen. It was literally PRUITT's time to shine. She was one of the few vessels that had radar and she was called upon to lead the invasion.

The radar allowed her to "see" ahead through the fog so she took up the lead position in front of the assembled landing craft and sailed into the gray, misty curtain. The large searchlight on her mast was turned aft so its powerful beam could cut through the fog and give the landing craft a beacon to follow. Like a mother goose followed by her goslings, PRUITT led the landing craft nine miles through the fog bank to make the successful landings.

PRUITT remained in Alaskan waters through the end of the month when she returned to the American West Coast for escort duties. After the summer of 1943 she was sent to the South Pacific. She laid mines off the coast of Bougainville in November. She spent the rest of the year in simple escort duties.

After an overhaul in San Francisco, PRUITT returned to Pearl Harbor where, for the rest of the war, she undertook escort and training duties.

FATE

Just prior to the end of the war, PRUITT was reclassified as an auxiliary vessel, AG-101. She set sail for the Philadelphia Navy Yard in September 1945, arriving there in October. She was decommissioned in December 1945, just three and a half months after the end of the war. The next year, 1946 she was broken up for scrap at the Philadelphia Navy Yard.

USS Pyro

AMMUNITION SHIP
AE-1
LAUNCHED: 1919

DECEMBER 7, 1941

With the exception of a few yard service boats, PYRO was pretty much alone in the most isolated part of Pearl Harbor known as West Loch. Loaded down with tons of ammunition and explosives, PYRO was relegated to the extreme reaches of the harbor in the event that disaster visited the ship and it should explode.

Other than routine ship's duties nothing was scheduled for this Sunday morning as she gently swayed at the ammunition depot's concrete pier. Below decks, sailor Johnny Sinatra and three of his friends were savoring a breakfast of ham, eggs and strong black coffee and already reminiscing about their just concluded weekend in Honolulu spent celebrating Sinatra's 21st birthday. On deck, standing near the gangway was the Officer of the Deck, Ensign Jack Sperling, chatting with 19-year-old Samuel Cassius, a black mess steward from Oklahoma. Cassius looked resplendent in his dress whites. He had just completed a ninety-day confinement to ship for a disciplinary infraction and was ready to hit the streets of Honolulu for his first liberty in three months. The two had formed an unusually close bond for an officer and an enlisted man. They had been brought together by a common adversary, a lieutenant, who disliked Sperling because he was Jewish and Cassius because he was black.

Muffled booms interrupted the conversation below decks and Sinatra noticed shock waves dancing in his coffee cup. As in many places across Pearl that day the sailors believed some demolition or training was taking place elsewhere in the harbor. On deck, Sperling and Cassius knew almost immediately that they were under attack, because they saw the Japanese planes flying at them, only 100 feet above the water. Sperling sounded general quarters and when the cry of "Man your battle stations!" bellowed over the ship's PA, Cassius, Sinatra and every other man onboard PYRO ran to his battle station.

A half dozen ways to send PYRO to hell threatened her. She herself was a floating bomb. Tied to her stern was a barge loaded with ammunition and on the pier itself were several boxcars of high explosives intended for USS NEVADA, BB-36. Any bomb or bullet hitting any of these rather large and immobile targets carried with it the potential of obliterating PYRO, her crew and a good portion of real estate around them.

The skipper of PYRO, Captain Nicholas Vytlacil, recognized the hazard instantly and ordered Ensign Sperling to move the boxcars on the dock. Sperling, with a group of brave volunteers, raced down the gangway to the pier to accomplish that.

Japanese planes strafed PYRO. Bombing runs were made on her also, perhaps because some of the enemy pilots recognized her as an ammunition ship. One near miss, at about 0900, hit the dock alongside and rained concrete debris down on the deck. Below decks the hoist that brought ammunition up to the guns was out of commission. Cassius was part of a line of men that were passing ammunition boxes, hand-to-hand and man-to-man up three decks, from the ammo locker to the guns on deck. When the bomb hit the dock the concussion rocked the men inside the ship like dice in a cup. A box of ammo fell through a hatch and hit Cassius in the face, splitting his lip and cracking a few teeth.

With the exception of minor cuts, bruises, cracked teeth and insignificant material damage to the ship, PYRO and her crew came through the attack relatively unscathed. Her anti-aircraft batteries hit at least one enemy plane but could not claim a kill.

The attack was over and PYRO began preparing the fleet for war. Ammunition was disbursed to any ship that wanted it and those that took it, took all they could hold. Rifles were also given to USS HONOLULU, CL-48.

Paranoia, understandably, ran rife for the rest of day. Rumors were flying as thick in the air as Japanese planes had been earlier in the morning. The entire Japanese Imperial Fleet was supposedly sighted off Diamond Head and invasions were occurring on other of the Hawai'ian Islands. None of this, of course, was true.

Facing the Navy that first night of war was one concern that was believed to be legitimate; sabotage. One surprise a day was all that the Navy wanted to handle and they were taking no chances whatsoever now. On board PYRO that concern was very seriously taken as a single saboteur could vaporize the entire ship and crew with ease.

Late in the day Samuel Cassius was told by the Chief Gunner's Mate to draw a rifle from the armory and stand guard over the ship during the night. Now, even under the unusual circumstances of the day, this was an extraordinary order. In the segregated navy of World War II, where black sailors were only allowed to work in menial jobs, giving a rifle to one was just plain unheard of. Captain Vytlacil heard what was going on and asked the Chief Gunner's Mate to explain his choice of Cassius. The Chief told the Captain that he had seen Cassius at a rifle range shooting holes through playing cards at a distance of about twelve feet. When Vytlacil commented that he could do the same thing himself, the Chief elaborated saying that Cassius wasn't shooting the cards face on, but rather he was splitting them in half with the card facing edgewise. Vytlacil approved the selection of Cassius as guard.

When Cassius arrived for guard duty he was told not to take any chances, he was to shoot first and ask questions later. Luckily he didn't have to follow that order as the night passed quietly.

THE WAR

Only seven days after the attack PYRO was headed back to the west coast of the United States to load up on ammunition for the battles to come.

At 0430 on the morning of December 14, 1941 a marauding Japanese submarine launched a torpedo at PYRO. In the pitch-blackness of the moonless night none of the lookouts spotted the tell tale sign of a periscope slicing through the water. Often times in war, luck is the deciding factor between survival and disaster. On this night luck was with PYRO. Having unloaded virtually all of her cargo in Pearl Harbor she was riding high in the water and the Japanese torpedo passed harmlessly beneath her keel.

For most of the first year of the war, until September 1942, PYRO routinely sailed between Hawai'i and San Francisco, loading up with munitions on the West Coast and then depositing them at Pearl Harbor and repeating the process. For the rest of the war PYRO wandered the Pacific like a camp follower, supplying the fleet with bullets, bombs, mines and shells as the slow but inevitable march towards Tokyo proceeded. She traveled as far north as the Aleutians and south to Australia in her mission to keep the guns firing.

PYRO was in the Admiralty Islands being overhauled when the Japanese surrender came.

FATE

She arrived in Seattle, Washington on November 21, 1945 delivering very happy troops returning from the war and then on to San Francisco to unload ammunition. PYRO returned to Seattle in June where she was decommissioned and turned over to the War Shipping Administration. For almost four years she sat waiting for the inevitable, which finally arrived in March 1950 when she was sold for scrapping to the National Metal and Steel Company.

USS Rail

LAPWING CLASS MINESWEEPER
AM-26
LAUNCHED: 1918

DECEMBER 7, 1941

Like most sailors at Pearl Harbor that day, 23 year old machinist Leland James didn't believe it when a fellow crewman rushed into the engine room and loudly announced that the Japanese were attacking. So, like all the other non-believers, James scrambled topside to see for himself. What he saw when he got there was a Japanese pilot flying overhead and looking straight at him from inside his cockpit. After that, James believed.

It took RAIL fifteen minutes to get her three-inch gun into action and twenty minutes for her .30 caliber machine guns to come alive. Despite this delay RAIL claimed shooting down one plane during the raid. RAIL, along with the other minesweepers berthed at the Coal Docks, moved out into the channel in order to get a better field of fire and also to make smaller targets for the enemy. When the last Japanese plane departed, RAIL commenced rescue and salvage operations in the harbor. Even though shrapnel fell on the minesweeper during the attack, RAIL suffered no damage or causalities.

THE WAR

RAIL was designated as a fleet tugboat, AT-139, in June 1942. She remained in Hawai'i until January 1943 when she headed out into the Pacific. There she performed the plethora of duties inherent to a tug.

In late June 1943 RAIL was dispatched to New Georgia Island to assist one of her Pearl Harbor sisters, USS ZANE, DMS-14, which had run aground during invasion operations. RAIL pulled her free from the rocks and towed her to Tulagi in the Solomons for repair. In late January 1945 she performed a similar service for another ship in distress: the attack transport USS CAVALIER, APA-37, was torpedoed near Manila Bay and left unable to maneuver. Once again RAIL arrived and took the wounded vessel in tow, delivering her to Leyte for repairs.

RAIL performed the critical chores of an ocean going tug for the rest of the war in the Philippines.

FATE

She remained in the South Pacific through the end of 1945, reporting to San Francisco the first week of February 1946. The naval career of RAIL was over when she was decommissioned in April 1946. She was then transferred to the Maritime Commission in January 1947.

USS Raleigh

OMAHA CLASS LIGHT CRUISER
CL-7
LAUNCHED: 1922

DECEMBER 7, 1941

Christmas was coming. Three-year-old Mary Jane Coleman was waiting for Santa to arrive. Whether he came in a sleigh pulled by magical reindeer or arrived on a surfboard made no difference to Mary Jane. Even though she didn't know it, she was also waiting for the ship to arrive from the States that would deliver the Christmas trees under which, her gaily-wrapped presents would be placed.

Mary Jane lived with her mother Agnes and her father William J. "Red" Coleman who was a Petty Officer 1st Class in the Navy and was assigned to the galley on board the light cruiser USS RALEIGH, CL-7. Their house was on Sierra Drive in Kaimuki, a quiet suburb of Honolulu that lay in the shadow of Diamond Head. "Red" had been at Pearl Harbor since 1939 when RALEIGH was switched from the Atlantic Fleet to the Pacific Fleet. Agnes and Mary Jane arrived in the summer of 1940. Life in Hawai'i was good.

At Pearl Harbor RALEIGH was tied up on the north side of Ford Island where the aircraft carriers were normally berthed. The first torpedoes dropped from enemy planes were meant for the carriers and RALEIGH took one directly amidships. The commanding officer, Captain Robert

Simons, was in his cabin when he felt the shudder of the explosion. He immediately reported to the bridge. He didn't take time to change out of the Annapolis bathrobe he was wearing.

RALEIGH began to list within minutes of being struck. Counter-flooding was begun but it was feared even that would not prevent the ship from capsizing. Simons gave the order to jettison anything and everything that could be to lighten her and make her less top heavy. The entire crew turned to and began stripping the ship. Items thrown overboard included, *"...torpedoes, minus their warheads, were pushed overboard by hand and beached at Ford Island. Both torpedo tubes, both catapults, the steel cargo boom, were all disconnected and jettisoned by hand power. Also, all stanchions, boat skids and life rafts and booms were jettisoned. Both anchors were let go."* [47] The cruiser's two SOC[48] biplanes were also lowered into the water by hand. They then taxied across the harbor, under their own power, to the air station on Ford Island.

On Sierra Drive in Kaimuki "Red" Coleman got into his uniform and hightailed it for his ship. Agnes was left to wonder if she would ever see her husband again. She stood in her living room and looked out the window toward Pearl Harbor. In the distance she could see planes swarming in the air.

Despite the hit from the torpedo and the ever-increasing list the gun crews of RALEIGH fought back. All her anti-aircraft batteries were firing and had been since the beginning of the air raid. By the end of the day RALEIGH claimed shooting down or assisting with shooting down five enemy planes.

There were few wounded on board and Capt. Simons sent the senior doctor to the hospital ship USS SOLACE, AH-5. He also sent a party of men over to the former battleship USS UTAH, AG-16, which had rolled over on her port side in the first minutes of the raid. They brought with them an acetylene torch to try to cut men out of their steel tomb. During the lull between the first and second wave of the attack, Simons returned to his cabin. Once there he finally got out of his bathrobe. Fully expecting to

---

47 From after action report, dated December 13, 1944 by Captain Robert B. Simons.
48 Scout Observation Curtiss

die sometime in the ensuing hours, he put on his full dress white uniform and reported back to the bridge.

After the initial torpedo in the opening seconds of the attack, RALEIGH received little, if any, attention from the enemy. The second wave took more interest in her and soon bombs were falling all around the cruiser. At 0908 a 500-pound armor-piercing bomb struck her main deck aft. The projectile passed completely through the ship, including traveling through a tank full of fuel oil, finally exiting the hull and exploding in the muddy bottom of the harbor. This wound did not help with her stability problems.

After the attack RALEIGH was tended to by several tugs that delivered pontoons to help keep her afloat. They also supplied electric power, steam and food. By the end of the day "Red" Coleman and the rest of the crew had returned and all hands went about saving their ship. Commander William Wallace, the Executive Officer, was not on board during the attack. He was also among the late arrivals. In his after action report, he made an interesting observation, "...*all officers and men on the USS RALEIGH...were tried and found not wanting, especially those officers and men who were fortunate enough to be aboard during the action.*" [49]

In the afternoon Agnes Coleman walked to the top of the hill behind her house to get a better view of Pearl Harbor. When she got there she saw nothing. A blanket of black, malevolent smoke obscured her view of the harbor. That night, darkness, fear and the radio kept her and Mary Jane company.

Later on the radio announced that the harbor was being bombed again and Agnes could see from her living room window the light show of tracers arcing through the sky. That excitement was followed by a period of silence that was shattered once again by a frantic radio announcement. This time the erroneous announcement was made that the Japanese had landed on O'ahu. Terror now replaced fear.

The next few nights were spent the same way. A blackout had been ordered, but knowing they would be evacuated soon, Agnes didn't bother

---

49   From after action report, dated December 12, 1941 by Commander William H. Wallace.

with blackout curtains. At night she went into a small walk-in closet that had a single light bulb in it to read and write. Three days after the attack "Red" managed to get a note to Agnes telling her he was fine. The next day, December 11th, he made it home for a quick visit.

The Christmas tree never did show up in Mary Jane's living room, so a poinsettia stood in. Santa Claus did visit Mary Jane and she got gifts in her stocking and opened presents. The best gift was that her father "Red" got to hold her in his arms.

THE WAR

Some quick repairs were made on RALEIGH at the Pearl Harbor Navy Yard. The hole in her hull was simply plugged up with cement. Under her own power she then sailed to Mare Island for more permanent repairs.

Through July 1942, when her repairs were completed, to November 1942 RALEIGH was occupied with mostly escort and patrol duties in the Pacific. Then in November she sailed north to the Aleutian Islands where she spent the next two years. While en route, she managed to damage her hull and once again the problem was solved with copious amounts of cement, this time contributed by the Navy Construction Battalions, better known as the "Sea Bees."

While in the frozen north, RALEIGH participated in all major actions of the Aleutians campaign. She shelled Attu and Kiska and covered the landings on Amchitka and Attu.

For a time, an invasion of the Japanese mainline from the north was considered by the United States. That plan was eventually discarded. But deception is as much a part of war as direct action. The United States continued efforts to make the Japanese believe that despite the steady march of allied forces through the South Pacific, the real thrust might come from the north. Sporadic harassment of Japanese bases in the Kuril Islands, north of Japan, by aerial and naval bombardment, helped to convince the enemy of just such an alternative. From 1943 to 1944 the Japanese more than quadrupled the troops there from 8,000 to 41,000. In the first week of February 1944 RALEIGH became part of that deception.

RALEIGH, along with another cruiser and six destroyers, proceeded to Paramushiro Island.[50] There they conducted a severe bombardment of Japanese outposts. In 1944, the Kuril Islands were part of Japan, so for the crew of RALEIGH, bombarding Japanese soil was considered immense payback for Pearl Harbor.

RALEIGH fired on coastal batteries while the other ships focused on airfields and hangars. The bombardment wreaked havoc on the Japanese. The installations that were hit burned for five hours afterward and RALEIGH expended over 500 six-inch shells. The bombardment of Paramushiro was the last major action for RALEIGH of the war.

Shortly after Paramushiro, RALEIGH underwent overhaul at Puget Sound Navy Yard and then returned to the Aleutians for a short time. Damage to one of her engines forced a return to Puget Sound. She never went to war again. Her last duty during the war was to conduct training cruises for Midshipmen from the Naval Academy at Annapolis.

FATE

The last voyage of RALEIGH was to the Philadelphia Navy Yard where she was decommissioned on November 2, 1945. She was sold for scrap in February 1946.

50　Now, Paramushir Island of the Russian Federation.

USS Ralph Talbot

BAGLEY CLASS DESTROYER
DD-390
LAUNCHED: 1936

DECEMBER 7, 1941

Louis A. Wilson was unique among his shipmates. First, at 27, he was older than most of them. Secondly, by December 1941, he had already been in the Navy for over six years. Thirdly, and perhaps more significantly, in a Navy where transfers to other ships were the norm, Wilson was a "plank owner" of the RALPH TALBOT. That meant that he was a member of the original crew assigned to her when she was commissioned in October 1937. Wilson was a Boatswain's Mate and his battle station was the No. 2 five-inch gun. On this day he was nowhere near it.

He was, in fact, at the southern end of the harbor at Merry Point Landing. Along with other sailors there he heard the bombs falling on the airplanes at nearby Hickam Field. The first Japanese planes successfully neutralized the Army Air Corps at that base giving the enemy almost absolute control of the skies over Pearl Harbor.

The sounds of bombs exploding at Hickam almost immediately were drowned out by the roar of engines only 100 feet above his head. Looking up he saw the source of those roars, the first torpedo planes flying over the submarine base heading straight for Battleship Row. It was only seconds later that the realization came that the Japanese were attacking.

A launch approached the Merry Point dock and Wilson along with his shipmates commandeered it in order to return to their ship nested in East Loch. Once out in the harbor a patrol boat pulled along side the launch and ordered them to report to Ford Island. The sailors reluctantly turned about. As they sailed for their new destination, the whoosh of a deafening explosion and the accompanying shock wave washed over them as ARIZONA, BB-39, blew up just a few hundred yards distant. Before the rumble had a chance to die away, flaming debris from the battleship rained down around the launch. For Wilson and his shipmates the harbor was becoming a very dangerous place, but Lady Luck was still with them. Having been missed by the falling metal from ARIZONA, they continued on to Ford Island only to have a "Kate" torpedo plane, with its torpedo still attached, crash in the harbor directly in front of them. The watery obstacle course finally showed some mercy and they docked, unscathed, on Ford Island.

Onboard their ship, the rest of the crew of RALPH TALBOT was preparing to get underway. She was firing both her main five-inch batteries and her small caliber anti-aircraft guns and claimed probable hits on at least three enemy planes. One of the ship's boats was sent to disengage the anchor chain but was having difficulty getting to it. Coxswain, Edward J. Chavies took it upon himself to go over the side near the bow, where he grabbed onto the anchor chain. He then went hand over hand down the chain, dropped into the water, swam over to the buoy and released the chain so the ship could get underway. RALPH TALBOT sortied around 0900 and exited the harbor via the North Channel, passing the #1 sea buoy at 0934.

On Ford Island, Louis Wilson and his shipmates had been dragooned into fighting fires and when they were put out, they helped pull the dead and wounded out of the ravaged battleships. They were stuck in Pearl Harbor as their ship sailed without them. They didn't see her again for three days.

THE WAR
The first months of 1942 found RALPH TALBOT escorting and screening. She helped screen ENTERPRISE, CV-6, during a raid on the Marshall

Islands in January and covered the flattop once again in February for a raid on Wake Island.

In August she found herself in the Solomons at the outset of Guadalcanal operations. In the early morning hours of August 9th, RALPH TALBOT was acting as a picket northeast of Savo Island, searching for a Japanese task force heading for Guadalcanal. Shortly after 0200, she spotted the unmistakable flashes of a surface battle taking place south of her position and she rushed to join the fray. Minutes later a searchlight raked her and within seconds she was under attack. In rapid succession, the enemy gunners, who were superbly trained for nighttime naval battles, landed four direct hits on the destroyer. One shell each obliterated the chart house, the wardroom, a torpedo tube, and the No. 4 five-inch gun. RALPH TALBOT also fired, getting off four torpedoes and some five-inch rounds. Unfortunately, her fire was either inaccurate or ineffective.

The shelling and resulting fires gave her a twenty-degree list to starboard and reduced her speed drastically. She sailed to nearby Savo Island where the fires and flooding were brought under control. Minimum repairs were made and by noon she was able to make it back to Tulagi. The encounter with the enemy cost twelve dead, two missing and presumed dead, and twenty-five wounded. Her next stop was Mare Island Naval Shipyard for a month's long stay to fully repair her damage.

A year later RALPH TALBOT was once again in the Solomons, where the efforts to remove the Japanese from those islands continued. On the night of July 12/13, 1943, she was part of a force of three cruisers and ten destroyers that mixed it up with one enemy cruiser and five destroyers in the Battle of Kolombangara. RALPH TALBOT came out of the engagement unscathed but not so USS GWIN, DD-433. GWIN had taken a single Japanese torpedo amidships, which spelled her doom. About seven hours later, after all attempts to save the wounded destroyer had come to naught, RALPH TALBOT took on survivors and then stood off to deliver the coup de grâce. She let loose four torpedoes which struck GWIN and sent her to the bottom of the Pacific.

Throughout the rest of 1943 and all of 1944, RALPH TALBOT seemed to be everywhere there was action in the Pacific. She provided shore bombardments at New Britain, Saidor, Garapan Harbor and Tinian. She covered landings at Kiriwina, Cape Gloucester and Garapan Harbor and participated in operations at the Bonon Islands, Yap and Palau. When she wasn't performing those jobs, she was patrolling for the enemy or providing convoy escorts.

RALPH TALBOT was just one of the 97 destroyers that took part in the siege of Okinawa from March 26th through June 21, 1945. Of those 97 ships, 88 were damaged in battle. RALPH TALBOT was one of those. She survived April 6th when seven individual kamikazes sank two destroyers and five more planes damaged three other ships. The following day fleet forces around Okinawa shot down 54 attacking kamikazes, an indicator of the ferocity with which the Japanese intended to wield this new and terrible weapon.

On April 27th at 2200, RALPH TALBOT was conducting an antiaircraft patrol off of Hagushi, Okinawa. Hunting in the darkness were two kamikazes that found the destroyer. The first slammed into her stern on the starboard side. The second plane splashed into the water off her port quarter narrowly missing her. Casualties inflicted by the attack were 5 dead and 9 wounded. In less than fifteen minutes, flooding was brought under control. She reported to nearby Kerama Retto for repairs and in less than a month she was back in action.

RALPH TALBOT played a small but vital role in the closing days of the war. The cruiser USS INDIANAPOLIS, CA-35, delivered the enriched uranium and other parts for the atomic bomb that was to be dropped on Hiroshima to the island of Tinian on July 26, 1945. Four days later INDIANAPOLIS was sunk in mid-ocean by the Japanese submarine *I-58*. Over 800 of her crew went into the Pacific Ocean, and there, they fought to stay alive against nature for another four days. Patrolling aircraft on August 2nd spotted survivors. RALPH TALBOT, along with other ships, received orders to rescue their fellow bluejackets. She searched until August 8th ultimately saving 24 INDIANAPOLIS sailors.

FATE

As part of the occupation of the defeated Japanese, RALPH TALBOT sailed into the port of Sasebo, Japan on September 16, 1945, helping to establish an American naval presence that continues still.

In July 1946, the atomic tests known as Operation Crossroads took place at Bikini Atoll. RALPH TALBOT, one of the most decorated American destroyers of World War II, was chosen to participate, but not as a working vessel. She was chosen to be a target. After suffering the blasts and radiation of the air burst test "Able" on July 1st and the underwater burst test "Baker" three weeks later on the 25th, she was nothing more than 2,245 tons of radioactive steel. She was towed to Kwajalein where she sat until she was unceremoniously sunk on March 8, 1948.

USS Ramapo

PATOKA CLASS OILER
AO-12
LAUNCHED: 1919

DECEMBER 7, 1941

On board RAMAPO, docked at the Navy Yard, Quartermaster 1st Class J. A. Moses heard the sound of planes overhead and looked up. He spotted a gray plane in a steep dive a half-mile away over the hangars of the Ford Island Naval Air Station. Following the plane's progress until it was about 100 feet off the deck, he watched the "Val" drop the first Japanese bomb against American forces in World War II and then pull up rapidly. Five more planes followed in rapid succession, all bombing the naval air station.

For the next hour and fifty minutes RAMAPO fought back and quickly fell into the rhythm of war, shooting first at the dive bombers than the high level horizontal bombers then back to the dive bombers with the occasional distraction of fighters. One bomb that was probably meant for the heavy cruiser USS NEW ORLEANS, CA-32, berthed at the pier on RAMAPO's port side, exploded in the water between the two ships causing minor shrapnel damage to both. Heavy fire was put up by RAMAPO for the entire attack with the possibility of one kill. There were no casualties to the crew and only minor damage.

THE WAR

RAMAPO made two trips to Bora Bora at the onset of hostilities. She spent the rest of the war supplying oil from refineries and storage depots on the American west coast to the Aleutians and to ships operating in the North Pacific.

FATE

When the war was over RAMAPO was decommissioned and turned over to the Maritime Commission on July 1, 1946, which placed her in the Reserve Fleet in Suisun Bay, California. RAMAPO was sold and resold three times until she was finally flagged as a Liberian tanker in 1950.

USS Ramsay

WICKES CLASS DESTROYER / LIGHT MINELAYER
DM-16
LAUNCHED: 1918

DECEMBER 7, 1941

Her first 23 years of life were rather uneventful in a peacetime navy. RAMSAY missed out on participating in the conflict she was built for: World War I. Between the end of that war and the attack on Pearl Harbor she had been decommissioned and recommissioned twice. Her time had finally come. This day she fired her first shots in anger.

In the opening minutes of the war she engaged the enemy planes with both her three-inch main guns and .50 caliber machine guns. Berthed in Middle Loch near Pearl City she was underway an hour after the raid began. As she sailed out of the channel her .50 caliber machine gunners targeted a plane and brought it down.

RAMSAY was one of the many ships that got underway and sortied from the harbor during the attack. Upon exiting Pearl Harbor she commenced anti-submarine patrols. At 1120 she made sonar contact with what she believed to be an enemy submarine. She commenced an attack dropping 10 depth charges. An oil slick was reported as a result of her offensive action. But, like many American ships that day, no positive proof of a sinking manifested itself. Japanese records indicate that no submarines assigned to the Hawai'i operation were sunk or lost that day except the five mini subs which have all been accounted for.

THE WAR

She started off the first several months of the war engaged in patrol and escort duties in and around Hawai'i. Late February 1942 found her setting sail for Fiji where she completed her first mine laying operations of the war, followed in rapid succession by mine laying in Samoa and Efate. For the next three years RAMSAY criss-crossed the Pacific from the west coast of the United States to Eniwetok and from the Aleutians to Samoa. She engaged in escort and patrol duty, screening and anti-submarine patrols and towards the end of the war, submarine training activities.

FATE

In October 1945 RAMSAY was decommissioned for the third and last time. After 27 years of service she was sold for scrap in November.

Reedbird

REEDBIRD CLASS COASTAL
MINESWEER
AMc-30
LAUNCHED: 1935

DECEMBER 7, 1941

Every morning two of the coastal minesweepers from the Bishop Point, Section Base would venture into the Pacific Ocean outside Pearl Harbor and sweep for mines. This was done religiously. On December 7, 1941, according to the 14th Naval District Duty Logs, REEDBIRD and COCKATOO, AMc-8, were supposed to sweep that morning. For some reason a change was made and CROSSBILL, AMc-9, and CONDOR, AMc-14, went out instead.

During the attack the Section Base was pretty much ignored by the enemy planes. The best REEDBIRD could do was to take potshots with her .30-caliber guns at any stray planes that happened by. At 0915, according to her log, she was underway and sailing out of the channel towards open ocean. By 1020 she was sweeping for mines outside the Pearl Harbor entrance. She continued sweeping for almost six hours ceasing operations at 1710.

THE WAR

As with all the other coastal minesweepers, REEDBIRD spent the entire war keeping local Hawai'ian waters cleared of mines for inter-island shipping. This entailed sweeping for mines around a particular island and then reporting back to the Section Base. The process would then repeat itself, rotating through the islands on a regular basis. Lieutenant Charles Winfrey, who was captain of REEDBIRD at the end of the war, said that compared to battle, being in command of a coastal minesweeper was easy, but that it could be "intense, pressure packed duty."

FATE

Within months of the war's end REEDBIRD returned to the United States, arriving in San Diego, where she was placed out of service in January 1946. She was turned over to the Maritime Commission for final disposal in November of the same year.

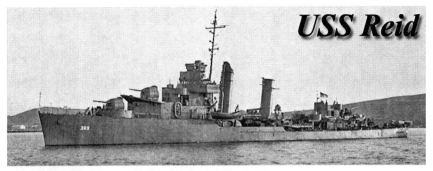

MAHAN CLASS DESTROYER
DD-369
LAUNCHED: 1936

DECEMBER 7, 1941

Nested alongside the tender USS WHITNEY, AD-4, with four other destroyers, REID was tucked away quietly at the far northeastern edge of Pearl Harbor in East Loch. Undergoing routine maintenance, her crew was marking time awaiting a December 11th departure for several weeks' leave in the States. That trip, of course, never came.

It took fifteen minutes for her machine guns to get into action and twenty-five minutes for her main five-inch guns to respond. REID and the ships in her nest were subject to a couple of strafings but other than that no direct enemy action was taken against them. In his after action report, REID's captain, Commander Harold F. Pullen, reported expending 200 five-inch shells and 5,000 rounds of .50-caliber ammunition. He credited one enemy plane shot down to the collective fire of the nest. She sortied from the harbor twenty-five minutes after the end of the attack at 1010.

THE WAR

Throughout early 1942 REID carried out patrol and escort duties in the central and eastern Pacific. After escorting several convoys to the west coast REID sailed to the Aleutians where she participated in the efforts to dislodge the Japanese from that American territory.

On August 31, 1942 the pilot of a PBY Catalina spotted a Japanese submarine running on the surface just north of Atka Island and dropped depth charges on it. He then notified REID, now captained by Lieutenant Commander Harry McIlhenay. Upon arrival, McIlhenay discovered an oil slick indicating a probable hit by the PBY's depth charges. A sonar search soon found a target and, like a hound on the scent of a fox, REID went after it.

One hundred and thirty feet beneath the surface of the icy Bering Sea, Lieutenant Commander Tokutomi Toshisada was desperately trying to save his damaged submarine, *RO-61*. The first depth charges from the PBY did indeed wound the sub and the initial series of depth charges dropped by REID forced the sub to dive to two hundred feet in order to escape further harm, but REID was relentless. Another pattern of depth charges wreaked havoc on *RO-61* and her engine rooms began to flood. For more than an hour REID dropped depth charges on the Japanese submarine, severely injuring it. Fires broke out on board and a petty officer died from inhaling chlorine gas from damaged batteries. At this point Lieutenant Commander Tokutomi had no option left but to order his boat to surface.

When the enemy sub arose from the depths, its crew immediately manned the deck gun but REID was waiting and soon had the sub in her sights. The destroyer raked the sub's deck with 20mm fire and decimated the Japanese sailors there. McIlhenay then unleashed his main five-inch battery on *RO-61*. Her shells ripped holes in the sub and it capsized taking with it Commander Tokutomi and the crew, save five survivors who were picked up by REID.

After having spent time in late 1942 supporting the ongoing battles on Guadalcanal, a year later REID was off the coast of New Guinea. There, on Wednesday, September 22, 1943, she was covering the Australian landings near Finschhafen. Onboard REID were Army Air Corps spotters whose job it was to call in and direct air cover for the ships. Late in the morning, after a beachhead had been firmly established, over 50 enemy planes arrived to attack both the landing forces and the ships protecting them. The Air Corps spotters called in an opposing force of approximately 90 American P-38 and P-40 fighter planes. In the ensuing air battle the Americans shot down over 35 enemy aircraft. Despite the terrific dogfights many of the Japanese got through the air cover. Two torpedo planes targeted REID but the destroyer's anti-aircraft batteries destroyed both. Unfortunately, before they were blown up, each one had dropped their torpedo and they headed straight for REID.

The destroyer's fate had been sealed. There was nothing to do but wait for the inevitable. The two deadly torpedoes inexorably sliced their way through the water. The crew let loose a collective sigh of relief as the first torpedo missed, passing directly in front of the bow. The reprieve was only temporary as the second onrushing torpedo could be clearly seen headed directly amidships. But the gods of modern ocean warfare once again smiled on REID as this torpedo, set to run too deep, passed harmlessly underneath the hull.

Eight months later, in June 1944, she was once again off New Guinea, this time off the northwest coast island of Biak, participating in covering Allied landings of that island. Around 1100 on the morning of the 3rd, a flight of almost 20 Japanese planes - comprised of level bombers, dive bombers and fighters - flew out of some low clouds and dropped over a ridge on the island heading out to strike the ships supporting the landings. As they approached, the closest ship to them and the only one in the immediate area was REID. A least 14 of the planes swarmed the lone destroyer.

Every man on board REID knew that they were in a fight for their lives. The Japanese were merciless. While the bombers dropped their explosives, the fighters strafed. Commander Samuel A. McCornock, the captain of REID, ordered flank speed and commenced a violent and random zigzag pattern as an evasive maneuver. Many bombs hit uncomfortably close but there were no direct hits. Planes came at REID from every angle, they were virtually everywhere. Anti-aircraft guns ripped into the attacking planes, bringing one down by shearing a wing off of it and splashing at least two more. During the onslaught, two of the destroyer's 20mm anti-aircraft batteries were fired with such intensity that they malfunctioned. Only one was repaired and brought back into action during the fight. For more than twenty minutes REID stood alone against the flock of raptors determined to kill her. Eventually, like the cavalry in a western movie, some American P-40 and P-47 fighters arrived and drove off the remaining attackers. REID survived the vicious assault but one sailor was killed and four wounded. For his brilliant leadership and superb seamanship, Commander McCornock was awarded the Bronze Star.

From Pearl Harbor, Hawai'i to Biak, New Guinea REID met, almost exclusively, an enemy that came at her from the sky and she prevailed over that enemy with extraordinary skill, amazing courage and a good share of luck. The final act of the war would test her again as she faced the last and most deadly Japanese threat from the air – the kamikaze.

FATE

The Battle of Ormoc Bay on the island of Leyte was but one very small part of the recapture of the Philippines. On December 7, 1944 the United States Army 77th Infantry Division was landed there. Four days later, REID was the lead ship in a convoy sailing north that was resupplying that invasion. In the late afternoon, around 1700, radar picked up a flight of 12 enemy planes flying south, straight for the convoy. Four American escort planes rushed ahead to engage the enemy, but being outnumbered they couldn't stop them all. As before, at Biak, the Japanese planes swarmed REID, this time because she was the lead ship. At least five of the Nakajima B6N2 "Jill" bombers concentrated on REID.

The difference now, however, was that Japan was desperate to bring the United States to the negotiating table and obtain almost anything other than a humiliating unconditional surrender. In order to meet that end they were willing to try anything. Thus was born the kamikaze. The enemy planes were now guided missiles whose payloads were bombs, high-octane aviation fuel, and the willingness of the pilot to die for the Emperor.

Once again, the anti-aircraft batteries on REID were firing as fast as they could and they rapidly brought down three attacking planes. But this airborne "banzai" charge was guaranteed to overwhelm the destroyer's ability to protect itself. Lady Luck, at last, abandoned REID.

The wing of one plane struck REID causing the aircraft to cartwheel into her hull at the waterline, its bomb exploding. Two other planes narrowly missed her but crashed on either side of her bow, exploding. One last plane did its job superbly. It crashed directly into the No. 3 gun astern and skittered along the superstructure coming to rest on the port side 40mm gun tub. The bomb it was carrying dislodged and penetrated into the interior of REID and exploded, detonating the ship's magazine. All these planes crashed into the destroyer within the space of 60 seconds.

The ship began to sink immediately. She was so mauled she didn't know which way to sink. She lunged to her starboard side and then began to right herself and then repeated this seesaw motion several more times. While this went on she began to settle rapidly by the stern. In fact, she was sinking so fast that men were waist deep in water at their battle stations on the exposed deck as they fired at the still attacking planes. Even as she sank, her impetus kept her sailing forward. She was still moving at twenty knots but slowing rapidly.

Although it was patently unnecessary, Commander McCornock ordered abandon ship. His vessel was now lying on her starboard side and under water up to her No. 1 smokestack. Standing with the port side of the ship under his feet instead of the deck, he took one final look at what was left of his ship and his crew and he dove into the ocean. In the best tradition of the sea, he was the last man to leave the ship. It took just three minutes total for REID to cease to exist. From the last hit of the kamikazes to the time REID disappeared only two minutes elapsed. After REID was beneath the water, several explosions occurred, more than likely her boilers blowing up. The concussion from these explosions killed several of the survivors in the water.

The convoy commander assigned LCI(L)-661 (Landing Craft Infantry, Large), to pick up survivors, which she did expertly, recovering 66 sailors from the sea, all within about thirty minutes.

There were 120 who survived the sinking and 106 lost. When the survivors were debriefed back in the States they were told to say that they had been torpedoed. The sailors asked why they were to lie about what happened to them and their ship. They were told that information on how effective kamikazes were wasn't to leak out.

USS Rigel

RIGEL CLASS DESTROYER TENDER
AR-11
LAUNCHED: 1918

DECEMBER 7, 1941

A lazy Sunday morning is the perfect time to enjoy the natural wonders of the island of O'ahu. It was 0615 when Chief Electricians Mate W. H. Moore and Machinist Mate H. H. Vanaman departed RIGEL to revel in the simple joys of a hike in the hills above the town of Aiea overlooking Pearl Harbor. Just before 0800 they reached a vantage point that gave them a great view of the island. They couldn't help but notice that their calm idyll was disturbed by more than a hundred planes flying directly over them from the north. They watched as the planes split off, some heading for Pearl Harbor and some heading for the airbase at Hickam Field.

Miles away in the harbor, RIGEL, undergoing significant alterations, sat helpless at a Navy Yard pier with no power and no armament. With no way to help herself, her crew did the only other thing they could do: they helped others. The senior officer on board was Lieutenant Commander Loar Mansbach who promptly ordered repair parties organized that could go to the aid of other ships when the inevitable need arose.

Two other officers, Ensign Charles R. Hake and Ensign James P. Bienia took charge of two of RIGEL's motorboats, organized volunteer crews for them and ventured into the chaotic harbor to help where they could. Bienia and his crew had no sooner gotten into the water when a bomb passed directly through their boat and exploded underneath it, sinking it and throwing him and his crew into the water, severely injuring two of his men.

Hake managed to get his boat out into the harbor in one piece and headed straight for Battleship Row and the already battered USS WEST VIRGINIA, BB-48. If any man-made scene could be out of Dante's Inferno, this was certainly it. The water around WEST VIRGINIA was an oily conflagration punctuated with the cries for help of sailors who had jumped off or been blown off the crippled battleship. Hake and his crew began picking men out of the water, men who were injured or exhausted or on fire or unconscious. The sailors in RIGEL's motor launch pulled so many men out of the hellish harbor that they lost track of the number, but they estimated at least fifty and perhaps as many as one hundred.

All during their rescue efforts the Japanese attack continued to swirl around them. Bombs fell all about them, bullets whizzed past their heads and torpedoes coursed beneath their tiny boat. Of these men, the commanding officer of RIGEL, Captain Roy Dudley said, *It is considered that Ensign Hake and the crew of #1 motor launch...are deserving of special commendation for the initiative, resourcefulness, devotion to duty and personal bravery displayed on this occasion*.[51]

In the hills above Aiea, Moore and Vanaman watched the drama unfold before them like a tableau. To the east they saw high-level bombers dropping their loads of destruction on Hickam Field, expertly neutralizing the Army Air Corps and preventing them from intervening over the skies of Pearl Harbor. As if they were sitting in the balcony of a great movie palace looking at a Cecile B. DeMille spectacular the two men watched in awe as the "Kate" torpedo planes decimated the Pacific Fleet.

THE WAR

RIGEL remained in Pearl Harbor for the next four months until work on her was complete. This included the installation of four three-inch guns. She would never be defenseless again.

---

51   After action report by Captain Roy Dudley, dated December 9, 1941.

On paper RIGEL was a destroyer tender, but like many naval vessels she was called on to do more than just what she was designed for. She repaired or maintained not only destroyers, but also everything from landing craft to battleships. She helped to convert civilian ships to military use and even installed new 20mm anti-aircraft guns on herself. Her crews also assisted in construction jobs on shore. RIGEL became an itinerant repair ship roaming the South Pacific staying in a port for a few weeks or a few months and then moving on to the next port. Several times she was even used to transport troops and cargo. Her last port of call was San Pedro Bay, Philippines where she stayed for the last seven months of the war.

FATE

Less than a year after the Japanese surrender, RIGEL was back in the states where she was decommissioned and turned over to the Maritime Commission in July 1946.

USS Sacramento

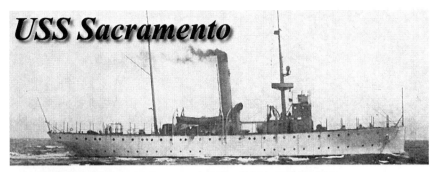

SACRAMENTO CLASS GUNBOAT
PG-19
LAUNCHED: 1914

DECEMBER 7, 1941

In 1939 Jack Moore was a 17-year-old high school kid who joined the Navy on a dare. In December 1941 he was a 19-year-old Gunner's Mate, reading the Sunday morning paper below decks aboard SACRAMENTO. Lieutenant Commander F. F. Knachel, the Executive Officer of SACRAMENTO, was in command of the vessel that morning. She was docked at berth B-6 in the Navy Yard between 1010 dock and the yard craft pier.

When the attack began it was discovered that her four-inch gun couldn't be adequately elevated to fire at the planes, so that gun's crew was issued Browning Automatic Rifles (B.A.R.) and Thompson .45 caliber sub-machine guns and stationed on the pier to fire at low flying planes. Jack Moore was the first one to arrive at his battle station, a .50 caliber machine gun. He didn't wait for the rest of the crew. He just loaded it and started firing. Standing there on the deck of his ship, Moore looked closely at the low flying enemy planes. Many of them, on strafing or torpedo runs, flew below 100 feet. At one point a Japanese plane flew by and Moore and the enemy pilot saw each other, and, for an instant, their eyes locked. The moment so burned itself into his memory he would be able to recall it clearly 68 years later. Many, many others later recounted almost identical incidents in the harbor that day.

SACRAMENTO's other anti-aircraft guns fired unrelentingly helping to splash two planes in conjunction with fire from other nearby ships. One of these crashed near the Naval Hospital.

As on other ships, those crewmembers that weren't fighting were helping others. One of the motor launches was sent to help fish survivors from sunken ships out of the burning water. When the attack concluded, SACRAMENTO handed out ammunition and dry stores to the destroyer MUGFORD, DD-389, which had been berthed next to her. She gave a rescue breathing apparatus to CALIFORNIA, BB-44. The atmosphere of danger, teamwork, and urgency was such that SACRAMENTO issued a fire extinguisher to an unknown boat that came alongside and just asked for one.

As the sun went down that evening, SACRAMENTO had suffered no damage, reported only two minor injuries, and had expended almost 20,000 rounds of small arms ammunition.

THE WAR

SACRAMENTO was assigned to patrol the Hawai'ian Sea Frontier and she did so through September 1942. She was then transferred to Palmyra Island, just over 1,000 miles south of Hawai'i, and attached to Motor Torpedo Boat Squadron 2, as a tender. The Naval Air Station there also utilized her services for air-sea rescue duties. She remained there only two months as she was ordered to San Diego in late November 1942. For all intents and purposes the war ended here for SACRAMENTO.

For the next two years and four months SACRAMENTO was used to train sailors as gun crews for the war that she had left behind. Then towards the very end of the war, in March 1945, SACRAMENTO moved north to San Francisco where she performed weather patrols.

FATE

Having been named after its capital, it seems fitting that SACRAMENTO spent almost the entire war operating in California and when the war was over she didn't have to go far. She was decommissioned in Suisun Bay, California, near Mare Island and then transferred to the War Shipping Administration. In August 1947, she was sold for use as a merchant vessel under the Italian flag and renamed *Fermina*.

USS San Francisco

NEW ORLEANS CLASS HEAVY CRUISER
CA-38
LAUNCHED: 1933

DECEMBER 7, 1941

SAN FRANCISCO was supposed to be in Dry Dock #1 at the Navy Yard in Pearl Harbor. Work on the battleship USS PENSYLVANIA, BB-38, was taking longer than expected and she was still in the dry dock, so SAN FRANCISCO was berthed at a pier waiting her turn. However, she was ready for her scheduled work. Much of her ammunition had been removed and some of her machinery was already disassembled and sitting on the dock. None of her guns, from her large eight-inch main batteries down to her small caliber anti-aircraft guns, was operational.

Richard Freeman and his twin brother Reese were native Georgians. They were assigned to SAN FRANCISCO and had joined the Navy at Macon in June 1939. The brothers had turned twenty years old three months before. Like most of the crew, they were enjoying their lazy Sunday morning on board. On deck, just before 0800, was Boyd Williamson, waiting for the ship's Marine detail to raise the flag for morning colors.

James Sherrell had just finished breakfast and was also heading on deck to witness the raising of the flag. Just as he stepped out of the hatch he was greeted with the sight and sound of planes rocketing down Southeast Loch toward Battleship Row. Even at the speeds the planes were flying, the faces of the pilots were clearly visible. Sherrell also clearly saw the large red circle contrasting against the dark green paint of the fuselage.

Orders were quickly given for all hands to report below decks to give them shelter from the storm about to break over the harbor. The only avenue of offense available to SAN FRANCISCO was small arms, so that locker was opened and weapons distributed. Richard Freeman was issued a 1903 .30 caliber bolt action Springfield rifle. He stood, alongside shipmate Ted Tupper and others with rifles, totally exposed on deck, firing at passing enemy planes. Years later Freeman admitted that he had no idea if he hit anything that he shot at that day.

Since her gun crews had nothing to do onboard SAN FRANCISCO they were sent to assist with the guns on the heavy cruiser USS NEW ORLEANS, CA-32, berthed directly across the pier. The light minelayer, USS TRACY, DM-19, was just ahead of SAN FRANCISCO in the slip and .50-caliber ammunition was passed to her for her guns.

Boyd Williamson was ordered out into the harbor in a motor launch. Once on the water he proceeded to recover bodies. They were everywhere. He and the other sailors in the boat pulled the dead from the water until the launch was full. The bodies were then ferried to an improvised morgue on Ford Island. A return trip to the harbor would then follow and the entire procedure then repeated. This went on throughout the raid and into the night. Only after it was dark did Williamson return to his ship.

In his after action report the commanding officer of SAN FRANCISCO, Captain Daniel J. Callaghan, related that there were no casualties to personnel and the only damage was to a searchlight.

THE WAR

If examined closely, almost any person, group, organization or country has its "day of days," that time or event that defines it, or changes it forever; that day that is remembered eternally and inexorably connects the subject with the occurrence. For some it may go unnoticed at the time, only to be recognized days, months, or even years later. For others, it is quite obvious as the experience takes place and unfolds around the participants that the time and event is significant.

For USS SAN FRANCISCO and her crew, the day of days was the twenty-four hour period of November 12-13, 1942. That time, and the events that occurred during it, both defined the ship and her crew, changed them forever and placed them and their deeds in a hallowed niche in American Naval history.

Shortly after Pearl Harbor, in April 1942, Captain Daniel Callaghan was promoted to Rear Admiral. In November he was made a Task Group[52] commander and it was only natural that he chose his old ship, SAN FRANCISCO, as his flagship.

Another change was made onboard SAN FRANCISCO in early November. On the 9th she received as her new commanding officer, Captain Cassin Young. Young was awarded the Medal of Honor for his actions as the captain of the repair ship USS VESTAL, AR-4, at Pearl Harbor. He had been promoted to captain in February 1942.

On November 12, 1942 SAN FRANCISCO was covering the unloading of supplies and personnel to reinforce Henderson Field, the airbase on Guadalcanal. The invasion of that Japanese stronghold was just over two months old and the outcome was still in doubt. The key to the American success was control of the skies and the continued occupation of Henderson Field was the key to that control. On the other hand, the Japanese could not allow Henderson Field to continue to operate in American hands. To that end they had a simple plan; destroy the field, the men on it, and the ships supporting it, then take back Guadalcanal.

At 1317, upon receiving notice of a flight of enemy planes approaching, SAN FRANCISCO and other ships screening the unloading cargo and troop ships, formed a picket line that the attackers would have to cross to get to their targets. Shortly thereafter a flight of about twenty, twin-engine, enemy torpedo planes were seen coming in from the north. They had flown in over Florida Island, hugging the contours of the land. Once over the water, they flew a mere fifty feet above the surface. At that altitude the green silhouette of the island behind them would blend in with their dark forest green colored planes, making it difficult for the anti-aircraft gunners to see them.

On SAN FRANCISCO Lieutenant, (jg) Albert T. Harris was in command of the aft 20mm anti-aircraft battery. He had reported to the

52 A group of ships attached to a larger Task Force.

cruiser as a new Ensign in January and had only recently been promoted. Helping to man one of those guns was Seaman Second Class Frank Slater a young Alabaman who had been on board seven months. In the aft control room for the main eight-inch batteries, just twenty feet above Harris, in Control Aft, was Lieutenant (jg) John G. Wallace. Wallace had graduated from Annapolis on December 19, 1941, just twelve days after the Pearl Harbor attack. He had been assigned to SAN FRANCISCO since his graduation. Not far from Wallace, Lieutenant (jg) John E. "Jack" Bennett was on the aft superstructure deck also directing ant-aircraft fire.

When the enemy planes started coming in, the screening ships opened fire and two planes were immediately destroyed. The eight-inch guns on SAN FRANCISCO did not have air burst shells in them, so rather than shooting directly at the planes, they fired at the ocean in front of them. The impacting shells sent up an enormous wall of water that the planes would have to either fly through or radically maneuver around to avoid. At best this might cause the plane to crash and at the least it would cause the pilot to interrupt his torpedo run and have to reacquire his target. The tactic had some small effect as several planes were observed making violent course changes to avoid the mountainous geysers. The anti-aircraft fire from the secondary five-inch and 20mm batteries was right on target as they splashed one plane and damaged two others.

In contrast to their success at Pearl Harbor, the Japanese torpedo planes struck out, scoring no hits at all. One torpedo was seen to skim off the water's surface like a skipping stone, leap back into the air and almost hit the plane that dropped it. Another ran erratically and doubled back in a circular path. Two torpedoes came at SAN FRANCISCO. But by turning, the cruiser avoided both of them, one passing ahead and another running along the starboard side.

As the attack waned almost all of the enemy planes had been shot down or forced to withdraw. There were only a few left and they were taking fire from all sides. Both SAN FRANCISCO and a transport, USS McCAWLEY, AP-10, had the same plane in their sights. It was making a run on SAN FRANCISCO. McCAWLEY had already hit the enemy aircraft causing the plane's starboard engine to erupt in flames. Even as it burned, the plane dropped its torpedo. The TNT fish cut through the ocean and as with all the others, missed, this one passing down the starboard side.

After releasing the torpedo the plane did not pull up. It just kept coming, heading straight for the heavy cruiser. Lt. (jg) Harris had all three of his 20mm guns pumping away at the plane. Inside the cockpit, one of three things had happened: either the pilot was dead at the stick and could not maneuver; or the plane was damaged with the same result; or the pilot had determined he and his plane were done for and he was going to take out SAN FRANCISCO anyway he could.

What orders, if any, Lt. (jg) Harris gave to Frank Slater and the other twenty men at the 20mm guns is unknown. What is known is that those guns continued firing with a white-hot rapidity, without pause or break. They continued firing, unerringly, unceasingly, until the big plane crashed directly into their gun platform killing all of them.[53] The plane's wing hooked on the mast, and the aircraft pirouetted around it, crashing in the water off the ships side. Like a liquid filled bladder ripped open by a knife, the plane's gas tank ruptured, spewing flaming aviation fuel everywhere.

Lt. (jg) Jack Bennett, was standing on the superstructure deck just as the plane hit. The aircraft's starboard wingtip sliced off and went twisting through the air and across the deck. The wingtip struck a glancing blow to Bennett's right elbow and spun the officer on his heels. Nearby, Lt. (jg) John Wallace heard the rate of fire from Harris' 20mm guns increase and he stepped out of his fire control room to see what was going on. Just before the enemy plane hit the ship, Wallace saw it and dove back into the compartment. A split second later the aircraft impacted and exploded, the concussion slamming Wallace against a bulkhead and knocking him out.

---

53 Almost all written recollections of this attack state the ship was struck by a Mitsubishi G4M "Betty" bomber. The official after action report dated November 16, 1942, by Lt. Cdr. H. E. Schonland states, *"Name plate from the plane which crashed this ship was obtained and is forwarded separately via airmail...Plane appears to have been a Mitsubishi 97 twin engine landplane, painted dark"*. The Mitsubishi 97 was the Japanese Army land based variant of the Mitsubishi Ki-21, code named "Sally".

When Wallace regained his senses he found himself on fire. He immediately jumped onto the canvas cover of a nearby motor launch and rolled until the flames were extinguished. He then made three separate trips into flaming compartments and retrieved three sailors, all of them severely burned. Reaching into his pocket, he retrieved a pack of six morphine syrettes[54] each officer had been issued before the battle and administered one to each of the men he rescued. Wallace then helped to organize firefighting details to extinguish the multiple fires started by the burning fuel.

The afternoon was spent cleaning up and repairing. Twenty-two wounded men were transferred to the transport, USS PRESIDENT JACKSON, AP-37. Refusing evacuation was Commander Mark Crouter, the executive officer of SAN FRANCISCO. Despite severe burns on his legs, he insisted on remaining on board.

With anti-aircraft flack still in the air, SAN FRANCISCO trails smoke from an enemy plane that crashed into her. The cruiser's wounded were later transferred to the transport USS PRESIDENT JACKSON in the left foreground

The early afternoon aerial attack was only phase one of the Japanese plan to kick the Americans off of Guadalcanal. Already on its way was a naval task force with a three-fold mission: bombard the Marines at Henderson Field; engage and destroy American Naval forces attempting to

---

54 A disposable syringe with a small tube of a premeasured drug attached to it, designed for one-time use.

interdict; and lastly, land reinforcement troops on the island. The formidable fourteen-ship flotilla sent down The Slot that day was comprised of eleven destroyers, one cruiser, and to top it all off, two battleships. American planes spotted the enemy ships long before they arrived. The speed they were traveling and the number and type of ships was relayed to those officers in charge. The Americans knew exactly what they were facing and what time they would be arriving.

The Americans put together a Task Group to meet the enemy. It had thirteen ships, made up of eight destroyers and five cruisers. Rear Admiral Daniel Callaghan on SAN FRANCISCO was placed in command of the Task Group and Rear Admiral Norman Scott, on board the light cruiser USS ATLANTA, CL-51, was second in command. When Callaghan met with Captain Cassin Young and informed him of the nature of their mission, Young expressed his opinion that it would be suicide to meet a superior Japanese force at night. Callaghan agreed but informed Young that there was no other choice if the American claim to Guadalcanal was to be retained and the Marines on the island were to be saved.

Capt. Young encountered Lt. (jg) Bennett later in the evening and noting blood on the junior officer's elbow, where it was clipped by the Japanese plane earlier in the day, he ordered Bennett to his quarters to rest. Bennett obeyed the captain's order and reported to his quarters. He rested for a moment, then slipped out and reported to the gunnery officer for a battle assignment.

Throughout the ship, the crew was preparing for battle. Below decks was Mess Attendant 3rd Class, Leonard R. Harmon. Born in Cuero, Texas, the young black sailor had enlisted in June 1939 and reported on board SAN FRANCISCO in October 1939. On his way to his battle station as a litter bearer he passed by the Executive Officers quarters and looked in on Commander Crouter, who was recuperating from his wounds received earlier. Admiral Callaghan and his staff mustered on the Flag Bridge while Capt. Young and his staff gathered on the Navigation Bridge. With Young on the Navigation Bridge was Lieutenant Commander Bruce McCandless[55] the ship's 31-year-old communications officer.

---

55 McCandless was the father of Bruce McCandless, II, NASA astronaut, who flew on two Space Shuttle Missions.

To say there was concern in the fleet would be an understatement. Even though the numbers of the opposing forces were almost even, everyone from the most exalted admiral down to the lowliest seaman knew that they were up against it. Besides facing two battleships, the Japanese were well known for their abilities to fight at night. Their lack of radar technology forced them to perfect that particular discipline. They practiced night sea battles on a regular basis. The proof was in the brutal mauling eight Japanese ships gave a superior force of twenty-three American vessels only two months prior in the Battle of Savo Island, just a few miles away from where the American fleet was now.

The group sailed in a single column just over a mile long with the destroyers in the front and rear and the cruisers in the center, making their way in a northwesterly direction only a few miles off the north coast of Guadalcanal. Near 0130 radar picked up the Japanese fleet eighteen miles away. Continuous monitoring indicated the presence of three columns of enemy ships advancing on the Americans. In the next twenty minutes Admiral Callaghan desperately tried to interpret the information he was receiving from those ships with radar, (SAN FRANCISCO had none). The night was black as coal as the moon had set earlier. Radar was now the eyes of the Admiral. Preliminary instructions given in order to gain a favorable firing position only seemed to confuse some of the ships. Before the battle even started the American ships lost their column.

Callaghan kept the Americans moving, not realizing that the opposing fleets were not only dangerously close to each other, but were, in fact, beginning to sail through each other. High in the superstructure of SAN FRANCISCO was Electrician's Mate Ted Tupper, manning his battle station, one of the large thirty-six inch searchlights. Just before 0148, without warning of any kind he and the rest of SAN FRANCISCO were drenched in blinding light from the searchlights of the Japanese battleship *Hiei*. Tupper and the three other sailors manning searchlights didn't wait for any orders. They immediately switched on their searchlights, which danced across the enemy battleship only 3,000 yards away. They were so close that Tupper could clearly see Japanese sailors on the deck of the enemy vessel. Other ships in the vanguard passed within 500 feet of Japanese ships at this time.

Realizing that the two fleets were hopelessly entangled and that he was sailing through the center of multiple Japanese columns, Callaghan gave the order, "Odd ships fire to starboard, even ships fire to port." With that order, the most vicious, close-quarters naval battle of World War II was underway.

The darkness, which brought the opposing forces into such dangerous proximity, was also the cause of much confusion and misidentification during the battle. Despite the best efforts of Admiral Callaghan, the darkness and "the fog of war" caused the battle to quickly degenerate into a street brawl, with ships taking individual action based on the best judgment of their captains. The star shells that burst above the combatants and the powerful searchlights that reached out into the night to aid in recognition, only succeeded in creating a disconcerting surreal and nightmarish environment. Seventy years after the battle it is still questionable, in some instances, exactly what ships fired on others.

As soon as the lights went on, ships on all sides opened fire at the nearest enemy ship. SAN FRANCISCO and ATLANTA were hit immediately as were *Hiei* and the Japanese destroyer *Akatsuki*. No less than six American ships hit *Akatsuki* which blew up and was gone within two minutes.

SAN FRANCISCO then targeted a cruiser just off her starboard bow and let fly with a salvo each from her two forward main batteries. Both volleys were direct hits. Several more shots came from the main batteries of SAN FRANCISCO, until a total of nineteen direct hits registered on the cruiser. Fires were seen breaking out everywhere, her mast collapsed and she was going dead in the water.

By the time the mistake was discovered it was too late. SAN FRANCISCO had been firing on ATLANTA and Rear Admiral Norman Scott was dead. Rear Admiral Callaghan realized what was happening and ordered, "Cease Fire!" This order unfortunately went out to the entire fleet not just to SAN FRANCISCO. For a moment, all the American guns fell silent.

In the fleet, the guns came alive again almost as soon as they went quiet. On SAN FRANCISCO regret passed in a flash and the time for questions would come later. The crew moved on. *Hiei* came within the sights of SAN FRANCISCO and she fired on the battleship and *Hiei* fired back. For a minute or so, the two behemoths slugged it out at point blank range. Artillery shells flew across the black sea in flat trajectories and each ship shuddered with every blow.

A Japanese shell penetrated the hull and exploded inside the cabin of Executive Officer Crouter, killing him. The Navigation Bridge was riddled with shellfire, and Lt. Cdr. McCandless was knocked unconscious. What he awoke to was unbelievable carnage. He was wounded and bleeding. Capt. Cassin Young, Medal of Honor winner from Pearl Harbor, was dead along with every other officer on the bridge. The only other person alive on the bridge was Quartermaster 3rd Class Harry Higdon. In fact, not only was he alive, he didn't have a scratch on him.

McCandless, finding himself still alive, quickly ran to the Flag Bridge to inform Rear Admiral Callaghan of Young's death. Upon arrival there, the other shoe dropped. Callaghan and everyone on the Flag Bridge were also dead. McCandless, then only three and a half years out of Annapolis, on his own initiative, took command, not only of SAN FRANCISCO, but of the entire fleet, and began issuing orders. He did realize that there was one other officer on board who was senior to him. He sent word below decks, by messenger, to Lieutenant Commander Herbert E. Schonland, the Damage Control Officer, that he, Schonland, was now the senior officer on SAN FRANCISCO.

When the messenger found Schonland, he was, literally hip deep in water. The enemy shells had holed SAN FRANCISCO badly and she was taking on water rapidly. Power was also temporarily gone and all work was being conducted by flashlight. When informed he was the senior officer on board and McCandless was temporarily in command, Schonland decided that he was needed more, there, below decks, doing his job as damage control officer. He informed the messenger to tell McCandless to take command.

On deck, things were heating up. Mess Attendant Leonard Harmon, along with Pharmacist Mate 3rd Class Lynford L. Bondsteel was caring for the wounded. In the midst of the battle Harmon heard an incoming shell from *Hiei*. He yelled at Bondsteel to watch out and then leapt on the Pharmacist Mate to protect him. Harmon successfully shielded Bondsteel but was shot through with shell fragments. Bondsteel attempted to save the young Texan, but to no avail. Harmon died; he was twenty-five.

Amidships, the hanger for the cruiser's scout plane was on fire. Boatswain's Mate 1st Class Reinhart J. Keppler grabbed a fire hose and was attacking the flames single-handedly. Even as the slugfest between SAN FRANCISCO and *Hiei* continued, Keppler fought the flames with shot and shell literally bursting around him. When help arrived, he directed the firefighting efforts. When he wasn't doing that he was ministering to the wounded. Only when he collapsed did anyone realize that not only was he wounded, but also he had also been bleeding to death as he stood there. Keppler died; he was twenty-four.

At his battle station, Gunner's Mate 3rd Class Kenneth J. Spangenberg was also in the thick of the fighting. Despite being wounded, the boy from Allentown, Pennsylvania, stayed at his post. By the time the battle was over nothing could be done for him. Spangenberg died; he was twenty.

On the bridge McCandless was attempting a find a way to advise the captain of the light cruiser HELENA, CL-50, Captain Gilbert Hoover, that he was now the Senior Officer Present Afloat. All communication on SAN FRANCISCO was out. McCandless discovered a five-cell flashlight and using Morse code signaled his message to HELENA.

At 0220 USS STERETT, DD-407, fired some parting shots at a retreating Japanese destroyer. With that the Naval Battle of Guadalcanal was over. The encounter lasted just thirty-two minutes. Both forces withdrew almost simultaneously to lick their wounds.

The Japanese lost one battleship, *Hiei*, which was sunk later that day by American planes. Also lost were two destroyers. The Americans lost one cruiser, ATLANTA, and four destroyers. SAN FRANCISCO took forty-five hits during the engagement. Sixteen of them were from large caliber rounds, either fourteen-inch or six-inch shells. She had 106 sailors killed and 237 wounded.

Despite heavier losses, the victory went to the Americans. The Japanese were turned back. They did not bombard Henderson Field. Though they took another licking, the American Navy was still there and the landing of Japanese reinforcements did not take place.

An incredible four Medals of Honor, 33 Navy Crosses and 23 Silver Stars were awarded to men of SAN FRANCISCO for the November 12th / 13th actions. Those awarded the Medal of Honor were, Rear Admiral Daniel J. Callaghan, Lt. Cdr. Herbert E. Schonland, Lt. Cdr. Bruce McCandless and Boatswain's Mate 1st Class Reinhart J. Keppler. Among those who received the Navy Cross were Lt. (jg) John E. Bennett, Cdr. Mark H. Crouter, MAtt 1st Class Leonard R. Harmon, Lt. (jg) Albert T. Harris, GM 3rd Class Kenneth J. Spangenberg, Seaman 2nd Class Frank O. Slater, Lt. (jg) John G. Wallace and Capt. Cassin Young.

The high regard with which the Navy holds the crew of SAN FRANCISCO and their performance of November 12-13, 1942 is also manifested in other ways. One of the highest honors that can be given any sailor or Marine is to have a ship named after them. Between 1943 and 1981 the Navy named twenty-four ships after twenty-three men[56] of SAN FRANCISCO. Among them was Leonard Harmon, who became the first black sailor to have a U.S. Navy warship named after him, the destroyer escort USS HARMON, DE-678. It was commissioned in 1943, saw service in the Pacific during the war, including duties at Iwo Jima, and was decommissioned in 1947.

Elam Slater, brother of Frank Slater, recipient of the Navy Cross, served for the entire war onboard the ship named for his brother, the destroyer escort, USS SLATER, DE-766. Robert E. Spangenberg, Kenneth's younger brother also served on the ship named for his brother, another destroyer escort, USS SPANGENBERG, DE-223.

FATE

SAN FRANCISCO was second only to the aircraft carrier USS ENTERPRISE, CV-6, as the most decorated United States Naval Vessel of World War II. When the war was over SAN FRANCISCO sailed home,

---

56 Rear Admiral Daniel J. Callaghan had two ships named after him, a destroyer, commissioned in 1943 and sunk in 1945 and a guided missile destroyer, commissioned in 1981 and decommissioned in 1998. It was sold to Taiwan in 2005 and was still in service as of 2011. Technically, the frigate, USS McCANDLESS, FF-1084, was named after Lt. Cdr. Bruce McCandless and his father, Commodore Byron McCandless.

arriving at the Naval Yard of Philadelphia, Pennsylvania in January 1946. She spent the next thirteen years quietly in the Atlantic Reserve Fleet. In September 1959 she was sold. In 1961, in Pensacola, Florida she was cut into pieces by the scrapper's blowtorch.

*   *   *   *   *

In the city of San Francisco, on a windswept plot of earth called Lands End overlooking the Pacific Ocean, is the USS SAN FRANCISCO Memorial. The main components of the memorial are remnants of the ship's bridge where brave men fell. Holes put there by enemy shells on November 13, 1942, are prominent. The memorial points toward Guadalcanal.

WICKES CLASS DESTROYER
DD-103
LAUNCHED: 1918

DECEMBER 7, 1941

SCHLEY was a member of that group of destroyers built for World War I but that never saw action in that conflict. She was commissioned only three weeks before the armistice of November 11, 1918. In preparation for the next "Great War" she was taken out of "mothballs" in San Diego where she had been since 1922 and recommissioned in October 1940. Only two months later, in December 1940, she reported to Pearl Harbor. What followed was a year of patrolling the Hawai'ian Islands. She did not receive a major overhaul when she was brought back into service and was sorely in need of one. As a result she was put in berth #20 in the Pearl Harbor Navy Yard in late November 1941. Almost every major piece of equipment on her was being repaired, replaced or refurbished so when the Japanese raid began she could do almost nothing.

John Baskette was an 18-year-old sailor assigned to SCHLEY and like most sailors whose ships were in the yards, he was staying at the receiving barracks. As the first planes buzzed in low over the water, a Chief Petty Officer ordered him into a 50 foot launch with some other men and sent them out to the already flaming Battleship Row. The boat hugged the shoreline and piers for as much cover as possible on its way. Once out in the open harbor, fear washed over Baskette as he saw the onslaught of enemy planes seemingly sinking ships at will. His fear soon turned to rage and through tears he screamed profanities at the swarming enemy.

Off Battleship Row he repeatedly dipped his arms into the oily water and pulled out the dead, the dying, and the wounded. After three round trips into the harbor and back, Baskette was covered in oil and the blood of others. At the end of the third trip he was told to return to his ship. Making his way toward the Navy Yard, a "Zero" strafed him and others around him, but he was unhurt.

Upon arrival at SCHLEY, a shipmate, seeing Baskette's oily and blood soaked condition, asked him if he was OK. Baskette replied that he was. His shipmate then pointed at the hem of Baskette's bell-bottoms. Only then did Baskette see five bullet holes in his pants from the failed strafing run on him.

He then reported to the bridge and commenced firing at enemy planes after he helped to mount a .50-caliber machine gun. Only two .50-caliber machine guns on SCHLEY fired at the enemy and between the two of them they expended only 150 rounds. SCHLEY claimed neither kills nor even any hits.

THE WAR

Her overhaul was quickly completed and two weeks later SCHLEY joined the ships patrolling and escorting other ships in Hawai'ian waters. In these rather mundane, backwater duties SCHLEY remained for a year. In December 1942 she received new orders to begin a new life.

The Navy made the decision to take some of the older World War I destroyers that were being replaced by destroyers that were newer, faster and better armed, and convert them into high speed transports with the hull classification of APD. SCHLEY was sent to the Puget Sound Naval Shipyard in Bremerton, Washington to undergo her conversion, which was completed in two months. In February 1943 SCHLEY, now APD-14, was once again underway and arrived in Pearl Harbor on the 22nd.

In late March, SCHLEY was at Espiritu Santo with the 4th Marine Raiders for a month-long training in beach landings. Three months later, in her first outing as a fast transport, N Company of that battalion boarded

SCHLEY, which then headed for the New Georgia group. On June 30th at 0300, SCHLEY landed N Company on the beaches of Oliana Bay for the invasion of Vangunu Island.

SCHLEY left the South Pacific in August and spent the remainder of 1943 undergoing overhaul and major engine repairs at Mare Island and Pearl Harbor. When work was completed SCHLEY returned to the war. During the first six months of 1944 SCHLEY participated in the invasions of Kwajalein, Eniwetok and further incursions in New Guinea and in doing so landed troops on ten different islands.

The last months of 1944 found SCHLEY heavily involved in the retaking of the Philippines. On December 7th she was part of the force of at least fourteen ships landing troops in Ormoc Bay or screening the landings. SCHLEY landed members of the 1st Battalion, 305th Infantry. Shortly after the troops were deposited on the beach, a force of twenty-one kamikazes swarmed the destroyers and transports. The enemy attack, comprised of multiple types of aircraft was intense and coordinated.

The ships shot down at least ten of the attackers, but other kamikazes got through the umbrella of bullets and shells attempting to protect the ships. Two ships – USS MAHAN, DD-364 and USS WARD, APD-16 were so severely mangled by the suicide planes they had to be scuttled. A Landing Ship, Medium, LSM-318 was sunk outright and four other ships were badly damaged. SCHLEY came through without a scratch.

A week later she was at Mindoro and once again subject to kamikaze attack. At one point a kamikaze was directly in front of SCHLEY and headed straight for her. Only her forward guns could be brought to bear on the plane but even they were silent. The fire directors saw an American fighter on the enemy plane's tail attempting to shoot it down before it struck SCHLEY. The ship held its fire for fear of missing the Japanese plane and hitting the American. The only thing the crew could do was wait and watch and hope that the American pilot and his F4U Corsair were good enough. The pursuing American finally found his mark and brought the kamikaze down. The Japanese plane was so close to the ship when it was shot down that when it crashed into the sea, SCHLEY ran over it.

SCHLEY remained in the Philippines through late February, 1945 and continued in the Western Pacific escorting convoys until April. Her age and her very strenuous duties took a toll on her and she was sent to San Diego in mid 1945 for much needed repairs. While there, it was determined that SCHLEY was no longer fit for front line duties against the enemy. In a rare occurrence for ships that had been redesignated, it was decided to return SCHLEY to her original designation as a destroyer and she reverted once again to DD-103. She never performed her newly assigned duties of escorting and training as the war ended while she was still under repair.

FATE

Her last orders were to report to Philadelphia in order to be deactivated and decommissioned, all of which happened between September and December 1945. In an unusual turn of events, SCHLEY was not sold to some scrap dealer, but was rather scrapped by the Navy itself at the Philadelphia Navy Yard in March 1946.

USS Selfridge

PORTER CLASS DESTROYER
DD-357
LAUNCHED: 1936

DECEMBER 7, 1941

SELFRIDGE had pulled into Pearl Harbor in the late afternoon on Saturday the 6th after having been deployed since early November. Her fuel tanks were bone dry and she was totally bereft of food and other supplies. Being Sunday, none of these situations were being addressed; time enough for those things tomorrow.

Nineteen-year-old Seaman John Ross was standing on deck with a friend. They were waiting to catch a boat from their berth out in the harbor to the shore. Their agenda for the day was hiking the hills of O'ahu and enjoying nature and some spectacular panoramic views. Those plans of course all came to an end once the Japanese started bombing.

Ross' battle station was manning one of the .50-caliber machine guns adjacent to the bridge. The ready ammunition box at his weapon was full but when he reported to his station the box was still locked, so Ross grabbed a marlinspike[57] and broke the lock off. The machine gun was soon loaded and within three minutes of the sounding of general quarters Ross had it chattering away at the enemy.

SELFRIDGE fired at targets within range with both her .50-caliber and 1.1-inch anti-aircraft guns, throughout the raid. The captain, Lieutenant

---

57 A tapered metal rod between 6 and 12 inches in length used for shipboard rope work such as splicing.

Commander Wyatt Craig, in his after action report claimed hits on four Japanese planes but did not specifically call them kills. He also reported the expenditure of 850 rounds of 1.1-inch ammunition and 2,340 rounds of .50-caliber.

Crewmen not manning guns or loading ammunition belts brought supplies on board from the tender WHITNEY, AD-4 throughout the attack. SELFRIDGE was hurriedly fueled and got under way at 1000. When they exited the harbor Ross expected to find the whole Japanese Navy waiting for them. He was not disappointed to find he was wrong. SELFRIDGE stayed out for several days patrolling around O'ahu.

THE WAR

SELFRIDGE carried out patrol duties in the Hawai'i area until late December when she was assigned to the task force built around the aircraft carrier SARATOGA, CV-3, that was sent to relieve Wake Island. That mission was terminated when Wake fell to the Japanese and the task force returned to Hawai'i.

During the second week of January SELFRIDGE was once again screening SARATOGA as the carrier sailed for the central Pacific. In the early evening of January 11, John Ross was enjoying some relief from the stifling atmosphere below, by bathing in the tropic breezes on deck. He was casually scanning the horizon when something caught his eye. There in the distance Ross saw the unmistakable phosphorescent trail of a torpedo in the water and it was heading straight for SELFRIDGE. Ross yelled out that a torpedo was heading their way but nobody seemed to hear. Transfixed he could do nothing but stare at the onrushing doom. The torpedo crossed the distance rapidly and it was apparent that it would hit the destroyer amidships, directly beneath where Ross was standing. Ross watched as it raced towards him and braced for the impact and resulting explosion. But there was no impact and no explosion. Momentarily confused Ross soon realized that the TNT laden fish had been set for something with a deeper draft than the destroyer and had passed harmlessly beneath her.

In short order Ross and the entire task force found out that SARATOGA was the intended target when one of three torpedoes fired by the Japanese submarine *I-6* slammed into the carrier killing six sailors. SELFRIDGE immediately raced to the estimated position of the submarine and dropped depth charges but came up empty. SARATOGA, injured and listing, slowly returned to Pearl Harbor with SELFRIDGE escorting her. The following month she escorted the carrier to Bremerton, Washington for further repairs.

Shortly after SELFRIDGE returned to the Pacific, John Ross, who had been working in the sick bay, received orders off the destroyer for training as a medic back in the States at Mare Island Naval Hospital. When he completed that training, he was transferred out of the Navy and into the Marine Corps. He spent the rest of the war as a medic with the Marines serving at both Bougainville and Guam.

SELFRIDGE was called on to perform multiple functions at Guadalcanal in early August 1942. She screened the invasion force from air attack, escorted landing craft and helped sink a schooner carrying gasoline. On August 9th, SELFRIDGE reported to assist allied vessels that had been severely mauled by Japanese ships off Guadalcanal in the Battle of Savo Island. When she arrived on scene the crew of the Australian cruiser, HMAS CANBERRA, D33, was being evacuated off the burning ship. She was ordered scuttled and the job was given to SELFRIDGE. The destroyer fired four torpedoes at the cruiser but only one exploded. SELFRIDGE then tried to sink her with five-inch shells and fired 263 of them at the cruiser, but she stubbornly refused to sink. Finally, the American destroyer USS ELLET, DD-398, came up and with one well-placed torpedo put the cruiser down.

In October 1943 SELFRIDGE was still in the Solomons participating in the prolonged actions removing the Japanese Army from their entrenched position in those islands. On the 6th SELFRIDGE was part of a three-ship vanguard of six ships sent to interdict a Japanese force attempting to evacuate 600 soldiers from the island of Vella Lavella. With SELFRIDGE were USS CHEVALIER, DD-451 and USS O'BANNON, DD-450.

Just before 2300 the three American destroyers stumbled upon the Japanese evacuation force that consisted of nine enemy destroyers. The other three American destroyers were still twenty miles away and unable to help. When the Japanese headed for them, SELFRIDGE and the other two destroyers were forced to engage.

The Americans were aggressive and fired first, the three ships letting loose a total of fourteen torpedoes, immediately following up with all their main guns. One of the Japanese destroyers, *Yagumo*, dashed towards the Americans firing both torpedoes and guns as she did. One of her torpedoes blasted into CHEVALIER causing her magazine to detonate. The resulting explosion took off the entire forward section of the ship up to her bridge. CHEVALIER went dead in the water. O'BANNON, following close behind, rammed CHEVALIER in the stern severely damaging her bow and also taking her out of the battle. The brave *Yagumo* took out two of the American destroyers but at the cost of her own life. The three Americans all fired on *Yagumo*, as she made her bold attack and the enemy ship was mortally wounded.

With CHEVALIER and O'BANNON both out of action, SELFRIDGE was left to face the remaining eight Japanese destroyers her-self. She didn't have a chance. Multiple enemy destroyers fired a total of sixteen torpedoes at SELFRIDGE and one found her. In a massive explosion that lit up the night, the torpedo took her bow off back to her second turret.

The Japanese sighted the three other American destroyers and beat a hasty retreat thinking that they were cruisers. The Battle of Vella Lavella was over. SEL-

The severely crippled SELFRIDGE after the Battle of Vella Lavella.

FRIDGE had thirteen killed, eleven wounded and thirty-six missing and presumed dead.

On the following day CHEVALIER was scuttled and O'BANNON, the least damaged of the three was repaired and eventually returned to the war. Despite the immense damage to her, SELFRIDGE was still seaworthy and made it back to a safe harbor. Once there temporary repairs were made to her, including the installation of a make shift bow. She then made her way to Mare Island Naval Shipyard for permanent repair and overhaul. SELFRIDGE was out of action for six months and by April 1944 she had a new bow and a new paint job.

In June SELFRIDGE was once again in the Western Pacific. Now she was engaging the enemy at Saipan bombarding the island for pre-invasion operations. On the 15th she screened the landing craft as they hit the beaches. Just five weeks later, on July 21st, she was off the coast of Guam providing support fire and screening for the invasion there. On August 10, after Guam was secured, SELFRIDGE set a course for Pearl Harbor. Shortly after her arrival there she received a very unusual set of orders for a ship assigned to the Pacific Fleet; she was ordered to the Atlantic.

Pearl Harbor and the warm Pacific were left behind and SELFRIDGE sailed to New York via the Panama Canal, arriving there in September. While there she underwent a brief overhaul. When completed she was tasked with escorting convoys across the Atlantic to Africa.

SELFRIDGE on April 10, 1944 on a shakedown cruise in San Francisco bay after being rebuilt at Mare Island.

At the end of April 1945 SELFRIDGE was one of the escorts for convoy UGS-89 heading for Oran, Algeria. Like all convoys, the slower cargo ships and transports sailed along in columns as the swifter escorts circled them as a constant shield against German U-Boats and as they shielded they simultaneously searched for them. On May 8, 1945, as they neared the end of their crossing, news was announced over the radio that Germany had surrendered and the war in Europe was over.

In the early morning hours of the 12th the darkness ahead of the convoy was broken by the glare of flares in the sky. SELFRIDGE steamed ahead to investigate. When she arrived on scene she discovered a German U-Boat that had surrendered and was being escorted by two American destroyers. Her last mission of the war was escorting a convoy from Algeria back to New York.

FATE

Perhaps the Navy wasn't quite sure what it wanted to do with SELFRIDGE, because she was sent out for training on the East Coast from July to September only to be called back to New York to begin deactivation. She was struck from the Navy rolls in November 1945. In December 1946 she was sold to the George H. Nutman Company of Brooklyn, New York for $11,041.28. In October 1947 she was scrapped.

USS Shaw

MAHAN CLASS DESTROYER
DD-373
LAUNCHED: 1935

DECEMBER 7, 1941

SHAW had been sitting in YFD-2, one of Pearl Harbor's floating dry-docks, ever since she was rammed by the oiler SABINE, AO-25 a few weeks earlier. She had suffered a significant gash in her starboard bow below the waterline and repairs were being made in the floating dry-dock anchored near the south channel.

When general quarters sounded, 19-year-old Yeoman 3rd Class John DeFields promptly reported to his battle station on the bridge. He was the captain's "talker" and it was his job to relay the captain's orders to the proper people or departments. The only problem was that the captain wasn't on board, nor were any of the other officers normally on the bridge, so DeFields had nothing to do but watch the Japanese devastate Battleship Row.

About fifteen minutes into the attack an enemy plane strafed SHAW and riddled the bridge with bullets, narrowly missing DeFields and some other sailors there. DeFields headed for the main deck where he thought he might do some good.

As SHAW was in dry-dock, it wasn't deemed wise to fire the main five-inch battery for fear that the recoil would knock the ship off the huge wooden blocks holding her up. The only other options were her four .50-caliber anti-aircraft machine guns and small arms. DeFields reported to the small arms locker and strapped on a cartridge belt, but there were no more rifles so once again he had nothing to do. The officer in charge ordered all men without weapons to report to their abandon ship stations.

DeFields went below decks to his office. His responsibility for abandoning ship was to save the crew's personnel files. While in his office a Japanese bomb punched through several decks and exploded inside the destroyer just below his compartment. DeFields was launched into the air and slammed against the overhead. When he landed back on the deck the entire compartment was in flames. The young yeoman then, with the aid of some others, took a wounded crewmate up to the main deck. When they arrived they discovered that a wall of flames blocked the gangway to safety. They then raced to the stern and climbed down some scaffolding to the deck of the dry-dock and then climbed up a ladder to the top of its side. Safety was now only inches away; all DeFields had to do was jump off the dry-dock into the harbor and swim 150 feet to shore. Still wearing the cartridge belt weighed down with ammunition, he started to take it off before he leapt into the water. When he looked down to remove the belt he noticed that his shirt was soaked red with his own blood. He hurriedly lifted his shirt and was shocked to find a one and a half inch wound in his stomach.

A moment earlier, escaping his burning ship was his main purpose but now he hesitated, thinking that jumping into the now oil covered water might contaminate his wound. Just as this internal debate was raging, the Chief Pharmacist Mate came upon him. When DeFields explained his dilemma the Pharmacist Mate told him they needed to get off before the magazine exploded and then promptly pushed DeFields into the water. As if DeFields didn't have enough troubles already, when he swam to shore an enemy plane dove on him and others in the water and strafed them. Little fountains of white foam erupted all around him as the bullets struck the water, but amazingly neither he nor any of the others in the water were hit. He dragged himself out of the water and onto the shore. Then he walked to the Naval Hospital.

Aboard SHAW, the fires went on unabated. About twenty minutes after being penetrated by the bombs, the flames finally reached the forward magazine and the resulting massive explosion shook the entire harbor. The bow was violently severed from the rest of the ship, with a small portion of the keel the only thing keeping it attached to the rest of the hull. The floating dry-dock was now ordered flooded to save it and SHAW from further damage.

The bombs had seriously damaged the dry-dock also and it began to sink. Remarkably, as it sank, the two thirds of SHAW that remained were still water tight and it began to float! YFD-2 listed heavily to port as it sank. Attempts to counter flood, to allow it to sink on an even keel were prevented by fires that blocked access to the valves on the starboard side.

Photo taken from Ford Island just as the forward magazine on SHAW blew up at about 0930

At the end of the day SHAW had suffered massive damage and twenty-five killed. John DeFields was one of the sixteen wounded from the destroyer. He had survived his walk to the Naval Hospital and was finally brought into surgery twelve hours later at around 2100 where the surgeon removed the single piece of shrapnel in his stomach.

THE WAR

The third wave of the Japanese attack was supposed to target the fleet's fuel storage tanks and the Navy Yard, but Admiral Nugumo Chuichi, who was in command of the Pearl Harbor attack force, cancelled the third wave fearing the Americans might find and ambush his battle group. It was a decision with significant consequences for Japan.

SHAW, with her temporary bow, docked at Mare Island after her arrival from Pearl Harbor.

SHAW was towed out of YFD-2 so initial evaluations could be made of her and so the floating dry-dock could be raised and repaired. It was determined that SHAW could be rebuilt and when YFD-2 was raised only seven weeks after the attack, SHAW was the first ship to enter it for repairs. Initial preparations for her rebirth took place in the Navy Yard. A new temporary bow was also manufactured there and the two were joined together in the resurrected dry-dock. On February 4th, just short of eight weeks after having been almost totally obliterated, SHAW sailed out of the floating dry-dock under her own power. For the next few days she conducted trials to ensure her temporary bow was sea worthy. SHAW sailed out of Pearl Harbor two months and two days after the attack and headed for California. Also on board was John DeFields. Recovered from his wounds after spending three weeks in the hospital, the repaired sailor rejoined his repaired ship.

The miracle workers at Mare Island got busy. They rebuilt, repaired and revitalized SHAW until she looked the same way she did the day she was sent down the ways at the Philadelphia Navy Yard in 1935. The job was completed in just five months. The first days of June 1942 she was taken out for sea trials. She returned to Pearl Harbor on August 31, 1942, ready to go to war.

In October, SHAW headed out to her first battle in the Santa Cruz Islands. She was part of a force that was screening the aircraft carrier ENTERPRISE, CV-6. During the battle another destroyer, PORTER, DD-356, was torpedoed and SHAW was dispatched to help her. Upon arriving on scene, PORTER was deemed too far gone and SHAW began to take aboard her crew. SHAW then scuttled PORTER with gunfire.

SHAW remained in the Solomons for some time in support of the Guadalcanal operation. In January 1943, while navigating the harbor at Nouméa, she ran aground on a reef and severely damaged her hull, propellers and sound gear. Five days passed before she was finally pulled off the reef. The holes in her hull were patched up with concrete. However the temporary repairs made at Nouméa weren't enough and she returned to Pearl Harbor. Hitching a ride back to the States on this trip was one of the oldest correspondents of the war, 67-year-old Edgar Rice Burroughs, creator of Tarzan. Once at Pearl she underwent repairs to the damage incurred on the reef plus extended overhaul and refurbishment, which kept her there until September.

SHAW conducting trials in San Francisco Bay on July 5, 1942 just seven months after she blew up in Hawai'i.

By the end of the year, SHAW was back in the thick of things in the South Pacific. She was constantly conducting convoy escorts, screening missions, covering landings or bombarding enemy positions on islands. On

December 26, 1943 while participating in the invasion of Cape Gloucester on the island of New Britain, two "Val" dive bombers attacked SHAW, damaging her and inflicting three fatalities. Other than the twenty-five men lost at Pearl Harbor, these were the only deaths for SHAW from enemy action during the war. The damaged destroyer once again limped back to the United States where she underwent repairs at Hunters Point Naval shipyard in San Francisco, remaining there until May, 1944.

Upon her return to the battlefront SHAW took up where she left off, participating in the invasions of Saipan and Guam and then on to Luzon and Pawalan Islands in the Philippines. During her duties in the Philippines in April 1945 she once again ran aground, this time south of Bohol Island. And, as before, temporary repairs were made that enabled her to return to the west coast of the United States. There she was made whole and had new equipment installed. This work was completed on August 20, 1945, six days after the Japanese surrendered.

FATE

Despite being freshly overhauled, the addition of new apparatus and being only ten years old SHAW was ordered to the east coast for decommissioning which occurred in New York in October. She was scrapped in July 1946.

USS Sicard

CLEMSON CLASS DESTROYER / LIGHT MINESWEEPER
DM-21
LAUNCHED: 1920

DECEMBER 7, 1941

SICARD was undergoing overhaul in the Navy Yard and was rather limited in her ability to respond to the attack. Her main batteries were unable to fire because her boilers were down and couldn't provide power. Two .30-caliber machine guns were manned and fired at the enemy, hitting but not downing any Japanese planes. That was the extent of her offensive actions. What SICARD did have was plenty of men and she dispersed them to help as needed.

Two fire fighting parties were formed on SICARD to combat flames should the ship suffer bomb hits. Other men were detailed to ships in the immediate area. Twenty men were sent to USS CUMMINGS, DD-365, on the opposite side of the pier to help handle and pass ammunition. Four gunner's mates were dispatched to USS NEW ORLEANS, CA-32, docked further down the wharf.

Part of the crew was staying in the Receiving Barracks nearby. There, sailor John Deusterman and some of his SICARD shipmates were getting into their dress white uniforms for a day of relaxation and fun in the sailor's paradise that was Honolulu. When the attack started, ten of them were ordered to the battleship USS PENNSYLVANIA, BB-38, to assist in damage control. Deusterman and 18-year-old Seaman 2nd Class Warren P. Hickok of Kalamazoo, Michigan were among them. They arrived at the dry dock that held PENNSYLVANIA, and went aboard. Hickok went to assist on the No. 7 five-inch gun. Deusterman and the rest went to retrieve ammunition. When they returned with it, a bomb had killed Hickok and the other men at the gun.

In his after action report, the commanding officer, Lieutenant Commander, William C. Schultz, reported no damage to his vessel and no casualties. He also reported that Seaman 2nd Class Hickok was the only crewmember not aboard, but he was presumed to be on CUMMINGS, which had exited the harbor. However, neither CUMMINGS nor PENNSYLVANIA had any records of Hickok being onboard or being a casualty on their vessels.

THE WAR

SICARD had begun life as a destroyer but in 1937 was converted to a minelayer. It was in this capacity that she performed many of her duties during the war. In 1942 alone, in between anti-submarine and escort duties in and around Midway and Hawai'i, she assisted in laying minefields off French Frigate Shoals, northwest of Hawai'i, and off the coast of Kodiak Island and the Aleutian Islands in Alaska.

In May 1943 she was again in Alaskan waters preparing for the invasion that would remove the Japanese army from Attu Island on the extreme western end of the Aleutians. The evening before the invasion, while maneuvering in a dense fog, SICARD collided with USS MACDONOUGH, DD-351. No casualties resulted from the collision but SICARD had to tow MACDONOUGH to Adak and she then proceeded to San Francisco for repairs.

After her stay stateside she returned to Alaska one last time for the invasion of Kiska in mid-August. With that mission completed she sailed for sunnier climes in the South Pacific where she remained for the rest of the war. In October and then again in November, SICARD laid two separate minefields off the coast of Bougainville. In late November she planted more mines off the coast of the Shortland Islands at the western end of the Solomons. In May of 1944 SICARD laid her last minefield off the island of Buka east of New Guinea. This was essentially the end of her participation in the war.

The rest of the war was spent either in the States undergoing overhaul or in the backwaters of the Pacific participating in submarine training. In June 1945 she was once again reclassified, this time as an auxiliary vessel with the new hull designation of AG-100.

FATE

The end came quickly for SICARD. In October 1945, only a month after the Japanese surrender, she was in the Philadelphia Navy Yard being inactivated and a month later she was decommissioned. In June 1946 she was sold for scrap to the Hugo Neu Company of New York.

*   *   *   *   *

In November 2003, Ray Emory, a Pearl Harbor survivor and amateur forensic detective contacted historian Heather Harris of the Joint POW/MIA Accounting Command, (JPAC). This governmental agency, located in Hawai'i, is tasked with identifying the remains of American military personnel. Emory said that he believed he had identified, through his research, the remains buried in a grave marked "Unknown, Dec. 7, 1941" at the National Cemetery of the Pacific in Honolulu, (The "Punchbowl"). The staff at JPAC reviewed and agreed with Emory's research. The remains were exhumed and, using dental records, the body was positively identified as that of Seaman 2nd Class Warren P. Hickok, the SICARD sailor, who was killed onboard PENNSYLVANIA.

Hickok was reburied on March 29, 2006, with full military honors, at The Punchbowl, no longer unknown.

USS Solace

HOSPITAL SHIP
AH-5
LAUNCHED: 1927

DECEMBER 7, 1941

Perhaps more than any other ship, the crew of SOLACE saw the tragedy and personal carnage of the attack on Pearl Harbor. Even though she was fourteen years old at the time, she was like new, having just completed a three and a half million-dollar conversion from her original incarnation as the passenger ship *SS Iriquois* to a state-of-the-art 400-bed hospital ship. Her medical staff consisted of physicians, dentists, hospital corpsmen and 13 nurses. SOLACE was commissioned only four months before and arrived at Pearl Harbor on October 27, 1941. The senior medical officer was Captain Harold L. Jensen and the ship's commanding officer was Captain Benjamin Pearlman.

When the attack began all preparations were immediately made to accept casualties. Patients already on board were moved from lower bunks to uppers, to make it easier to accommodate the new casualties. Cots were set up wherever there was space and when they ran out of cots and space, makeshift beds were made by laying blankets on deck. Corpsmen made plaster of Paris and rolled bandages in order to make casts. Gallons and gallons of tea were boiled up, because the tannic acid in it was a treatment for burns at the time.

All motor launches and boats were lowered into the water and sent out. Once in the harbor, the #1 and #2 motor launches headed for Battleship Row where the USS ARIZONA, BB-39 had just exploded. Arriving at the scene, stretcher parties went on board the blazing battleship and, with total disregard for their own safety, began gathering up the burned and maimed sailors and loaded them on the launches. The coxswains then revved the engines and returned to SOLACE, delivering the first wounded within fifteen minutes of the ARIZONA blowing up. After that first delivery, the wounded came in a continuous flood of broken and blackened humanity, deposited by boats from all over the harbor.

Once the casualties started arriving, medical staff began doing whatever they could to save the lives they could and make dying easier for those they couldn't. Many of the casualties were severely scorched, with their hair, ears, lips or noses burned off. The eyes of some sailors - through injury or burns - couldn't close and a Pharmacist Mate applied lubricant to them so they wouldn't become painfully dry. Morphine was liberally administered to ease pain or death. To say that medical personnel were overwhelmed would be a gross understatement. All would go without sleep for days. Civilian doctors and those from other ships arrived to help with medical duties and chaplains also from other vessels in the harbor came to aid with spiritual ones.

Out on the flaming waters of Pearl Harbor, SOLACE's two launches made repeated and continuous trips back to Battleship Row, particularly to ARIZONA and WEST VIRGINIA, BB-48. On one trip, launch #1 fished over thirty-six men from WEST VIRGINIA out of the water and delivered them to SOLACE. At one point, Seaman 1st Class J. V. Saccavino, the coxswain of the #1 launch, had to jump into the water to douse his uniform which began smoldering from the intense heat of the fires. These forays continued for the rest of the day until there was no one living left to save in the water.

For days after the attack, the crew of SOLACE trolled the harbor with the gruesome duty of recovering bodies and body parts, which were brought to the morgue onboard. Efforts were then made to identify them, using teeth or fingerprints or any other distinguishing characteristic to match a body to a name.

There is no doubt that had SOLACE not been there in the middle of Pearl Harbor, in the middle of the action, in the middle of the chaos, the death toll would have been higher than what it was. There is also no doubt that the crew of SOLACE earned and deserved the Navy Unit Commendation that was awarded to them by Navy Secretary James Forrestal, for the courage they displayed and the services they rendered on December 7, 1941.

This photo shows what is very possibly one of the motor launches from SOLACE rescuing sailors from the fiery waters around WEST VIRGINIA

It should be noted that SOLACE was clearly marked as a hospital ship. Painted white, she had four large red crosses painted on her stack and a large green stripe running horizontally around her hull with another red cross amidships on both sides. Captain Pearlman clearly states in his after action report that SOLACE suffered no material damage and no casualties because the attacking Japanese planes took no offensive action against her at all, recognizing and respecting her status as a non- combatant.

THE WAR

For a time SOLACE was the only hospital ship in the Pacific Ocean. The first casualties she received from a major battle were in May 1942 from the Battle of the Coral Sea. With that, she was off and running, criss-crossing the Pacific from one battle to another, picking up wounded, treating them and then dropping them off in Australia or New Zealand or the United States for further treatment. Once done, she was resupplied and returned to the Pacific.

To the sailors, marines and soldiers of the Pacific she had many nicknames, "The Work Horse of the Pacific," "The Great White Ship," "The Ice Cream Ship," "The Bandage Barge," "Our Navy's Luxury Liner" and "The USS Agony." But no matter what they called her, they were always happy to see her because her presence meant that a wounded man's chances of survival increased a hundred fold.

In some strange, bizarre way, the wounded were anxious, almost happy, to be on board, because they saw and experienced things there that they hadn't experienced in months or maybe even years: hot showers, clean sheets on clean mattresses, pillows, good hot food, fresh fruits and vegetables, ice cream, (lots and lots of ice cream), movies every night on deck and of course, nurses, women, American girls! SOLACE was a small slice of heaven in the midst of a very large hell.

On more than one occasion SOLACE nestled among ships just off of a beachhead, where fighting was taking place, to accept casualties that only an hour before had been whole healthy men. SOLACE was the first U.S. Navy hospital ship ever to receive orders to an active combat area. Because of this ability to be on scene and being able to treat injuries

Nurses enjoying a tropical breeze on the quarterdeck of SOLACE somewhere in the South Pacific in 1945.

within minutes if not one or two hours of their infliction, the wounded that came aboard had a survival rate as good as, if not better than, a stateside, shore based medical facility. This capability was imperative in the later stages of the war during the battles of Iwo Jima and Okinawa.

Four days after the Marines hit the beach at Iwo Jima, SOLACE was there. She lay only 2,000 yards off shore and within forty-five minutes of her arrival the first wounded were being boarded and cared for. The next morning, with every bed and cot occupied by a casualty, she set sail for Saipan to deliver her charges. She then returned to Iwo Jima. In the three weeks from February 23 to March 17, SOLACE made three round trips from Iwo Jima to Saipan or Guam and evacuated and treated over 2,000 casualties.

Okinawa was the last major invasion of the Pacific war and once again SOLACE was there. This time she was ahead of the game, arriving in the area four days before the invasion started. There she repeated the Herculean tasks of Iwo Jima, transporting and treating over 4,000 injured in seven separate round trips in a three-month period. After Okinawa SOLACE reported to Portland, Oregon for a much-needed major overhaul, which is where she was when the war ended.

During her war service, SOLACE traveled over 170,000 miles and cared for approximately 25,000 patients, or about 560 a month. Of those patients, over 17,000 were battle casualties. It is almost impossible to calculate how many of those men lived, or how many men kept their arms or legs, or how many walked instead of being confined for life in a wheelchair, or how many have sight instead of being blind or how many countless generations are alive today because SOLACE was there. In an endeavor such as war that is designed to kill, maim and destroy, SOLACE and her medical staff were shining stars of humanity that saved, healed and provided great solace.

FATE

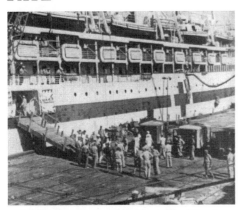

SOLACE unloads Iwo Jima casualties to waiting ambulances on Saipan.

SOLACE completed her overhaul on September 12, 1945. She was then assigned to "Operation Magic Carpet", repatriating service men from the Pacific war zone back to the United States. She made her last voyage in that capacity in January 1946, after which she sailed for Hampton Roads, Virginia.

After being decommissioned, SOLACE was turned over to the War Shipping Administration, which sold her to the Turkish Maritime Lines in April 1948. Under control of that company SOLACE was converted back to her original incarnation as a passenger liner and renamed SS ANKARA. She sailed on for another thirty years carrying passengers, until she was laid up in 1978. SS ANKARA / USS SOL-ACE finally came to an end at the demolition yard in Aliaga, Turkey in 1981.

USS *Sotoyomo*

DISTRICT HARBOR TUG
YT-9
LAUNCHED: 1903

DECEMBER 7, 1941

SOTOYOMO was trapped and defenseless during the attack on Pearl Harbor. Being defenseless wasn't unusual. As a tug she had no weapons of any kind. She was trapped because she was undergoing maintenance and repairs in YFD-2, the floating dry dock. Being trapped prevented her from maneuvering and removed any chance at all she might have to escape the onslaught. She was forward in the dry dock and aft of her was SHAW, DD-373. Late in the attack the Japanese found SHAW and blew her up. The massive explosion devastated the destroyer. The explosion also damaged the floating dry dock and it began to sink. At the end of the day the YFD-2 was underwater along with SHAW and the tiny tug berthed with her.

THE WAR

On January 9, 1942 the floating dry dock, YFD-2 was refloated; bringing SHAW and SOTOYOMO back to the surface with her. On the 17th the badly burned SOTOYOMO was floated out of the dry dock. She was eventually placed in Dry Dock 2 in the Navy yard and rebuilt. In June SOTOYOMO left the dry dock and was taken to the repair basin for the finishing touches of her restoration. In August she was completed and returned to service in Pearl Harbor. SOTOYOMO plied her trade as a tugboat for the rest of the war in Pearl Harbor.

FATE

SOTOYOMO was struck from the Naval Register and destroyed on February 15, 1946. However there doesn't seem to be any record to explain if she was destroyed because she had been struck from the register or if she was struck from the register because she had been destroyed.

ST. LOUIS CLASS LIGHT CRUISER
CL-49
LAUNCHED: 1938

DECEMBER 7, 1941

While at sea, a ship is always moving and the engines always running. This continuous use is the reason they are in constant need of repair and overhaul. Technology also is in constant motion which is another reason ships are always being added onto and modified. On Friday December 5, 1941 ST. LOUIS entered Pearl Harbor to attend to these very needs. She pulled into a berth in the Navy Yard to have her boilers and guns worked on. She also was going to have new radar installed. Being in for service also meant liberty for the crew.

The Orders of the Day for ST. LOUIS on that December Sunday morning called for light and easy duties. On the schedule were Protestant and Catholic church calls and liberty parties. At *"0930 Knock off work. Holiday routine. All hands shift into clean uniform of the day. Keep the ship, boats, brow and accommodation ladder neat. Keep all hands in clean uniform of the day. Sun bathing from 0930 – 1130."*[58] There was also another round of sunbathing scheduled from 1300 to 1700. Planned to be shown that evening at 1920, was a movie, "When Ladies Meet," starring Joan Crawford, Robert Taylor and Greer Garson. After 0755 the sunbathing and the movie were cancelled.

On the fantail, just prior to 0755, was a detail of four Marines. They were waiting for the bugler to arrive so they could proceed with morning colors. One of the Marines, Max Schmeling, (not the German heavyweight boxer), held the flag as they waited.

---

58 Orders of the Day for U.S.S. St. Louis, December 7, 1941 by Commander C. K. Fink, Executive Officer.

All these men saw the first wave of Japanese planes fly in over the harbor. They observed the first bombs falling on Ford Island and they heard the staccato chatter of the enemy machine guns as they opened fire. They all stood there, momentarily bewildered at what was unfolding before their eyes. What shook them back into reality was the sight of a "Kate," just aft, flying toward Battleship Row only twenty or thirty feet above deck height. The Marines didn't wait for the bugler. Schmeling raised the flag and they all ran for their battle stations.

Below decks, the commanding officer of the cruiser, Captain George A. Rood, was notified by the Executive Officer, Commander Carl K. Fink of the air raid. Rood jumped up and threw his uniform shirt and pants on over his pajamas, then, still in his slippers, he raced to the bridge. By the time he arrived there several things were already happening. The crew of ST. LOUIS was directing 1.1 inch and .50 caliber anti-aircraft fire at the enemy planes. Throughout the cruiser preparations were being made to get underway. Later in the day Captain Rood asked Fink if he had given orders for either one of these operations. Rood and Fink realized that neither of them had given these orders and attributed their initiation to the initiative of a well-trained and motivated crew.

Below decks in engineering one boiler was operating to supply electricity and steam for only the most basic operations while in the Navy Yard. Two boilers had been dismantled for overhaul and the other five boilers were cold. Those cold boilers were lit and great efforts were made to instill fire, heat and steam in them.

On deck, hasty and unorthodox operations were taking place to facilitate the entry into war. Ropes and wires holding ST. LOUIS in her berth were severed with axes. To the despair of Gunner's Mate Charles Loud, the ornate wood and brass accommodation ladder that he had spent countless hours polishing was, with a few swift, strong, strokes sent to the bottom of the harbor. Procedures for getting underway were not the only unorthodox things happening on deck. One sailor, Alva Jones, saw another, obviously very frustrated, bluejacket on the fantail throwing potatoes at the low flying planes as they zoomed by.

Orders had been received that clearly stated, *"Sortie according to Plan 1 – locate and destroy the enemy."* Plain, simple and direct, Captain Rood had every intention of following them. At 0931 with Rood at the conn59, ST. LOUIS backed out of her berth in the Navy Yard. There were no tugs available for this complex maneuver and Rood accomplished it himself - an amazing piece of seamanship. Wanting to get out of the mousetrap of a harbor as quickly as possible, Rood began moving at 15 knots and was soon at 20 knots. The standard speed limit inside the harbor was 8 knots.

ST. LOUIS, on the right, makes her run for the sea, here, passing Ford Island at about 0940. The battleship CALIFORNIA is burning on the left. In the distant center, a destroyer, probably USS PHELPS, makes her sortie.

After leaving her berth, Captain Rood gave the order to "strip ship." This meant that all loose or superfluous materials were to be removed from the main deck, lest they pose a danger during action. Swabs, brooms, lockers, paint cans and anything else not attached to the ship were tossed overboard. One of the most hated and backbreaking jobs on board any ship was sanding the wooden deck with holystones. When the despised

---

59 "Conn" being the naval term for the person, or the action of, giving the orders controlling a ships movements.

sandstone rocks were seen being thrown overboard also, yells of jubilation could be heard throughout the ship.

Maneuvering in the harbor was a particularly dicey affair for Rood considering the cruisers 608-foot length and the high rate of speed she was traveling. Near Hospital Point she had to enter the main channel while avoiding the even bigger battleship USS NEVADA, BB-36, which was being beached and trying not to block the channel. The crew on the crippled NEVADA cheered ST. LOUIS on as the cruiser passed by.

Now heading down the main channel for the open sea, Rood was very worried. The dredged channel severely restricted the cruiser's direction to a straight line, making his ship an ideal target for any enemy submarines waiting outside the channel entrance. His only defense against this eventuality was to go just as fast as he could. By the time ST. LOUIS reached the channel entrance she was doing close to 25 knots.

Just as she neared the end of the channel, Rood's worst fears were realized. Almost every pair of eyes on deck spotted the telltale tracks of two torpedoes coming straight at their starboard side from about 1,000 yards distant. ST. LOUIS was trapped in the channel and could not maneuver to attempt to dodge the deadly fish. All eyes were fixed on the impending disaster that was racing toward their ship. Then, suddenly, the god of the sea or war or luck intervened. The two torpedoes struck a reef on the outside of the channel and detonated only a few hundred yards away, sending up plumes of water and coral. A black object, either the periscope or the conning tower of the mini-sub that fired the torpedoes was spotted. Several of the cruisers five-inch guns fired upon it, but neither the captain nor the executive officer noted any hits or claimed sinking it in their reports.[60]

At last free of the harbor and free to maneuver, ST. LOUIS formed a task group with several of the destroyers that had also managed to escape the harbor. They went hunting for the Japanese fleet. Several times during the rest of the day Captain Rood received orders to take his small group in different directions based on the latest intelligence or rumors circulating

---

60 There is also a controversial theory that this sub actually fired its torpedoes in Pearl Harbor at WEST VIRGINIA or OKLAHOMA and that the explosions seen by ST. LOUIS were errant anti-aircraft fire.

as to the whereabouts of the enemy ships. Around 1600 Captain Rood finally took the time to return to his cabin and get out of his pajamas and slippers.

ST. LOUIS stayed out searching and patrolling for over three days, returning to Pearl Harbor on the evening of Wednesday, December 10th. When the cruiser entered the harbor the crew was greeted with the sight of broken battleships and bodies still being fished out of the water.

ST. LOUIS was credited with shooting down three enemy planes on the 7th. She suffered no causalities, and damage was restricted to a few inconsequential bullet holes.

THE WAR

During the early months of 1942 ST. LOUIS was occupied as an escort, shepherding convoys back and forth from the west coast to Pearl Harbor or from Pearl Harbor to Midway. One of the Midway trips was to deliver two companies of the 2nd Marine Raider Battalion, better known as Carlson's Raiders, to help reinforce the island defenders. She also participated in a raid on Japanese bases in the Marshall and Gilbert Islands. ST. LOUIS spent from May to October 1942 in the Aleutian Islands where she shelled Kiska Island and covered the landings at Adak.

After a period of overhaul at Mare Island she sailed south where the struggle for the Solomon Islands continued. For months ST. LOUIS, in conjunction with other U.S. and Allied ships, sailed The Slot in efforts to interdict the enemy's efforts to reinforce and resupply its garrisons throughout the island chain. On July 6, 1943 they met the Tokyo Express head on in Kula Gulf.

At approximately 0145, a radar contact was made at a distance of 17,000 yards. She opened fire at 0157 and the fight was on. With her that night were two Pearl Harbor sisters, the cruisers USS HELENA, CL-50, and USS HONOLULU, CL-48, along with four destroyers. What they had run into were ten Japanese destroyers. The battle in the darkness raged for almost a half hour. Shells cut through the night sky and torpedoes sliced through the coal black water. Intermittent fighting continued for a full hour until the final cease-fire call was made at 0251. When it was all over the Japanese were down two destroyers and the Americans had lost HELENA.

After her escape from Pearl Harbor on December 7, 1941, many began to refer to ST. LOUIS as "The Lucky Lou." It was here at the Battle of Kula Gulf that she really earned the name, however. The Japanese Type 93 torpedo, was one of the best and most reliable torpedoes, of any country, used during the war. Three of these struck HELENA and brought her down. Two days after the battle, while undergoing inspection by divers in Espiritu Santo, at least one large dent was discovered in the hull of ST. LOUIS where she had been struck by an enemy torpedo that failed to detonate.

A week later, on the 13th, ST. LOUIS was once again patrolling The Slot, this time with twelve other ships. What followed was an almost exact replay of what happened the week before. Radar contact was made at 0042, this time at a distance of 22,000 yards. At 0105 the enemy ships were in sight and at 0111 ST. LOUIS opened fire. Once again a donnybrook in the dark ensued. Muzzle flashes from six-inch guns illuminated the night. Searchlights danced across the water. A symphony of bright and black enveloped the steel combatants.

Workers conduct preliminary repairs on the bow at Espiritu Santo.

ST. LOUIS engaged several different targets in the first eighteen minutes of the battle. During this time her entire radar system stopped working, but returned to power in slow increments. At 0156 the 608-foot length of the cruiser shuddered violently as her luck finally ran out. An enemy torpedo struck her forward, adjacent to the chain locker, and blew off the lower half of the bow. Although the ship's luck had run out, the crew's luck had not. There were no casualties as a result of the torpedo, and even though the wound looked dire and her bow was twelve and a half feet out of line, she was still seaworthy

The Americans lost one destroyer in the battle. Three cruisers, including ST. LOUIS, were severely damaged and had to withdraw from the theater of operations for repairs. Her bow was welded closed and she made for the States where the wizards of Mare Island made her like new once more. Repairs were completed in November 1943.

ST. LOUIS returned to the South Pacific and spent the rest of 1943 there shelling targets in the Solomon Islands as their liberation from the Japanese continued. By early 1944 the campaign had reached and passed Bougainville in the extreme Northwest of the chain. In February, landings were to take place on the Green Islands just north of Bougainville.

In the late evening of the 14th ST. LOUIS was en route to those islands. A flight of enemy planes spotted the small task group and attacked. Two Val dive-bombers picked the cruiser out as a target and dove on her. ST. LOUIS increased speed to 27 knots and began a violent zigzag pattern to avoid the bombs that would soon be falling. Her gunners sent a heavy anti-aircraft barrage skyward. The first Val released its load of three bombs. They all missed but impacted very close. The second plane pressed its attack much closer than the first and did not let loose its load until much later. Of the three bombs released, two of them missed, but again they were very close. The third bomb hit amidships. As it traveled the last few feet before impact, it struck a glancing blow to a steel seat of a quad 40mm gun mount. The gun's trainer, a sailor named Parnett, occupied the seat. He was completely unharmed.

The bomb penetrated the gun mount platform and detonated below decks killing 23 and wounding 20. Two years and two months into the war "The Lucky Lou" finally suffered her first casualties from enemy action. If there was any consolation in this at all it was that the Japanese pilot's bravery in pressing his attack to insure a hit cost him his life, as the cruiser's gunners splashed him. Although her wounds were not critical ST. LOUIS headed for Tulagi for repairs. The following day the 23 dead were ceremoniously committed to the deep.

Her mending did not require a major shipyard and the repairs were completed at Tulagi. Afterward she spent more time in the Solomons. She sailed north in June to the Marshall and Mariana Islands where she engaged in operations off Eniwetok and Guam respectively. In July she returned to the United States for overhaul. Upon completion and after training in Hawai'i, she sailed to the Philippines in November.

The United States Army had returned to the Philippines on October 20, 1944 when they landed on Leyte. ST. LOUIS and a large flotilla were there to support the massive operation. Ever since her arrival in the area in mid November she, along with all the other ships, was subject to severe and almost constant aerial attack by the enemy, sometimes two or three alerts in a day.

On November 27, 1944 ST. LOUIS and other vessels were in the middle of refueling operations when another of these daily attacks occurred. The Lucky Lou was about to be subjected to her worst fifty minutes of the war.

Arvid L. "Swede" Newman was a 20mm gunner on a portside fantail mount. When word arrived at 1130 that enemy planes were coming in, he and his crew were waiting for them and they didn't have long to wait. Within minutes the planes were in range and headed straight for their cruiser. The first plane was a Val dive-bomber coming in at approximately 200 miles an hour at a fairly steep angle. All the anti-aircraft batteries were firing on it. In seconds it was apparent that the plane was hit, but it kept on coming. Newman had the plane squarely in his cross hairs and was pumping 20mm rounds at the plane just as fast as he could.

Then came the point that everyone on the fantail realized that the Val was going to hit right where they were, and they all began to scatter. "Swede" Newman didn't move. He too realized that if it continued on its current trajectory the plane was going to hit very near to where he was sitting. He also came to the conclusion that his only chance of survival was to kill the plane, disintegrate it, before it struck. So he kept firing and it kept coming. As the Val crossed the last hundred yards, it nosed up, rolled on its back, then crashed, inverted into the fantail.

The plane plowed through the deck, its 500-pound bomb and fuel exploding into a massive fireball, enveloping the stern of ST. LOUIS. Many of those sailors who ran seeking cover were caught and killed in the explosion. "Swede" Newman, who stayed at his post, was wounded by shrapnel and covered in blood.

One minute later, a second plane came in attempting to crash the cruiser. This time the plane missed, but only barely. It appeared that it was going to hit the superstructure amidships, but the plane amazingly flew between the two smokestacks, its wingtips missing each stack by only inches. The kamikaze passed over the ship and splashed in the water only one hundred yards away.

Damage control parties rushed to the stern to fight the fire caused by the plane strike. Of all the stern 20mm gun's crewmen, only three men came out alive. Medical teams also arrived to help with the dead and wounded. Sailors were quickly found to man the guns and they were soon in action again.

ST LOUIS, under attack by kamikazes and fighting for her life in Leyte Gulf, November 27, 1944.

Ten minutes after the first two planes attacked, two more were seen to be aiming for ST. LOUIS. The smoke and flame may have enticed them to attack seeing that she was already wounded and hoping to finish the job. The enemy planes came in from the port side. The first plane was brought down by anti-aircraft fire and crashed into the ocean. The second plane closely followed the first and was clearly on fire as it approached. The Japanese pilot was determined and did not flinch. He struck the port side of the hull punching numerous holes in it and taking out a twenty-foot section of armor belt.

As soon as one attack was complete, there was barely time to take a breath when another threat appeared. Minutes later several planes launched torpedoes at ST. LOUIS, but quick maneuvers avoided the deadly fish.

In the aftermath of the attack, Eddie Niziolek, a sailor from Chicago, went looking for his friend, "Swede" Newman. They had reported to ST.

LOUIS together and had promised that should something happen to one of them, the other would tell their family what occurred. Niziolek couldn't find "Swede" among the survivors or the wounded. He presumed then that his buddy was dead and went to the part of the deck where the deceased had been laid out beneath some canvas. He lifted the canvas and sure enough he saw Newman's body laying there. Before he dropped the canvas he noticed something about Newman's bloody body. It was breathing. Niziolek called for help and Newman was taken to get medical treatment.

The final tally from the kamikaze was 16 dead and 43 wounded. Two days after the attack, the body of the Japanese pilot was found in a compartment below deck. He was buried at sea. ST. LOUIS headed to the United States for repairs.

After three months of repair at Mare Island, ST. LOUIS set sail for her last battle, arriving off Okinawa in March 1945. As with all invasions, the job of the fleet off shore is to first provide bombardment of the enemy island prior to the landings, protect the troop ships and assault craft during the landings, protect support vessels from air and submarine attack after the landings, and to provide call fire[61] support for land operations.

On the 26th, after just arriving in the area, the Japanese greeted ST. LOUIS with her second mini-sub attack of the war. While off Kerema Retto, lookouts spotted the tracks of two torpedoes headed straight for her as she was getting into position to commence shore bombardment. The helm was quickly notified and the ship was turned. One torpedo passed just in front of the bow and the second one passed astern.

The invasion of Okinawa took place on April 1, 1945. On that day, in support of the landings, ST. LOUIS fired 1,500 shells from both her main six-inch and secondary five-inch batteries. For a total of 70 days at Okinawa, ST. LOUIS was a workhorse for the Army, Navy and Marines. With the exception of only a few days in that time, she performed call fire operations, clearing away enemy strongholds in caves and pill boxes, blowing up ammo dumps and raining destruction down on enemy vehicles.

---

61   "Call fire" is a request by ground forces for artillery support usually for a specific target.

She sounded general quarters for 87 air raid alerts. Eleven of those alerts resulted in attacks on her or ships in her sphere of protection. She shot down or assisted in shooting down ten enemy planes.

Throughout her tour at Okinawa, ST. LOUIS is believed to have set the record for most rounds fired by a surface vessel during a single operation. When the mission was completed she had fired 26,265 six-inch and five-inch shells, for a total of 1,059 tons of artillery dropped on the enemy. She was at Buckner Bay, Okinawa when the Japanese surrendered.

FATE

Her post-war duties included three runs to the United States for operation "Magic Carpet," returning Americans home for discharge. In February 1946 she sailed to Philadelphia where she was decommissioned and placed in the reserve fleet there.

In January 1951, ST. LOUIS was sold to Brazil. She was renamed *TAMANDARE*, C-12, and became the flagship for the Brazilian Navy. She sailed for Brazil for twenty-five years, until 1976. She was sold four years later to a scrap yard in Hong Kong. While being towed there, she developed a severe leak and began taking on water. The tow cable was released and on August 24, 1980, *TAMANDARE*/ST. LOUIS slowly rolled over and sank in the South Atlantic.

For some who sailed on her this was considered a much more fitting end than being broken up and turned into razor blades.

USS Sumner

BUSHNELL CLASS SUB TENDER /
SURVEY SHIP
AG-32
LAUNCHED: 1915

DECEMBER 7, 1941

Only four minutes after the first bombs started dropping, the gun captain of SUMNER's #3 anti-aircraft gun, Boatswains Mate 2nd Class H. L. Campbell had his gun firing at the enemy. Two minutes after that, Campbell's 8-man crew brought down an enemy plane. In fact, the #3 gun saw so much action that by the end of the day the gun's barrel had expanded from the heat, increasing the diameter by one quarter inch about four inches from the muzzle. Campbell by the end of the attack had somehow managed to break a finger and his Pointer, Machinist Mate 2nd Class J. N. Pastor had a ruptured ear drum.

Although not a ship designed for combat, from her vantage point at the submarine base, SUMNER put up an amazing amount of firepower that morning. Her standard armament was one five-inch gun, four three-inch guns and four .50 caliber machine guns. In addition to these weapons, Captain I. W. Truitt had four Lewis machine guns brought out and mounted and manned on the boat deck. He then issued standard rifles and Browning Automatic Rifles to other crewmembers and sent them up into the rigging to fire on the enemy. When the sun set that night, SUMNER had fired 234 rounds from the three-inch guns, 8,000 rounds of .50 caliber ammunition and an untold amount of small arms ammunition, all of which shot down one enemy plane and assisted in bringing down two other Japanese aircraft.

As with many ships that day, SUMNER continued firing at almost anything that flew for hours after the Japanese attack was over. She fired a total of nineteen three-inch rounds between 1000 and 1130 at American planes. Luckily, most of the planes were at high altitude and all the shells missed.

THE WAR

During the war SUMNER's job as a survey ship was to travel the Pacific Ocean and create navigation charts of islands, passages and harbors for use by the Navy. She would find the channels for safe sailing and locate the underwater rocks and shoals that were a constant danger to ships.

In September 1944, just days after the American Army took Ulithi atoll SUMNER sailed into the massive lagoon there to survey it. She discovered that the anchorage could accommodate approximately 700 ships. Her figures were correct, because at one point 617 ships were safely anchored there at one time.

In March 1945 her job brought her into harm's way. Only weeks after the invasion of Iwo Jima, SUMNER was brought in to survey the waters around that still embattled rock. On the 8th a Japanese battery fired on and hit SUMNER. Even though the enemy shell didn't detonate, it killed one sailor and injured three others.

During the war SUMNER sailed to every corner of the Pacific, surveying as far south as Tonga and as far north as Korea and hundreds of places in between. When the war ended she was completing duties in the Philippines.

FATE

Among SUMNER's final duties was to report to Bikini Atoll where she surveyed the area for the atomic bomb tests that would soon take place there. That mission completed, she sailed back to the United States and was decommissioned at Norfolk Naval Base in September 1946. She was immediately transferred to the National Defense Reserve Fleet, James River Group in Virginia. Her stay in the mothball fleet was short lived. She was sold in February 1948 to the Patapsco Scrap Corporation.

USS Sunnadin

BAGADUCE CLASS HARBOR TUG
AT-28
LAUNCHED: 1919

DECEMBER 7, 1941

17-year-old Donald Raymond was standing the gangway watch on board SUNNADIN on the morning of December 7th. Strapped to his duty belt was his .45 caliber pistol that was totally useless because it wasn't loaded. After all, why would he need bullets in his weapon with the Pacific fleet thousands of miles away from any possible enemy? So at 0755 when a Japanese plane strafed his boat and him, he dove for cover because he couldn't shoot back. When the firing stopped he discovered a spent Japanese bullet on the deck. He grabbed the bullet and jammed it in his pocket before he ran to alert the rest of the crew that World War II had started.

SUNNADIN was called upon to serve many masters that day and to perform many different jobs. She assisted with beaching the battleship USS NEVADA, BB-36, and later she came to the aid of the torpedoed and listing cruiser USS

The SUNNADIN delivers a pontoon barge to USS Raleigh.

RALEIGH, CL-7, on the north side of Ford Island. SUNNADIN brought a jury-rigged pontoon barge alongside the cruiser to help with keeping it upright.

THE WAR

SUNNADIN spent the entire war in and around Pearl Harbor, which soon became one of the busiest ports in the world, and in desperate need of an expert and dedicated crew manning a tough, versatile ship.

FATE

In 1945 SUNNADIN reported to the west coast in order to be decommissioned, which she was in 1946. The following year she was turned over to the Maritime Commission for final disposition, ending an almost thirty year career with the Navy.

USS Swan

LAPWING CLASS MINESWEEPER / SEAPLANE TENDER
AVP-7
LAUNCHED: 1918

DECEMBER 7, 1941

Pete Limon was on the deck of SWAN eating an apple. There wasn't much for the 17-year-old radioman to do that day. Work was being done on her boilers and SWAN was high and dry in the Navy Yard. As he ate his apple he casually looked up at some unfamiliar looking planes flying above. Then the planes started dropping bombs. Limon saw the red "Rising Sun" painted on the planes and was confused as to why the Japanese would be dropping bombs since we weren't at war. Limon and his shipmates wasted no time. SWAN's three-inch gun began firing within minutes of general quarters being sounded. The ship was made watertight and engineers were sent to get the boilers up and running. Her crew claimed one torpedo plane shot down and a possible partial credit on two other planes. One crewman was slightly injured by enemy machine gun fire and no damage to the ship occurred. By 1315 she was ready to be placed back in the water and get underway.

THE WAR

SWAN spent most of 1942 wandering the Pacific hauling men and materials to islands and outposts. In March she was sent to the island of

Puka Puka in the Danger Islands. The Navy had been notified that three sailors had landed there in a rubber life raft. When SWAN arrived she picked up Chief Machinist Mate Harold F. Dixon, and his two man crew, Aviation Ordinanceman 2nd Class Anthony J. Pastula and Radioman 3rd Class Gene D. Aldrich. These 3 men had ditched their TBD Devastator bomber on January 16 and spent the next 34 days at sea logging 1,200 miles to travel only 450 miles between where they ditched and finally washed ashore.

Other than a few side trips to French Frigate Shoals, halfway to Midway, SWAN stayed in the Hawai'ian Islands from 1943 through 1945 assisting in the instruction of both ships and planes by towing targets and recovering training torpedoes.

FATE

SWAN underwent a lengthy overhaul in the summer of 1945 in Los Angeles. She left for Pearl Harbor on August 13th. The next day, while she was at sea, the Japanese surrendered and the war was over. She remained in Pearl Harbor until October when she was ordered back to the States. SWAN was decommissioned in Boston on December 13, 1945. In October 1946 she was delivered to the Maritime Commission for final disposition.

USS Tangier

SEAPLANE TENDER
AV-8
LAUNCHED: 1939

DECEMBER 7, 1941

As the tender for the PBY Catalina flying boats of Patrol Wing 2, TANGIER was moored near the seaplane base on Ford Island. TANGIER was in the thick of things almost immediately, because the first bombs fell on the seaplane base. Her three-inch, 40mm and .50 caliber guns joined the fray within minutes and kept up almost continuous fire for the nearly two hour long attack.

Forty-five minutes into the attack TANGIER and almost every other ship in that part of the harbor spotted the only Japanese mini-sub confirmed to have made it inside the harbor and fire its torpedoes. Every ship that saw the sub opened fire on it including

An amazing photograph taken on December 7, 1941 from TANGIER of a Japanese bomb exploding in the harbor about twenty feet away.

TANGIER. But all firing stopped when USS MONAGHAN, DD-354, made it attack run on the intruder and sank it.

TANGIER came under attack when the second wave of the air raid began. The enemy pilots began to seek out targets of opportunity, because all of the battleships were already sinking, burning or both. TANGIER's gunners now had a good opportunity to give back some of what they were getting and they brought down at least four planes by themselves or in combination with fire from other ships.

The intense fire TANGIER sent skyward probably had a lot to do with the fact that all five dive-bombers that specifically targeted her missed. The closest of the bombs dropped missed by only fifteen feet. The crew suffered only three minor wounds and the only tangible damage was two insignificant holes above the waterline from bomb fragments.

Of all the reported expenditures of ammunition that day, TANGIER can claim the record for the most .50 caliber ammunition fired with a total of 23,000 rounds. That means her gunners fired an average of more than 3 rounds a second for almost two straight hours.

THE WAR

TANGIER was assigned to the Task Force being sent to reinforce and resupply the besieged garrison on Wake Island. She was loaded with anything and everything that might be helpful to the Marines there who were expecting a Japanese invasion: radar equipment, 21,000 three-inch and five-inch shells, 3 million rounds of machine gun ammunition and barbed wire. As welcome as this wealth was going to be, the most important cargo TANGIER loaded was several hundred Marines from the Fourth Defense Battalion.

The Task Force set out for Wake on December 13th. Ten days later, while still at sea, it was learned that Wake had fallen. The ships were redirected to Midway where all the Marines and supplies were unloaded for the defense of that island. TANGIER returned to Pearl Harbor on New Year's Eve.

In early March, TANGIER arrived at Nouméa, the capital of the French colony of New Caledonia. There she did exactly what she was designed to do, be a tender for seaplanes. Squadron VP-14, comprised of PBY Catalina flying boats was stationed there. The purpose of VP-14 was to utilize the long-range search capabilities of their PBYs to keep a vigilant eye on the Japanese. On March 8, 1942 TANGIER took on board her first plane ever for servicing. In May the PBYs of VP-14 were used to look for survivors of the Battle of the Coral Sea.

For the rest of the war TANGIER's life was a cycle of repairs and overhauls followed by extended deployments to the Pacific. She was a loving caretaker of her charges. The PBY Catalina flying boats and the PBM Mariners that she serviced, repaired, and kept flying were an integral part of the American advance against the Japanese strongholds throughout the Pacific. These seaplanes, with their extended range and multiple capabilities, were invaluable to the Navy. The flying boats engaged in duties as varied as long range patrols, bombing, search and rescue, and supply missions. Just in their capacity as search and rescue planes the Catalinas and the Mariners saved the lives of countless downed pilots and sailors cast adrift from sinking ships.

If TANGIER hadn't been there to keep these planes flying many lives would have been lost, many ships would have been sunk and the war would have been just that much longer. Her extensive journey took her to almost every major base in the Pacific and eventually took her back to San Francisco for another overhaul in July 1945, which is where she was when the war ended.

FATE

TANGIER reported to Japan in September 1945 to support occupation forces there. She stayed in the Far East until March 1946 when she returned to the United States to be decommissioned in Philadelphia in 1947. TANGIER was then laid up as part of the Atlantic Reserve Fleet for the next 14 years when she was struck from the Navy roles and sold to Union Minerals and Alloys Corporation. The all too familiar routine would be that she was then scrapped; however, the case of TANGIER is different. Union Mineral and Alloys turned around and resold her to the shipping company Sea-Land Service. They converted her into a containerized cargo ship and renamed her *SS Detroit*. As any good veteran she gave her new owners years of faithful service until she made her last stop in Valencia, Spain where she was finally scrapped in December, 1974.

USS Tautog

TAMBOR CLASS FLEET SUBMARINE
SS-199
LAUNCHED: 1940

DECEMBER 7, 1941

On December 5th TAUTOG returned to Pearl Harbor from a Pacific cruise of more than 40 days. Despite the fact that the Japanese had not yet attacked Pearl Harbor, in his reports, the captain, Lieutenant Commander Joseph H. Willingham referred to this as the 1st war cruise. Willingham berthed his boat at the submarine base in Pearl Harbor. As a result of the long cruise, three quarters of her crew were on liberty, leaving fewer than twenty sailors on board.

Just before 0800, some of them spotted Japanese planes making their first bomb runs and immediately manned the machine guns on board. The enemy Kates making torpedo runs on Battleship Row flew on a straight course down South East Loch, directly astern of the vessels at the sub base. Some of the planes were as close as 150 feet. This allowed the gunners onboard TAUTOG a clear field of fire. By the end of the attack her gunners claimed one kill and at least one assist on another downed plane.

The Japanese totally ignored the sub base during the attack not even bothering to make a strafing run on the subs firing at them. TAUTOG suffered no damage of any kind or any causalities. The Japanese folly of not sinking, damaging, or even attacking TAUTOG that Sunday morning would come back to haunt them.

THE WAR

TAUTOG wasted no time in bringing the war to the enemy, leaving on her first war patrol only 19 days later on December 26th. She sank her first enemy ship, a submarine, four months later in April 1942 during her second war patrol. Only three weeks after that she sank a second Japanese submarine. By November 1942 TAUTOG had sunk six enemy ships.

On November 11, 1942, while traversing the Makassar Strait off of Borneo, TAUTOG encountered a tempting freighter being escorted by a lone Japanese ship. Willingham set up a shot and fired a single torpedo, which unfortunately missed its target. As a precaution, Willingham rigged for silent running and dove his boat to 250 feet and it was a good thing that he did. The escort vessel saw the torpedo, calculated its origin and went hunting. TAUTOG could hear the active pinging of the escort vessel's sonar. The Japanese sonar operator, quartermaster and captain were all good at their jobs. Fifty-five minutes after TAUTOG fired her torpedo, the first depth charge dropped.

That first depth charge shocked TAUTOG like a Jack Dempsey uppercut, rocking the ship violently. In rapid succession four more depth charges exploded within 100 feet just above and to the port of the submarine. The crew bounced off of bulkheads and decks. Water spewed from ruptured valves and electrical arcs sparked like 4th of July fireworks. Very soon the engine bilges were under two feet of water. For the next hour and a half the Japanese escort dropped a total of eleven depth charges on TAUTOG, leaving the Americans significantly shaken. Finally around 1330 the enemy had lost the scent and could be heard moving away.

Even though TAUTOG didn't suffer any major damage as a result of the shellacking she took, she did have a long laundry list of minor ills which when totaled added up to one severely injured submarine. Captain Willingham called off the patrol and headed back to the submarine base at Freemantle, Australia, where she arrived ten days later.

In late December 1943, TAUTOG dodged a similar bullet when it fired two spreads of three torpedoes each at three merchant ships. At least four enemy anti-submarine ships charged TAUTOG and dropped a total of eighty-nine depth charges on her over the next four hours. Although the amount of depth charges and elapsed time was far more than her previous brush with death, this was far less distressing, as the closest depth charge was estimated to be over 200 yards away.

Throughout her thirteen war patrols TAUTOG spent a total of one year and seven months at sea hunting and killing the enemy, a job at which she excelled. She also spent time planting mines and spying on enemy facilities.

TAUTOG completed her last war patrol on February 1, 1945 at Midway Island. In April she arrived on the west coast, where for the rest of the war, in cooperation with the University of California, she helped with the experimentation of new safety equipment for submarines.

FATE

TAUTOG was decommissioned at Portsmouth, New Hampshire in December 1945, however her service to the Navy and the country was not yet complete. In December 1947 she found herself on the way to the Great Lakes Naval Reserve Training Center in Illinois. There she served as a static training ship for over a decade. She was finally stricken from the Naval rolls in 1959 and sold for scrap to the Bultema Dock and Dredge Company of Manistee, Michigan in November of that year.

After the war, when American records were compared to Japanese records, it was determined that TAUTOG had sunk a total of 26 enemy naval and merchant ships during the war - more than double the number of ships the Japanese sank at Pearl Harbor and more than any other American ship. She was responsible, by herself, for sending to the bottom more than 72,000 tons of enemy shipping.

USS Tennessee

TENNESSEE CLASS BATTLESHIP
BB-43
LAUNCHED: 1919

DECEMBER 7, 1941

TENNESSEE was possibly the most well protected ship in the harbor. She was berthed at F-6, one of the quays[62] of Battleship Row. To her starboard was Ford Island. Berthed a mere seventy-five feet aft of her was ARIZONA, BB-39. To her port was WEST VIRGINIA, BB-48, and just off her bow was MARYLAND, BB-46. The only way to really get at her was from above and even there the Japanese were to be thwarted by some good luck for the Americans.

The first wave of attacks on Battleship Row was by "Kate" torpedo planes. When they were unleashed WEST VIRGINIA, by virtue of her position, took all the blows. TENNESSEE was left untouched. Within minutes the second attack came from above with horizontal bombers. Two armor piercing bombs found TENNESSEE. One hit turret No. 2 and a second hit turret No. 3. Fate once again intervened and protected TENNESSEE. Both bombs were duds. Neither of them detonated, although the explosives inside the one that hit turret No. 3 did catch fire and burned intensely. Some men were killed and the guns were put out of commission but the damage was negligible.

---

62 Pronounced "key" it is a freestanding concrete structure used for berthing ships.

At approximately 0810 the forward magazine on ARIZONA blew up after being hit with a bomb. TENNESSEE was showered with debris that fell from the sky like steel hail. This flaming wreckage started numerous fires. A torrent of fuel oil gushed from the shattered hull of ARIZONA and ignited almost instantaneously. On her port side WEST VIRGINIA was also an inferno.

After ARIZONA blew up, the threat from attack by the Japanese disappeared for TENNESSEE. The thick, roiling black smoke from ARIZONA flowed over TENNESSEE and totally obscured her. The enemy could no longer see her and not one more bomb was dropped on her.

The fire that surrounded her was her biggest enemy. The fires on board were controlled relatively easily. Fire-fighting parties on board TENNESSEE played water onto the inferno engulfing WEST VIRGINIA. The oil fire from ARIZONA, however, quickly floated to TENNESSEE and soon her stern was cooking inside and out. Damage control parties inside reported the paint on interior bulkheads was smoldering and letting off a choking black smoke that made it impossible to see anything below decks and made it almost impossible to move around. The heat was so intense that an interior fireproof hatch that had been only dogged[63] at the top warped at a ninety-degree angle.

Japanese photo of Battleship Row after ARIZONA blew up. On the right is NEVADA in the clear. The burning ARIZONA is in front of her. Smoke from her fires obscures TENNESSEE and other ships alongside Ford Island.

---

63 A "dog" is one of multiple heavy metal latches around a hatch to secure it. To dog a hatch is to close it.

Captain Charles E. Reardon arrived on board from his home just after the attack ended. He immediately took command while still wearing his civilian clothes and a straw hat. There were already crews standing on the stern spraying heavy streams of water into the harbor to keep at bay the ever-threatening burning fuel oil floating on the surface. Reardon now ordered the engines engaged to turn the propellers. The idea was that the screws would create a wake that would push the oil fire away from the stern. It worked. Later in the morning it was pointed out to Reardon that he was still in his civilian clothes and that he might want to change. The captain agreed and replaced his straw hat with a helmet. He then continued with his duties.

By 1030 the fires on board were out. By the end of the day those surrounding her, though still burning, were no longer a serious threat. TENNESSEE suffered only five men killed and claimed four enemy planes shot down.

THE WAR

The battleship's position in the harbor that helped protect her during the attack also trapped her after the battle. Even if she hadn't been blocked in, she still had another problem. When WEST VIRGINA began to list and then was counter–flooded, her position in her berth shifted. WEST VIRGINIA was now firmly wedged against TENNESSEE pinning the latter against the concrete quay on her starboard side. TENNESSEE couldn't move. While initial repairs and clean up were commenced on board, a demolition crew was sent to the quay to remove it so the battleship could escape. She was freed from Battleship Row on the 16th and on the 20th she sailed east for America, arriving at the Puget Sound Naval Yard on December 29th.

As with all the battleships from Pearl Harbor, when TENNESSEE went in for repairs, the opportunity was taken to significantly improve her. After two months in the yard she sailed down the West coast for training. She then escorted the carrier USS HORNET, CV-8, to Pearl Harbor. When she completed that assignment she returned to Puget Sound for a complete modernization. While there her radar was upgraded, her anti-aircraft defenses were heavily increased and the silhouette of her superstructure markedly reduced. When she left Washington she looked like a different ship.

The door was closing on the time of the grand battleship. World War II was the last time that giant dreadnaughts would meet in great ship-to-ship surface battles and even then those engagements were few and far between. She did participate in the last major confrontation between battleships in the war, the Battle of Surigao Strait in October 1944. For the most part TENNESSEE spent the war as a moving artillery platform, roaming the Pacific like a gun for hire delivering her big 14-inch main batteries to where ever they were needed.

She was there at almost every major landing of the Pacific war. Arriving a day or two prior to the invasion she would launch her spotter planes that would direct her fire and call for adjustments as needed. Some of the pre-invasion bombardments would last for hours, expending hundreds of shells. The day of the landings she provided cover fire for the assault boats going into the beaches. After the beachhead was established, she stood by for call fire assignments to aid in the ultimate conquest of the island. If needed, she contributed to night operations by hurling star shells into the sky. And of course, in between all these assignments, her formidable array of anti-aircraft weaponry protected the fleet and ground troops from aerial attacks.

The big fourteen-inch guns of TENNESSEE provide support for the landings at Okinawa on April 1, 1945

On several occasions TENNESSEE got into duels with enemy shore batteries. While bombarding Kavieng on New Ireland, in March 1944, a shore battery got her range and several salvos straddled the battleship. TENNESSEE responded with a ten-minute barrage on the Japanese position and the enemy guns were silenced. In June 1944, while bombarding Tinian, TENNESSEE had another set-to with a Japanese shore battery. The enemy guns specifically targeted TENNESSEE just after the first wave of Marines landed. Three artillery rounds struck the battleship that resulted in the deaths of eight sailors and the wounding of twenty-seven more. Occasionally her shelling operations brought her so close to shore she was in range of enemy small arms. At Eniwetok in 1944 a sailor on deck was wounded by rifle fire from the island.

At Okinawa the last ditch weapon from a desperate Japanese military was the kamikaze. The enemy would send in waves of them in an effort to disrupt, dislodge and destroy the American invaders. The gale of the "divine wind" blew across the American fleet almost every day after the initial landings and almost every day an American ship was damaged or sunk. On April 12th a large flight of kamikazes went after the fleet. There were so many that it was inevitable that some would get through the outer defense perimeter.

Five of them got through and aimed for TENNESSEE. The battleship let loose with every anti-aircraft gun on board. One plane was shot down, then another and another and another, till there was just one left. The last plane, a "Val," took a beating as it approached. One wheel was shot off and the engine spewed smoke from the hits it took, but the plane kept coming. The kamikaze hit the signal bridge then skittered along the superstructure finally coming to rest near turret No. 3. The bomb it carried penetrated the main deck and exploded. The death toll was twenty-two, with 107 others wounded. The damage was minor for the great dreadnaught and she fought on.

TENNESSEE remained in the Western Pacific until the end of hostilities. Her record during the war was outstanding. TENNESSEE was representative of the vast majority of Allied ships during the march across the Pacific. She was engaged mostly in some very basic and very necessary work. One step at a time, one battle at a time she was part of a vast team that set a goal and ultimately achieved it. She didn't make any heroic dashes to the rescue, nor was she involved in any great close quarters surface battles. But she was always there and she always did her job well.

During the conflict TENNESSEE sailed over 170,000 miles, fired 158,218 rounds of small and large caliber ammunition and spent 339 days in actual combat operations. She downed, by herself or with others, at least twenty-four enemy airplanes. She also lost forty-four men and suffered 175 wounded. She was one of only two battleships during the war to receive the Navy Unit Commendation. Awarded to her by Secretary of the Navy James Forrestal, it read in part, "...*The TENNESSEE's splendid record of achievements, from the Aleutians to the Ryukyus, reflects the superb teamwork and gallantry of her valiant officers and men and is in keeping with the highest traditions of the United States Naval Service.*"

FATE

TENNESSEE stayed in the Pacific through October 1945 with stops in Japan and China. She returned home, arriving in Philadelphia, coincidentally, on December 7, 1945. She was decommissioned in 1947 and placed in the reserve fleet. She sat in peaceful retirement waiting for the next call to duty until 1959. That call never came. In her career she had received many orders and had followed them all to completion. Now, the last order she received was to leave America's service for good. This order she also followed.

In July 1959 she was sold as scrap to the Bethlehem Steel Company.

USS Tern

LAPWING CLASS MINESWEEPER
AM-31
LAUNCHED: 1919

DECEMBER 7, 1941

B. F. Marshall was a 31-year-old radioman that had already served 4 years in the Marine Corps and 2 years in the Navy. He reported for duty aboard TERN just 3 days before and was expecting to have a very slow day. TERN was tied up at 1010 dock undergoing a major overhaul and there was little if anything for the crew to do on a Sunday morning. Marshall was leisurely reading a book on deck waiting for the liberty boats to start crisscrossing the harbor. He intended to catch one to go visit a friend of his who was in the sickbay on board USS ARIZONA, BB-39. His quiet day suddenly vaporized when the bombs began falling. Marshall reported to the radio room to monitor any orders or instructions that came from Commander in Chief, Pacific, (CincPac) over the harbor frequency.

Below decks, 21-year-old fireman Arthur Cooper was off duty also reading a book. He reported to his battle station in the boiler room at the beginning of the raid. Since the ship was undergoing overhaul and receiving all power and steam from the dock the boilers were off and completely cold. Cooper and the rest of the boiler room crew immediately set to firing them up using flashlights for illumination since the power from the dock was cut off at the onset of the attack.

Up on deck other crewmembers opened fire on the enemy with .30 caliber Lewis machine guns claiming a kill early in the attack.

In the radio room, Marshall got an occasional glimpse at the devastation out in the harbor. He saw debris falling from the sky after ARIZONA exploded and he watched as USS OKLAHOMA, BB-37, turned turtle and capsized.

Cooper and the boiler room crew got the boilers going and fired up in record time and TERN pulled away from 1010 dock just as the raid was ending. The speed and efficiency exhibited by all of the crew is even more remarkable when one re-alizes that there was not a full compliment on board. Fully half the crew was on leave because of the over-haul. TERN pulled out into the harbor and com-menced hauling survivors from the water. One by one, 47 oil soaked, ex-hausted, half dead men

USS TERN, right, fighting fires on the sunken USS WEST VIRGINIA

were fished out of the harbor. Shortly before 1100 TERN reported to ARIZONA to assist with fighting fires on board the doomed vessel. She then received orders to report to USS WEST VIRGINIA, BB-48, where Lieutenant Walton B. Pendleton, the captain of TERN, was put in charge of fighting the fires on that battleship. Down in the boiler room Arthur Cooper was keeping the pressure pump up and running to feed water to the five fire hoses being used.

THE WAR

For the next two days TERN continued fighting fires on battleship row. The following day TERN bounced around the harbor fulfilling minor duties. Finally on Thursday the 11th TERN returned to the Navy yard to complete her overhaul, which had been interrupted, by the beginning of the war.

The following month, January 1942, TERN set sail for Bora Bora, where she would remain for a year. While there she was reclassified as a fleet tugboat, AT-142. In November 1942 TERN was sent out to help escort USS PENSACOLA, CA-24, back to Pearl Harbor. The cruiser had been badly damaged at the Battle of Tassafaronga. After accomplishing this mission, TERN reported to San Pedro, California for overhaul.

Upon completion she returned to Pearl Harbor where she stayed for over a year. There she retrieved practice torpedoes for submarines and towed targets for everything from shore artillery to high-level bombers, sometimes towing targets with as much as a mile of cable behind her. In May 1944, TERN, like most of the other LAPWING Class minesweepers her age, was redesignated as an ocean going tugboat, old, ATO-142.

TERN spent the rest of the war in the South Pacific in and around Eniwetok, Ulithi and Guam, towing other craft and targets as needed.

FATE

The end came quickly for TERN. In December 1945, less than four months after the Japanese surrender, she was struck from the rolls of the Navy after 26 years of service.

USS Thornton

CLEMSON CLASS DESTROYER / SEAPLANE TENDER
DD-270 / AVD-11
LAUNCHED: 1919

DECEMBER 7, 1941

The Pearl Harbor submarine base was a good place to be on that Sunday morning. American ships there were virtually ignored by the enemy. Japanese planes making torpedo runs on Battleship Row had to pass within range of American guns at the sub base. Sometimes the enemy planes were flying as low as twenty-five to fifty feet and only several hundred feet away. They made excellent targets. The men of THORNTON shot at the enemy planes with everything from .50 caliber machine guns to Springfield rifles.

The combined fire of THORNTON and HULBERT, AVD-6, which was docked at the next pier, brought down one "Kate" torpedo plane. The plane splashed into Southeast Loch in flames. THORNTON continued firing at anything that came into range. Three planes made a strafing attack on the oiler USS NEOSHO, AO-23, but were either driven back or changed direction by the intense fire of THORNTON and other ships.

As with almost all of the ships in this part of the harbor, when the skies were empty and the guns went silent, THORNTON had suffered no damage or casualties.

THE WAR

Built as a destroyer and remade into a seaplane tender, THORNTON, as did many ships like her, plied the waters of the Pacific in many guises. One day she was a rescue vessel and two weeks later she was a cargo ship, then next month she might be transporting Marines to an invasion and six months later she was screening a convoy or towing a damaged ship.

The American destroyer of World War II was, perhaps more than any other type of ship, the workhorse of the Navy. Their versatility made them invaluable. They could be called upon at any time to do almost anything.

THORNTON was much like this. At times she actually performed in her design function as a seaplane tender. Her wartime career took her literally across the Pacific. She was in the North Pacific, in the Aleutians, during the days of the Japanese occupation of Attu and Kiska. She was in the Western Pacific at the end of the war for the invasion of Okinawa. Guadalcanal in the South Pacific was no stranger to her and she even spent time on the west coast of the United States.

Every one of the forty-four destroyers or converted destroyers that were at Pearl Harbor on December 7, 1941 met the enemy in the Pacific theater of operations. Each one played and mastered the role of "jack-of-all-trades."

FATE

THORNTON was assigned to the Search and Reconnaissance Group of the Southern Attack Force in 1945 and on April 5th she was a part of a convoy near Okinawa. Somehow, in the darkness of the early night, THORTON's convoy crossed into another American convoy. Chaos reigned. Suddenly ships were running into each other like a demolition derby. Nine ships were damaged; the most serious was THORNTON, which had been rammed by two oilers, USS ESCALANTE, AO-70 and USS ASHTABULA, AO-51. ASHTABULA did the most damage, cutting a neat slice into THORNTON amidships on her starboard side.

The damage can be clearly seen in this photo showing where ASHTABULA's bow cut into THORNTON.

Because of the severity of her damage THORNTON was beached at Kerama Retto near Okinawa. She was stripped of anything and everything that might possibly be useful to the Navy and the war effort, decommissioned, struck from the Navy roles and left to rust on the beach. Her abandoned hulk was donated to the government of the Ryukyu Islands by the United States in 1957.

USS Tracy

CLEMSON CLASS DESTROYER /
LIGHT MINELAYER
DM-19
LAUNCHED: 1919

DECEMBER 7, 1941

As TRACY was undergoing overhaul at Berth 16 in the Pearl Harbor Navy Yard the crew was billeted at the Receiving Barracks there. A small duty section and four officers were on board that Sunday morning. The senior officer on board was Ensign L.B. Ensoy, who had graduated from the U.S. Naval Academy only months earlier. All power was off and all ammunition had been sent to the ammunition depot. TRACY was essentially helpless. So when the attack began there were only two courses of action for Ensign Ensoy to take: somehow bring his ship to life and to help those ships that could fight to fight. He did both.

Immediately crewmen began assembling both .30 and .50 caliber machine guns. As this went on other crewmen were dispatched to other ships. Some were sent to USS CUMMINGS, DD-365, which was berthed two ships over. Other crewman from the Receiving Barracks were sent to USS PENNSYLVANIA, BB-38, in the dry dock. While on board PENNSYLVANIA, a Japanese bomb struck the battleship killing three TRACY sailors.

A half hour into the attack, on board TRACY, the machine guns were finally assembled but firing was limited due to meager stores of .30 caliber ammunition and no .50 caliber rounds at all. By 0915 .50

caliber ammunition "appeared miraculously" as the captain, Lieutenant Commander George Phelan, described in his after action report.

THE WAR

In March 1942 TRACY laid a minefield off French Frigate Shoals northwest of Hawai'i. She then headed for the South Pacific to participate in the Guadalcanal offensive. During that invasion she acted as an escort and engaged in anti-submarine duty.

By early 1943 the Japanese had finally realized that Guadalcanal was lost and set about evacuating the remainders of its garrison there. The Navy received information on one of these runs and attempted to interdict it. On February 1, 1943 TRACY, along with two other ships, laid 300 mines in the path of the "Tokyo Express." The Japanese destroyer *Makigumo* struck one of those mines that evening. Badly damaged, 237 men were evacuated from the ship. Another Japanese destroyer then scuttled the *Makigumo* by firing a torpedo at her. She sank off the cost of Savo Island.

After several more months of duty TRACY sailed for the States and some overhaul work at Mare Island. Following that she spent several months of relatively quiet duty escorting convoys between Hawai'i and the west coast.

All of 1944 was spent either escorting convoys throughout the Pacific or in overhaul at various yards.

With the war drawing ever closer to the Japanese mainland, the enemy developed desperate suicide weapons such as the kamikaze. Along the same lines, the enemy created explosive motorboats called "Shinyo," (translated as "sea quakes" or "sea shakers"). These were one-man speedboats filled with explosives designed to be rammed into a ship to sink it.

On April 4, 1945 a Shinyo rammed and sank a Landing Craft Infantry, Gunboat, the LCI (G)-82, off the coast of Okinawa. The attack killed eight crewmen. TRACY was dispatched to rescue the survivors.

She continued her varied duties in the South Pacific until she was sent to the Philippines for overhaul. When that was completed she headed for Okinawa. She was at sea when the Japanese surrender was announced.

FATE

As rapidly as the Navy geared up for war, it just as rapidly turned toward peace. After the surrender, TRACY was sent to Nagasaki Bay. There she commenced clearing that vital seaport of mines in order to allow much needed supplies to enter that city which had been devastated by the second atomic bomb.

She left Japan on October 25, 1945 and arrived in New York City in December. Her 26-year long career with the Navy was ended when she was decommissioned in January 1946. She was then sold on May 16, 1946 to the Northern Metals Company of Philadelphia, Pennsylvania.

USS Trever

CLEMSON CLASS DESTROYER MINESWEEPER
DMS-16
LAUNCHED: 1920

DECEMBER 7, 1941

Arnold Schwichtenberg had arrived in Pearl Harbor in November of 1940. The day after his arrival the 19-year-old was assigned to TREVER. He was just in time to see the ship reclassified after her conversion from a destroyer to a destroyer-minesweeper and had been on her ever since. The year he spent in Honolulu, from November 1940 to December 1941,was a true paradise for the boy who turned 20 while he was there. He had spent Saturday the 6th shuttling sailors between the ship and shore on a 26-foot whaleboat. Right before 0800 Sunday morning he was at the boat waiting to be relieved. There was a rumble of planes in the air that caught his attention. He turned to look at the source of the noise in time to see two Japanese planes let loose their torpedoes at Battleship Row.

General Quarters was sounded and the crew rushed to their battle stations. The .50-caliber machine guns were manned and firing almost immediately because they were already loaded. The gunners, eager to defend their ship, started firing at any plane they saw even though it was out of range. They were soon instructed to fire only at planes that were within range. Schwichtenberg ran up the ship's ladder to his battle station on the No. 4 four-inch gun, however the gun couldn't target the high-speed low-flying planes, so it wasn't fired.

TREVER and the other ships of Mine Division Four that were nested together in Middle Loch, took a toll on enemy aircraft. At one point an enemy plane attacked the nest head-on, drawing fire from all four ships. The combined blitz of .50-caliber bullets ripped the wings off the plane, leaving only the fuselage to crash and burn near Beckoning Point.

TREVER was ready to get underway at 0930 and she sailed along with the rest of Mine Division Four out of the harbor while the attack was in its waning moments. TREVER remained on patrol for the rest of the morning and early afternoon, returning to Pearl Harbor at 1500. Later on she exited the harbor once again to recommence patrol duties.

THE WAR

Seven days after the start of the war TREVER was called upon to save lives in a war setting for the first time. The Japanese submarine *I-4*, captained by Commander Nakagawa Hajime torpedoed the Norwegian commercial vessel *HØEGH MERCHANT* just 29 miles off of Cape Makapuu, O'ahu. *I-4* was one of the Japanese submarines that had been assigned to sink American naval vessels escaping from Pearl Harbor on December 7th and, having failed in that mission, she had hung around to see what other victims she could find.

Just before 0400 on December 14, 1941, TREVER spotted a bright light cracking through the darkness and went to investigate. When she arrived she found *HØEGH MERCHANT* sinking and 40 passengers and crew in four lifeboats. The ship sank around 0530 and by 0700 all the survivors had been taken on board.

After her rescue of the passengers and crew of the *HØEGH MERCHANT* she spent the majority of 1942 in rather routine patrol and escorting duties in Hawai'i and the American West Coast. After getting a refit at Mare Island Naval Shipyard, TREVER joined in the invasion of Guadalcanal and the Solomons.

In the early morning hours of August 7, 1942, the day of the Guadalcanal landings, TREVER was assigned bombardment duties.

Along with other ships, TREVER fired her main four-inch batteries at enemy shore targets 3,000 yards away. The Japanese responded with their own gun emplacement targeting the ships. This duel went on for almost a half hour until TREVER placed a four-inch shell directly on the gun destroying it.

The Japanese heavily utilized air power to prevent the Americans from gaining a toehold on Guadalcanal. On the second day of the invasion, TREVER was screening the landing force when a flight of Mitsubishi "Betty" bombers attacked. Heavy anti-aircraft fire from TREVER and other ships brought down four of the enemy planes.

TREVER spent many months in the Solomons going where she was needed to help secure America's first land victory of the Pacific war. On October 13, 1942 she was sent out to search for survivors of the Battle of Cape Esperance. The nighttime battle between American and Japanese ships cost the U.S. one cruiser and one destroyer, and cost the enemy one cruiser and three destroyers. TREVER found and rescued 34 Japanese seamen during the operation. She also found another raft with eight more enemy sailors on it. These men, in a scenario that was very common in the Pacific, fought their rescuers, forcing the men of TREVER to fire on and destroy the men they were trying to save.

In December 1944, TREVER was caught in Typhoon Cobra with 90-knot winds. The seas were vicious enough to tear two whaleboats out of their davits and swallow them up. In the midst of this tempest a sailor was washed overboard. Luckily, this was known and a search was begun. With an incredible amount of luck and some excellent seamanship the sailor was plucked out of the angry sea two hours later, alive. The lucky seaman was transferred to a hospital on Guam the next day.

Like many ships of her type, TREVER was a jack-of-all-trades. At times she transported troops, or cargo. Once, she became an impromptu tanker, when she had 175 fifty-five gallon drums of gasoline lashed to her deck for delivery to Tulagi. TREVER escorted convoys, patrolled for submarines, and protected landing craft during invasions. After her last overhaul of the war in San Diego in January 1945, she returned to Pearl Harbor where she remained for the rest of the war. Here she towed targets and assisted in other fleet training. In June 1945 she was reclassified as a miscellaneous auxiliary and given the new designation AG-110. TREVER was performing these duties when the war ended.

FATE

In the aftermath of the war the end came quickly for TREVER. She was in Norfolk just six weeks after the surrender, and was struck from the Navy roles in December 1945. She was sold in November 1946 to be scrapped.

MAHAN CLASS DESTROYER
DD-374
LAUNCHED: 1936

DECEMBER 7, 1941

Among all of the claims made concerning who fired at the enemy first that day is that of Lieutenant Commander William R. Terrell, captain of TUCKER. His assertion, made in his after action report, is that Gunner's Mate 2nd class Walter E. Bowe fired the initial American response from the aft .50-caliber machine gun of TUCKER.

Unlike the vast majority of ships in Pearl Harbor, TUCKER had almost her entire complement on board, missing only about seven men. With the exception of the No. 3 five-inch battery, all guns were firing at the Japanese planes within minutes. They fired almost continuously throughout the attack ultimately claiming to have splashed 3 or 4 planes. TUCKER got underway around 1000 and exited the harbor and began patrolling, having come through the raid without casualties or damage.

THE WAR

TUCKER spent the opening months of the war in the Eastern Pacific, first patrolling in Hawai'i and then escorting convoys from the islands to the west coast and back.

In April 1942 TUCKER was assigned as the escort for the seaplane tender WRIGHT, AV-1. Together they traveled to multiple ports-of-call throughout the South Pacific. During the spring and into the summer of

1942, TUCKER settled into the routine of escorting convoys or individual ships. Late July found her in Suva, the Fiji Islands awaiting orders for her next mission. She soon received them, instructing her to escort the merchant ship *SS Nira Luckenbach* to Espiritu Santo. On August 1st the two ships set sail.

FATE

Late in the night of August 3rd TUCKER and *Nira Luckenbach* turned into Segond Channel off Espiritu Santo, only a few miles from their destination. Unfortunately, Captain Terrell was never informed that just after midnight on that same day, three of TUCKER's Pearl Harbor sisters, the minelayers BREESE, DM-18, GAMBLE, DM-15 and TRACY, DM-19 set out on a mission from Espiritu Santo to lay 171 mines in three separate channels around the island, Segond Channel being one of them.

The black Pacific night was suddenly illuminated as TUCKER struck one of the mines in the channel. The blast lifted the destroyer out of the water. The mine had detonated directly under her amidships, killing three sailors outright and splitting her keel. The captain of *Nira Luckenbach* halted his ship and immediately lowered boats and sent them to the stricken destroyer.

Within several hours the patrol boat YP-346 arrived and took TUCKER under tow in an attempt to get her into a harbor or at least ground her in order that she might be saved. During this process TUCKER slowly but surely began to sink. Terrell had the anchor dropped and ordered the crew to abandon ship. BREESE also arrived on scene to assist if she could with survivors and salvage. When the sun came up it became quite apparent that TUCKER was going to be lost. When the surviving crew had been rescued, it was discovered that three sailors were missing and presumed dead, in addition to the three killed in the initial blast. Late on August 4th TUCKER sank in about 70 feet of water, although her bow took several more days to pass beneath the surface.

In the inquiry that followed Lieutenant Commander Terrell was completely exonerated for the loss of his ship and on the recommendation of Admiral Chester Nimitz no action was taken against him.

William Terrell retired from the Navy as an Admiral and moved to Lawrence, Kansas. In the 1960's a recreational scuba diver exploring the wreck of TUCKER found Terrell's Naval Academy sword in his sunken cabin. The diver sent it to Terrell who then had it framed.

The bow section of TUCKER slowly sinks into the Pacific

USS Turkey

LAPWING CLASS MINESWEEPER
AM-13
LAUNCHED: 1918

DECEMBER 7, 1941

TURKEY, along with the three other minesweepers nested with her at the coal docks, was in the eye of the storm that Sunday morning. The opening action of the Pacific war whirled around them while they were left untouched. The Officer of the Deck, Ensign R. J. Melchor[64], reacted quickly and appropriately to the attack, sounding general quarters, preparing the ship for getting underway and manning the guns. The crew could only fire at planes that strayed nearby. It is possible that the combined fire of the nest brought down one enemy plane but that was the extent of their contribution. TURKEY fired only 37 three-inch rounds and just over 2,000 rounds of .30 caliber ammunition during the raid. She suffered no damage or casualties, although her captain, Lieutenant Commander T. F. Fowler, in his after action report noted that, _"considerable shrapnel and spent machine-gun bullets fell on and near the ship and this danger was accepted calmly."_ After the attack TURKEY joined the flotilla of ships engaged in rescue and salvage operations.

---

64 Later in the war Melchor promoted to Lieutenant and became captain of TURKEY.

THE WAR

TURKEY remained at Pearl Harbor until April 1942 when she sailed for Samoa. Shortly after her arrival she became AT-143 when she was reclassified as an ocean going tug. During her Pacific career she performed all the normal duties of a tug including towing targets and barges, recovering practice torpedoes and running supplies.

In October 1944 while operating out of Ulithi she assisted the USS MONTGOMERY, DM-17, one of her Pearl Harbor sisters, after a mine struck her. Towards the end of November TURKEY fought fires aboard the tanker USS MISSISSINEWA, AO-59, after that ship became the first victim of a Kaitan, a Japanese manned torpedo. TURKEY ended the war operating between Ulithi and Leyte.

FATE

Soon after the end of the war TURKEY found herself in San Francisco where she was decommissioned and struck from the Navy's list of ships in November 1945. One year later in December 1946 after almost thirty years of service she was sold to the Hawley Forge and Manufacturing Company of San Francisco.

USS Vestal

FLEET REPAIR SHIP
AR-4
LAUNCHED: 1908

DECEMBER 7, 1941

The most interesting thing about the after action report written by Commander Cassin Young, the captain of VESTAL, is not what he wrote. His report reads very much like most of the others written by commanding officers all across the harbor. Some are short and to the point with little detail. Others are extremely detailed with specific times and specific actions recorded. Young's report is noticeably average. It is only eight paragraphs long and gives pertinent information about the performance of his crew and the actions of his ship. But Young leaves out some extremely important information about what happened on board VESTAL that morning and the information he left out gives some telling insight into his character. What he left out was an account of his actions that day; the actions that would earn him the Medal of Honor. There is no mention of those. It took other people to tell the tale of his courage and leadership. He doesn't say a word about it.

VESTAL was tied up alongside ARIZONA, BB-39, on Battleship Row, providing repair and maintenance services to the battlewagon. When the attack began VESTAL's guns answered the threat almost immediately. Commander Young left the bridge and went out on deck to take personal command of a three-inch anti-aircraft battery. Literally side-by-side she fought along with ARIZONA. Only minutes later the horizontal bombers came and targeted Battleship Row. VESTAL was hit with two bombs, which were almost assuredly meant for ARIZONA. One plunged all the way through her and punched a hole in the bottom of her hull. The other exploded inside her. Both bombs started fires. Young ordered the magazine flooded to preempt an explosion of their live ordinance. Moments later that exact thing happened on ARIZONA, a bomb detonated her magazine. When the battleship erupted, the massive concussion from the explosion blew everyone off of the deck of VESTAL and into the harbor, including Commander Young.

There were dozens of men that day who were literally blown off of their ships and found themselves in the burning, oily waters of Pearl Harbor. When they regained their wits, many of them swam for safety to Ford Island or to some boat plucking sailors out of the water or to any other place that would improve their plight. But that morning when a dazed Cassin Young broke the surface of the water after his shockingly abrupt departure from VESTAL, he looked around, got his bearings and swam back to his blazing and ravaged ship. No one would have thought the less of him if he hadn't. No one would have blamed him for thanking his lucky stars that in a strange way he had been absolved of all responsibility for his ship and his men. After being blown off the deck of his ship who could fault him if he threw up his hands and thought, "Well, I gave it my best shot!" and then swam to safety? But Young didn't think that way. He swam back to his ship because she was his responsibility. He swam back to his crew because they were his responsibility. He swam back because it wasn't in him to swim away.

When Young reached the accommodation ladder and climbed onto it he was met by a large group of sailors coming down. The oil soaked captain asked them where they were going and they told him they were abandoning ship. Young shot back at them in the clearest possible terms that no one was abandoning his ship and to get back on board. He coolly retook command and began to save his ship which was on fire and surrounded by a mass of flaming oil spewing from ARIZONA. Young ordered the lines cut that were keeping his ship attached to the doomed battleship. With a tugs assistance, VESTAL maneuvered away from ARIZONA and got underway about 0845 hours although she was listing and sinking.

VESTAL headed for McGrew Point, about 900 yards away in a corner of the harbor. En route an inventory of her condition was done and it was discovered that she had a six and a half degree list and her stern was down by twenty-seven feet. Young deduced that his ship was going to sink and the best thing to do was to beach her. The course was changed and VESTAL headed for Aiea Landing several hundred yards beyond McGrew Point. At about 1000 hours she was safely grounded.

In early 1942 Admiral Chester A. Nimitz awarded the Medal of Honor to Commander Young for his

VESTAL grounded off Aiea landing scarred by the fires on ARIZONA.

actions on December 7th. The citation reads in part: *"For distinguished conduct in action, outstanding heroism and utter disregard of his own safety, above and beyond the call of duty...Commander Young...took personal command of the three-inch antiaircraft gun. When blown overboard by the blast of the forward magazine explosion of the U.S.S. Arizona...he swam back to his ship...Despite severe enemy bombing and strafing at the time, and his shocking experience of having been blown overboard, Commander Young, with extreme coolness and calmness, moved his ship... and subsequently beached the U.S.S. Vestal upon determining that such action was required to save his ship."*

Of his own heroism he said nothing but Commander Young did have something to say about his crew, *"The conduct of all officers and enlisted personnel was exemplary and of such high order that I would especially desire to have them with me in future engagements."* No higher praise could come from a commanding officer.

THE WAR

VESTAL remained in Pearl Harbor until August of 1942. While there, she provided much needed repair and salvage services not only to her devastated sister ships but to herself. When August arrived, VESTAL departed to bring the war to the Japanese in her own way and to demonstrate the folly of the enemy's target choices the previous December.

VESTAL spent almost the entire war in the Pacific expertly doing her job: repairing damaged ships. Her highly skilled crew consisted of electricians, plumbers, painters, mechanics, carpenters, welders, machinists and sheet metal workers. They could repair anything, from a doorknob to a 16-inch gun. If you were a cruiser with a missing bow, VESTAL could fix you. If you were a landing craft with broken steering, VESTAL could fix you. If you were an aircraft carrier with a bomb hole in your flight deck, VESTAL could fix you. If you were a battleship that had been torpedoed, VESTAL could fix you. In the three and a half years of the war VESTAL performed over 10,000 individual repair jobs on over 400 ships.

Ships with minor to moderate damage could be repaired and sent back into war within a few days if not a few weeks. Vessels with major damage were made sea worthy so they could return to a major shipyard in the United States, be repaired and get back in the fight with minimum delay.

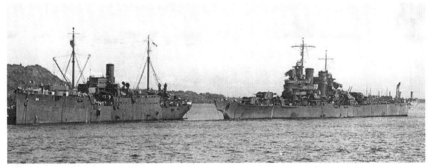

With a large piece of her bow missing as a result of a torpedo hit USS ST. LOUIS, CL-49, on the right, pulls alongside VESTAL for repairs.

In a way, VESTAL posed more of a threat to the Japanese than any ten warships. If she could have been put out of commission that would also put out of the war all the ships that she could have repaired. But because she was there, ships that may have been severely crippled or even lost lived to fight another day and remained on the battle line.

FATE

When VESTAL returned to the United States after the war she helped to prepare other ships for decommissioning by stripping them of useful material. She did this work up until the time came for her own decommissioning, which occurred on August 14, 1946, one year to the day after the Japanese surrender. She then spent two and a half years in inactive reserve before she was sold for scrapping in 1949 to the Boston Metals Company of Baltimore, Maryland.

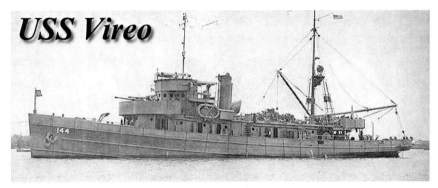

USS Vireo

LAPWING CLASS MINESWEEPER
AM-52
LAUNCHED: 1919

DECEMBER 7, 1941

VIREO, along with the other minesweepers, was berthed at the Coal Docks adjacent to Hickam Field on the Pearl Harbor entrance channel. On this Sunday morning both of her engines had been dismantled for overhaul. When the Japanese began swarming, VIREO could only stand and fight. About a half hour into the attack, an enemy plane flew across the minesweeper's bow and was caught in the fire of her anti-aircraft guns. The plane went down near Hickam Field. When the shooting had stopped, VIREO was undamaged. The only casualty was Radioman 2nd Class Aubrey Price who received a serious, but not life threatening, shrapnel wound to the neck.

By 1400 her engines had been put back together and she was busily sailing around the harbor doing whatever job needed to be done. She was first sent to West Loch where she removed a lighter[65] loaded with ammunition from the Ammunition Dock. Returning to the dock she picked up more ammunition and delivered it to USS ARGONNE, AG-31.

Around 2100, shortly after VIREO pulled alongside USS CALIFORNIA, BB-44, to commence with salvage efforts, guns awakened all over the harbor in response to the sound of incoming aircraft. There were planes, but they were Americans sent ahead from USS ENTERPRISE,

---

65 An engineless barge used for transporting cargo to and from ships in a harbor.

CV-6. Four F4F Wildcats from fighter squadron VF-6 were shot down by anti-aircraft fire as they attempted to land on Ford Island. One of these pilots, Lieutenant (jg) Eric Allen, bailed out and splashed into the water astern of VIREO who promptly rescued him. Unfortunately, Allen died the following day from a bullet wound and internal injuries.

THE WAR

VIREO conducted minesweeping and other duties in and around the Hawai'ian islands through the first months of 1942. In late May she was assigned to escort the tanker USS KALOLI, AOG-13 to Midway Island, in preparation for the impending battle there. While at sea the Navy changed the designation of VIREO from a minesweeper to an ocean going tug, AT-144.

On June 5th, two days after arriving in the Midway area, VIREO received an urgent call to perform her first mission as a tug. She quickly got underway for the coordinates indicated and arrived there at 1135. When she arrived she found the American aircraft carrier USS YORKTOWN, CV-5, with a heavy list to port and on the verge of capsizing. YORKTOWN had suffered numerous bomb and torpedo hits inflicted by Japanese planes during the American victory at Midway. It took VIREO and her crew several hours to rig a towline and when this was accomplished she got underway. Unfortunately VIREO wasn't really equipped to tow a badly damaged vessel that was over one hundred times her own weight and four times her length in the open sea. She couldn't even muster 3 knots.

Surrounded by an escort of destroyers, VIREO, with YORKTOWN in tow, was still struggling along the following day. A damage control party had been put back aboard the crippled carrier in an effort to correct the 26-degree list and hopefully save her, and their efforts were succeeding. The destroyer USS HAMMANN, DD-412, was brought alongside YORKTOWN to assist the damage control party, furnishing pumps and electrical power. It was to be all for naught however.

Several miles away just beneath the waves was the *I-168*, an Imperial Japanese Navy submarine, under the command of Lieutenant Commander Yahachi Tanabe. With great skill and patience, Yahachi stalked the Americans for nine hours, slowly but surely closing in and breeching the protective screen of the destroyers. In the early afternoon the Japanese skipper fired a spread of four torpedoes. The first hit the HAMMANN, which sank in only four minutes. Two more struck the YORKTOWN and sealed her fate. As HAMMANN sank, multiple explosions came from underwater. These are believed to have been her own depth charges exploding. The concussion from these killed sailors that had been tossed into the sea, further crippled YORKTOWN, and damaged VIREO's rudder.

Fearing the distinct possibility of the YORKTOWN rapidly sinking, Lieutenant James C. Legg[66], the captain of VIREO, ordered the tow cable to be cut, which was quickly done with an acetylene torch. As soon as she was free, Legg turned his ship around to rescue as many sailors as he could. Survivors of the HAMMANN were plucked from the ocean. In a daring and dangerous move, Legg then brought the tiny VIREO alongside the critically wounded aircraft carrier to rescue the damage control party before she sank. The huge carrier's hull banged against VIREO's all during the rescue operation. The skill and bravery exhibited by Legg during the rescue earned him the Navy Cross.

Because of her damaged rudder, VIREO ran aground when she returned to Midway and ultimately had to be towed to Pearl Harbor for repairs. She took this opportunity to undergo a complete overhaul.

Four months later in October 1942, VIREO, along with five other vessels, including the destroyer USS MEREDITH, DD-434, were towing fuel and ammunition laden barges to the besieged Marines on Guadalcanal. The small convoy was informed of the threat of enemy forces nearby and four of the ships turned about but VIREO and MEREDITH kept going.

Not long afterwards, the two vessels engaged two enemy planes that quickly retreated, but were then notified of two Japanese cruisers that were headed their way at high speed. Discretion was deemed to be the better part of valor and the two American ships turned around. Unfortunately VIREO was no match for the fast destroyer in the speed department. The decision was made to abandon the slower VIREO for the retreat and to continue solely on the destroyer. The transfer of VIREO's 68 crewmen

---

66 Legg was 52 years old and had enlisted in the Navy in 1919. He received his officer's commission only a month before after over 20 years as an enlisted man.

was made and the tug was left adrift. The intention of MEREDITH was to sink VIREO in order to prevent her from being captured intact by the enemy. Just as she was maneuvering to do this she was set upon by 38 enemy planes that ravaged her. The destroyer was struck by 14 bombs and 7 torpedoes and in the space of only 10 minutes she had broken into three pieces and was gone.

Of VIREO's 68-man crew, only 17 were alive, swimming in the Pacific Ocean along with approximately 73 survivors of MEREDITH. Six of MEREDITH's men managed to swim to the drifting VIREO and clamber aboard. They were unable to start the ship's engine and went wherever the tides and currents wanted to take them for the next four days until they were picked up by a PBY Catalina flying boat. Once again VIREO was placed under tow and brought to a safe harbor.

Having barely survived the first year of the war VIREO followed the fleet on its inexorable march across the Pacific towards the Japanese mainland. In her capacity as a tug she pushed, pulled and towed her way to victory. During the final stages of the war she supported the invasion of Okinawa and the Philippines.

FATE

After the surrender, VIREO spent the remainder of 1945 performing towing duties in the Philippines. She then took a leisurely and roundabout journey from the South Pacific to San Francisco, arriving in the City by the Bay on February 5, 1946. After being redesignated twice in her lifetime and almost fifty years of service, VIREO's end had finally come. She was decommissioned in April and transferred for final disposal to the Maritime Commission in February 1947.

Wapello

NET TENDER
YN-56
LAUNCHED: 1941

DECEMBER 7, 1941

WAPELLO was assigned to the Station Base at Pearl Harbor where she tended the anti-submarine nets at the mouth of the harbor entrance. When the attack began, the captain of WAPELLO, Ensign J. Young, Jr. received orders to stand by to patrol the harbor or for his ship to be used as a possible *"submarine ramming vessel."*[67] After the Japanese air raid, WAPELLO opened up the nets protecting the harbor and then returned to her berth. She suffered no casualties or damage as a result of that first day of war.

THE WAR

The threat of submarines never left Pearl Harbor during the next three and a half years and neither did WAPELLO. She remained there for the duration tending the nets and performing other duties as needed.

FATE

WAPELLO left Hawai'i in 1946 and was sent to Bremerton, Washington where she was placed out of service on October 23rd. In May 1947 she was

---

67   From the WAPELLO's deck log of December 7, 1941.

turned over to the War Shipping Administration and sold for commercial purposes. WAPELLO went through several name changes and owners. She eventually wound up in Panama with the name GORGONA II. While working in one of the locks of the Panama Canal she was seriously damaged by a larger vessel and was towed to the adjoining Miraflores Lake where she sank.

USS Ward

WICKES CLASS DESTROYER
DD-139
LAUNCHED: 1918

DECEMBER 7, 1941

Of all the ships involved in the attack on Pearl Harbor the USS WARD and its crew hold a special place. One of the World War I vintage "flush deck" destroyers it was delegated to patrol duty outside Pearl Harbor, condemned to sailing its lazy figure eight pattern for eternity. A crew of naval reservists from Minnesota manned it. But when fate dealt WARD an unexpected hand, she and her crew played it expertly and won a significant place in the annals of American naval history.

At approximately 0408 on December 7, 1941, WARD was signaled by the coastal minesweeper USS CONDOR, AMc-14, that they believed they had sighted a submarine following close astern. The WARD's commanding officer, Lt. William W. Outerbridge, who was a graduate of the Naval Academy and in his second day as captain, ordered general quarters and rushed WARD to the indicated position but found nothing. After twenty-seven minutes of unsuccessful searching WARD secured from general quarters and returned to her patrol duties. Only a half hour later, at 0506 WARD was once again contacted, but this time by the general stores cargo ship USS ANTARES, AKS-3. ANTARES radioed that she had sighted a submarine, between her stern and the target she was towing. WARD jumped into action again. As she approached the scene, a PBY Catalina flying over the area, also responded to ANTARES' call and, spotting the enemy submarine from the air, dropped two smoke pots to mark the position.

WARD sighted the small submarine and began its attack run. The sub was on WARD's starboard side and the No. 1 gun spat fire at it. The four-inch shell sailed over the mini-sub and impacted in the water a few yards beyond. As WARD continued its attack run the mini sub presented itself to the No. 3 gun, which fired a four-inch round directly through the base of the conning tower. Not content with the direct hit WARD commenced a depth charge run, dropping four on top of the doomed sub as she passed over it. The first American engagement in World War II took all of one minute. It was an American victory and cost the Imperial Japanese Navy two brave sailors, Ensign Hiroo Akira and Petty Officer 2nd Class Katayama Yoshio.

After the engagement WARD radioed the Commandant of the 14th Naval District that they had sighted and fired upon a submarine in their patrol area. Immediately WARD spotted a sampan in the vicinity, approached it and had the Coast Guard escort it to Honolulu.

At 0703 a sonar contact was made and WARD commenced a depth charge run on the new target. The attack did not generate any positive confirmation of a kill. However, WARD sighted a "black oil bubble" about 300 hundred yards astern. At the end of WARD's very busy early morning she spotted squadrons of Japanese planes flying towards Pearl Harbor to start a war that had already began with WARD's sinking of the submarine.

WARD maintained her patrol duties for the rest of the morning and made six more depth charge attacks on sonar or visual contacts. She was also subject to several bombing and strafing attacks by Japanese aircraft. One attack was repulsed by machine gun fire and she suffered no damage or causalities. In the early afternoon WARD was relieved by USS CHEW, DD-106, and she returned to Pearl for replenishment of supplies.

THE WAR

In the days immediately following December 7th, 1941, WARD continued her duties patrolling the entrance to Pearl Harbor. Those days were tense and everyone reacted with a hair trigger, not wanting to be surprised again. No one was taking any chances and that included the men of the WARD. As a result WARD dropped 170 depth charges on sonar contacts in the three days following the attack, however no kills were noted.

1942 dawned with the boredom of routine. Her duties consisted mainly of escorting shipping traffic in and around the Hawai'ian Islands, as more modern vessels became available and took over patrol and sub-hunting assignments. In a navy that was ramping up for war and strapped for inventory, no ship could be written off as obsolete. So aging "four stackers" like the WARD were refurbished, remodeled and reincarnated. The navy decided that in the island hopping march toward Tokyo fast maneuverable ships would be needed to transport troops. As a result WARD and other ships like her were sent back to the mainland for conversion. She arrived at Puget Sound Navy Yard in Bremerton, Washington on Christmas Eve, 1942.

The conversion was twofold; turn her into a troop transport and make her a more effective and modern weapon. The first order of business was to create space for 150 soldiers. To accomplish this, her forward boilers and two forward funnels were removed establishing berthing areas for ground troops and their equipment. To accommodate the extra men WARD also received new storerooms, refrigeration units, blowers for air circulation, an 8,000-gallon per day distillation unit and a new generator, which was salvaged from her Pearl Harbor sister, the USS NEVADA. Topside, her bridge was redesigned and new radar installed. Four davits were added to carry the 36 foot long LCPR's, (Landing Craft, Personnel, Ramped), which themselves were armed with two .30 caliber machine guns. The second task involved newer weaponry. Two "K" guns for firing depth charges were added, along with 20mm Oerlikon anti-aircraft guns and three-inch multi-purpose guns.

With her conversion completed in only 43 days, WARD was now an Armed Personnel Destroyer and was designated, APD-16. She sailed from Bremerton on February 6, 1943, under the command of Lt. (jg) L. G. Benson. Her destination was the island of Espiritu Santo in the New Hebrides Islands.[68]

---

68 Now the island nation of Vanuatu.

Upon her arrival in the south pacific WARD joined Transport Division 22. She was assigned to escort duties, anti-submarine patrols and resupplying troops on Guadalcanal. After one such resupply run on April 7, 1943, Japanese planes appeared in the sky as she approached Tulagi harbor. At 1510 WARD went to general quarters and along with other vessels in the harbor defended against the air raid. Her gunners shot down two of the attackers.

WARD now began in earnest the routine of war. She participated in training exercises with Marines, escorted merchant ships, screened convoys and patrolled for submarines. On the 16th of June WARD shot down four more enemy planes during an air raid in the Guadalcanal area. She was, for the most part, amply engaged in her primary duties of landing troops. In July and August WARD landed troops on New Georgia and Vella Lavella in the Solomons, respectively. On October 4th she landed New Zealand troops on Mono Island in the Treasury Islands in the morning and in the evening landed a force of Marine commandos, under cover of darkness on Choiseul Island. On December 26th she landed two companies of Marines at Cape Gloucester, New Britain and made a return trip three days later to land 200 more Marines. For her next mission, the invasion of Cape Sudest, New Guinea on January 2, 1944, WARD landed a company of soldiers from the Army's 126th Infantry Regiment.

For a brief period WARD enjoyed the relative comfort of training and cargo operations at Espiritu Santo. Then on February 15th she took part in the landings at Nissan Island. During this operation she struck something underwater and damaged her sonar dome and her port propeller, which were repaired in a floating dry-dock. In March, still another landing took place on Emirau Island, where WARD disembarked a company of Marines, after which she anchored in Purvis Bay and performed maintenance for the remainder of the month. The repair period was followed by landing members of the Army's 163rd Regimental Combat Team at Aitape, New Guinea on April 22nd. After completing this mission she took up a fire support position off of Tumleo Island and commenced a shore bombardment for a half hour with her three-inch batteries and then, once again proved her versatility by immediately performing screening duties.

She continued off of Aitape the following day transporting reinforcements and providing fire support.

The next several months were even busier for the WARD. On the 25th of April she screened a convoy from Buna to Saidor, returning to Aitape to screen the beachhead there. She then, along with the attack transport HENRY T. ALLEN, AP-30, escorted a small convoy to Humboldt Bay. After provisioning and an overhaul at Port Harvey, WARD set sail for Biak Island with men from the Army's 186th Infantry Regiment, landing them there on May 27th. Throughout June she conducted anti-submarine patrols in the Humboldt Bay area until the 24th when she rendezvoused with the destroyer tender USS DOBBIN, AD-3 for overhauls. WARD conducted escort duties in the Milne Bay area and finished off her assignments there by once again screening a convoy from Humboldt Bay to Maffin Bay. WARD's last action in the New Guinea area was to land troops from the Army's 1st Infantry Regiment at Cape Sansapor.

After a well-deserved ten days of liberty in Port Jackson, Australia, WARD returned to Milne Bay where she picked up troops from the Army's 124th Infantry Regiment for landings on Morotai Island on September 15th. Four days later WARD rescued 1st Lt. Edgar B. Scott who had crashed his P-38 Lightning in the ocean.

October 1, 1944 found WARD at Cape Cretin loading soldiers of the Army's 6th Ranger Battalion in preparation for the beginning stages of the liberation the Philippines. 11 days later she made way for Dinagat Island in the Philippines, landing the Rangers there on the 17th.

Amazingly, in all of the landings WARD had participated in up to this time, she had not lost one man, one boat or failed to deliver her charges safely to any beachhead. Every mission had gone like clockwork, perfectly. Up to this time, that is.

On the morning of the 17th WARD, along with British minelayer, HMS ARIADNE, M65, took up position off the beach of Dinagat Island and released her landing craft. The waters were unusually rough owing to swift currents in the channel and the effects of a distant typhoon. Although conditions made it difficult all of WARD's landing craft made it to the beach safely where they deposited the Rangers. A second trip was required to pick up even more troops from ARIADNE and bring them to the landings. A third trip was needed from the beach, back to WARD and then back to the beach in order to bring the Rangers' equipment to them. All of this was accomplished in very heavy seas. After the last trip two of WARD's LCPR's could not get off the beach due to the increasingly mad wind and seas. The stormy seas necessitated one of WARD's boats being picked up by USS SCHLEY, APD-14, and WARD picking up one of SCHLEY's. Ensign Guy Thompson, the WARD's Boat Officer, was on the beach and ordered the men to "dig in" for the night. The WARD herself weighed anchor and headed out to deeper water to better ride out the storm. The next morning dawned with tropical beauty and WARD returned to the beach to gather up her sailors.

After the Dinagat landings, while at sea and returning to New Guinea, a lifeline parted as two of WARD's crew were leaning on it. Both sailors fell into the ocean. Immediately "man overboard" was called and WARD came about to rescue the men. USS HERBERT, APD-22, was following WARD and quickly launched one of her landing craft and fished one of the men out of the water. The other was not as lucky. WARD searched but could not find her missing man and listed him as "presumed lost."

On November 12th, WARD screened three LST's during a landing operation at Dulag Bay. That evening she proceeded to Hollandia escorting a convoy. Thirteen days later she arrived in San Pedro Bay, Philippines with a 15-ship convoy.

FATE

On December 7, 1944, under the command of Lt. R. E. Farwell, USNR, WARD participated in the Ormoc Bay landings on Leyte Island in the Philippines. It was just one in a long string of landings WARD had engaged in. She launched her boats at 0626 and by 0755 all her boats were back on board, having successfully landed soldiers of the Army's 77th Division on the beach. As always WARD performed multiple missions. As soon as her boats were secure she turned to picket duty, protecting the invasion force from marauding enemy submarines. About two hours later her lookouts spotted a formation of Japanese aircraft coming in from the north at approximately 5000 feet. WARD began evasive maneuvers and fired her 20mm and .50 caliber anti-aircraft guns but no hits were detected and the Japanese flew on without molesting the fleet.

Shortly afterward three Japanese twin-engine bombers attacked WARD. The first of the three dove on WARD. The men of WARD soon realized that this plane wasn't making a bombing run. It was a kamikaze and it intended to crash into the ship. She responded to this threat with a wall of anti-aircraft fire and although the bomber was hit it was not stopped. The plane leveled off only feet above the water and headed full speed at WARD's port side. In moments it was all over. The Japanese plane struck WARD just above the waterline on the port side. It hit with such force that one of the plane's engines passed completely through the ship and came out the other side. Despite the mortal wound to the ship, the crew continued firing at the two other planes. The second plane strafed the ship and then crashed into the water 200 yards off the starboard bow and the third plane plowed into the water 600 yards off her starboard quarter.

Although the attack was over, the men of WARD were in great peril. The plane had crashed into the now vacant troop compartment and the fireroom. The volatile aviation fuel spewed into the ship's interior and ignited. In short order WARD was ablaze and no fire fighting effort was going to put it out. The fire affected the boilers, steam pressure dropped rapidly and WARD was soon dead in the water. Efforts were made both on the ship and from the water to quench the wild flames but to no avail. Two of the ships landing craft were launched to fight the fire with portable pumps but this effort was also futile. Any firefighting efforts only bought the WARD time, nothing else. As the fire spread, ammunition began cooking off, further endangering the crew.

In order to save his crew, Captain Farwell gave the order to abandon ship. The kamikaze had succeeded. Less than a half hour after it crashed into WARD, she was finished. Through the thick black smoke that engulfed WARD, her crew was picked up by USS SCOUT, AM-296, USS CROSBY, APD-17 and USS O'BRIEN, DD-725. Amazingly not one man was killed by the kamikaze and only one man was seriously injured.

In a bizarre twist of fate, the commanding officer of the O'BRIEN was William Outerbridge, now a Lieutenant Commander, the same man that had captained the WARD on the first day of the war and expertly sank the mini-sub outside Pearl Harbor. The irony however, continues. After WARD was successfully evacuated it was determined that nothing else could be done for the critically wounded ship and Outerbridge was ordered to sink the ship that was his first command. All other ships left the immediate vicinity to give O'BRIEN a clear field of fire. O'BRIEN fired her main batteries and at 1130, December 7, 1944, three years to the day after she fired the first American shots of the war, WARD slipped beneath the waves of Ormoc Bay between Poro Island and Apali Point.

The USS WARD on fire after the kamikaze attack, Dec. 7, 1944.

CLEMSON CLASS DESTROYER
MINESWEEPER
DMS-15
LAUNCHED: 1920

DECEMBER 7, 1941

WASMUTH was at the north end of the harbor nested with the other ships of Mine Division 4 at the entrance to Middle Loch. Lieutenant (jg) J. R. Grey, the senior officer on board, ordered general quarters. The four .50-caliber anti-aircraft machine guns were quickly manned and brought to bear on the enemy aircraft. One of her gunners, Seaman 1st Class James Hannon was credited with shooting down one Japanese plane.

Before the attack was over, WASMUTH got underway and exited the harbor. Anti-submarine patrols began immediately. An hour later WASMUTH dropped a single depth charge on a suspected submarine with no results. Thirteen minutes later she dropped a pair of depth charges on a second target and sighted "*large quantities of oil.*"[69]

After several hours of patrolling WASMUTH and USS ZANE, DMS-14, teamed up to do a mine sweep of the channel into Pearl Harbor. They conducted the sweep until the 2,400-foot sweep wire between the two vessels parted. The sweep gear was recovered and WASMUTH returned to patrol duties outside the harbor.

---

69   After action report dated December 12, 1941 by Lieutenant Commander John L. Wilfong.

WASMUTH expended 6,000 rounds of .50-caliber ammunition against the enemy that day. One ensign suffered a minor hand wound from flying shrapnel and the ship received no structural damage at all.

THE WAR

Escorting and patrol duties throughout the Hawai'ian Islands kept WASMUTH occupied for the first few months of 1942. She then escorted a convoy to San Francisco in May. During her stay in California she underwent work at Mare Island Naval Shipyard where she had been built 22 years earlier. She made the return trip to Pearl Harbor escorting another convoy in August.

On August 14th WASMUTH headed north to the Aleutian Islands where she would screen and escort convoys in the campaign to dislodge the Japanese from the only American territory occupied during the war.

FATE

On December 27, 1942, just four months after arriving in the Aleutians, WASMUTH was escorting a supply convoy through a rather vicious storm. Somewhere near Unimak Island, a wave reached up out of the sea and ripped two depth charges out of their rack on deck. The TNT filled drums fell into the ocean and promptly sank. Then they exploded and tore away part of WASMUTH's stern. Amazingly the explosions killed no one.

The oiler, USS RAMAPO, AO-12, one of WASMUTH's Pearl Harbor sisters, came to the rescue. The captain of RAMAPO, Commander Alfred J. Homann, pulled his 447-foot tanker perilously close to the smaller 314-foot long destroyer. With the tempest tossing both ships about, the operation of transferring the crew off of WASMUTH and onto RAMAPO began. Through three and a half hours of angry ocean and superb seamanship all 136 men were transferred off the sinking minesweeper.

The sea finally took WASMUTH two days later on the 29th when she sank 35 miles off of Unimak.

USS West Virginia

COLORADO CLASS BATTLESHIP
BB-48
LAUNCHED: 1921

DECEMBER 7, 1941

The last Japanese plane left the skies above Pearl Harbor at 0945. By that time WEST VIRGINIA was literally a wreck whose keel rested heavily on the floor of Pearl Harbor. Her captain was dead, along with 105 other men of her 1,400-man crew. Her future was very much in question. Her blackened hull and twisted and warped remains gave silent witness to the hour and fifty minutes of hell she and her gallant crew had just been through, and to the destructive power of seven well-placed torpedoes. The fires that engulfed her were so intense that her steel deck glowed red like hot iron in a blacksmith's forge.

The crew was scattered among numerous facilities throughout the harbor. Some were still taking cover in ditches on Ford Island, others were at the Receiving Barracks at the shipyard, some were at the submarine base and still others were on board the battleship USS TENNESSEE, BB-43, berthed next to WEST VIRGINIA.

The only thing that saved WEST VIRGINIA from total destruction was the quick actions of her crew and the shallowness of Pearl Harbor. Had she been on the open ocean and taken the shellacking that she did, she would have gone to the bottom of the Pacific and taken most of her crew with her.

Battleships and carriers were the top priorities on the Japanese list of targets for the Pearl Harbor attack. WEST VIRGINIA was totally exposed, being berthed outboard of the double column of ships on Battleship Row. When the enemy planes attacked she was one of the first ships hit. Unlike other ships in other places in the harbor she had almost no warning. What warning she did have lasted no more than a few seconds. She was rudely introduced to the war.

For the majority of the crew the first sign of trouble was the first torpedo hitting the battlewagon amidships. The full 33,500 tons of warship jumped into the air a few feet and shuddered as she settled back into the water. Then in quick succession two more torpedoes hit and she began to list to port almost immediately. In the first thirty seconds of the battle the fate of WEST VIRGINIA had been sealed. Within the next few minutes at least four and perhaps as many as six more torpedoes hit the battleship.[70]

The 54-year-old commanding officer, Captain Mervyn S. Bennion from Utah, was one of the first people at his battle station. The ship's navigator, Lieutenant Commander Thomas T. Beattie, ran down the passageway, right behind Bennion. The captain led the way to the bridge, high in the conning tower. By the time they got there the list to port was already at least six degrees. The two officers soon discovered that power and communications were also out. The captain was speaking with Beattie when a Japanese bomb struck the No. 2 turret of TENNEESSEE. Shrapnel from the explosion whipped across the narrow space between the battleships and ripped into Capt. Bennion's stomach. Like his ship, in that instant, Bennion's fate was also sealed.

Beattie and others on the bridge took their stricken captain and sat him on the deck, leaning against a bulkhead. Medical help was sent for and Chief Pharmacist Mate Leslie N. Leak soon arrived. The captain was holding both hands over the heavily bleeding wound. Leak moved Bennion's hands so he could examine the injury. When he did the captain's intestines were protruding from his abdomen. In spite of his injuries, Bennion continued to give orders to the officers gathered on the bridge. Seeing the seriousness of his wound it was advised to move Bennion as quickly as possible.

---

70 It is possible that two torpedoes struck WEST VIRGINIA by passing through holes in the hull already made by previous torpedo hits.

Below on the boat deck, sailor William W. Hardeman responded to the call for general quarters and was removing the cover from the anti-aircraft gun to which he was assigned. As he waited for the rest of the gun crew to arrive he looked toward the Merry Point landing. Coming directly at him, just slightly higher than eye level, was a flight of three "Kate" torpedo planes. The lead plane in the "V" formation dropped its torpedo, which headed straight for Hardeman at the forward port side gun. The two other planes dropped their torpedoes only seconds later. Hardeman watched the planes as they pulled up out of their attack runs, missing the antennas and superstructure of WEST VIRGINIA by mere feet as they did. The three torpedoes struck the hull directly beneath him. The concussion from the last one was so powerful that it threw him against the splinter shield[71] and knocked him out.

For some crewmen, the news of danger to their ship and the start of a war came later than most. In the lush hills of Aiea, east of Pearl Harbor, were Lieutenant (jg) Charles Nicholas and Ensign Harold W. Sears on a wild pig hunt. They were being guided through the valleys when the noise of distant explosions disturbed their adventure. They climbed to the top of a ridge. Wayward antiaircraft shells were exploding nearby and showering them with dirt. At the crest of the ridge they could see the fleet under attack. The hunt for wild pigs was cancelled and the hunt for a way to get back to WEST VIRGINIA was on.

On the bridge of WEST VIRGINIA was one of the officer's stewards, Mess Attendant 2nd Class Doris "Dorie" Miller. The big black man from Waco, Texas was the ship's heavyweight boxing champion and he, along with others on the bridge, picked up the severely wounded captain, Mervyn Bennion, to get him to safety. It was soon discerned that the bridge of a battleship was not designed for the removal of wounded men. The ladders and narrow passageways high in the conning tower would not allow several men carrying a wounded person out. The captain was placed back on the deck. Several other efforts were made to jury rig some kind of stretcher with ropes in order to lower Bennion to the deck or over to the much less damaged TENNEESSEE, but to no avail. Even then, Bennion continued to inquire into the condition of the ship and give directions to his crew.

71   Light armored partition designed to protect from flying shrapnel.

Two events were very apparent and of much concern to the men of WEST VIRGINIA. Berthed in front of her was the battleship USS OKLAHOMA, BB-37. She was also hit in the opening seconds of the attack and had already capsized. Aft of WEST VIRGINA was ARIZONA, BB-39. Her magazine had blown up and pretty much destroyed the battleship. The crew of WEST VIRGINIA had no intention of going out in that fashion.

In a somewhat ironic way her best friend was now water. Her list had increased to as much as twenty-five degrees and it needed to be corrected or she would very soon, like OKLAHOMA, turn turtle. Lieutenant Claude V. Ricketts, the Assistant Gunnery Officer, with the assistance of Boatswain's Mate 1st Class Garnett S. Billingsley, ventured below decks and in the darkness found and opened the valves that would flood spaces on the starboard side to level her off. This was done and the list soon began to even out. Everyone on board knew she was going to sink, but this way she would settle to the bottom in an upright position. When efforts were made to flood the forward magazine it was discovered that the Japanese torpedoes had already accomplished that mission.

The bridge was becoming untenable. Oil from ARIZONA had caught on fire. The wind and current had carried it down Battleship Row. Flames from the oil and from fires on WEST VIRGINIA had leapt up to the bridge. Avenues of escape were rapidly closing.

While officers and men on the bridge fought fires, others fought the enemy. Lieutenant (jg) F. H. White and the mess attendant Miller, manned the two .50 caliber machine guns forward of the conning tower. Miller, although trained as a loader, had never been trained on this weapon. He fired at the low flying enemy planes, scoring a possible kill on at least one. After about fifteen minutes of firing, the ammunition ran out. Like all the guns on WEST VIRGINIA, once the ready ammunition was gone, that was it. There was no way to get more to the weapons.

An escape route was finally devised for those threatened by the smoke, heat and flames closing in on the bridge. An ensign on the boat deck had climbed the starboard boat crane and from there thrown a line up to the bridge. The line was attached to a fire hose that was then hoisted up. Captain Bennion told the men on the bridge to evacuate. As they made their way down the fire hose, Bennion literally shed his last drop of blood and died. With nothing more that could be done for the ship or the Captain, the bridge was abandoned.

On the boat deck, William Hardeman regained consciousness. When he did he realized two things, the first one was that he was naked. The concussion from the torpedo blast had been so powerful that it literally blew his clothes off him. He lay there on the deck, nude, except for his shoes and socks. The second thing was that he heard people yelling, "Abandon ship!" With the deck covered in oil and water and still listing, walking was almost impossible. Hardeman half crawled, half climbed across the deck. He made it to the starboard forecastle, which seemed to be a relatively safe place. It was away from the burning oil that was on the port side facing the harbor. The crew was gravitating there to leave the ship and move the wounded onto boats for evacuation.

In a somewhat strange occurrence, many sailors noticed that men abandoning ship had taken their shoes off and placed them side-by-side on the deck. Soon there was a neat row of shoes lining the deck of the burning and sinking battleship. Joining the orderly row of shoes was the discarded uniform of the Communication Officer, Lieutenant Commander Doir C. Johnson. Johnson stripped naked before he eased himself onto the anchor chain and swam to Ford Island.

The water between WEST VIRGINIA and Ford Island was alive with swimming men and boats. Hardeman also swam to Ford Island and was helped up the coral embankment. A warrant officer saw Hardeman's exposed condition and told him to go find some clothes in one of the houses on the island. In the second house he entered he found a pair of pants and shirt that fit. He also discovered that the residents had quite obviously left in a big hurry. He helped himself to some beans and potatoes that had been left cooking on the stove, which he conscientiously turned off before he left.

WEST VIRGINIA was never really abandoned. After the last living man left her, officers on Ford Island put together fire fighting parties and returned to the ship. Others of the crew remained on the island to help with wounded or just try to stay out of the way of strafing enemy planes. One bluejacket took cover underneath a truck and yelled at some others to come join him during one strafing attack. The other sailors began yelling back at him in return. They had noticed that he was taking cover under a fuel truck. The young bluejacket quickly found other protection.

The pig hunters, Nicholas and Sears, finally made it to Pearl Harbor after the attack was over. They caught a whaleboat that was delivering personnel to ships throughout the harbor. As they set out they saw their ship burning at its berth. Sitting on the bottom of the harbor, the blue Hawai'ian waves now lapped at her deck and an umbrella of oily black smoke shaded her. Figuring they could do nothing there that wasn't already being done, they searched for other avenues of action. They could see the cruiser USS PHOENIX, CL-46, was getting underway and they instructed the coxswain to take them to her. Once on board they went where they thought they could help. Nicholas was a scout plane pilot so he reported to the aviation division. Sears, a Gunnery Officer on WEST VIRGINIA reported to the bridge. He asked Captain Herman Fischer if he was in need of a turret officer. Fischer replied that all of his guns were fully manned and didn't need any assistance in that area. Sears excused himself and walked down to the main deck. As PHOENIX sailed passed Battleship Row, Sears saw the flaming hulk that was his ship. He decided that WEST VIRGINA might need him after all. He stepped to the edge of the deck and dove into Pearl Harbor from the moving cruiser. He swam over to WEST VIRGINIA.

For his *"...conspicuous devotion to duty, extraordinary courage, and complete disregard of his own life..."*[72] Capt. Mervyn Bennion was posthumously awarded the Medal of Honor. Doris Miller became the first black sailor to receive the Navy Cross. His citation reads in part, *"For distinguished devotion to duty, extraordinary courage and disregard for his own personal safety...despite enemy strafing and bombing and in the face of a serious fire...manned and operated a machine gun directed at enemy Japanese attacking aircraft..."*[73]

---

72 Medal of Honor citation. The destroyer USS BENNION, DD-662, was named for Capt. Bennion in 1943.

73 Navy Cross citation. Miller died on November 24, 1943 when the escort carrier he was on, USS LISCOME BAY, CVE-56, was torpedoed and sank. In 1973 a frigate named in his honor, USS MILLER, FF-1091 was commissioned.

As for the rest of the crew, if the men of WEST VIRGINIA demonstrated anything it was that sometimes just surviving is heroic.

THE WAR

With the aid of tug boats and barges the fires on WEST VIRGINIA were extinguished by 1400 on Monday the 8th. The Navy wasted no time in making examinations. A cursory look at damages was conducted and a very preliminary estimate of one year to eighteen months was given to raise and repair her. The estimates were optimistic.

To facilitate the raising of the dreadnought and repairs to other ships, WEST VIRGINIA became a parts supplier for the rest of the fleet. Many guns were removed and reinstalled on other ships. Some guns were given to the Army to become shore batteries.

WEST VIRGINIA, like other ships, had a small detail of her own crew assigned as part of the salvage team. One of the jobs assigned to them was clean up. The deck was littered with debris from the aftermath of the battle and fires. They also began the process of removing smaller damaged items from the deck such as stanchions, lifelines, boat cradles and hatches. Within three weeks, fifty tons of material had been taken off.

Another duty assigned to this crew was standing guard over their ship. At night, they reported hearing tapping coming from inside the sunken battlewagon. Their reports were explained away as nerves or the sounds of floating debris banging against the hull.

In order to raise the battleship the holes in the hull from the torpedoes had to be repaired. Once that happened the water could be pumped out and the ship refloated. In February 1942 the first patches, made from wood, concrete and steel, were delivered to WEST VIRGINIA. Work continued for months and on May 12, 1942 nine 10-inch pumps were turned on. The water level inside began to go down and the ship began to rise. The ship eventually floated free of the bottom. On June 9th, six months and two days after she was sunk she was brought into dry dock.

Once the ship was unwatered the final recovery of bodies could be completed. Sixty-seven bodies were removed from the ship, including three that were discovered in a storeroom. Found with those three was evidence of consumed emergency rations and water and a calendar that had days marked off indicating the three lived, trapped inside WEST VIRGINIA, for over two weeks before the food, water, air and hope finally ran out. The last day marked off the calendar was December 23rd. The mysterious tapping was now explained.

Work was begun on WEST VIRGINIA at the Pearl Harbor Yard and continued for almost a year. On May 7, 1943 she sailed out of Pearl Harbor under her own power and headed for the Puget Sound Navy Yard in Washington to be rebuilt.

WEST VIRGINIA, rebuilt and reborn, at the Puget Sound Navy Yard, Bremerton, Washington, July 1944

While in the yard she was dramatically altered in looks and firepower. She retained her eight 16-inch guns and added multiple batteries of anti-aircraft guns. To accommodate new protection against torpedoes her beam was widened by six feet, which was just enough to make her too big to transit the Panama Canal. She made her trial runs in July 1944. A shakedown cruise down the west coast followed. She sailed for Pearl Harbor, arriving there September 14, 1944, becoming the last ship damaged in the Japanese attack to return to the fleet.

WEST VIRGINIA finally got into the war on October 19, 1944 when, in preparation for the invasion of the Philippines she stood off the island of Leyte and provided a shore bombardment on enemy targets there. She stayed there and provided anti-aircraft support for the landings through the 23rd. While undertaking this mission she damaged three of her four screws transiting some shallow water. Her speed was reduced to sixteen knots from twenty-one knots.

On October 25, 1944, still suffering from her reduced speed, WEST VIRGINIA took part in the Battle of Surigao Strait, the last surface engagement between battleships in history. WEST VIRGINIA, along with other U.S. battleships, met a Japanese force that was sent to repulse the allied invasion of the Philippines. At 0352 WEST VIRGINIA opened fire on the Japanese battleship *Yamashiro*. The first salvo WEST VIRGINIA fired hit *Yamashiro* and the American dreadnaught continued to pound the enemy ship with her big sixteen-inch guns. Seventeen minutes later the firing had stopped and *Yamashiro* retreated, mortally wounded. Ten minutes later *Yamashiro* sank.[74] WEST VIRGINIA had finally avenged herself for her sinking and the deaths of her captain and crew at Pearl Harbor.

No matter what name you use, be it shore bombardment, call fire, harassment fire, interdiction fire or support fire, WEST VIRGINIA spent the rest of the war doing just that. For the remainder of the long march across the Pacific, the battleship was called upon to bring her massive sixteen-inch guns into play to protect and defend American troops. With her state-of-the-art radar-controlled firing system she provided extremely accurate gunfire from many miles off shore.

In the Philippines she used her guns on enemy positions on the island of Mindoro and San Fernando Point. Standing off in Lingayen Gulf she pounded the Luzon cities of Rosario, Santo Tomas and obliterated the town of San Fabian. She moved on, and in February 1945 she brought her considerable might to the invasion of Iwo Jima and in April to Okinawa.

The diversity of targets that she was called on to hit was amazing. Big targets were certainly easy, such as large compounds, installations, crossroads, supply dumps and enemy troop concentrations. What was even more remarkable were the small targets that WEST VIRGINIA could hit with pinpoint accuracy. On many occasions, call fire was requested for a truck or a tank or even a specific mortar position or machine gun nest.

---

74 One of the ships contributing to the sinking of *Yamashiro* was the destroyer USS BENNION, DD-662, named in honor of WEST VIRGINIA's captain at Pearl Harbor, Mervyn Bennion.

When her considerable firepower was not being used on shore installations it was turned skyward as protection against enemy aircraft. During the time she was in the Okinawa operation she downed at least three enemy planes. On April 1st, Easter Sunday, a kamikaze managed to make it through the battleship's air defenses and crashed into the superstructure killing five sailors and wounding many others. The ship's damage was insignificant and her performance was not affected.

The battleship was at Okinawa when the Japanese called it quits. On August 31, 1945, WEST VIRGINIA sailed into Tokyo Bay. She and her crew witnessed the end of the war when the Japanese surrendered on September 2, 1945, three years, eight months and twenty-seven days after she witnessed the beginning at Pearl Harbor.

FATE

After a short stay in Japan, WEST VIRGINIA moved on and soon was delivering tired and victorious Americans to their ultimate victory - home. She then returned to the place of her rebirth, Bremerton, Washington, where she was deactivated and placed in the Pacific Reserve Fleet. On August 24, 1959, without fanfare or ceremony noble WEST VIRGINIA was sold to the Union Minerals and Alloys Corporation of New York as scrap.

USS Whitney

DOBBIN CLASS DESTROYER TENDER
AD-4
LAUNCHED: 1923

DECEMBER 7, 1941

Every ship in Pearl Harbor was getting ready for morning colors at 0755. The traditional raising of the American flag at 0800 is as much a part of the military as saluting. The day cannot start without it. Onboard WHITNEY, 19-year-old Marvin Kaufman stood at the bow with his nation's ensign folded in his arm waiting to raise it. But the flag was never raised that day. Kaufman eyed a plane skimming over the surface of the harbor and as it pulled up he spotted the unmistakable red ball of Japan on the underside of the wing; and the attack began.

As a tender, WHITNEY did what it was best at: during the attack it helped other ships. As with all armed ships that morning, it fired at the enemy whenever the opportunity presented itself. But the men of WHITNEY were primarily occupied with assisting the destroyers nested with her. For a time she continued providing steam, water and electricity until the destroyers could do so for themselves. The crew provided ammunition and other provisions to aid in their preparations for getting underway. Pumps were also sent over to the heavily listing USS RALIEGH, CL-7 and two of WHITNEY's doctors reported to the hospital ship USS SOLACE, AH-5 to assist with the wounded. Young Marvin Kaufman watched in utter amazement as USS ARIZONA, BB-39, just a few hundred yards away, rose out of the water in its devastating death throe. He then crisscrossed Pearl

Harbor in a small boat throughout the morning pulling fellow bluejackets from the fiery waters. One distressed sailor that Kaufman rescued was covered in oil and wearing only his skivvies and a .45 caliber pistol. At the end of the day, Kaufman returned to WHITNEY to discover that his ship had suffered no damage or casualties during the enemy raid.

THE WAR

WHITNEY was bounced all across the Pacific during the war. The longest she stayed in any one port was an eight-month period in Noumea, New Caledonia from August 1942 through April 1943. During the war WHITNEY supported destroyers from the Third, Fifth and Seventh American Fleets and vessels from the Australian, French and Dutch navies. WHITNEY and her crew not only performed regular maintenance, but repaired battle damage, including some of the first victims of kamikaze attacks.

In March 1945 WHITNEY was servicing ships at San Pedro Bay in Leyte Gulf in connection with the liberation of the Philippines. On the 31st USS FOOTE, DD-511 tied up alongside WHITNEY. After a short thirty-minute stay FOOTE prepared to leave until it was discovered that the newest member of FOOTE's crew was missing.

Only two weeks before, miles out at sea during an intense storm a lost, tired and very errant pigeon landed on the bridge of the destroyer. The bird took an immediate liking to her surroundings. The captain of FOOTE thought its presence to be a good omen. The bird was named "Pattie" and soon became a fixture on the bridge.

When "Pattie" came up missing the captain ordered an immediate search. Almost 200 men from FOOTE and WHITNEY were pressed into service. An intense bird-hunt commenced on both ships. After forty minutes the squab was nowhere to be found and an extremely reluctant captain and crew untied from WHITNEY and sailed off without their mascot. It was believed that "Pattie," although much loved, grew tired of her steel island and human companions and flew the coop for the nearby Philippine mainland in search of more avian company. The Philippines was home to WHITNEY until the end of the war.

FATE

WHITNEY remained in the Pacific through late 1945 and then returned to San Diego. She was decommissioned in October 1946 and sent to the "mothball fleet" in Suisun Bay, California in November. On March 18, 1948 she was sold for scrap to Dulien Steel Products of Washington.

USS Widgeon

LAPWING CLASS MINESWEEPER / SUBMARINE RESCUE VESSEL
ASR-1
LAUNCHED: 1918

DECEMBER 7, 1941

When the first Japanese planes flew in low over the Pearl Harbor submarine base, they were met with both mounted machine gun fire and rifle fire from the crew of WIDGEON. She stayed tied up there throughout the raid, her crew firing at targets when available and watching the destruction unfold the rest of the time. When the attack was over WIDGEON got into action in a different way.

She steamed over to Battleship Row to help with the stricken CALIFORNIA, BB-44, arriving along side the sinking dreadnaught at 1125. Her divers were soon in the water inspecting the damaged hull of battleship.

THE WAR

Because she was a submarine rescue vessel WIDGEON's divers were skilled at working underwater. The talents of these men were used extensively in the next

WIDGEON alongside ARIZONA conducting salvage dives.

428

months following the attack. WIDGEON's divers made hundreds of dives on the sunken battleships, primarily on NEVADA, BB-36. These dives consisted of inspecting and reporting on the damage and then assisting with the repairs.

For the next two years WIDGEON supported submarine training in the Pacific. She towed targets for gunnery exercises and acted as a target for torpedo practice and then recovered the training torpedoes. She performed these functions first at Pearl Harbor and then on the west coast of the United States. In 1944 she returned to Pearl Harbor where she served the same function for the duration.

FATE

WIDGEON made her way to Bikini Atoll in 1946 as part of the salvaging unit for the Operation Crossroads atomic tests. After each test the crew would remove equipment and scientific instruments from the target vessels and assist with decontaminating the ships.

WIDGEON prepares the submarine APOGON, SS-308, to be a target vessel for Operation Crossroads, July, 1946

After her atomic duties the Navy decommissioned and struck her from the roles in 1947. She was then sold for scrap to the Basalt Rock Company of Napa, California.

FARRAGUT CLASS DESTROYER
DD-352
LAUNCHED: 1932

DECEMBER 7, 1941

WORDEN and the rest of Destroyer Squadron One were berthed in East Loch resting from their routine of Pacific Fleet duties. For months WORDEN went on patrols lasting three to four days and engaged in repeated training missions. She and her crew fired practice torpedoes, practiced anti-aircraft defense by shooting at a target sock towed behind a plane, and she practiced surface battles by shooting at a target towed behind a tug. Life in the fleet was a merry-go-round of monotonous practice.

Before dawn Seaman 2nd Class Herbert Young arose from his bunk and made his way to the galley where his job was preparing breakfast for his crewmates, among them his older brother, Richard. As the sailors trailed haphazardly into the mess, Young fixed their eggs as requested, fried for this one, scrambled for the next. After the line dwindled down to nothing, Young walked out on deck to get some relief from the heat of the galley. Now 17, the Louisiana native had lied about his age to join the Navy a year earlier. He stood out on deck eating an apple, simply enjoying the tropical Hawai'ian morning. Aft of the ship, Young saw planes flying over Ford Island. Then he saw something fall from one of them. Seconds later the bomb exploded on the seaplane ramp. Young immediately ran below to awaken his brother in the berth they shared and tell him they were under attack. They both headed to their respective battle stations, Richard to the No. 4 gun and Herbert to the No. 1.

Due to the overnight liberties granted to many of the crew and early morning church call on shore, when Young arrived at the No. 1 gun there were only five men there, including himself, of the twelve men assigned. It took the crew almost thirty minutes to begin to return fire, not because they were untrained or disorganized, but because they were undergoing maintenance and the shells that they needed had been stowed or removed to the tender DOBBIN, AD-3 that they were berthed next to. Soon ammunition had been brought aboard, two .50 caliber machine guns were mounted and WORDEN began to fight back. During the battle, all the guns received word to avoid firing in an easterly direction as many large caliber anti-aircraft shells were landing in and around Honolulu.

Towards the end of the attack, a bomb exploded in the water just aft of WORDEN. A large wave from this bomb lifted the destroyer's stern causing the lines securing her to DOBBIN to part. From his vantage point Herbert Young thought the ship had been hit and he rushed back to check on his brother. Seeing that he was OK, Young ran back to his battle station.

By 1040 WORDEN was getting underway, taking only 2½ hours to get up enough steam to move, an operation that normally took 4 to 8 hours. The captain, Lieutenant Commander William Pogue, moved his ship into the channel and headed out of the harbor. As they passed Battleship Row the heat from the blazing dreadnaughts was so intense that Richard Young had to retreat behind a bulkhead to shield himself from it. Once outside the harbor, WORDEN formed up with other ships that had escaped and commenced looking for the Japanese.

The crew remained at their battle stations for the next four days, patrolling, searching for the enemy, and occasionally dropping depth charges on suspected submarines. Herbert Young returned to his assignment in the galley as needed over the next few days to make sandwiches for the No. 1 gun crew and bring them back.

Although subjected to several strafing attacks during the raid, WORDEN suffered no damage or casualties and claimed a kill on a "Val" dive-bomber.

THE WAR

The first months of the war were extremely hectic for WORDEN. The week after the attack WORDEN was kept busy with escorts and on December 14th she joined the relief force heading for Wake Island. When it was determined that it was too late to save Wake, WORDEN returned to Pearl Harbor. In February WORDEN escorted two ships to Nouméa, New Caledonia. Two days after her arrival there she was called upon to rescue the crew of the merchant ship *SNARK*, which had struck a mine. In the first week of June she screened the carriers ENTERPRISE, CV-6 and HORNET, CV-8 as part of the armada that met and defeated the mighty Imperial Japanese Navy at the Battle of Midway. In July she once again rescued men at sea. This time it was the Dutch vessel *TJINEGARA*, which was being used as an Army transport. The Japanese submarine *I-169* torpedoed it 75 miles southeast of Nouméa and WORDEN saved 36 survivors that she discovered drifting in a lifeboat.

In August 1942, WORDEN participated in the invasion of the Solomon Islands screening the carrier SARATOGA, CV-3, during the initial phases of the landings at Guadalcanal. When a Japanese torpedo damaged SARATOGA, WORDEN escorted her back to Pearl Harbor. From there WORDEN returned to the United States arriving in early October.

While in California, Richard Young decided to leave WORDEN and his brother Harold. Richard and his boss, a Chief Boatswains Mate, to put it mildly, did not get along at all and Richard had had enough. Acting on the advice of one of the officers, Richard put in for a transfer.

The destroyer stayed on the west coast, escorting other ships until December 27th when she left for Alaska. Arriving on January 1, 1943 she wasted no time in getting involved in theater operations.

FATE

Eleven days later on January 12, 1943, WORDEN, along with the transport ARTHUR MIDDLETON, AP-55, was tasked with assisting in landing Army troops on Amchitka Island in the Aleutians. The ships entered Constantine Harbor and made their way toward the beaches. WORDEN unloaded her 50 troops into rubber boats and they paddled their way to shore. The transport had many more soldiers and unloaded them in Higgins boats.[75] The landings were unopposed and as a result were routine in the extreme. Her mission was complete by 0720 and WORDEN turned about to exit the bay. As she did, a wind came up and coupled with a strong current they grabbed the destroyer and ran her aground on a large outcropping of rocks. Immediately her hull was punctured between the boiler room and the engine room, which both began to flood rapidly.

Pumps were turned on and damage control started. Captain Pogue passed a towline to the destroyer DEWEY, DD-349, one of WORDEN's Pearl Harbor sisters. DEWEY took a strain on the line and began to pull WORDEN off the rocks. The sound of her steel hull scraping across the rocks could be heard and she moved ever so slightly. The tension on the rope was too much however and the line parted. Pogue dropped anchor to prevent the ship from drifting and incurring more damage. The Alaskan waters were not kind and the increasingly rough seas slowly and surely pushed WORDEN onto some exposed rocks. The waves had their way with the vessel. They repeatedly slammed the ship onto and against the rocks. It soon became abundantly clear that she was doomed. Captain Pogue gave the order to abandon ship.

Below decks Herbert Young was in the galley along with the other cooks making sandwiches to be placed in the life rafts. When the order was given to abandon ship he reported on deck. By this time WORDEN was going fast. She had a severe list and was beginning to break up. All the boats and life rafts had already departed. Those left on board had to swim for it. Ensign R. P. Barker, the ship's disbursing officer, was a former member of the University of California swim team. He stood on the forecastle and did a swan dive into the icy bay. Young clambered up one of the starboard boat davits and just as WORDEN began to roll on her side he too jumped into the sea. Captain Pogue was also on deck directing the abandoning of his ship. As the ship began to list heavily a rogue wave reached up out of the ocean and knocked Pogue off the ship.

---

75 The Higgins boat was the standard landing craft used by the United States during the war. It featured a flat bottom and a bow that doubled as a ramp that dropped down for exit.

Once in the water boats from DEWEY and ARTHUR MIDDLETON fought the roiling ocean to pick up survivors. Ensign Barker was picked up. Captain Pogue was pulled unconscious but alive from the sea. Herbert Young drifted in the freezing bay for an hour holding on to a benevolent crate of dehydrated potatoes that floated his way. Just as a boat came along to pluck him from the water, a wave knocked the crate out of his grasp. Because he was nearly frozen he was unable to swim and he began to sink. A sailor from the rescue boat dove into the water and pulled him out.

For five more days the seas pounded WORDEN until on January 17, 1943 she finally broke up and disappeared below the waves. Fourteen of her crew died with her.

WORDEN breaking up on the submerged rocks of Constantine Harbor, Amchitka Island, January 12, 1943.

CLEMSON CLASS DESTROYER
MINESWEEPER
DMS-14
LAUNCHED: 1919

DECEMBER 7, 1941

Ensign David M. Armstrong was the Officer of the Deck and had been since the weekend began. The 22-year-old North Carolina native graduated from Annapolis just a little more than ten months before and ZANE was his first ship. ZANE was a World War I era "flush-decker"[76] that had been converted into a minesweeper in 1940. Armstrong's duties that morning were varied as is evidenced by the following deck log entry: *"0640: Received the following...provisions for use in the general mess...3 ½ gallons ice cream. Inspected as to quantity and quality by Ensign D.M. Armstrong, USN."*[77]

On deck was 20-year-old Warren Coligny, a native of Baltimore, Maryland. He saw planes coming in over the harbor and like most witnesses that day thought the Army was being over zealous with mock maneuvers on a Sunday morning. He also thought that painting the red Japanese "meatball" on the wings was very realistic. Moments later he found out just how "realistic" the planes were.

Watching from the quarterdeck, Armstrong saw the war start for America as Japanese planes dropped the first bombs on Ford Island. He

---

76 A type of destroyer whose exposed deck has no vertical breaks.
77 From the deck log of USS ZANE, December 7, 1941.

immediately called for General Quarters. Running down a passageway he found the captain, Lieutenant Commander Louis M. LeHardy, coming out of the wardroom and told him the Japanese were attacking. LeHardy bounded up the ladder toward the bridge with Armstrong close on his heels. There, Armstrong, who was also Communications Officer, received the order for all ships to sortie.

Only minutes into the attack, all four of the .50-caliber machine guns on ZANE were engaging the enemy. During the second wave Armstrong looked through his binoculars at a "Val" dive-bomber bearing down on ZANE and the three other ships of Mine Division Four. All of the ships opened fire on the plane and Armstrong clearly saw pieces flying off of it. One or more of the ships in the area had found the target. In a desperate game of "chicken" the plane continued its dive as the ships' machine guns ate away at it. The plane released its bomb, which fell harmlessly into the waters of Middle Loch. The plane couldn't pull out of its dive and it crashed into the sugar cane fields of Waipio Peninsula astern of ZANE. The death of the enemy plane elicited spontaneous and enthusiastic cheers from the sailors on deck.

At 0945, just as the attack was ending, ZANE backed out of her berth and sailed down the channel and out of the harbor at a reckless 25 knots. Once on station she began anti-submarine patrol. After several hours of patrolling and minesweeping, ZANE was ordered back to Pearl Harbor to investigate a report of a mini-sub north of Ford Island.

As they returned to the harbor the men of ZANE got their first good look at the devastation. Battleship Row was a shambles. Every one of the old dreadnaughts was on fire. OKLAHOMA, BB- 37, was capsized, ARIZONA, BB-39 was spewing smoke and flame. Everywhere they looked there was a vision to rival Dante's Inferno. On the bridge of ZANE, Armstrong turned to look at Captain LeHardy and saw tears running down his commanding officer's cheeks. Only then did Armstrong realize he was crying too.

A thorough sonar search of the harbor confirmed that the sighting of the mini-sub was only a case of frazzled nerves and just one of dozens of false sightings that were reported after the attack. Late in the afternoon

ZANE returned to a patrol station outside the harbor and remained there for the rest of the night.

THE WAR

After performing the rather mundane patrol and escort duties around Hawai'i in the early months of the war, ZANE was assigned to the armada participating in the invasion of Guadalcanal. ZANE and three other destroyer-minesweepers swept the waters off the invasion beaches to discover and destroy any mines there. There were none found. During this sweep Japanese shore batteries fired on the minesweepers but hit nothing.

On October 25, 1942, ZANE and her Pearl Harbor sister, USS TREVER, DMS-16 were off the north shore of Guadalcanal when they spotted three Japanese destroyers 12 miles away. The enemy spotted the Americans as well and altered their course to intercept them. TREVER was also an old "flush-decker" and the two aged vessels would be no match for the more modern and heavier armed enemy ships. In this case discretion was indeed the better part of valor, and the two minesweepers took off running.

The Japanese ships had a slight speed advantage and in short order ZANE and TREVER were within range. The enemy gunners were very good and shells peppered the sea all around ZANE, shaking the ship and showering her with fountains of water. One shell eventually found its mark and crashed into her forward three-inch gun mount killing the three sailors manning it. The only thing ZANE could do was to continue to run on her zigzag course and hope that something would happen to change the situation. Something did happen. The Japanese ships suddenly broke off the attack and changed directions, giving ZANE and TREVER the reprieve they needed. What the enemy had spotted were two other American vessels - a tug and patrol craft - and for whatever reason they were deemed to be better targets. The Japanese destroyers engaged and sank both of those vessels. ZANE slipped away to lick her wounds.

Early 1943 found ZANE in Australian waters where, on January 25, she was sent out to tow the steamer *PETER H. BURNETT* that had been torpedoed by the Japanese submarine *I-21*. ZANE rescued 14 men from a lifeboat and towed the steamer safely back to Sydney.

ZANE returned to Guadalcanal in February 1943, where a new officer by the name of Herman Wouk reported on board. Guadalcanal had been secured and the Allies continued the campaign in the Solomons with the invasion of New Georgia, northwest of Guadalcanal. In late June, ZANE and another ship picked up elements of the U.S. Army's 169th Infantry Regiment as part of the New Georgia operation.

In the early morning hours of June 30th ZANE and her charges sailed through the darkness into Onaiavisi channel toward the landing beaches. Bad weather had hampered the operation since its inception and tonight was no different. As ZANE was disembarking the 169th, a squall hit and grounded ZANE. The accident didn't hamper the main operation and the soldiers made it to the beach. ZANE now had to extricate herself. She put her engines into reverse and freed herself only to run aground on some rocks aft. This time she was stuck solid and she couldn't free herself. Finally after 0930 another Pearl Harbor sister, the tug USS RAIL, AT-139 arrived and pulled ZANE free. RAIL then towed the minesweeper to Tulagi.

After repairs made her seaworthy enough to get to the States on her own, ZANE made her way to Mare Island Naval Shipyard. This ended her involment in the campaign for Guadalcanal and the Solomons. As a result of her actions there, she received the Navy Unit Commendation from John L. Sullivan Secretary of the Navy, which read in part: *"For outstanding heroism in action against…Japanese forces in support of the Solomon Islands Campaign from August 7, 1942, to August 1, 1943…U.S.S. ZANE participated in the…assaults against Guadalcanal, Russell Islands and New Georgia, braving concentrated enemy shore battery fire, major and minor strafing and bombing, and air torpedo attacks to complete minesweeping, fire support, anti-submarine and antiaircraft screen missions. Constantly vigilant and ready for battle, she fought her guns valiantly against hostile planes and shore guns, inflicting serious damage on vital enemy units; she transported troops, ammunition and supplies, conducted navigational reconnaissance missions and escorted convoys…During long periods of combat operations… she steamed boldly through enemy-infested waters in support of our assault forces and contributed directly to the success of the Solomon Islands Campaign. Her own gallant fighting spirit and the skill and courage of her entire company reflect the highest credit on the U.S.S. ZANE and the United States Naval Service."*

ZANE didn't return to the war until late January 1944 when she participated in the invasion of Kwajalein Atoll in the Marshall Islands. She followed that with operations in the Marianas. The last year of the war kept ZANE busy in the backwaters of the Pacific performing the boring but necessary jobs of escorting and towing targets. ZANE was reclassified for the second time in her life in June of 1945 when, with the stroke of a pen, she was turned into AG-109, a miscellaneous auxiliary vessel.

FATE

When Japan capitulated, ZANE was stationed at San Pedro Bay in the Philippines. After the surrender she continued in the Southwest Pacific with her miscellaneous duties until October 1945 when she made her long and last voyage home arriving at Norfolk, Virginia on November 29th. Less than a month later she was decommissioned and just over three weeks after that, in January 1946, she was removed from the Navy's rolls. ZANE was sold to Luria Brothers of Philadelphia in autumn 1946 and scrapped by them in March 1947.

*   *   *   *   *

Herman Wouk, who joined ZANE in 1943, started his first book while assigned to her. In 1951 he wrote *The Caine Mutiny* based on his experiences both on her and USS SOUTHARD, DMS-10. The book earned him a Pulitzer Prize. He went on to write many other books including *The Winds of War* and *War and Remembrance*.

PART II

THREE GRAVES

PENNSYLVANIA CLASS BATTLESHIP
BB-39
LAUNCHED: 1915

DECEMBER 7, 1941

World War II lasted all of about ten minutes for USS ARIZONA, yet in a different way she fights it every day and will be fighting it forever. ARIZONA is without question the most famous American ship of the attack on Pearl Harbor. She is the symbol of the "dastardly" attack by the Japanese and is known more for the way she died than how she lived.

In preparation for the attack on Pearl Harbor the Japanese made some modifications to two key pieces of ordinance. One was the type 91 torpedo, modified to run in the shallow harbor. The second was a 1760-pound artillery shell, which was modified into an airplane delivered armor piercing bomb.

Two hours before the attack, Lieutenant Commander Kusumi Tadashi along with his radioman/gunner, Fukuda Maseo and bombardier/observer Lieutenant, (jg) Kondo Seijio took off from the carrier *Hiryu* in his Nakajima B5N "Kate" bomber. Strapped to the underside of his plane was one of the modified artillery shells. They were going hunting. Their prey was, in order of priority, aircraft carriers, battleships and cruisers. They had long studied the layout of Pearl Harbor and were anxious to get to work.

Like all other ships in the harbor that morning, the men of ARIZONA were slowly awakening to just another day in the Pacific Fleet. Lieutenant Commander Samuel G. Fuqua, the ARIZONA's Damage Control Officer, was already up and eating breakfast in the wardroom. Ensign A. R. Schubert was in the head shaving. Ensign W. J. Bush was still in his rack in that hazy twilight zone between being asleep and awake. Ensign Jim D. Miller was in his quarters slipping into his uniform and Chief Gunner's Mate J. A. Doherty was in the chief's quarters.

They all noticed the vibrations in the ship as the first bombs and torpedoes exploded nearby. Three blasts on the warning howler was the signal for an air raid but for some reason only one was sounded shortly after 0755 followed by the announcement of "Air Raid!" That got everyone's attention. Lieutenant Commander Fuqua called the officer of the deck by phone and ordered him to sound general quarters. He then ran out to the quarterdeck only to be greeted by the sight of a Japanese plane flying by with guns blazing only a few feet above his head. Seconds later he found himself flat on his back, having been knocked down by the blast of the first bomb to hit ARIZONA.

Aft in Turret No. 3, Ensign Miller had hurried to his battle station but was fighting smoke, flame and gas and not the Japanese. A bomb had hit near Turret No. 4 and exploded below decks. All power went out, the lower handling room was flooding and the compartment was filling with smoke. Miller ordered the turret evacuated. The last men out, Ensign J. P. Field, Jr. and Ensign G. S. Flanagan, Jr. reported the turret clear and secured.

Lieutenant Commander Fuqua was on the quarterdeck when the bomb exploded beneath Turret No. 4 and he was knocked out by the concussion. When he regained consciousness the deck was an inferno. He immediately organized the crews that had evacuated Turrets 3 and 4 into fire fighting and rescue parties. One group retrieved CO_2 extinguishers and held back the flames as best they could while the other men gathered the scores of wounded men and placed them in the ARIZONA's boats that were lying off the stern. Fuqua supervised the loading of the injured men.

At 10,000 feet above Pearl Harbor, Lieutenant Commander Kusumi was leading his group of five Kates on their bombing run. Behind him, his bombardier Lieutenant Kondo peered through his sight and ARIZONA came into view. Kondo pressed the release button and the modified artillery shell dropped from the plane. Twenty six seconds later it crashed through the teak covered steel deck between Turrets 1 and 2 and exploded deep inside the doomed lady. The detonation set off the black powder magazine and the resulting secondary explosion ripped the ship apart, her forward deck leaping into the air and then smashing down into the void left by the massive blast. She was mortally wounded and nothing could be done to save her.

Chief Gunner's Mate Doherty, who had reported to his anti-aircraft battery on the boat deck, was knocked senseless by the explosion and in moments found himself in the flaming oily water.

Ensign D. Hein was on the Navigation Bridge with Captain Franklin Van Valkenburg when the deathblow came. Van Valkenburg was solidly in command at the time, on the phone issuing orders and coordinating the defense of his vessel. The blast turned the bridge into a hell of smoke and flame from which only Hein emerged. He climbed down a jungle of twisted metal until he reached the port quarterdeck, finally making his way to a barge alongside.

Fuqua still fought to save as many lives as he could. He had sent several men in search of Captain Van Valkenburg and Admiral Isaac C. Kidd, the commanding officer of Battleship Division One. They couldn't be found and he assumed them to be dead, leaving him the senior officer on board. With the ship now nothing more than a raging mass of flames, smoke and melting steel and with no means of defending herself, he gave the order to abandon ship. He commanded his little flotilla of small boats ferrying wounded men to nearby Ford Island where make shift first aid stations were set up. After ensuring that there were no men left on board the ship to be rescued, he took one boat back out into the flaming harbor to search for men in the waters around the ship.

Three Medals of Honor were awarded to men of the ARIZONA, one each posthumously to Captain Van Valkenburg and Admiral Kidd for staying at their stations while coordinating the defense of their ship and battleships respectively. The third was awarded to Lieutenant Commander Fuqua for his courageous and masterful leadership in saving the lives of so many of his shipmates.

In his after action report, Fuqua wrote, *"I could hear the guns firing on the ship long after the boat deck was a mass of flames."* Commander Ellis H. Geiselman, ARIZONA's Executive Officer, was not on board during the attack. He submitted a report based on the statements of others and eyewitness testimony, in which he wrote, *"The anti-aircraft battery and .50 caliber machine guns fired on the enemy planes as long as personnel at the guns were alive."* As long as the guns were operational men fired them and the guns fired until the men at them were dead. ARIZONA had fought to the last.

THE WAR

Despite having been sunk, the fires on board ARIZONA continued to burn for two days sending billowing clouds of black, acrid smoke into the blue Hawai'ian sky. Recovery became the first order of business. For days bodies floated to the surface and, as the flames died down, bodies that were now nothing more than ashes and bones could be recovered from the melted and smoldering deck. Admiral Kidd's Annapolis ring was found on the Signal Bridge, welded to the metal deck by the infernal heat of the fires. The first dives into the wreck began on the 8th, while she still burned, in an effort to collect essential paperwork and some of the $139,000 in cash on board.

From the beginning opinions in the Navy went back and forth as to whether or not the ship was salvageable. At times it was thought she could be raised and saved. Some thought she could be cut up in place and removed in pieces and other opinions were voiced that it was impractical or impossible to do either and that she should rest on the bottom of the harbor forever. Until a final decision could be made, what work could be done would be done. On the 22nd of December work commenced at recovering anything useable from her and some searchlights and five-inch guns were removed. One week later everything that could be easily salvaged had been and work ceased for a week. In early January serious work began on removing the number 3 and 4 turrets.

Several weeks later a second effort to recover bodies began; this time however it was the dead that remained trapped inside the ship. To say the task was grisly would be a gross understatement. The remains were so ghastly after over a month underwater and the task became so gruesome that recovery efforts were halted after about 45 bodies were retrieved. That was the last attempt to collect bodies. The rest of ARIZONA's crew would remain at their battle stations.

Work continued and on February 10th the first of ARIZONA's main guns were recovered when the right hand gun of the No. 3 turret was lifted from the water. The middle and left gun were raised by the end of the week. While this work went on, the 14-inch shells for the guns were also being salvaged.

Depending on the weather, equipment availability and the current prevailing thought on salvage or abandonment, work on ARIZONA continued off and on for almost two years. The guns from Turret No. 2 were finally removed in September 1943 and the last day of work was October 11, 1943.

ARIZONA was finally at rest.

FATE

On March 7, 1950 Admiral Arthur Radford, Commander in Chief, Pacific Fleet, had a flagpole attached to the still exposed mainmast of ARIZONA and hoisted the American flag, stating, "From this day on, Arizona will fly our country's flag just as proudly as she did on the morning of 7 December, 1941. I am sure the Arizona's crew will know and appreciate what we are doing." A simple wooden platform had been erected spanning the wreck with a commemorative plaque attached. This was the beginning of the Arizona Memorial.

Admiral Radford attempted to get funds several times for a more suitable and permanent memorial but was denied. In 1956 the U.S. Navy began running boats out to the wreck for the general public. The average was about 600 visitors a day.

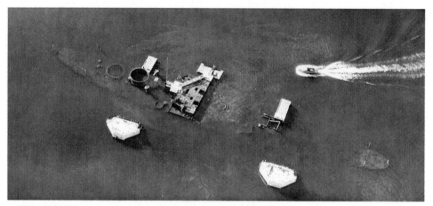

**The USS Arizona with the original wooden "memorial" in place in a 1958 photo.
Leaking fuel oil is clearly visible.**

Almost ten years after her death there was still debate over what to do with ARIZONA. Some families wanted the remains of loved ones recovered and returned. Others thought of removing the wreck completely. Finally in 1958 President Dwight D. Eisenhower approved the creation of a memorial. The original stipulation for the half a million dollar memorial was that no public funds were to be used, however only $300,000 was raised and the remaining $200,000 was paid for by the government. Elvis Presley raised over $64,000 by giving a benefit concert on March 25, 1961 at Pearl Harbor's Bloch Arena.

Alfred Preis, an Austrian born Honolulu architect was chosen to design the memorial that the Navy required should look like a bridge floating above the ship. Preis described his design this way, "...the structure sags in the center but stands strong and vigorous at the ends, expresses initial defeat and ultimate victory...The overall effect is one of serenity. Overtones of sadness have been omitted to permit the individual to contemplate his own personal responses...his innermost feelings." The three sets of seven windows individually represent December 7th, the day of the attack. Together the twenty-one windows represent a permanent twenty-one-gun salute to the fallen. The memorial is supported on either end by underwater pylons. Neither the pylons nor the memorial touches the wreck. The dedication ceremony for the completed memorial took place on Memorial Day 1962. Since then millions of people have taken the short boat ride across Pearl Harbor to visit the gallant lady and pay respects to the fallen heroes who sleep eternally inside her.

Surviving crewmen who were serving on her on December 7, 1941 are allowed to have their cremated remains placed inside the ship.

All these years later ARIZONA still sheds "black tears" of oil at the rate of about a quart a day. There is a legend, a belief, that the ARIZONA will stop crying oil on the day that the last survivor dies. That remains to be seen.

The Navy and the National Park Service are actively studying ways to slow or stop the leakage and to control the structural deterioration of the wreck, while at the same time preserving her and respecting her status as a war grave.

The 1,177 men that died on ARIZONA still stand today as the greatest single loss of life in U.S. Navy history. ARIZONA was declared a National Historic Landmark and placed on the National Register of Historic Places in 1989.

The completed Memorial hosts 1.4 million visitors a year and appears to serenely float over USS ARIZONA.

USS *Oklahoma*

NEVADA CLASS BATTLESHIP
BB-37
LAUNCHED: 1914

DECEMBER 7, 1941

Twelve-year-old Rose Marie DeCastro lived with her little sister, three brothers and parents in a small home five miles from Pearl Harbor. Her forty-year-old father, Julio "Lefty" DeCastro, was a civilian worker at the Pearl Harbor Navy Yard. A distinct thrumming from the sky noticeably disturbed the Sunday morning peace and young Rose went outside to see the cause. Looking up she saw dozens of planes flying over their home. She waved at them.

At Ford Island in Pearl Harbor, OKLAHOMA rested at her berth on Battleship Row, outboard of her sister ship USS MARYLAND, BB-46. The call for battle stations and the shudder of the first torpedo hits happened within seconds of each other. In the first seventy seconds of the attack, no fewer than five Japanese torpedoes slammed into her port side. The 583-foot long, 27,500-ton behemoth started to list immediately. Once that happened, the laws of physics took over. OKLAHOMA was going to capsize and nothing could be done to prevent it or the deaths of 429 of her crew.

George A. DeLong, a sailor studying to become a helmsman, was in his quarters in Steering Aft, a compartment far astern on the lowest deck of the ship. Almost the instant the torpedoes hit, water came gushing into the space through an air vent. He and the others with him were dropped into a living nightmare. Up was rapidly becoming down, air was being replaced with water and the Sunday morning silence suddenly became screaming men, ear shattering explosions, and the roar of rushing water.

Lieutenant (jg) Aloysius Schmitt was a thirty-two-year-old Catholic priest from Dubuque, Iowa and the Chaplain on OKLAHOMA. He had completed 0615 mass in the ship's chapel only a short time before. His battle station was the sick bay, where his duties were to help care and pray for the injured and dying. He reported there immediately.

Ray Turpin, a twenty-year-old Marine Private 1st Class had just finished his breakfast of pancakes and bacon. He was assigned to a five-inch anti-aircraft gun and he headed for it when the call to battle stations was sounded. He quickly made it out to the main deck before the list became too severe.

The explosions at Pearl Harbor could be clearly heard at the DeCastro home in the Damon housing tract. Local radio stations put out the call for all civilian shipyard employees to report to work. Rose watched as her father got ready to leave, not really understanding what was happening. When she said good-bye him she didn't know that she wouldn't see him again for three days.

The amount of time that passed from the first torpedo strike to the moment OKLAHOMA came to rest upside down on the bottom of Pearl Harbor was twelve minutes. OKLAHOMA died before she ever fired a single shot. The only thing for her crew to do now was to try to survive.

Deep inside OKLAHOMA in Steering Aft, George DeLong and his fellow sailors were desperately trying to plug up the two-foot square air vent where tons of water were quickly invading their living space. They finally managed to stuff a mattress into the opening and then cover it by lashing down a wooden game board over the opening. They also managed to open the hatch to an adjacent unflooded compartment, greatly increasing their breathable air. Now the only thing they could do was sit, wait, and pray for rescue.

As OKLAHOMA slowly rolled to port, Pvt. Ray Turpin walked, crawled, and then climbed until he was standing on the starboard hull. Turpin hesitated to jump into the harbor, as he wasn't a great swimmer. Besides that, the mass of humanity already in the water seemed to be dangerously chaotic. His mental debate as to whether or not to jump or stay was interrupted by cries for help. He turned to see a sailor climbing out of a porthole below him. With the help of another sailor, Turpin reached over and helped pull the grateful sailor out. As soon as that one was out, another one appeared in the porthole. He was pulled out too. This happened three more times until Turpin had helped extricate five men.

A sixth man next popped through the porthole. It was Chaplain Schmitt who had been on the other side of the porthole pushing the men out as Turpin pulled. Schmitt tried to fit through the opening and promptly got stuck. He struggled for a few moments but couldn't seem to budge. Turpin proffered his hand and told Schmitt to grab it and he would help him out. Schmitt replied that he couldn't fit through the porthole and it was no use. He told Turpin he was going back in to help others.

When Schmitt dropped back into the compartment he found more sailors there. As the ship continued to roll and the compartment slowly filled with water, Schmitt helped push them out the porthole one by one. He did this until he had helped a total of twelve men escape. OKLAHOMA slowly rolled until the porthole was underwater. Chaplain Schmitt never made it out[78]. Ray Turpin made it over to the MARYLAND where he joined a line of men supplying ammunition to her anti-aircraft guns.

Around 1100 Julio DeCastro and his crew arrived at the capsized OKLAHOMA. There, other workers were already attempting to cut trapped men out of the hull using acetylene torches. However, the searing blue flame ate up the oxygen in the compartments and the sailors inside asphyxiated. The situation called for more direct means. DeCastro was a caulker and chipper and his tool was a pneumatic jack with a chipping blade on the end. With this he could punch holes into the steel hull and that's what he and his men set out to do.

The steel of OKLAHOMA did not yield easily. Hours went by. Slowly and inexorably the long steel plates that made up the hull were bent back and the rivets gave way under the unrelenting pneumatic blade of "Lefty"

---

78 Chaplain Lieutenant (jg) Aloysius Schmitt was awarded the Navy and Marine Corps Medal for his selfless act. A destroyer escort, USS SCHMITT, DE-676, was named after Chaplin Schmitt and commissioned in 1943. She was sold to Taiwan in 1968 and scrapped in 1976.

DeCastro. The sun set and DeCastro and his team worked by the light of the fires from ARIZONA. The lanky and balding DeCastro stood on the battleship's upturned hull all night. As he pounded into the steel his muscles vibrated to the rhythm of the hammer and his ears grew numb with the music of steel striking steel. At 0600 Monday morning DeCastro and his crew pulled six living sailors out of the tomb that was OKLAHOMA. But the work was not complete. The tapping of other trapped sailors still called out from deep inside the sunken ship. Later, on Monday afternoon, DeCastro and his crew succeeded in punching a hole into Steering Aft where he helped pull out George DeLong and the others that had been trapped with him for a day and a half.

DeCastro and his crew stayed through Monday, through Tuesday, through Wednesday. They kept pulling men out of OKLAHOMA. Ten, fifteen, twenty-five. When they finished on Wednesday a total of thirty-two sailors emerged from their dark fetid crypt to breathe fresh air again.

After three days of intense labor, Julio "Lefty" DeCastro left Pearl Harbor and went home. He was tired and hungry. He walked back to his mother's home where his family had taken refuge. Young Rose was happy to see him, but not nearly as happy as the men he helped pull out of OKLAHOMA.

THE WAR

From the outset it was fairly evident that OKLAHOMA was going to be a difficult job no matter what her final disposition. Short of cutting her up in place, no matter what was to be her fate, the first thing to do was to raise her. An enormous amount of study and preparation was done toward this end. It was determined that a huge and complex winch system needed to be built along with lightening her and dredging the harbor bottom around her.

All this work - from planning to implementation - took fifteen months. On March 8, 1943, twenty-one large winches and miles of rope and cable went into motion to bring upright the sunken dreadnaught. This was not a one day, one week, or even a one month process. It took over three months, until June 16, 1943 to bring the ship level again. Once this was accomplished she still had to be refloated.

A massive job on its own, bringing her back to the surface took another five months and she finally floated free on November 3, 1943. Even then she leaked like a sieve and it took pumps and pontoons to keep her from sinking again. On December 28, 1943, two years and three weeks after she sank at her berth, she was brought into the dry dock at Pearl Harbor.

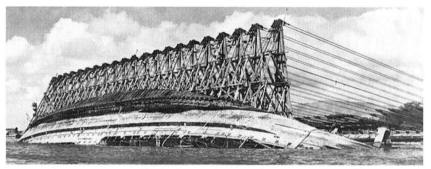

After over one year, with frames, rigging and winches in place, the righting process begins on March 8, 1943

OKLAHOMA was an anachronism by this time. She was almost thirty years old and the new IOWA class battleships, 887 feet long and 45,000 tons, dwarfed her in size, speed and firepower. On top of that it was almost 1944 and it was clear that the age of the battleship was finished and the dawn of the fast carrier group was already here. OKLAHOMA just plain wasn't worth fixing.

After she was decommissioned in September 1944 she was stripped of anything that was still useful, which included her main fourteen-inch guns. For the rest of the war and beyond she sat at anchor in a lonely corner of Pearl Harbor waiting for the destruction that everyone knew would come.

FATE

OKLAHOMA was sold for $46,000 to the Moore Dry Dock Company of Oakland, California in December 1946. When she finally left Pearl Harbor, OKLAHOMA was really nothing more than a floating pile of junk. She had to be towed on her final journey back to San Francisco where the blowtorches of the scrapper awaited her.

In a way, OKLAHOMA had the last laugh. En route to San Francisco, while being towed, a storm came up. Even now there were pumps on her that were staying ahead of the leaks she still had. But the storm put a strain on her repairs and she began to take on more water than the pumps could handle. She became too heavy for her towlines and they parted.

At 0140 on May 17, 1947, OKLAHOMA sank into the Pacific Ocean 540 miles northeast of Hawai'i, never to be raised again.

429 marble stanchions each engraved with the name of a fallen sailor or Marine stand in neat rows at the OKLAHOMA Memorial on Ford Island.

FLORIDA CLASS BATTLESHIP / TARGET SHIP
AG-16
LAUNCHED: 1909

DECEMBER 7, 1941

Eighteen minutes after World War II started for the United States, USS UTAH was dead. Her 32-year career as a United States naval vessel was over. She had been converted, and at the time of the Japanese attack, was being used as a target ship and as a gunnery training ship for fleet practice. Above decks her five-inch and 1.1-inch guns were protected by steel shelters rendering them inoperable. All of her smaller .50 and .30 caliber guns had been dismantled and put in storage below decks. The decks themselves were covered with a dual layer of 6" x 12" lumber to protect her from the practice bombs that were actually dropped on her. UTAH was no longer the magnificent dreadnaught BB-31, but instead was now designated AG-16. Stripped of all her weapons and buried beneath tons of protective lumber she was virtually defenseless. Tied up at berth F-11 on the north side of Ford Island, she was a sitting duck.

Members of her crew saw the attack begin when they spotted three planes dropping bombs on the seaplane hangars at the south end of Ford Island. At 0801 two of the first torpedoes launched by the enemy struck UTAH in quick succession on her port side and she began to list immediately. Within minutes the initial 15-degree list increased to 40 degrees. Peter Tomich, an Austrian born Chief Watertender was in the engineering spaces below decks. Realizing that the ship was capsizing, he insured that his men evacuated the area and then he proceeded to secure all the boilers. The senior officer on board, Lieutenant Commander S. S. Isquith, gave the order that no commanding officer ever wants to give, "Abandon ship!" As the crew abandoned ship via the starboard side they were subjected to strafing by Japanese planes.

At 0810, a mere nine minutes after being hit, UTAH was listing a full 80 degrees and Commander Isquith, Lieutenant, (jg) P. F. Hauck and Machinist Stanley A. Semanski were the last to leave her, exiting through portholes in the Captain's cabin. The men in the water scrambled for the safety of the heavy concrete quays of berth F-11, to afford some protection from the strafing planes. Several launches and whale boats plied the harbor picking men out of the water and depositing them on Ford Island while being continually exposed to enemy fire. The water and oil soaked survivors took refuge from the battle in trenches on the island that had been dug for a public works project.

UTAH after being hit by several torpedoes is listing in this photo taken from TANGIER minutes into the attack

Six officers and fifty-two of UTAH's crew died as a result of the attack on Pearl Harbor. One of those was Chief Watertender Peter Tomich, who posthumously received the Medal of Honor for his selfless acts on that day.

THE WAR

On December 29, 1941 UTAH was declared "in ordinary," a naval term meaning a ship that was being taken off the rolls of active ships and placed in reserve. In January what munitions that could be, were removed from her. As with ARIZONA, BB-39, and OKLAHOMA, BB-37, the debate began as to what to do with UTAH. It was finally determined to bring her upright and refloat her, solely for the purpose of scrapping her and clearing the berth for use. After much study, delay and preparation, the process was begun on February 9, 1944. As she was righted, she also sank further into the mud; so much so, that about four weeks into the operation all work was halted. It was finally determined to cease all

Salvage efforts underway for UTAH in early 1944.

salvage efforts on her. The attempts to raise her having been foiled, UTAH was left were she fell, at berth Fox-11 on the north shore of Ford Island. There was really nothing else to do with her. UTAH spent the duration of the war lying on her port side on the bottom of Pearl Harbor.

FATE

UTAH was officially decommissioned on September 5, 1944 and struck from the Navy's rolls on November 13th of the same year. For 31 years she lay there, pretty much ignored, while her more famous sister, USS ARIZONA, received the lion's share of fame, glory and honor, not to mention a beautiful and elaborate memorial. Finally on May 27, 1972, a memorial was dedicated overlooking her wrecked hulk.

On May 5, 1989 she was designated a National Historic Landmark and placed on the National Register of Historic Places. Access to viewing the rusting, partially exposed remains of UTAH and visiting the memorial on Ford Island is restricted.

As seen from her stark memorial, the hulk of UTAH lies on her port side just off the north shore of Ford Island.

PART III

THE JAPANESE

The Japanese

IMPERIAL JAPANESE NAVY
COMBINED FLEET
CREATED: 1924

DECEMBER 7, 1941

The Japanese sent over sixty vessels in the armada to attack Pearl Harbor. It included aircraft carriers, battleships, cruisers, destroyers, oilers for refueling on the long trip, five midget subs and almost half of the submarines in the inventory at that time.

They also brought planes. They sent 353 in two waves to attack the American Pacific Fleet resting peacefully at anchor that Sunday morning. The initial attacks hit all airbases on the island of O'ahu. The planes of the Navy, Marines and Army Air Corps were essentially neutralized. A few American planes got off the ground but for all intents and purposes, the skies over O'ahu were Japanese.

The attack on Pearl Harbor began at 0755. All the torpedo planes utilized by the Japanese came in the first wave. Of the eight ships that were sunk it was the torpedo planes that sank half of them in the first minutes of the attack. Nine Japanese planes were lost to the American defenders in the opening wave.

The second wave arrived at 0845. It was comprised mostly of level bombers and dive-bombers. These bombers demolished three destroyers in the Navy Yard. They also caught the battleship USS NEVADA, BB-36, in the harbor as it made a run for the open ocean. They succeeded in sinking it but they failed to block the harbor with it. The attack ended at 0945. In this wave, the alert defenders brought down twenty Japanese planes. The last plane to leave was that of Fuchida Mitsuo, the commander of the aerial attack force. He made one last circle of the harbor to assess the damage inflicted and then flew north to return to his carrier.

Any history of the Pearl Harbor attack always notes that the Japanese lost "only" twenty-nine planes. However there is almost no mention ever made of the ten to fifteen planes that were unceremoniously dumped from the decks of the carriers into the ocean by the Japanese because they were so shot up they couldn't be repaired. So the count of Japanese planes lost at Pearl Harbor is actually thirty-nine to forty-four. For some strange reason it appears that no one kept an exact count of how many planes were jettisoned into the sea. That's as much as a twelve percent loss of the attacking force. Fuchida Mitsuo counted twenty-one holes from anti-aircraft fire in his plane when he landed. One control cable on his "Kate" was shot almost completely through and held together only by a single strand of wire.

Of the five midget submarines that were part of the attack, only one is confirmed to have entered the harbor during the attack and fire its torpedoes. It was spotted almost immediately coming into the main channel and was set upon by a half a dozen ships that fired on it. A destroyer rammed and depth charged it, sending it to the bottom of Pearl Harbor. Three other midget subs never made it into the harbor. One was sunk by the destroyer USS WARD, DD-139, an hour before the attack as it attempted to sneak into the harbor. A third sank in Keehi lagoon off the main entrance and a fourth ultimately ran aground off Bellows Field on the east shore of O'ahu and was captured.

The fifth midget sub remains somewhat of a mystery. Although some believe it to have made it into the harbor and fired its torpedoes at Battleship Row, the more accepted theory is that it fired its torpedoes at the light cruiser USS ST. LOUIS, CL-49, as ST. LOUIS exited the harbor, missing with both, then made its way into West Loch.

No matter what you believe, no midget submarine sank any American ships. At the most, one might have helped to sink one of two battleships, USS OKLAHOMA, BB-37, or USS WEST VIRGINIA, BB-48. But both these ships were sunk by multiple torpedo strikes, and the addition of one or two more hits would have made little or no difference as to their ultimate fate.

Twenty-eight enemy submarines were sent to Hawai'i. In fact there were so many Japanese submarines lurking beneath Hawai'ian waters that you could have walked from island to island and never gotten your feet wet. They had multiple missions. Five delivered the midget subs. After the attack, several were to rendezvous with the midgets and pick up their crews off the coast of Lana'i. Others had life saving duty and were to pick up downed pilots. No Japanese pilot ditched in the ocean so the subs were not needed for that service. No matter what their other assignments, all the submarines were tasked with sinking any ship exiting the harbor.

At least fifteen ships exited the harbor while the attack was underway and another eleven made it out shortly afterwards. By midday the waters around O'ahu were lousy with American ships. The destroyers that escaped the harbor rained down a plague of depth charges on numerous sonar contacts believed to be enemy submarines. So many depth charges were used in fact, that they were later admonished for their uninhibited use. These prolific attacks may have hindered the Japanese submariners in their mission. However the fact remains that not one American ship that left Pearl Harbor was sunk by enemy submarine action. Late in the day *I-69* fired two torpedoes at an American destroyer just off O'ahu. The destroyer made a sudden maneuver, indicating that it probably spotted the torpedo wakes, and the two metal fish missed. *I-69* received a depth charging for its troubles, but escaped unharmed.

THE WAR

The feeling of success Japan felt after Pearl Harbor was short lived. Even though the first days of the war brought them victories in Hong Kong, the Philippines, Indonesia and islands scattered throughout the Pacific, the long string of defeats they suffered began within months and continued until their demise in 1945.

The beginning of the end for the Japanese Navy and Japan was at Midway, in June 1942, when four of the carriers that brought the war to America at Pearl Harbor were sent to the bottom. The vaunted carrier force that so clearly demonstrated the potential and abilities of naval air power six short months earlier was soundly defeated by just such a force made up of American carriers and airplanes. The final ship sunk, of the flotilla that sailed against Pearl Harbor, the cruiser, *Tone*, last saw daylight on July 24, 1945.

After their defeats at the Coral Sea, Midway and Guadalcanal, all within months of Pearl Harbor, the Japanese were on a downward slope from which they never recovered. The Allies marched across the Pacific and didn't stop until they were standing on Japan's doorstep at Okinawa and then, at great cost, took it from them. Slowly, surely, methodically, from on the sea, from above the sea, and from under the sea the Japanese Navy and its brave sailors paid the price for the ambitions of their government.

FATE

By the end of the war the Japanese Navy, or *Nihon Kaigun* in Japanese, wasn't even a shadow of its former self. It had been swept from the Pacific Ocean, ceasing to exist in any meaningful way. Every ship involved in the task force that assaulted Pearl Harbor was sunk during the war.

SHIP	TYPE	PLACE	DATE LOST
1941			
Midget #1	Submarine	Pearl Harbor	Dec. 7, 1941
Midget #2	Submarine	Pearl Harbor**	Dec. 7, 1941
Midget #3	Submarine	Pearl Harbor	Dec. 7, 1941
Midget #4	Submarine	Pearl Harbor	Dec. 7, 1941
Midget #5	Submarine	Pearl Harbor	Dec. 7, 1941
I-70	Submarine	Molika'i	Dec 10, 1941

**Captured

SHIP	TYPE	PLACE	DATE LOST
1942			
I-173	Submarine	Midway	Jan 27,1942
I-23	Submarine	O'ahu	Feb 14, 1942*
Hiryu	Carrier	Midway	Jun 4, 1942
Kaga	Carrier	Midway	Jun 4, 1942
Soryu	Carrier	Midway	Jun 4, 1942
Akagi	Carrier	Midway	Jun 5, 1942
Arare	Destroyer	Kiska Island	Jul 5, 1942
I-22	Submarine	E. Solomons	Oct 4, 1942*
I-172	Submarine	Guadalcanal	Nov 3, 1942*
I-15	Submarine	Guadalcanal	Nov 10, 1942
Hiei	Battleship	Savo Island	Nov 13, 1942
Kirishima	Battleship	Guadalcanal	Nov 15, 1942
I-3	Submarine	Guadalcanal	Dec 9, 1942
I-4	Submarine	New Britain	Dec 21, 1942

SHIP	TYPE	PLACE	DATE LOST
1943			
Toei Maru	Oiler	Truk	Jan 18, 1943
I-1	Submarine	Guadalcanal	Jan 29, 1943
I-18	Submarine	Coral Sea	Feb 11, 1943

SHIP	TYPE	PLACE	DATE LOST
Toho Maru	Oiler	Celebes	Mar 29, 1943
Kagero	Destroyer	Rendova	May 8, 1943
I-9	Submarine	Kiska	Jun 10, 1943*
I-24	Submarine	Kiska	Jun 11, 1943
I-7	Submarine	Kiska	Jun 22, 1943
I-168	Submarine	New Hanover Isl.	Jul 27, 1943
I-17	Submarine	Noumea	Aug 10, 1943
I-25	Submarine	Solomons	Aug 25, 1943
I-20	Submarine	Espiritu Santo	Sep 3, 1943
I-19	Submarine	Makin Island	Nov 25, 1943
I-21	Submarine	Tarawa	Nov 29, 1943

1944

Kenyo Maru	Oiler	Sorol Island	Jan 14, 1944
Nippon Maru	Oiler	Sorol Island	Jan 14, 1944
I-171	Submarine	Buka Island	Feb 1, 1944
I-175	Submarine	Marshall Islands	Feb 4, 1944
Shinkoku Maru	Oiler	Truk	Feb 17, 1944
I-169	Submarine	Truk	Apr 4, 1944
I-2	Submarine	New Ireland	Apr 7, 1944
Akigumo	Destroyer	Zamboanga	Apr 11, 1944
I-174	Submarine	Truk	Apr 12, 1944
I-16	Submarine	Solomons	May 19, 1944
Tanikaze	Destroyer	Basilan	Jun 9, 1944
I-6	Submarine	Saipan	Jun 16, 1944
Shokaku	Carrier	Yap Island	Jun 19, 1944
I-5	Submarine	Saipan	Jul 19, 1944
Kokuyo Maru	Oiler	Philippines	Jul 30, 1944
Kyokuto Maru	Oiler	Philippines	Sep 21, 1944
Chickuma	Cruiser	Samar	Oct 25, 1944
Zuikaku	Carrier	Cape Enganao	Oct 25, 1944

SHIP	TYPE	PLACE	DATE LOST
Abukuma	Cruiser	Philippines	Oct 26, 1944
Shiranui	Destroyer	Panay	Oct 27, 1944
Akebono	Destroyer	Philippines	Nov 13, 1944
Urakaze	Destroyer	Formosa	Nov 21, 1944

1945

I-8	Submarine	Okinawa	Mar 31, 1945
Hamakaze	Destroyer	Japan	Apr 7, 1945
Isokaze	Destroyer	Japan	Apr 7, 1945
Kasumi	Destroyer	Japan	Apr 7, 1945
Tone	Cruiser	Kure Island	Jul 24, 1945

*Last date reported, presumed lost.

"We are gathered here, representatives of the major warring powers, to conclude a solemn agreement whereby peace may be restored. The issues, involving divergent ideals and ideologies, have been determined on the battlefields of the world and hence are not for our discussion or debate. Nor is it for us here to meet, representing as we do a majority of the people of the earth, in a spirit of distrust, malice or hatred. But rather it is for us, both victors and vanquished, to rise to that higher dignity which alone befits the sacred purposes we are about to serve, committing all our people unreservedly to faithful compliance with the understanding they are here formally to assume. It is my earnest hope, and indeed the hope of all mankind, that from this solemn occasion a better world shall emerge out of the blood and carnage of the past -- a world dedicated to the dignity of man and the fulfillment of his most cherished wish for freedom, tolerance and justice."

General Douglas Macarthur,

Statement at the surrender ceremonies on the deck of the U.S.S. Missouri, September 2, 1945.

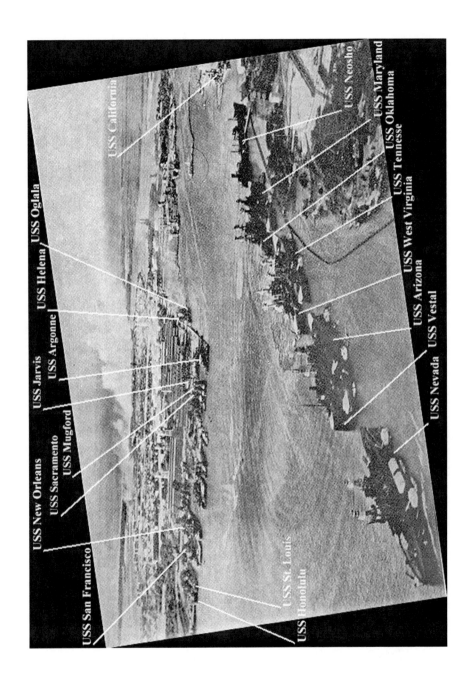

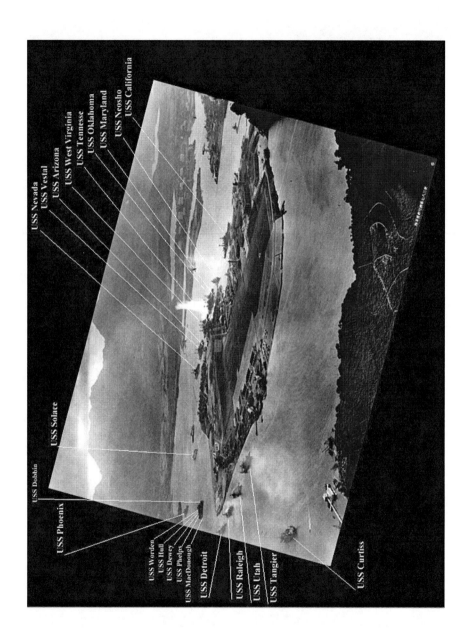

USS Nevada
USS Vestal
USS Arizona
USS West Virginia
USS Tennesse
USS Oklahoma
USS Maryland
USS Neosho
USS California

USS Dobbin

USS Solace

USS Phoenix

USS Worden
USS Hull
USS Dewey
USS Phelps
USS MacDonough
USS Detroit
USS Raleigh
USS Utah
USS Tangier

USS Curtiss

APPENDIX

DAMAGE ROSTER
of ships at Pearl Harbor Dec. 7, 1941

SUNK OR CAPSIZED: 11
Requiring raising and extensive repair and rebuilding.
(8 of these ships returned to the fleet)

USS Arizona, BB-39	Never salvaged	*still on bottom at Pearl Harbor*
USS California, BB-44	Raised & rebuilt	*rejoined the fleet 1-31-44*
USS Cassin, DD-372	Rebuilt	*rejoined the fleet 2-6-44*
USS Downes, DD-375	Repaired & rebuilt	*rejoined the fleet 11-15-43*
USS Nevada, BB-36	Raised & rebuilt	*rejoined the fleet 5-43*
USS Oglala, CM-4	Raised, repaired	*rejoined the fleet 2-44*
USS Oklahoma, BB-37	Raised, sold for scrap	*hulk sank 5-47 while under tow*
USS Shaw, DD-373	Repaired & rebuilt	*rejoined the fleet 8-31-42*
Sotoyomo, YT-9	Rebuilt	*rejoined the fleet 8-42*
USS West Virginia, BB-48	Raised & rebuilt	*returned to the fleet 9-14-44*
USS Utah, AG-16	Never salvaged	*still on bottom at Pearl Harbor*

HEAVILY DAMAGED: 2
Requiring significant repairs.

USS Helena, CL-50	Repaired	*rejoined the fleet June 1942*
USS Raleigh, CL-7	Repaired	*rejoined the fleet July 1942*

MODERATE DAMAGE: 4
Damage had no major effect on performance & easily repaired

USS Maryland, BB-46	Repaired & modernized	*rejoined the fleet 2-26-42*
USS Vestal, AR-4	Repaired	*rejoined the fleet February 1942*
USS Pennsylvania, BB-38	12-20-41, left PH for repairs	*rejoined the fleet 3-30-42*
USS Tennessee, BB-43	Repaired	*rejoined the fleet March 1942*

MINOR DAMAGE: 8
Damage immediately repaired with no consequence

USS Argonne, AG-31	USS Bagley, DD-386	USS Cummings, DD-365
USS Curtiss, AV-4	USS Helm, DD-388	USS Honolulu, CL-48
USS Jarvis, DD-393	USS Pyro, AE-1	

INSIGNIFICANT DAMAGE: 7
Damage requiring little or no repair

USS Dobbin, AD-3	USS Monaghan, DD-354	USS New Orleans, CA-32
USS Ramapo, AO-12	USS Rigel, AR-11	USS Tangier, AV-8
USS Wasmuth, DMS-15		

NO DAMAGE: 90
No damage whatsoever*

USS Allen, DD-66	USS Aylwin, DD-355	USS Antares, AKS-3
USS Avocet, AVP-4	Ash, YN-2	USS Blue, DD-387
USS Bobolink, AM-20	USS Breese, DM-18	USS Cachalot, SS-170
USS Case, DD-370	USS Castor, AKS-1	Cheng-Ho, IX-52
USS Chew, DD-106	Cinchona, YN-7	Cockatoo, AMc-8
Condor, AMc-14	USS Conyngham, DD-371	Crossbill, AMc-9
USS Dale, DD-353	USS Detroit, CL-8	USS Dewey, DD-349
USS Dolphin, SS-169	USS Farragut, DD-348	USS Gamble, DM-15
USS Grebe, AM-43	USS Henley, DD-391	Hoga, YT-146
USS Hulbert, AVD-6	USS Hull, DD-350	USS Keosanqua, AT-38
USS Macdonough, DD-351	Manuwai, YFB-17	Marin, YN-53
USS Medusa, AR-1	USS Montgomery, DM-17	USS Mugford, DD-389
USS Narwhal, SS-167	USS Neosho, AO-23	Nihoa,YFB-17
Nokomis, YT-142	USS Ontario, AT-13	Osceola, YT-129
USS Patterson, DD-392	USS Pelias, AS-14	USS Perry, DMS-17
USS Phelps, DD-360	USS Phoenix, CL-46	USS Preble, DM-20
USS Pruitt, DM-22	MTB Squadron #1,12 PT Boats	USS Rail, AM-26
USS Ralph Talbot, DD-390	USS Ramsay, DM-16	Reedbird, AMc-30
USS Reid, DD-369	USS Sacramento, PG-19	USS San Francisco, CA-38
USS Schley, DD-103	USS Selfridge, DD-357	USS Sicard, DM-21
USS Solace, AH-5	USS St. Louis, CL-49	USS Sumner, AG-32
USS Sunnadin, AT-28	USS Swan, AVP-7	USS Tautog, SS-199
USS Tern, AM-31	USS Thornton, AVD-11	USS Tracy, DM-19
USS Trever, DMS-16	USS Tucker, DD-374	USS Turkey, AM-13
USS Vireo, AM-52	Wapello, YN-56	USS Ward, DD-139
USS Whitney, AD-4	USS Widgeon, ASR-1	USS Worden, DD-352
USS Zane, DMS-14		

* Some of these vessels had wires, rigging or antennas shot away either by the enemy or by friendly fire but there was no structural damage.

476

FATE OF PEARL HARBOR SHIPS BY YEAR

12/7/1941:

USS Arizona	sunk at Pearl Harbor		*enemy action*
USS Oklahoma	sunk at Pearl Harbor		*enemy action*
USS Utah	sunk at Pearl Harbor		*enemy action*

1942:

USS Neosho	sunk in Coral Sea,	May	*enemy action*
USS Blue	sunk off Guadalcanal,	Aug	*enemy action*
USS Jarvis	sunk off Guadalcanal,	Aug	*enemy action*
USS Tucker	sunk off Espiritu Santo,	Aug	*enemy action*
USS Wasmuth	sunk off Aleutian Islands,	Dec	*enemy action*

1943:

USS Worden	sunk off Amchitka,	Jan	*enemy action*
USS Grebe	destroyed by hurricane,	Jan	
PT-22	badly damaged in storm,	Jan	scrapped
PT-28	wrecked in storm,	Jan	
USS Helena	sunk in Kula Gulf,	Jul	*enemy action*
USS Henley	sunk in Huron Gulf,	Oct	*enemy action*
PT-21	stricken for obsolescence,	Oct	
PT-23	reclassified as small boat,	Oct	
PT-25	reclassified as small boat,	Oct	
PT-26	reclassified as small boat,	Oct	

1944:

USS Perry	sunk off Palau,	Sep	*enemy action*
USS Ward	sunk off Leyte,	Dec	*enemy action*

USS Reid	sunk off Leyte,	Dec	*enemy action*
USS Hull	sunk by typhoon,	Dec	
USS Monaghan	sunk by typhoon,	Dec	
PT-20	stricken for obsolescence,	Dec	
PT-29	stricken for obsolescence,	Dec	
PT-42	stricken for obsolescence,	Dec	

1945:

USS Thornton	rammed by other US ships,	Apr	beached & abandoned
USS Gamble	scuttled off Guam,	Jul	*enemy action*
USS Narwhal	sold for scrap,	Nov	

1946:

Cheng-Ho	returned to owner	Feb
USS Detroit	sold for scrap,	Feb
USS Raleigh	sold for scrap,	Feb
Sotoyomo	destroyed,	Feb
USS Montgomery	sold for scrap,	Mar
USS Schley	scrapped by the Navy	Mar
USS Breese	sold for scrap,	May
USS Tracy	sold for scrap	May
USS Sicard	sold for scrap,	Jun
Condor	to Maritime Commission	Jul
USS Oglala	to Maritime Commission,	Jul
USS Ramapo	to Maritime Commission,	Jul
USS Shaw	sold for scrap	Jul
USS Dolphin	sold for scrap,	Aug
USS Vega	sold for scrap,	Aug
USS Allen	sold for scrap,	Sep
Cockatoo	to Maritime Commission,	Sep
USS Sumner	to Maritime Commission,	Sep
USS Swan	to Maritime Commission,	Oct

USS Chew	sold for scrap,	Oct	
USS Zane	sold for scrap,	Oct	
USS Preble	sold for scrap,	Oct	
USS Hulbert	sold for scrap,	Oct	
Reedbird	to Maritime Commission,	Nov	
USS Ramsay	sold for scrap,	Nov	
USS Trever	sold for scrap,	Nov	
USS Selfridge	sold for scrap,	Nov	
USS Turkey	sold for scrap,	Dec	
USS Aylwin	sold for scrap,	Dec	
USS Dale	sold for scrap,	Dec	
USS Dewey	sold for scrap,	Dec	
USS Macdonough	sold for scrap,	Dec	
USS Pruitt	scrapped by the Navy		

1947:

USS Cachalot	sold for scrap,	Jan	
USS Rail	to Maritime Commission,	Jan	
USS Sunnadin	to Maritime Commission,	Jan	
USS Vireo	to Maritime Commission,	Feb	
Marin	to Maritime Commission,	Mar	
Crossbill	to Maritime Commission,	Mar	
USS Ontario	sold to private party,	Apr	
Wapello	sold for commercial service,	May	sunk in Panama Canal
USS Keosanqua	sold for commercial service,	Jul	
USS Cummings	sold for scrap,	Jul	
USS Tern	sold,	Jul	
USS Sacramento	sold for merchant service,	Aug	
USS Farragut	sold for scrap,	Aug	
USS Patterson	sold for scrap,	Aug	
USS Phelps	sold for scrap,	Aug	
USS Antares	sold for scrap	Sep	

USS Helm	sold for scrap,	Oct
USS Bagley	sold for scrap,	Oct
USS Downes	sold for scrap,	Nov
USS Cassin	old for scrap,	Nov
USS Case	sold for scrap,	Dec

1948:

USS Pennsylvania	scuttled off Kwajalein,	Feb
USS Mugford	scuttled off Kwajalein,	Mar
USS Whitney	sold for scrap,	Mar
USS Ralph Talbot	scuttled off Kwajalein,	Mar
USS Conyngham	sunk as target,	Jul
USS Nevada	sunk as target,	Jul
USS Widgeon	sold for scrap	
USS Solace	sold for passenger service,	scrapped in 1981

1950:

USS Pyro	sold for scrap,	Mar
USS Vestal	sold for scrap,	Jul
USS Dobbin	sold for scrap	May
USS Argonne	sold for scrap	Aug
USS Medusa	sold for scrap,	Aug
USS Rigel	to Maritime Commission	

1951:

USS St. Louis	sold to Brazil, 1/51; sank under tow, 8/80
USS Phoenix	sold to Argentina, 10/51; sunk in Falklands War, 5/82

1954:

Manuwai	struck from Naval Register,	Sep

1959:

USS California	sold for scrap,	Jul
USS Maryland	sold for scrap,	Jul
USS Tennessee	sold for scrap,	Jul
USS West Virginia	sold for scrap,	Aug
USS New Orleans	sold for scrap	Sep
USS San Francisco	sold for scrap,	Sep
USS Honolulu	sold for scrap,	Nov

1960:

USS Tautog	sold for scrap,	Jul

1961:

USS Tangier	sold for scrap,	Jul

1968:

USS Castor	sold,	Dec

1971:

Ash	sold for scrap,	May

1972:

USS Curtiss	sold for scrap,	Feb

1973:

USS Pelias	sold for scrap,	Oct
Nokomis	sold for commercial service	1973
	abandoned in San Francisco	1994
	purchased for restoration	2002
	demolished in Alameda, Ca.	Aug 2010
Osceola	sold for scrap	

1976:

Cinchona	sold	Feb

2005:

Hoga	loaned to Oakland, CA.	1948
	returned to Navy	1994
	donated as a museum	2005

GLOSSARY & HULL DESIGNATIONS
Words, Terms and Names

A

Action Report: Written report usually by the senior officer of action with the enemy.

Aft: The direction of the stern of a ship.

Aground: When a ship's hull becomes stuck on the sea floor.

Attu: One of the Aleutian Islands in Alaska that was occupied by the Japanese.

B

Betty: American military code name for the Japanese G4M twin-engine bomber manufactured by the Mitsubishi Company.

Bikini Atoll: Atoll in the Marshall Islands.

Bluejacket: Another name for an enlisted sailor below the rank of Chief Petty Officer.

Boat deck: The deck aboard a ship on which lifeboats or other small boats are stowed.

Bonin Islands: Island chain 620 miles south of Japan.

Bulkhead: Naval term for a wall, or any vertical partition.

C

Call fire: A request by ground forces for artillery support usually for a specific target.

Convoy: A group of ships sailing together for mutual protection.

Cook off: Term used to describe ammunition exploding when it is exposed to heat or flame.

Crossroads: Atomic bomb tests conducted at Bikini Atoll in July 1946.

D

Draft/Draught: The depth a ship extends below the waterline or the depth of water it needs in order to float.

E

Espiritu Santo: The largest island of the New Hebrides Islands, (now the independent island nation of Vanuatu).

F

Flush-decker: A group of destroyers built during and after World War One whose exposed weather deck was unbroken from bow to stern and therefore flush. (see also "Four Stacker")

Forecastle: Pronounced, "foc'sel" the forward part of the main deck at the bow.

Four-stacker: A group of destroyers built during and after World War One that had four distinct smoke stacks. They were also known as "four-pipers".

G

Galley: A ship's kitchen.

General Quarters: A ship's battle stations. The alarm that tells the crew to report to their battle stations.

H

Head: Naval term for a toilet specifically or a bathroom in general.

Hunters Point Naval Shipyard: A major shipyard located in San Francisco, California.

I

I-Class Submarine: Japans large class submarine.

Ironbottom Sound: The name given by American sailors to that body of water in the Solomon Islands north of Guadalcanal, east of Savo Island and south of Florida Island. So called because of the large number of warships sunk there.

J

Jury rig: To temporarily or hastily assemble a facility or piece of equipment often from materials at hand.

K

Kaitan: A manned Japanese torpedo/submarine designed to be rammed into a target, sacrificing the pilot.

Kate: American military code name for the Japanese B5N single engine torpedo bomber manufactured by the Nakajima Company.

Kiska Island: One of the Aleutian Islands in Alaska.

Kwajalein: An atoll in the Marshall Islands.

L

Long Lance: The Japanese Type 93 torpedo, nicknamed "Long Lance" by American Naval historian Samuel Elliot Morison after the war.

M

Magic Carpet: The operation to repatriate American servicemen back to the United States.

Mare Island Naval Shipyard: A major shipyard, located at the extreme northern edge of San Francisco Bay, in Vallejo, California.

Maritime: The body established in 1940 to determine if ships should be sold, scrapped
Commission: or retained after their government use was over.

N

Nest: A group of ships berthed together, usually side by side in open water.

New Hebrides: Old colonial name for the Island Nation of Vanuatu, in the Southwest Pacific.

Noumea: Capital and port on the island of New Caledonia in the south Pacific.

O

Oscar: American military code name for the Japanese Ki-43 single engine fighter manufactured by the Nakajima Company.

P

PBM Mariner: American twin engine patrol/bomber flying boat built by the Glenn Martin Company.

PBY Catalina: American twin engine patrol/bomber flying boat built by Consolidated Aircraft.

Picket: A ship that patrols a defensive perimeter

Port: 1) Nautical term for "left." 2) A city on the water utilized by ships.

Q

Quarterdeck: That part of a ship's deck located at the extreme rear, whether raised or not.

R

Rate: The specialty a sailor works in, such as Quartermaster or Boatswain's Mate.

Ready Ammunition: Ammunition stored in a box at a weapons location ready for immediate loading.

RO-Class Submarine: Medium size Japanese submarine.

S

Saipan: Island in the Mariana Group in the Central Pacific.

Screen: The protecting of a larger ship or group of ships by other ships, usually smaller, by creating an outer perimeter with the smaller ships.

Scuttle: To purposely sink or otherwise destroy a ship so it will not fall into enemy hands.

Seeadler Harbor: A port on Manus Island in the Admiralty Islands.

Skivvies: Navy term for under shorts specifically and underwear in general.

Slot, The: The name given by American sailors to New Georgia Sound, the narrow body of water which runs northwest to southeast, forming a corridor, in the center of the Solomon Islands.

Striker: A sailor in training for a particular job or "rate".

Sortie: *French;* meaning to exit or go out, referring to a ship exiting a port.

Starboard: Nautical term for "right."

Stern: That part of a ship farthest to the rear.

Surigao Strait: A narrow body of water between Mindanao and Leyte Islands in the Philippines.

T

TBM Avenger: American single engine torpedo bomber designed by Grumman and built by General Motors.

1010 Dock: Pronounced "ten-ten" dock, it is a pier at the Pearl Harbor Navy Yard, so called because it is 1,010 feet long.

Tokyo Express: Name given by American sailors to the nighttime Japanese naval convoys resupplying garrisons on Guadalcanal and in the Solomon Islands in general.

U

Ulithi: Atoll in the Caroline Islands in the Western Pacific.

V

V-Boat: A series of nine submarines of varying design built for the United States Navy between the world wars.

Val: American military code name for the Japanese D3A Navy Type 99 bomber manufactured by the Aichi Company.

W

War Shipping Administration: An agency of the U.S. Government which purchased and operated civilian shipping during World War II.

X, Y, Z

Zigzag: Sailing along a straight base course by alternating port and starboard turns.

HULL DESIGNATIONS

Each Navy ship has a hull designation and number. The designation of usually two or three letters tells what type of ship the hull is for and the number tells what number that hull is in sequence. For example DD-337, USS ZANE, tells that it is a destroyer, (DD) and it is the 337th destroyer hull laid down. ZANE was later reclassified as AG-109, indicating it was the 109th miscellaneous auxiliary vessel in the Navy.

AD   Destroyer Tender

AE   Ammunition Ship

AF   Stores Ship

AG   Miscellaneous Auxiliary

AH   Hospital Ship

AKS   General Stores Ship

AM   Minesweeper

AMc   Minesweeper, Coastal

AN   Net Layer

AO   Oiler, (Tanker)

AP   Transport

AR   Repair Ship

ARD   Auxiliary Repair Dry Dock

AS   Submarine Tender

ASR   Submarine Rescue Vessel

AT   Tugboat

ATO   Ocean Going Tug, Old

AV   Seaplane Tender

AVD   Seaplane Tender, Destroyer

AVG   Auxiliary Aircraft Carrier

AVP   Seaplane Tender, Small

BB   Battleship

CA   Cruiser, Heavy

CL   Cruiser, Light

CM   Minelayer

CV	Aircraft Carrier
CVE	Escort Aircraft Carrier
DD	Destroyer
DM	Minelayer, Light
DMS	Destroyer, Minesweeper
IX	Unclassified Miscellaneous
LST	Landing Ship, Tank
PG	Patrol Craft, Gunboat
PT	Motor Torpedo Boat
SS	Submarine
YFB	Ferryboat
YN	Net Tender
YT	Harbor Tug

This list is of ship types mentioned in this book and is not a complete list of U.S. Navy hull designations.

BIBLIOGRAPHY

BIBLIOGRAPHY

Where available the after action reports written by the commanding officers of each ship formed the basis of the December 7, 1941 section of each profile. Also utilized for all ships was the Dictionary of American Naval Fighting Ships, generally referred to as DANFS. These were common to every ship in this book and are not listed in the ships' individual bibliography. Primary sources, such as ships' deck logs, memos and other official documents were used.

These documents were augmented by firsthand accounts of Pearl Harbor and Pacific war veterans. Their stories were gathered from a vast array of sources. Some of these were official, such as the Library of Congress Veterans History Project. Others came from unofficial sources such as the Pearl Harbor Veterans Association and the written histories of individual veterans and ships whether they were in book form or on the Internet.

The works of many authors were researched and referenced. Individual books used are listed with their appropriate ships. Several works were used extensively for general information on events or ships, including;

Blair, Jr., Clay, *Silent Victory: The U.S. Submarine War Against Japan*, Annapolis, MD, Naval Institute Press, 2001

Lord, Walter, *Day of Infamy: Sixtieth Anniversary Edition*, New York, NY, Holt Paperbacks, 2001

Madsen, Daniel, *Resurrection: Salvaging the Battle Fleet at Pearl Harbor*, Annapolis, MD, Naval Institute Press, 2003

Noel, John V. Captain, U.S. Navy (Ret), and Edward L. Beach, Captain, U.S. Navy (Ret), *Naval Terms Dictionary 3rd Edition*, Annapolis, MD, Naval Institute Press, 1971

Prange, Gordon W., with Donald Goldstein and Katherine Dillon, *At Dawn We Slept: The Untold Story of Pearl Harbor*, N.Y., NY, Viking Press, 1991

Prange, Gordon W., with Donald Goldstein and Katherine Dillon, *Miracle at Midway*, N.Y., NY, Penguin Books, 1983

Roscoe, Theodore, *United States Destroyer Operations in World War II*, Annapolis, MD, Naval Institute Press, 1953

Stillwell, Paul, *Air Raid, Pearl Harbor!: Recollections of a Day of Infamy*, Annapolis, MD, Naval Institute Press, 1981

*The Bluejackets Manual 12*th *edition*, Annapolis, MD, United States Naval Institute, 1944

The Internet has grown up and information, including primary sources, is readily available from both governmental and other web sites. Intelligent thought and facts are shared on many blog sites and forums where like-minded historians and interested parties discuss and exchange information. I utilized these sites extensively and harvested from them the hard work and research of others.

I would like to give special mention to the website that I used for all things regarding the Japanese Navy; http://www.combinedfleet.com. This site, founded by Jonathan Parshall and edited by Anthony Tully, authors of *Shattered Sword: The Untold Story of the Battle of Midway*, was unerringly correct and I deferred to it and them when it came to any information concerning Japanese ships and actions. The site is not only run by them but is contributed to by researchers from around the globe. If a fact or event was in dispute it was noted as such and evidence on both sides of the issue was given. That is the hallmark of historians whose only purpose is to learn and disseminate the truth. I found their research to be meticulous and impeccable. I am deeply in their debt.

For general information, the following Internet sites were used extensively for all ships:

- http://destroyers.org/
- http://digital.lib.ecu.edu/special/pearlharbor/index.html
- http://home.gci.net/~fourpiperdestroyer/html/ships.htm
- http://pacific.valka.cz/ships/index.htm
- http://pearlharbor-history.org/
- http://pearlharborsurvivors.homestead.com/names.html
- http://the.honoluluadvertiser.com/specials/pearlharbor60/pearl2truck.html
- http://wwiiarchives.net/
- http://www.combinedfleet.com/
- http://www.fleetorganization.com/1941commanders.html
- http://www.hazegray.org/
- http://www.history.navy.mil/
- http://www.hofferthistoryclass.com/Mr._Hofferts_Class_Website/Welcome.html
- http://www.ibiblio.org/hyperwar/
- http://www.justinmuseum.com/famjustin/usnbio.html
- http://www.loc.gov/vets/
- http://www.navsource.org/
- http://www.pearlharborattacked.com/
- http://www.researcheratlarge.com/Ships/FightingCans/index.html
- http://www.seawaves.com/newsletters/TDIH/TDIHarchive.asp
- http://www.uboat.net/index.html

PHOTOGRAPHS

All photographs except where noted are official United States Government photos courtesy of the National Archives or the Navy Heritage and History Command, (NHHC). Many were downloaded from the NHHC site or from the excellent Internet site navsource.org.

Photos on pages 299, 427 and 430 are by the author. The photo of the author is by Allyson West. All photos have been cropped and digitally edited for clarity by the author.

PART I: SURVIVORS
- After action reports
- Dictionary of American Naval Fighting Ships

USS Allen, DD-66
- http://www.smmlonline.com/archives/VOL1830.txt

USS Antares, AKS-3
- http://lcweb2.loc.gov/diglib/vhp/story/loc.natlib.afc2001001.00860/

USS Argonne, AG-31
- http://www.navsource.org/archives/09/36/3610.htm

Ash, YN-2
- http://lcweb2.loc.gov/diglib/vhp/story/loc.natlib.afc2001001 .66355/transcript?ID=mv0001

USS Avocet, AVP-4
- Deck log, USS Avocet, December 6, 1941 through December 8, 1941

USS Aylwin, DD-355
- Military History Magazine, *World War II: Interview with Burdick Brittin* by Jon Guttman, April 1995

USS Bagley, DD-386
- Sallet, George John, *Six Long Years on the USS Bagley*, unpublished memoir.

USS Blue, DD-387

- Naval Historical Center, Oral Histories of the Pearl Harbor Attack: Captain John E. Lacouture, USN

USS Bobolink, AM-20

- http://navyhistory.com/NAVY/MISC/Awahou.html
- http://www.historycentral.com/navy/cruiser/Atlanta2.html
- http://www.ussfoote.blogspot.com/

USS Breese, DM-18

- http://chronicle.augusta.com/stories/091601/met_079-3725.000 .shtml
- http://www.destroyerhistory.org/flushdeck/dm.html
- http://www.thehistorymakers.com/programs/dvl/files/Davis _Augustineb.html

USS Cachalot, SS-170

- United States Submarine Operations in World War II By Theodore Roscoe, Annapolis, MD, Naval Institute Press, 1949
- http://www.fleetsubmarine.com/ss-170.html

USS California, BB-44

- Mason, Theodore C., *Battleship Sailor*, Annapolis, MD, Naval Institute Press, 1982

USS Case, DD-370

- http://home.comcast.net/~wgoffeney/Case/usscase.htm
- http://lcweb2.loc.gov/diglib/vhp/story/loc.natlib.afc2001001.03742/
- http://pearlharborsurvivors.homestead.com/GoffeneyJoe.html
- http://www.freerepublic.com/focus/f-vetscor/1470185/posts
- http://www.ulongbeach.com/balanacan_bombing.html

USS Cassin, DD-372

- http://www.navsource.org/archives/05/372.htm

USS Castor, AKS-1

- Richardson, Kent D., *Reflections of Pearl Harbor: An Oral History*, Westport, CT, Greenwood Publishing Group, 2005
- Kelly, Carol Adele, *Voices of My Comrades: America's Reserve Officers Remember World War II*, Fordham University Press, 2007

Cheng ho, IX-52

- Fairchild, David; *Garden Islands of the Great East; Collecting Seeds from the Philippines and Netherlands India in the Junk "Cheng Ho"*, New York, NY, Charles Scribner's Sons, 1943
- http://www.chinahistoryforum.com/index.php?showtopic=16145
- http://www.nytimes.com/1990/08/26/books/a-travel-nut-s -library.html

I would like to thank Mr. Bill Douglas for his generous help in gathering information on CHENG-HO.

USS Chew, DD-106

- Pearl Harbor Attack: Hearings before the Joint Committee on the investigation of the Pearl Harbor attack, Congress of the United States, Seventy-ninth Congress, first session.

Cinchona, YN-7

- http://en.allexperts.com/e/u/us/uss_lst-84.htm
- http://www.hawaiireporter.com/story.aspx?739bc0ce-5b5b-48cc -9ec0-9e4371acd837
- http://www.pearlharborsurvivorsonline.org/html/The%20 Attack.htm

Cockatoo, Amc-8

- Personal interview with Elbert Lee Brown, November 22, 2009.
- Lahonton Valley News, Friday, December 7, 2007
- San Diego Sun, Tuesday, March 26, 1946

Condor, Amc-14

- http://lcweb2.loc.gov/diglib/vhp/story/loc.natlib.afc2001001.66355/transcript?ID=mv0001
- http://www.patriotfiles.com/index.php?name=Sections&req=viewarticle&artid=3410&page=1

USS Conyngham, DD-371

- http://ussfletcher.org/nov42.html, Deck log of USS FLETCHER, DD-445, November 2, 1942
- http://www.j-aircraft.com/research/rdunn/tuluvu/tuluvu_7.htm
- http://www.militaryhistoryonline.com/wwii/articles/aftermidway.aspx
- http://www.navweaps.com/index_oob/OOB_WWII_Pacific/OOB_WWII_Santa-Cruz.htm

Crossbill, Amc-9

- Telephone interview with Earnest Wilkins, November 17, 2009.
- http://www.patriotledger.com/homepage/x1307758946/Pearl-Harbor-survivor-honored-in-Randolph
- http://www.seawaves.com/TDIH/december/07Dec.txt

USS Cummings, DD-365

- Point Reyes Light, Thursday, February 26, 2004
- http://ww2il.com/?p=345
- http://www.navweaps.com/index_oob/OOB_WWII_Pacific/OOB_WWII_Cape_Engano.htm
- http://www.presidency.ucsb.edu/ws/index.php?pid=16543&st=&st1

USS Curtiss, AV-4

- The Brownsville Herald, Brownsville, Texas, Monday, August 31, 2009
- http://www.usscurtissav4.com/USSCURTMEMPAGE.html

USS Dale, DD-353

- Olson, Michael *Tales from a Tin Can: The USS Dale From Pearl Harbor to Tokyo Bay,* St. Paul, MN, Zenith Press, 2007
- http://www.microworks.net/pacific/battles/kommandorski_islands.htm
- http://www.seawaves.com/TDIH/march/10Mar.txt

USS Detroit, CL-8

- Telephone interview with Arthur G. Herriford, July 12, 2010.
- http://mws.mcallen.isd.tenet.edu/mchi/alumni/millner/account.shtml
- http://www.corregidor.org/chs_trident/uss_trout.htm
- http://www.history.navy.mil/faqs/faq66-3b.htm, Oral History of Lt. Ruth Erickson, Nurse Corps, USN
- http://www.world-war.co.uk/US/omaha_war.html

USS Dewey, DD-349

- http://www.angelfire.com/ca2/gormady/
- http://www.destroyerhistory.org/goldplater/ussdewey.html

USS Dobbin, AD-3

- War diary of Paul Fleshman, Chief Boatswain's Mate, USS MAHAN, DD-364
- Honolulu Star Bulletin, Sunday, December 7, 2003
- Los Angeles Times, Saturday, December 8, 1990
- http://lakeconews.com/content/view/10092/764/
- http://navysite.de/crewlist/commandlist.php?commandid=1391
- http://www.centredaily.com/2007/11/07/254974/chuck-bailey-remembering-attack.html
- http://www.kitsapsun.com/news/2008/Dec/06/67-years-after-pearl-harbor-fewer-survivors-but/
- http://www.pearlharbormemorial.com/html/wallofvalor/stansell.html

- http://www.pearlharborsurvivorsonline.org/html/Kleiss,%20 Victor%20J..wps.htm
- http://www.uscg.mil/history/weboralhistory/Ingham_Colbert _Carter.asp

USS Dolphin, SS-169

- First War Patrol report, USS DOLPHIN, dated February 5, 1942, by Lt. Cmdr. Gordon B. Rainer
- Second War Patrol report, USS DOLPHIN, dated July 30, 1942, by Lt. Cmdr. Royal L. Rutter
- Third War Patrol report, USS DOLPHIN, dated December 14, 1942, by Lt. Cmdr. Royal L. Rutter
- Historical Society of Laguna Woods, The Historian, Volume 1, Number 5, November-December 2007
- http://ezinearticles.com/?WWII-Veterans---3-Stories-From-This -Vanishing-Breed&id=3961020
- http://www.bowfin.org/december-7-1941

USS Downes, DD-375

- http://www.navsource.org/archives/05/375.htm

USS Farragut, DD-348

- USS ENTERPRISE, deck log, August 24, 1942
- New York Times, Sunday, April 13, 2003
- http://pearlharborsurvivors.homestead.com/MassaMario.html
- http://www.navweaps.com/index_oob/OOB_WWII_Pacific /OOB_WWII_Eastern-Solomons.htm
- http://www.tributes.com/show/88667294

USS Gamble, DM-15

- http://www.destroyerhistory.org/flushdeck/ussgamble/index.html
- http://www.cpedia.com/search?q=USS%20Pennsylvania&d =CURTISS

USS Grebe, AM-43

- http://blog.seattlepi.com/nowhearthis/category.asp?blogID =351&category=1806
- http://www.usmm.org/sunk43.html#anchor406099
- http://www2.fiu.edu/~thompsop/liberty/liberty_listT.html

USS Helena, CL-50

- http://lcweb2.loc.gov/diglib/vhp/story/loc.natlib.afc2001001 .10441/transcript?ID=sr0001
- http://lcweb2.loc.gov/diglib/vhp/story/loc.natlib.afc2001001.00964/

USS Helm, DD-388

- http://abbot.us/DD629/captains/carroll.shtml
- http://militarytimes.com/citations-medals-awards/recipient.php? recipientid=55372
- http://wp.scn.ru/en/ww2/f/1039/65/3
- http://www.pacificwrecks.com/aircraft/a6m2/5289.html
- http://www.pearlharborattacked.com/cgi-bin /IKONBOARDNEW312a/ikonboard.cgi?act=Print;f=34;t=30
- http://www.pearlharborattacked.com/cgi-bin /IKONBOARDNEW312a/ikonboard.cgi?act=ST;f=11;t=66;hl=helm
- http://www.researcheratlarge.com/Ships/FightingCans/index.html

USS Henley, DD-391

- Vallejo News Chronicle, *USS HENLY torpedoed in the South Pacific*, Wednesday, November 10, 1943
- http://web.mac.com/jptate/De_Leon_Handbook/Wayne _Chambers.html
- http://www.aracnet.com/~histgaz/pearlharbor/carsonj.html

Hoga, YT-146

- CNN News transcript, broadcast date, May 21, 2000
- National Association of Fleet Tug Sailors, The Towline, *Hoga's Home* by Don Bates, November, 2002

- Associated Press, *Survivor of Pearl Harbor a forgotten, rusting hero*, by James O. Clifford
- http://www.nps.gov/history/maritime/nhl/hoga.htm

USS Honolulu, CL-48
- Readers Digest, *Trapped*, by Len Karsian as told to Albert Rosenfeld, November 1958
- St. John, Philip A., *Battle for Leyte Gulf*, Turner Publishing Company, 1996
- http://navymemorial.ibelong.com/site/USS-Honolulu-CL-48
- http://www.hullnumber.com/crew1.php?cm=CL-48

USS Hulbert, AVD-6
- http://www.kadiak.org/ships/phyllis-s/phyllis_s.html
- http://www.vpnavy.org/vp43_history.html

USS Hull, DD-350
- Telephone interview with Pat Douhan, Saturday, April 2, 2011
- Drury, Bob and Thomas Clavin, *Halsey's Typhoon: The True Story of a Fighting Admiral, an Epic Storm, and an Untold Story*, New York, NY, Atlantic Monthly Press, 2007
- Henderson, Bruce, *Down to the Sea*, New York, NY, Smithsonian Books, 2008
- http://www.usshullassociation.org/

USS Jarvis, DD-393
- http://www.navsource.org/archives/05/393.htm

USS Keosanqua, AT-38
- Deck log, USS ANTARES, December 7, 1941
- http://shipbuildinghistory.com/history/shipyards/2large/inactive/bethstatenisland.htm
- http://www.nps.gov/archive/usar/survivors.html
- http://www.specwarnet.net/USSWard/history.htm

USS Macdonough, DD-351

- Drury, Bob and Thomas Clavin, *Halsey's Typhoon: The True Story of a Fighting Admiral, an Epic Storm, and an Untold Story*, New York, NY, Atlantic Monthly Press, 2007
- Henderson, Bruce, *Down to the Sea*, New York, NY, Smithsonian Books, 2008

Manuwai, YFB-17

- http://www.navsource.org/archives/14/350016.htm

Marin, YN-53

- http://www.navsource.org/archives/11/03031.htm

USS Maryland, BB-46

- Prange, Gordon W. with Donald M. Goldstein and Katherine V. Dillion, *God's Samurai: Lead Pilot at Pearl Harbor,* Brassey's, Inc., Washington, D.C. 1990, Kindle Edition
- *USS Maryland* by Turner Publishing, Paducah, KY, 1997
- ibid, USS MARYLAND Deck Log, November 1941 through July 1945

USS Medusa, AR-1

- http://royhyatt.bravehost.com/ussmedusa.html
- http://somdnews.com/stories/110907/indytop182908_32122.shtml

USS Monaghan, DD-354

- U.S. Navy Department letter to Mr. And Mrs. Joseph Guio from Water Tender 2nd Class Joseph C. McCrane, dated March 15, 1945
- Our Navy Magazine, *The Fury of the Sea*, April 1945
- Drury, Bob and Thomas Clavin, *Halsey's Typhoon: The True Story of a Fighting Admiral, an Epic Storm, and an Untold Story*, New York, NY, Atlantic Monthly Press, 2007

- Henderson, Bruce, *Down to the Sea*, New York, NY, Smithsonian Books, 2008
- http://www.bensonnews-sun.com/articles/2008/06/18/obituaries/aobit.txt

USS Montgomery, DM-17

- http://www.navsource.org/archives/05/121.htm

Motor Torpedo Boat Squadron #1

- Bulkley, Robert J., Captain, USNR, (Ret), *At Close Quarters: PT Boats in the United States Navy*, Washington, D.C. Naval History Division, 1962
- http://www.ptboats.org/20-01-05-ptboat-004.html

USS Mugford, DD-389

- http://suicidewheels.blogspot.com/2010/05/frank-duzick.html
- http://www.destroyersonline.com/usndd/dd389/dd389pho.htm
- http://www.fleetorganization.com/1941commanders.html
- http://www.ww2talk.com/forum/war-against-japan/14815-interactive-map-guadalcanal.html

USS Narwhal, SS-167

- 1st through 15th War Patrol reports
- Roscoe, Theodore, *United States Submarine Operations in World War II*, by Theodore Roscoe, United States Bureau of Naval Personnel, Naval Institute Press, 1949
- http://www.fleetsubmarine.com/ss-167.html

USS Neosho, AO-23

- http://www.delsjourney.com/uss_neosho/pearl_harbor/neosho_at_pearl.htm
- http://www.u-s-history.com/pages/h1734.html

USS Nevada, BB-36

- Ryan, Cornelius, *The Longest Day*, New York, NY, Simon and Schuster, 1959
- Proceedings Magazine, *Lest We Forget: Joseph K. Taussig Jr.* by Lt. Cmdr. Thomas J. Cutler, USN, (Ret), and A. D. Baker III, October 2004
- The Baltimore Sun, *Obituary, Captain Joseph Taussig Jr.,* December 18, 1999
- The Tulsa World, *Unsung Hero to Receive Silver Star After 57 Years* by Michael Overall, March 22, 1998
- The Virginian-Pilot and The Ledger-Star, Norfolk, VA, *Remembering Carl Brashear and Other Military Heroes*, Sunday August 6, 2006
- World War II Magazine, *Pearl Harbor Attack: Lieutenant Lawrence Ruff Survived the Attack Aboard the USS Nevada* by Mark J. Perry, January 1998
- http://digital.lib.ecu.edu/special/pearlharbor/ph/SSIG/hSSIG.html
- http://findarticles.com/p/articles/mi_qa4442/is_200409/ai _n16065904/pg_4/?tag=mantle_skin;content
- http://highdesertdigest.blogspot.com/
- http://ww2.dcmilitary.com/stories/120408/tester_28200.shtml
- http://www.ginfo.pl/more/505589,Mid+Receives+Gift+in+Honor +of+Captain+Joseph+K.+Taussig+Jr..html
- http://www.militaryhistoryonline.com/wwii/dday/
- http://www.pearlharborsurvivorsonline.org/html/USS%20 Nevada%20Patten%20Brothers.htm

USS New Orleans, CA-32

- Deck log, USS Yorktown, April 22, 1944
- After action report Battle of the Coral Sea, USS New Orleans, dated May 25, 1942
- Gwinnett Daily Post, Gwinnett County, GA, *Arthur Morsch Jr. Obituary*, February 26, 2011
- http://my.execpc.com/~dschaaf/praise.html

Nihoa YFB-17

- http://www.navsource.org/archives/14/350017.htm

Nokomis, YT-142

- http://www.hters.org/nokomis.php

USS Oglala, CM-4

- Bureau of Ships, Navy Dept., *USS Oglala Torpedo and Bomb Damage Report*, dated February 14, 1942

USS Ontario, AT-13

- http://www.nafts.net/images/Memories/hartley/Ontario1.htm

Osceola, YT-129

- http://www.ibiblio.org/maritime/media/index.php?cat=965

USS Patterson, DD-392

- http://usspatterson.tk-jk.net/index.htm

USS Pelias, AS-14

- http://www.navsource.org/archives/09/36/3614.htm

USS Pennsylvania, BB-38

- The Oakland Tribune, *Pearl Harbor Survivor Recalls Day of Infamy* by Jason Sweeney, December 7, 2009
- http://usspennsylvania.org/
- http://www.cpedia.com/search?q=USS%20Pennsylvania&d=CURTISS
- http://www.findagrave.com/cgi-bin/fg.cgi?page=gr&GRid=13831414
- http://www.personal.psu.edu/glm7/m486.htm

USS Perry, DMS-17

- The Sierra Star, Oakhurst, CA, *Pearl Harbor Veteran Gives Credit to God for his Safety* by Tiffany Tuell, May 27, 2010
- http://www.concordia.lib.la.us/rabb.htm
- http://www.pacificwrecks.com/ships/usn/DD-340.html
- http://www.ussperry.com/dms-17/story.htm

USS Phelps, DD-360

- http://www.navsource.org/archives/05/360.htm

USS Phoenix, CL-46

- http://en.mercopress.com/2009/04/23/captain-of-falklands-war-cruiser-general-belgrano-dies-in-argentina
- http://warship-pics.blogspot.com/2009/08/battle-of-surigao-strait.html
- http://www.navy.mil/navydata/navy_legacy_hr.asp?id=137
- http://www.thefirearmsforum.com/showthread.php?t=13987
- http://www.tributes.com/show/Milton-Kraut-85549693
- http://www.veterantributes.org/TributeDetail.asp?ID=855

USS Preble, DM-20

- Bulkley, Robert J., Captain, USNR, (Ret), *At Close Quarters: PT Boats in the United States*, Washington, D.C. Naval History Division, 1962
- http://oldbluejacket.com/bootcamp.htm
- http://www.concordia.lib.la.us/rabb.htm
- http://www.destroyerhistory.org/flushdeck/dm.html
- http://www.midway2009.com/battleofmidway.html
- http://www.pt171.org/PT171/writeups/stanvac.htm
- http://www.stonyroad.de/forum/showthread.php?t=3373
- http://www.usspreble.org/

USS Pruitt, DM-22

- http://findarticles.com/p/articles/mi_m0LFT/is_3_45/ai _n15686678/
- http://www.historynet.com/battle-of-the-aleutian-islands -recapturing-attu.htm

USS Pyro, AE-1

- The Record, Bergen County, NJ, *Nightmare on a Gorgeous Day* by William Lamb, December 7, 2006
- Albuquerque Journal, *Obituary, Natalie O. Vytlacil*, Friday, January 21, 2000
- http://www.usspyro.com/
- http://www.twilightsailor.com/default.htm
- http://www.sunymaritime.edu/stephenblucelibrary/pearlharbor.htm
- http://www.cossar.us/images/phpyro41.pdf

USS Rail, AM-26

- Oregon Dept. of Veterans Affairs Newsletter, *Freedom and Heritage Embodied through Oregon Tribal Celebrations*, Sept/Oct 2006
- http://findarticles.com/p/articles/mi_qn4191/is_20011207 /ai_n9997084/
- http://www.asbestos.com/navy/destroyers/uss-zane-dd-337.php

USS Raleigh, CL-7

- Damage report, USS Raleigh dated January 14, 1942
- Holt, Thaddeus, *The Deceivers: Allied Military Deception in the Second World War*, New York, NY, A Lisa Drew Book / Scribner, 2004
- http://www.legacy.com/obituaries/baltimoresun/obituary.aspx? page=lifestory&pid=135350537

USS Ralph Talbot, DD-390

- http://www.facebook.com/pages/Ralph-Talbot-Chapter-65 -Disabled-American-Veterans/280952301602

USS Ramapo, AO-12

- http://www.ibiblio.org/pha/comms/1943-09.html
- http://www.nap.edu/openbook.php?record_id=11635&page=184

USS Ramsay, DM-16

- The Daily Herald, Lake County, IL, *Pearl Harbor Survivors meet in Lake County,* by Russell Lissau, April 14, 2010

Reedbird, Amc-30

- The Beacon News, Aurora, IL, *Obituary Charles George Whinfrey, Jr.,* April 1, 2005
- http://www.i-16tou.com/crossing/crossing2.html
- http://www.producerschemical.com/news/?article=041105

USS Reid, DD-369

- Diary of Louis P. Davis, Jr., 7 December 1941, Louis Poisson Davis Jr. Papers, East Carolina University, Greenville, NC.
- Hammel, Eric, *Air War Pacific: Chronology,* Pacifica, CA, Pacifica Press, 1998
- Rielly, Robin, *Kamikaze Attacks of World War II: A Complete History of Japanese Suicide Strikes on American Ships, by Aircraft and Other Means,* Jefferson, NC, McFarland & Co., 2010
- USS Reid Newsletter, *Log of the LCI (L) 661,* November 1999, Vol. 3, No. 4.
- USS Reid Newsletter, *The Sinking of the USS REID* and *A Different USS REID Story,* March 2009, Vol. 13, No. 1
- USS Reid Newsletter, *Looks Can Be Deceiving,* December 2009, Vol. 13, No. 3
- http://schuylkillcountymilitaryhistory.blogspot.com /2008_08_01_archive.html
- http://www.pacificwrecks.com/airfields/png/finschafen/missions -finschafen.html
- http://www.ussreid369.org/History.htm

USS Rigel, AR-11

- http://www.navsource.org/archives/09/03/0313.htm

USS Sacramento, PG-19

- Highlands Today, Tampa, FL, *Pearl Harbor survivor, veterans honored* by Joe Seelig, December 9, 2009
- http://navalwarfare.blogspot.com/search?q=uss+sacramento

USS San Francisco, CA-38

- Bureau of Ships, damage diagrams of USS San Francisco, for November 13, 1942.
- The Morning Call, Allentown, PA, *Family Preserves Memory of Fallen War Hero*, by Frank Whelan, June 15, 1986
- http://www.usssanfrancisco.org/
- http://militarytimes.com/citations-medals-awards/recipient.php?recipientid=20495
- http://www.navalhistory.org/2010/11/12/matt1c-leonard-r -harmon-and-comdr-mark-h-crouter-gallantry-off-guadalcanal -12-13-november-1942/

USS Schley, DD-103

- After action report of Destroyer Division 80 by E. G. Fullenwider, dated December 12, 1941
- Extracts from the wartime diary of Chief Quartermaster Charley Madison Plummer, USS SCHLEY
- Rohwer, Jürgen, *Chronology of the War at Sea, 1939-1945: The Naval History of World War II*, Annapolis, MD, Naval Institute Press, 2005
- http://www.destroyerhistory.org/flushdeck/ussschley.html
- http://www.destroyerhistory.org/flushdeck/ussward.html
- http://www.stupakgen.net/mil/Robt_Marines.html
- http://www.usmarineraiders.org/chron4thbn.html

USS Selfridge, DD-357

- Lundstrom, John B., *First Team and the Guadalcanal Campaign: Naval Fighter Combat from August to November 1942*, Annapolis, MD, Naval Institute Press, 1994
- http://bobrosssr.tripod.com/515contribkcarlson.html
- http://pf69.grobbel.org/pf69timeline.htm
- http://www.delawarehospice.org/news-and-events/delaware -hospice-patient-and-veteran-remembers-pearl-harbor.html
- http://www.hmascanberra.com/history/hmascanberra1.html
- http://www.ussfoote.blogspot.com/

USS Shaw, DD-373

- Sea Classics Magazine, *USS Shaw: A Ship Too Tough to Die!* by Greg Sweatt, March 2006
- http://www.researcheratlarge.com/Ships/FightingCans/index.html
- http://www.specwarnet.net/USSShaw/

USS Sicard, DM-21

- American Forces Press Service, *Previously 'Unknown' Pearl Harbor Victim Reburied With Full Honors*, March 29, 2006
- Joint POW/MIA Accounting Command (JPAC) Public Affairs Release #06-11, March 22, 2006
- U.S. Department of Veterans Affairs, News Release, *Navy Seaman Missing From Pearl Harbor Attack is Identified,* December 16, 2005
- Block, Leo, *Aboard the Farragut Class Destroyers in World War II: A History with First Person Accounts of Enlisted Men*, Jefferson, NC, McFarland & Co., 2009
- Northwest Arkansas Times, *World War II Survivors: After the battle Deusterman recalls infamous day at Pearl Harbor* by Trish Hollenbeck, Sunday, December 7, 2008
- St. Petersburg Times, *Remember a date of infamy; Veterans honor Pearl Harbor Fallen*, December 8, 2004

USS Solace, AH-5

- Pearl Harbor Joint Information Bureau Press Release, *Navy Nurse Veterans Return to Pearl Harbor* by Lt. Cmdr. Mary Claire Lanser, May 30, 2001
- Mason, Jr. John T., *The Pacific War Remembered: An Oral History Collection*, Annapolis, MD, Naval Institute Press, 1986
- Associated Press, *Pearl Harbor memories still vivid for some. Survivor of 1941 surprise attack to return to scene for 68th anniversary*, December 6, 2009
- Hartford Courant, *The Last of the Survivors; 60 Years After Japan's Surprise Attack Jolted the U.S. into War, Many Who Lived Through Pearl Harbor Go Back* by Matthew Hay Brown, December 7, 2001
- Our Navy Magazine, *Dip Colors; Proudly We Salute the Hospital Ship USS Solace* by Catherine Shaw, May 1945
- The New York Times, *Navy Commissions New Hospital Ship*, Sunday, August 10, 1941
- http://crm.cr.nps.gov/archive/14-8/14-8-all.pdf
- http://tpzoo.wordpress.com/2008/12/07/the-story-of-a-great-white-ship/
- http://www.freerepublic.com/focus/chat/2355855/posts

Sotoyomo, YT-9

- U. S. Navy Pearl Harbor Salvage Diary, Entry September 8, 1942

USS St. Louis, CL-49

- Deck log, USS St. Louis, December 7, 1941
- http://www.multied.com/Navy/cruiser/St%20Loius.html
- http://www.usmarineraiders.org/midway.html
- http://www.ussstlouis.com/

USS Sumner, AG-32

- http://en.m.wikipedia.org/wiki/Ulithi
- http://www.history.noaa.gov/stories_tales/pathfinder6.html
- http://www.historycentral.com/navy/destroyer2/Walke%20II.html

USS Sunnadin, AT-28

- http://www.navsource.org/archives/09/64/64028.htm

USS Swan, AVP-7

- Los Angeles Times, *Pearl Harbor veterans recall infamous attack*, by Nicole Santa Cruz, December 6, 2009
- http://www.ww2f.com/war-pacific/32582-day-war-pacific-3.html

USS Tangier, AV-8

- http://www.navsource.org/archives/09/41/4108.htm

USS Tautog, SS-199

- 1st through 13th War Patrol Reports

USS Tennessee, BB-43

- Bureau Of Ships diagrams of bomb damage suffered December 7, 1941

USS Tern, AM-31

- http://www.navsource.org/archives/11/02031.htm

USS Thornton, AVD-11

- http://www.bangust.com/compiled.htm
- http://www.blountweb.com/blountcountymilitary/wars/ww2/timelines/1945_ww2.htm

USS Tracy, DM-19

- http://www.destroyerhistory.org/flushdeck/dm.html
- http://www.historycentral.com/navy/ap/WilliamWardBurrows.html
- http://www.tributes.com/show/George-Taras-87453494
- http://www.ww2pacific.com/suicide.html

USS Trever, DMS-16

- Deck log, USS Trever, December 14, 1941
- Dawson, Lon, *Cradle Cruise: A Navy Bluejacket Remembers Life Aboard the USS Trever During World War II*, Chicago, IL, Compass Rose Technologies, 2009
- http://www.warsailors.com/singleships/hoeghmerchant.html

USS Tucker, DD-374

- Memo from Admiral Chester W. Nimitz to the Secretary of the Navy dated October 23, 1942
- http://navalwarfare.blogspot.com/2008_05_01_archive.html
- http://www.michaelmcfadyenscuba.info/viewpage.php?page_id=37

USS Turkey, AM-13

- http://www.navsource.org/archives/11/02013.htm

USS Vestal, AR-4

- *Above and Beyond: A History of the Medal of Honor from the Civil War to Vietnam*, by the Editors of the Boston Publishing Company, 1985
- Medal of Honor citation, for Commander Cassin Young
- http://www.nps.gov/bost/historyculture/cassinyoung.htm

USS Vireo, AM-52

- http://members.iinet.net.au/~gduncan/maritime-2-1942.html
- http://usswashington.com/worldwar2plus55/dl04ju42d.htm
- http://www.cv6.org/ship/logs/ph/org-vf6-19411207.htm
- http://www.destroyerhistory.org/benson-gleavesclass/ussmeredith/lossofmeredith.html
- http://www.seawaves.com/TDIH/june/06Jun.txt
- http://www.ussnicholas.org/1942-3solomons.html

Wapello, YN-56

- Rough log, USS Wapello, December 7, 1941

USS Ward, DD-139

- Deck Log of USS Ward, dates December 1, 1941 through December 31, 1941
- Congressional Investigation into the Pearl Harbor Attack: Testimony of William W. Outerbridge, Commanding Officer, USS Ward
- http://www.ww2f.com/war-pacific/25602-japanese-midget-submarines-pearl-harbor.html

USS Wasmuth, DMS-15

- http://www.farragutpress.com/articles/2010/04/2230obituary.html
- http://www.nap.edu/openbook.php?record_id=11635&page=184
- http://www.ww2f.com/war-pacific/13817-today-history-pacific-theater-3.html
- http://www.maritimequest.com/daily_event_archive/2005/dec/29_uss_wasmuth_dms_15.htm

USS West Virginia, BB-48

- Medal of Honor Citation for Captain Mervyn S. Bennion
- Navy Cross Citation for Mess Attendant 2nd Class Doris Miller
- http://usswestvirginia.org/

USS Whitney, AD-4

- Honolulu Star-Bulletin, *Survivor's Memories Remain Vivid*, Wednesday, December 8, 2004
- http://www.afrh.gov/afrh/ussfoote.htm
- http://www.historycentral.com/NAVY/AD/Whitney.html

USS Widgeon, ASR-1

- http://www.warship.org/no31990.htm

USS Worden, DD-352

- Loss of USS Worden, Action Report dated January 17, 1943
- http://dd352.us/vets.shtml

- http://www.legacy.com/obituaries/bradenton/obituary.aspx?n
  =william-v-parent-bill&pid=145844392&fhid=5832

USS Zane, DMS-14

- Deck Log, USS Zane, December 7, 1941
- American History Illustrated, *Pearl Harbor! An Eyewitness Account* by David Armstrong, August 1974
- http://usswashington.com/worldwar2plus55/dl25oc42.htm
- http://www.blountweb.com/blountcountymilitary/wars/ww2
  /timelines/1942_ww2.htm

PART II: Three Graves

USS Arizona, BB-39

- National Parks Service USS Arizona Press Kit
- Honolulu Advertiser, *Pearl Harbor survivor's ashes laid to rest in USS Arizona* by Michael Tai, Saturday May 8, 2010
- http://www.ussarizona.org/

USS Oklahoma, BB-37

- Young, Stephen B., *Trapped at Pearl Harbor: Escape from the Battleship Oklahoma,* Bluejacket Books, 1998
- USS Arizona Memorial Newsletter, Fall 1997 article by Jack Henkels
- Las Vegas Review-Journal, *Looking Back to 1941* by Keith Rogers, December 7, 2008
- http://the.honoluluadvertiser.com/specials/pearlharbor60
  /chapter6.html
- http://www.catholicmil.org/index.php?option=com_content
  &view=article&id=794:fr-aloysius-schmitt-chaplain-thomas
  -kirkpatrick&catid=56:military-heroes&Itemid=90
- http://www.freerepublic.com/focus/f-vetscor/1033591/posts
- http://www.ussokcity.com/gbarchive4.html

- http://www.whshistoryproject.org/ww2/Interviews
  /phpInterviews/mr_halterman.php

USS Utah, AG-16
- http://www.military.com/Content/MoreContent?file=clark
  _simmons01
- http://www.ussutah.org/

PART III:

The Japanese
- Prange, Gordon W. with Donald M. Goldstein and Katherine V. Dillion, *God's Samurai: Lead Pilot at Pearl Harbor,* Washington, D.C. Brassey's, Inc., 1990, Kindle Edition
- Werneth, Ron, *Beyond Pearl Harbor: The Untold Stories of Japan's Naval Airmen*, Bushwood Books, 2008
- Naval War College Review, *Reflecting on Fuchida, or "A Tale of Three Whoppers"* by Jonathan Parshall, April 1, 2010.
- http://www.emersonkent.com/historic_documents/wwii_japan
  _war_declaration.htm
- http://www.friesian.com/pearl.htm

CPSIA information can be obtained at www.ICGtesting.com
Printed in the USA
BVOW07*1905180614

356757BV00001B/11/P